W9-BYL-175

Business Studies
for IGCSE

Robert Dransfield
David Needham
Leslie Garrett
Jane King

Nelson Thornes

Contents

Contents

Introduction

This book is designed specifically for University of Cambridge International Examinations (CIE) Business Studies (Syllabus 0450). Principal and Senior Examiners have been involved in all aspects of the book, including detailed planning to ensure that the content gives the best match possible to their syllabus.

Using this book will ensure that you are well prepared for the exam at this level, and also studies beyond the IGCSE level in Business Studies. The features below are designed to make learning as interesting and effective as possible:

EXAM TIP

These provide a chance for the IGCSE Principal Examiners to share with you their experience of many years in marking and setting examinations. They give you hints on how to avoid common errors or give useful advice on how to tackle questions.

LEARNING OUTCOMES

- These are at the start of each spread and will tell you what you should be able to do at the end of the spread.

CASE STUDY | Subject

These give real-life examples to illustrate the subject matter within the unit, and are accompanied by questions to test your understanding.

DID YOU KNOW?

These are not needed in the examination but are found throughout the book to stimulate your interest in business studies.

SUMMARY QUESTIONS

These questions are at the end of each spread and allow you to test your understanding of the work covered in the spread.

KEY POINTS

These summarise the most important things to learn from the spread.

At the end of each chapter, there is a double page of examination-style questions written by CIE Examiners, both short-answer summary questions to test your understanding and learning of the unit just covered, and longer-answer questions preceded by a short scenario, in the style of Paper 1. At the end of the book, you will find a set of longer case studies with questions, in the style of Paper 2. There is also a glossary of the key terms highlighted in bold in the text.

All the questions feature the command words that you will find in the exam. Explanatory notes on these, along with some guidance on answering the questions, are provided here.

How to use the practice exam questions
and Command words explained

The questions at the end of each unit in the book are to help you practise your exam technique after completing all the work in the unit. You should answer them without referring to the information in the book or your notes.

The short-answer questions test your knowledge and understanding of what you have learnt. Generally, these will ask you to state, identify, define and explain one or a number of factors, differences or meanings. Your answers will be fairly brief, perhaps bullet points, but avoid single-word 'lists', especially where an explanation is required. Do not spend too long or write too much – 2–4 lines is sufficient for these answers. Where an example is required, give one from your own experience, either as a consumer or as an observer of your local business environment.

The longer-answer questions, in the style of Paper 1, introduce you to the 'case study' approach, in which questions are based on a specific business scenario. Read the material carefully, because this will help you to give an answer that is appropriate to the business concerned. Marks will not be awarded where answers do not 'fit' the case. So, for example, do not recommend TV advertising for a small business; do not suggest 'access to raw materials' as a location factor for a retail business, as this is only really applicable to a production business. Read the case study carefully and try to put yourself in the role of the business person in the text.

Make sure you can answer the following:
- Is this business large or small?
- What are they selling – a product or a service?
- Is the business objective profit or another, such as public service?
- Who are the customers?
- What challenges does the business face (e.g. competition)?

Most 4-mark and 6-mark questions include some marks for Application, so make sure you refer to the circumstances of the business, rather than just mentioning the company by name. Analysis and Evaluation marks will be gained by considering both sides of an issue and coming to a supported conclusion.

The longer case studies at the end of the book are designed with a more integrated approach, including questions on several different areas of the syllabus. The questions also attract higher marks and therefore need you to demonstrate a range of different skills, with Evaluation and Application essential in 12-mark sections.

The instruction in the question is given by the command word: as the term suggests, this tells you what is required. The following is a list of the command words you are likely to see in your examination.

Analyse, e.g. 'Analyse the consequences of the merger between the two companies.' When asked to 'analyse', state or calculate the answer, use a linking word, such as 'because' before developing your response, using business theory concepts.

Calculate, e.g. 'Calculate the gross profit margin of a business.' You need to do some mathematics to produce an answer. Always show your workings.

Consider, e.g. 'Consider the two options given in the case study.' You need to weigh up the merits of a situation or decision and give the opposing view as well.

Define, e.g. 'Define market research.' State the exact meaning of the term; this will be a short answer, sometimes including an example to illustrate it.

Describe, e.g. 'Describe the management style of the business.' Give an account of something.

Discuss, e.g. 'Discuss the consequences for the business of producing a new product.' This requires you to put forward various points of view, advantages and disadvantages, or benefits and costs.

Explain, e.g. 'Explain what is meant by a price elastic demand.' This term enables you to show your understanding of a term or topic. You can do this by including an example or a descriptive development.

Give, e.g. 'Give an example of a fixed cost.' This is a short-answer command, requiring you to state a fact or provide an example to demonstrate your understanding.

Identify, e.g. 'Identify two factors a company should consider before deciding to issue more shares.' 'Identify' (or 'State') requires you to select from a number of possibilities. Only a brief answer is necessary, so a list may be fine, but if you are unsure, include a sentence of clarification or an example.

Justify, e.g. 'Should company X buy more machinery? Justify your answer.' This is a longer answer in which you should support your answer with reasons.

Outline, e.g. 'Outline the main features of a business partnership.' You should give a short description (in this example, of the main features of the partnership).

Recommend, e.g. 'Recommend which option the company should take.' You should make a positive suggestion, usually with reasons that support your ideas.

State, e.g. 'State two features of a sole-trader business.' Provide a short answer; this is usually intended for you to show your knowledge. (See also the notes for 'Identify' above.)

Why, e.g. 'Why has the market share of the company fallen?' You should give reasons for an event or outcome and provide some development of the points you make in your answer.

1 Business activity

1.1 Understanding business activity

ACTIVITY

Which of the following would you describe as your needs and which would you describe as additional wants? Justify the choices you make.

A midday or evening meal / a bed to sleep in / a bar of soap / a visit to the cinema / a blanket / a roof over your head at night / a toothbrush / a computer / a bottle of water / new clothes / a book to read.

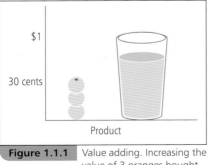

Figure 1.1.1 Value adding. Increasing the value of 3 oranges bought for 30 cents to a glass of orange juice sold for $1

Satisfying wants and needs

Businesses are usually set up to satisfy the wants and needs of customers. Everybody has wants and needs. We *need* food, drink, clothing, shelter and other essentials to stay alive. Other things are not quite so essential, but we still *want* them so our life can be enjoyable.

Business activity is concerned with satisfying these wants and needs. The act of preparing a good or service for sale is called production.

Businesses are set up to satisfy our needs by providing physical goods (manufacturing) and services. When you visit a restaurant not only are you provided with a physical product, the food, but you also receive a service in the form of a member of the restaurant staff bringing the food to the table and making sure that you have everything that you want to enjoy the meal.

Adding value

Businesses aim to provide products and services to customers that are more attractive than those of their competitors. Everything that a business does to make a good more desirable is **adding value**.

For example, cold fresh orange juice is enjoyed across the globe. Oranges are grown in temperate climates such as California (United States), Libya (North Africa) and Italy (Southern Europe). The oranges are transported in lorries, freight trains and ships across the globe. Hotels and restaurants buy and squeeze the oranges to make a fresh drink for the end customer. Ice may be added to cool the juice.

A restaurant selling fresh squeezed orange juice might buy three oranges at 10 cents each (totalling 30 cents) to make a glass of fresh orange juice which it sells to a customer for $1. The value added by the restaurant is therefore 70 cents. $1 – 30 cents = 70 cents.

Scarcity

We cannot have everything we want: we have to make *choices*. This is because resources are scarce: there are not enough for all the things that we would like to do. If we turn a field or park into a car park, then we lose the green space. Choices have to be made all the time.

In the same way, a business makes choices. Farmers make choices about when and how to improve their land. Farmers in Jamaica can decide to grow sugar cane or coffee. They sometimes make choices about who to sell their produce to (e.g. at a local market or to an agent of a food company).

Stage of production:	How value is added
1 Growing the oranges 	Farmers look after the orange trees for several years before they give fruit. Each year they must be treated against pests.
2 Transporting the oranges 	Fresh ripe oranges are transported closer to market.
3 Preparing the oranges 	The juice is squeezed from the oranges and ice added.
4 Serving the customer 	The juice is presented to the end consumer in a polite and friendly way.

Enjoying fresh cold orange juice – value is added in growing the oranges and also in serving the juice to the end consumer

Figure 1.1.2   Adding value to a product: the customer benefits from value being added at each stage of production

EXAM TIP

One way of making a product more desirable, and so adding value, is by branding. A brand is any distinguishing mark that is associated with a product. Consumers are often attracted by brand names and many people will pay more for branded products.

DID YOU KNOW?

A sugar cane farmer who invests in new cutting machinery may be giving up the opportunity to invest in a warehouse or to buy a new car. The next best alternative that is given up is the **opportunity cost**.

SUMMARY QUESTIONS

1 In your own words, write definitions for: needs, wants, scarcity, choice, opportunity cost, adding value.

2 How might packaging of a product add value to it? Explain your answers.

3 How would you explain the difference between wants and needs? Give further examples to show the difference.

KEY POINTS

1 Everyone has basic needs for food, shelter and clothing in order to survive. On top of these we have additional wants.

2 Businesses are set up to meet the needs of consumers.

3 Businesses produce goods to help consumers satisfy their wants and needs.

4 Businesses add value, to make products more desirable and suitable for customers.

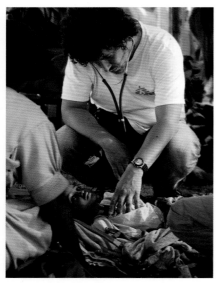

Médecins Sans Frontières is a non-profit organisation whose goal is to respond rapidly to medical emergencies in war and famine zones, and supply doctors, nurses and medical aid

Different goals

A goal is something that an individual or organisation tries to achieve. One of your goals may be to pass your exams with high grades. Having a goal gives you a sense of direction. You are then able to plan activities to achieve your goal.

Business organisations also have goals, but it is not always to make a profit. The table below outlines the goals of three types of organisations: not-for-profit organisations, private enterprise organisations and public enterprise organisations. These are the types of organisations covered in this book.

Not-for-profit organisations	Private enterprise organisations	Public enterprise organisations
Goals include	Goals include	Goals include
Providing healthcare Providing education Providing community activities	Making a profit Other secondary goals	Running public services well Providing ferry and postal services to rural communities Providing street lighting, police service

Figure 1.2.1 Types of business organisations and their goals

Non-profit-making activity

Many organisations exist to achieve goals other than profit. **Charities** are an example of not-for-profit organisations. The purpose of a charity is to achieve goals related to helping others rather than making a profit for a business owner. Médecins Sans Frontières is a charity that aims to help civilians, regardless of which side they are on, in danger from crises such as wars and famine. The organisation's purpose is to respond quickly by providing doctors, nurses and medical supplies. The charity runs over 500 projects in half of the world's countries. Most of its funds come from fundraising, with the remainder coming from government and business donations.

There are millions of other non-profit organisations involved in community work, education, medical projects, sporting activities and organising other activities.

Private enterprise

Most of the goods and services that we buy are provided by private enterprise. Private enterprises are often set up by an individual or small group of people who form a company (see Unit 5). The main goals of private enterprise are to make a profit.

You will see in Unit 2, however, that private enterprises may have additional, or secondary **objectives**. India's Tata Group of companies created India's first steel plant, hydroelectric plant and inorganic chemistry plant. Today the group has operations in six continents and produces many different goods. The group is not concerned solely with profits, however: in 1941 it created the Tata Memorial Hospital, India's first hospital for the treatment of cancer.

Setting up and running a private enterprise involves risk. The person who takes this risk is an **entrepreneur**. If the business succeeds, the entrepreneur makes a profit. Should it fail, he or she will be responsible for the losses. The loss could involve having to sell personal possessions, in order to meet the business debts.

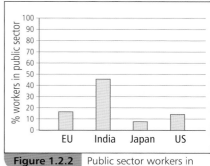

Figure 1.2.2 Public sector workers in four regions in 2007

Public enterprise

In many countries, the government is a major employer. Governments employ public sector workers to carry out work on their behalf, such as providing a police force, education and a health service. The size of the public sector varies from country to country. Figure 1.2.2 shows some of these differences.

The goal of a public sector enterprise such as Indian Railways is to provide an essential economic service for the nation. Hundreds of millions of people in India rely on the railway service to get around the country and to transport goods.

Public sector enterprises need to be carefully run. They are often funded by taxpayers' money, so they need to look after the taxpayers' interests by providing the best possible value for money.

SUMMARY QUESTIONS

1 Explain how goals of public sector organisations may differ from those in the private sector.

2 Read the following statements and then suggest whether the organisation is more likely to be in the private or public sector.

• Our goal is to make a profit for our owners. We will achieve this by providing excellent customer service.

• Our goal is to provide an efficient postal service to every single household in the country. This includes providing deliveries every day to out-of-the-way locations.

• Our goal has always been to make a profit. If we provide additional benefits to the wider community, this is a bonus.

3 Why does a not-for-profit business need to control its costs carefully and make sure that it has plenty of income coming into the business? Is this also true of a private enterprise? Explain your answer.

Classification of business

Describe and classify business activity in terms of primary, secondary and tertiary sectors.

- Understand the basis of classification.
- Use examples to demonstrate understanding.

Demonstrate an understanding of changes that have taken place in these sectors within your own country.

- Identify the key features of the structure of your own national economy.

A haircut is a service provided by a skilled hairdresser

EXAM TIP

The process of shifting resources from primary to secondary activities is industrialisation. More recent changes involving shifting more resources into tertiary activities is deindustrialisation.

Types of business activity

Business activity is often broken down into three types:

- extractive (**primary industry**)
- manufacturing and construction (**secondary industry**)
- services (**tertiary sector**).

Brazil is the world's second largest ethanol supplier after the United States. The following table shows the three stages involved in providing ethanol fuel for cars in Brazil.

Stage 1: Primary production	Stage 2: Secondary production	Stage 3: Tertiary production
Farmers grow sugar cane in Brazil	The sugar cane is refined to make ethanol	The ethanol is sold on service station forecourts to car owners and truck drivers in Brazil

Figure 1.3.1 The three stages involved in providing ethanol fuel for cars in Brazil

Extractive industries

Extractive, or primary, industries are concerned with using natural resources. They include farming, mining and oil drilling. Farmers grow and harvest crops and farm livestock, while miners take out fuel and minerals from the ground. Primary industries sometimes produce raw materials like iron ore (for making steel) and oil (for making petrol, plastics, fibres, etc.). They also produce finished products like fish and oranges.

Manufacturing and construction industries

Manufacturing and construction industries are concerned with making and assembling products. Manufacturers use raw materials and parts from other industries. Most products go through several stages of production: when the good is only partly made, it is a semi-manufactured good. Examples of manufactured products are furniture, cars, chocolate and oil rigs. An example of a semi-manufactured good would be the shell of an aeroplane that has not yet had the engine and inside furnishings (seats, etc.) added.

Service industries

Service, or tertiary, industries give something of value to people, but are not physical goods. You can physically touch or see a packet of biscuits, a bicycle or a computer. You cannot touch or hold a visit to the cinema or a lesson given to you in school: these are both services. Other services include banks keeping your money safe, public transport carrying people around or hairdressers cutting your hair.

CASE STUDY	Employment by major industry sector in the United States

The USA is frequently given as an example of a third-wave society. The following data are drawn from information provided by the US Bureau of Labor Statistics in 2007. The table shows recent breakdowns of employment by employment sector and likely future patterns in the United States.

	Percentage distribution by year		
	1996	2006	2016
Primary industry	2.4	1.8	1.6
Secondary industry	16.9	14.5	12.7
Tertiary industry	81.7	83.7	85.7

Source: US Bureau of Labor Statistics, 2007

Questions

1 Describe the key trends indicated by the data.

2 What is happening to jobs in the primary sector? Why do you think this is the case?

3 What is happening to jobs in manufacturing and services? Why do you think this is?

The data for the USA contrast with that of **newly industrialised countries (NICs)** like Brazil. In Brazil, roughly 20 per cent of the population is still engaged in agriculture and other primary industries, and a further 15 per cent in manufacturing, with the remainder working in services. In Ghana, West Africa, over half of the population still works in primary industries, including cocoa growing and other forms of small-scale agriculture. About 25 per cent of Ghana's population is engaged in services.

ACTIVITY

Group the following activities under the headings of Primary, Secondary and Tertiary Industry.

Building Cinema Attendant Electrican Sign Writing
Cloth Making Coal Mining Laundry
Fire Fighting Book Publishing Civil Service
Selling Lottery Tickets Banking Oil Drilling
Food Manufacture Key Cutting Public Transport Fishing
Retailing Food Selling

Figure 1.3.2	Primary, secondary and tertiary industries

SUMMARY QUESTIONS

1 The following statistics relate to employment by the industrial sector in China. (Source: *China Statistical Yearbook, 2008*)

	Primary (%)	Secondary (%)	Tertiary (%)
1978	70	18	12
1988	58	22	20
1998	50	23	27
2008	42	25	33

Describe the key trends that you see in the data. Explain why these changes might have occurred. Do you expect these trends to continue?

2 What are service industries? Give five examples of jobs in service industries.

3 State whether you would classify the following industries as primary, secondary or tertiary. Give reasons for your choices.

Construction / transportation and warehousing / retail trade / financial activities / manufacturing / mining / farming / educational services / leisure and hospitality / fishing.

KEY POINTS

1 It is helpful to classify business activity into primary, secondary and tertiary sectors.

2 There has been a global increase in the tertiary sector.

Business growth and measurement of size

How do you measure the size of a farm? This huge farm owns a lot of capital, and has a very high sales turnover, yet it only employs a small number of employees

Measuring the size of a business unit

You will often come across the terms small, medium and large businesses. However, it is not always clear what the difference is. In different industries, size is measured in different ways. Also, the definitions used will vary from country to country. The following table shows how the size of a business is measured.

Method	How is it done?
The **number of employees**	A small business might be one employing fewer than 50 employees.
The **level of sales turnover**	Determined by the value of sales in a year: a small business might be one selling up to $6.5m worth of goods.
The **market share of the business**	Determined by the share of the market that the business is responsible for: a small firm might supply less than 5% of the market.
The **value of the capital employed** by the business	Determined by the value of what the business owns.

The number of employees is a straightforward method. However, it is difficult to compare businesses in different industries. For example, a huge modern farm, working with the latest machinery, may employ just a few people. In contrast, a local supermarket may employ a hundred or more people.

The following table shows how the definition of small business in South Africa varies from industry to industry.

Sector (broad group of industries)	Size	Employees (less than)	Annual sales turnover (less than)	Capital employed (less than)
Agriculture	Medium	120	R4.00m	R4.00m
	Small	50	R2.00m	R2.00m
	Very small	10	R0.40m	R0.40m
	Micro	5	R0.15m	R0.10m
Manufacturing	Medium	120	R40.00m	R15.00m
	Small	50	R10.00m	R3.75m
	Very small	10	R4.00m	R1.50m
	Micro	5	R0.15m	R0.10m

Business growth

Businesses may be able to gain advantages over competitors by growing: they may be able to cut costs and win a greater share of the market. By growing they may also be able to develop new products or sell to new markets. Growth may be internal (inside the business) or external (joining together with existing businesses).

Internal growth

'Organic' growth takes place within a business. Money to finance the expansion can come from ploughing back profits or asking the owners to put in more 'capital'. Many small businesses grow organically in their early years. This is because the owners will not want to risk borrowing money from outside the business. However, it is quite a slow way of growing a business. Internal growth can then take place by investing in new products or selling more of existing products.

External growth

External growth involves the takeover of another business, or merger with another business.

An important way of raising finance in a large company is to sell shares. One **share** represents one unit of ownership in the business. (A **shareholder** is someone who is a part-owner of the business; they will typically have many shares.)

A merger occurs when two businesses combine to form a single company. The existing shareholders of both businesses retain a shared interest in the new business.

An acquisition occurs when one business gains control of part of another business. A business may be prepared to sell off one of its divisions that it no longer wishes to keep.

Businesses carry out external growth in order to:

- buy new and exciting brands where sales are likely to be high
- acquire new inventions and new technologies
- break into new markets, perhaps in other countries.

KEY POINTS

1 There are a number of ways of measuring the size of a business.

2 Businesses can grow 'organically' from within (e.g. ploughing back profits into the business, raising money from owners), or externally (e.g. by merger, takeover or acquisition).

SUMMARY QUESTIONS

1 Compare the merits of the following methods for classifying the size of retail units.
- Capital employed in the business
- Size of sales revenues
- Number of employees
- % market share

2 The following are methods for defining a business: the number of employees / sales turnover / market share / capital employed.

Which method/s do you think would be the most useful for classifying whether a business is small, medium or large? Explain your answer.

3 What methods of growth would you suggest to the owner of a small successful family hotel that has accumulated profits for several years?

The impact of business activity on the environment

Pollution and global warming

Business activity involves the creation of 'goods', such as food and clothing, that benefit people. However, during the last 20 years, scientists, politicians and the wider public have realised that it also creates 'bads' in the form of pollution and industrial wastes. These are substances that harm the environment.

Figure 1.5.1 There are different ways of causing pollution

Water pollution

Businesses such as paper mills and chemical factories are located near the sea and rivers in order to access the water needed for the manufacturing process. They release waste into water sources, which can lead to the depletion of fish stocks, as well as other harmful effects. Businesses need to budget for waste disposal that conforms to correct environmental standards.

Air pollution

Air pollution from business activity such as the generation of coal-fired energy used to heat and power factories, offices and other businesses is one of the most serious threats. Keeping to regulations in this area is a cost for businesses.

Global Warming

During the 20th century an increase in the average temperature of the earth, and the oceans, has been recorded. Although there is yet to be conclusive proof, many scientists believe that this is caused by human activity such as cutting down forests and burning fossil fuels.

People in societies that become more prosperous over time should be able to enjoy consuming more goods and live longer. This progress is 'development'. The challenge facing the planet is to make sure that this growth in prosperity increases over time. A continued growth in well-being is '**sustainable development**'.

In Bangladesh, freshwater prawn hatcheries provide one of the most important sectors of the economy. Bangladesh exports about $500m worth of fresh prawns each year. Prawns are hatched from two types of breeding stock – natural prawns that grow in the wild, and prawns that are developed in the new hatcheries. The wild prawns provide by far the superior stock. However, the number of prawns grown naturally in the wild is being rapidly reduced, as farmers increasingly reduce existing supplies to sell them in the market. Catching wild natural prawns in ever-increasing numbers in nets not only reduces their numbers, but also damages the breeding grounds of fish stocks.

Questions

1 Why do you think that farmers are increasingly reducing the supplies of natural prawns?

2 What are the possible long-term effects on the prawn industry in Bangladesh and prawn populations there?

Freshwater prawn farming in Bangladesh: depleting natural stocks of prawns means that the breeding capacity of the prawn population is being reduced

Sustainable development

Businesses contribute to well-being by providing goods and services for customers. Most businesses, however, create waste and some of this is harmful to the environment. It may be dangerous toxic waste or just discarded packaging. In extreme cases, business activity may lead to floods and famines. Trees that once prevented landslips are cut down for housing, rainforest that absorbed carbon dioxide and other gases is cleared for cattle ranches to provide meat for human consumption. Other damage can be caused by over-using resources: in this case the business will not be sustainable.

The challenge to business is to produce 'sustainable' goods that create less waste and pollution. There are now many businesses providing products or services to help protect the environment. These may be companies providing energy sources such as wind farms and solar energy plants, or non-polluting forms of transport such as electric cars. You can also buy items such as energy-saving light bulbs, rechargeable batteries, devices that measure electricity consumption in the home and washing powder that can be used with cold water.

In many countries, recycling is becoming more important. Recycling involves converting 'waste' products for reuse. In some Indian cities, many small enterprises have been set up to recycle waste. Small-scale collectors of rags, paper and metals collect materials from houses, the streets and even from refuse tips. This is then sold on to dealers who collect the materials in bulk. The materials are washed and reprocessed to make new goods such as textiles and newspapers. Many countries now have collection points for consumers to recycle materials such as glass, paper and plastic, and businesses exist that deal with the processing of these wastes.

KEY POINTS

1 As well as creating 'goods', business activity can result in pollution and waste.

2 Sustainable development involves minimising waste and pollution, while producing goods that enable people to enjoy a better life.

SUMMARY QUESTIONS

1 Write down definitions of the following terms: Pollution / greenhouse gases / sustainable development.

2 Explain two of the negative side effects of business activity on the environment.

3 Give three examples of non-renewable resources used by business to produce goods.

Key features of a national economy

Show understanding of the changing importance of different sectors and other factors causing change in your own national economy. These should be related to employment and contributions to national wealth.

- Show awareness of the structure and importance of different sectors in your own national economy.
- Illustrate such changes with reference to appropriate examples.

Changes in your country's economy

The **economy** consists of producers of goods and services who sell to consumers. Producers are classified according to the nature of their industry.

It is very important that you are aware of the changing structure of industry in your own country, as this makes it possible to compare your country with others, as well as providing a picture of the employment market that you will be entering.

ACTIVITY

Find out about your own national economy and recent changes that have taken place. Your teacher will suggest suitable newspapers and other publications to look at, and you will find information on the internet. Include the following details:

- current population
- main types of job in each sector of the economy
- main types of change to the industrial structure in recent years
- problems facing the economy, particularly in relation to employment/unemployment and pollution.

CASE STUDY | Changes in the Philippines

An economy in the process of change is the Philippines, made up of thousands of large and small islands off the coast of China. The Philippines has a population of 100 million, with 39 per cent of the population employed in agriculture. Farms tend to be very small and products include rice, coconut products, sugar, corn, pork, bananas, pineapples, mangoes and eggs. Some of these products will be for local consumption, while others will be traded for export. A major change taking place is that a smaller percentage of the population now earns a living from agriculture. Millions have moved into secondary and tertiary occupations in cities. Mining is also an important primary industry, for a range of metals including gold, silver, copper and nickel. In the secondary sector, the country has a range of manufacturing industries, including textile production, food processing, footwear, beverages, tobacco and paper. The country also produces cement, glass, fertiliser, iron and steel, and refined petroleum products.

In recent years, the Philippines has played a major part in developing two key industries which involve exporting (selling overseas). About

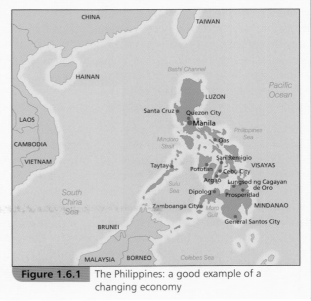

Figure 1.6.1 The Philippines: a good example of a changing economy

two-thirds of the money for exports comes from producing electronics goods. These include computer chips for US and Japanese computer manufacturers and the world's largest mobile phone companies.

The second major growth industry has been call centres. Nearly all of America's leading call centre firms operate in the Philippines, providing the benefits of steady and relatively well-paid work. The call centre workers provide low-cost labour with good levels of English language skills.

In 2009, the service sector in the Philippines produced about half of all the income generated in the economy. The major service employers are retailing and financial services, including banking. Tourism also provides a lot of income, and nearly half a million people are employed in hotels and restaurants. The Philippines also has a strong health care sector. Some of the hospitals are government-owned and run, while others are private enterprises. Because of the high number of hospitals, skilled doctors and nurses, people travel to the Philippines for medical treatment from other parts of the world.

A major cost of the economic success of the Philippines is some very high levels of pollution. This is particularly true for the area around the capital, Manila. Manila has been one of the fastest-growing cities in the world and millions of people live close to power stations and industrial plants. Smog constantly blankets the city and there are huge traffic jams.

To increase their income, many people travel to work in other countries to take on jobs, ranging from doctors and nurses to domestic workers and cleaners.

A further problem is that work created by foreign companies can rapidly disappear. The huge US company Intel has been producing computer chips in the Philippines for 35 years. However, in 2008, its workers there were informed that the company may move production to a new plant in Vietnam. The main reason for this is the lower cost of labour in Vietnam.

Questions

1 What have been the main changes in the economy of the Philippines?

2 What have been the main a) positive b) negative changes?

Costs and benefits

The sorts of changes described above have benefits and costs for society. Benefits are the ways in which members of society gain; costs are ways in which they lose out or are disadvantaged. Some of the costs and benefits of industrial change in the Philippines are illustrated in the following table.

Benefits of changes to the economy	Costs of changes to the economy
More people are able to gain employment in a variety of jobs.	New types of work may create pollution leading to medical problems.
Incomes rise over time.	Workers in declining sectors of the economy lose their jobs.
New service-sector jobs offer cleaner work in more pleasant conditions.	Foreign companies may close down their factories.
A wider variety of goods and services becomes available in the local economy.	

SUMMARY QUESTIONS

1 What are the three main sectors of the economy in your own country?

2 Compare the numbers of jobs in these three sectors in your economy. Which sectors are the largest employers?

3 Identify some of the costs and benefits resulting from the use of new computerised equipment in a particular industry in your own domestic economy.

KEY POINTS

1 Major changes are taking place in domestic economies.

2 Changes in the industrial structure have key costs and benefits, relating to employment, pollution and other side effects.

SECTION 1: Short-answer questions

1 Explain, using examples, the difference between a 'need' and a 'want'. [2]

2 Does the fast-food company KFC provide a product or a service? Explain your answer. [3]

3 Identify and explain THREE ways in which Levi Strauss & Co. adds value to the original blue denim material. [6]

4 A cup of coffee in a cafe of a well-known multinational company costs $4. The ingredient costs are: coffee – $0.10, milk – $0.02, takeaway cup – $0.07. Work out the added value in this example and analyse how the company adds this amount of value to each cup of coffee. [6]

5 Define and explain the business meaning of the term 'opportunity cost' and give your own example. [3]

6 If the government of your country spends $10 million on road improvements, what is the likely opportunity cost? Explain your answer. [4]

7 Identify and explain TWO reasons why a public enterprise must be careful how money is spent by the organisation. [4]

8 Give TWO examples of organisations in your country that are owned and run by the government. [2]

9 Give ONE example from your country of a charitable organisation and explain the business objectives it is trying to achieve. [4]

10 Identify and explain the link between scarce resources and the need for consumers and businesses to make choices. [4]

11 Identify ONE example of a business in your local area in each of the following sectors:
   • primary   • secondary   • tertiary. (3)

12 Identify and explain TWO examples of businesses which operate in two or more sectors. [4]

13 For each of your answers to Question 11, identify and explain one appropriate measure of business size. [4]

14 Identify and explain the best measure of business size for the following organisations:
   • a state-owned health service
   • a large multinational car production company. [4]

15 Identify and explain THREE examples of social costs that may arise from the creation of a new shopping mall on the outskirts of a big town in your country. [6]

16 Explain what you understand by 'sustainable development'. [2]

17 Why might an oil discovery by a multinational company not lead to sustainable development in the host country? [4]

SECTION 2: Longer-answer questions

The young enterprise company

A team of students from a private college in Dubai have set up their own company, Contact2U, selling computer and mobile phone accessories. They buy the accessories from a friend of one of their parents, who has a company based in China, and then repackage them, using their own business name and logo. The company also offers an installation service, for which a small fee is charged. The company aims to sell as many products as possible, but also to raise awareness of environmental concerns. They have pledged 75 per cent of all their profits to local 'green' organisations, which are trying to protect the area's natural marine species from pollution caused by the Dubai building and development programme. A combination of their low prices and charitable aims has led to very high sales and the company is going from strength to strength.

1 Identify and explain TWO ways that Contact2U adds value to its products. [4]
2 Identify and explain TWO suitable methods of measuring the size of the Contact2U company. [4]
3 Analyse how Contact2U's charitable aims may have led to increased sales. [4]

4 Identify and explain THREE possible social costs of the Dubai development programme. [6]
5 'This company cannot possibly have serious environmental aims, when products are produced in and imported by air from China.' Do you agree with this opinion? Justify your answer. [6]

The new malaria clinic

The new clinic in rural Uganda is being funded jointly by the government and charitable organisations. The aim is to become a centre for the programme of vaccination against malaria and also offer other support, such as supplying mosquito nets for beds. Money raised by the charity in the USA and Europe is sent directly to the charity representative in the local area, and government officials oversee the building and work of the clinic. Nurses at the clinic are mainly local, but they are supported by charity volunteers, who also provide basic training in the use of unfamiliar equipment.

1 Identify and explain TWO not-for-profit organisations that are involved in the malaria clinic project. [4]

2 Identify and explain ONE private benefit (to an individual) and ONE social benefit (to the whole society) that will be provided by the malaria clinic. [4]
3 Identify and explain TWO examples of opportunity cost for the organisations providing funding for the clinic. [4]
4 To what extent do malaria clinics help to provide sustainable development in countries such as Uganda? Explain your answer. [6]
5 Evaluate the view that 'clinics like these provide for an essential need, rather than a want, and should therefore be fully funded by the government'. [6]

The seed money enterprise

Lydia and Abigail are two young women from rural Zambia, who have received seed-money grants from the Camfed charity to start an enterprise in their village. They are very excited by this opportunity and have decided to lead a basket-making project, so that other women in the village can also benefit. The initial grant has been used to buy essential materials, such as dye, and they have found a way of selling the finished products in the nearest big town. The girls take the baskets to market each month and pay the women who make them 80 per cent of the selling price. The remaining 20 per cent is used to pay a small wage to each of the girls and cover extras such as transport.

1 Identify and explain TWO objectives of Lydia and Abigail's enterprise. [4]

2 Analyse ONE possible objective that the Camfed charity may be trying to achieve with 'seed money' grants. [4]
3 The materials for each basket cost $1 and the baskets sell for an average of $3. Explain how Lydia and Abigail's enterprise adds value in this example. [4]
4 Analyse the difference between the private benefits (to individuals) and the social benefits (to society) of this enterprise. [6]
5 Evaluate the view that seed-money enterprises like Lydia and Abigail's will make a major contribution to sustainable development in sub-Saharan Africa. [6]

2.1 The importance of business objectives

DID YOU KNOW?

Objectives should be **SMART**: **S**pecific, **M**easurable, **A**greed, **R**ealistic (or **R**elevant) and **T**ime-related.

One of Google's objectives is to provide a clear and simple interface

Aims and objectives

We read in Unit 1 how businesses set themselves broad aims, sometimes referred to as goals. Read the following case study about the internet search engine Google.

Business objectives

A courier firm might set out its specific objectives in a statement like the following:

'To ensure that 99 per cent of all packages received at our offices by 18.00 are delivered to their final destination before 10.00 the following day within Asia.'

You can see that this provides a SMART set of objectives that make the business goal more precise:

- It sets out specific details about the delivery times.
- Success in meeting the objectives is measurable – 99 per cent.

CASE STUDY | Google's objectives

Google is the most widely used internet search engine today. It organises the huge quantity of information that is available on the internet. Users can quickly find out information by carrying out a search. Google's goal is to be the best search engine available, by providing users with the best possible internet-based information.

Google knows that it is not perfect. One of the founders, Larry Page, states that: 'The perfect search engine would understand exactly what you mean and give back exactly what you want.' Google hopes that one day it will be able to achieve this. Google's website states that 'Google's goal is to provide a much higher level of service to all those who seek information, whether they're at a desk in Boston, driving through Bonn or strolling in Bangkok.'

To achieve its goal of providing the world's best search engine, Google has set itself a number of manageable objectives. These objectives are the end purposes towards which the organisation works. Two of Google's objectives are to make sure that:

- the interface is clear and simple
- pages load instantly.

Questions

1 What are Google's goals?

2 Give an example of one or more of Google's objectives that will enable it to work towards these goals.

- The figure of 99 per cent would be agreed by those responsible for delivering this high figure.
- The managers of the organisation will know from previous performance whether a figure of 99 per cent is realistic.
- The objectives are related to a given time period.

Business objectives:

- provide clear end purposes towards which to work
- enable everyone involved in a business to focus on these purposes
- make it possible to check on progress and to make improvements.

Businesses work towards a number of major objectives – for example, growth, profitability and market share. Some objectives will focus on profitable growth, while others may also set out the social responsibilities of the business, such as benefits to the local community.

Growth

A business can set out SMART objectives relating to growth. For example, it could seek to grow sales, or to grow the size of the company or the number of employees.

This could be set out in the following ways:

- to increase sales by 20 per cent by 2015
- to increase the number of employees by 10 per cent by next year.

Profitability

Profitability is an important business objective. Businesses require profits to stay competitive and to make improvements. A profit-related objective might be to increase operating profits by 5 per cent per year for the next 5 years.

Market share

The market share of a business is its percentage of sales in the market. The UK company Innocent sells 'smoothies', fruit drinks with no artificial additives. The company was set up in 1998; by 2009 it had a market share of 71 per cent of the UK's £169m smoothie market. A market share-related objective might be to increase market share to 75 per cent of the UK market.

KEY POINTS

1 Businesses work to broad goals, which may be broken down into objectives.

2 Objectives should be specific, measurable, agreed, realistic and time-related (SMART).

3 Broad objectives usually relate to profit, growth and market share.

EXAM TIP

One of the key functions of management is to direct and control a business. Without objectives, the managers of a business will not know exactly what they want the business to achieve.

SUMMARY QUESTIONS

1 Why do businesses need both goals and objectives?

2 An international soft drinks manufacturer already controls 80 per cent of the market in Europe and the United States, but has less than 5 per cent of the market in Asia and Africa. Which of the following objectives do you regard to be the SMARTest?
  - To maintain market share in Europe and the US and to grow market share in Asia and Africa.
  - To double market share in Africa and Asia over the next 5 years while retaining market leadership in the US and Europe.
  - To increase market share in Europe and the US by 1 per cent over the next 5 years, and to increase sales in Africa and Asia by 10 per cent within the next 10 years.

3 Choose a well-known global business, such as Tata, Toyota, Procter & Gamble, Nestlé, Shell or Nike. Explain how having clear business objectives will help its business managers to achieve targets.

EXAM TIP

Make sure that you know the difference between stakeholders and shareholders. It is a common error to think that they are the same.

ACTIVITY

Choose a local company – for example, a farm, a retail outlet, a manufacturing or transport company. Identify the key stakeholder groups. Set this out in the form of a diagram. Are there any clashes between the interests of the stakeholders in this business?

What are stakeholders?

A **stakeholder** is someone who has an interest in the decisions taken by the business. Some stakeholders are internal: they are part-owners of the business or they work within the business. Examples are shareholders, managers and employees. Other stakeholders are external – for example, the customers and suppliers.

CASE STUDY	Shell Nigeria

Nigeria is a leading oil-exporting country. The oil company Shell extracts oil in Nigeria and pumps it in pipelines to refineries on the coast. The company provides jobs for many Nigerians and offers scholarships for students. It is also involved in a number of community projects. Tax revenues from the company make a major contribution to the Nigerian government. However, there are criticisms that oil production pollutes large areas of the countryside, and that the removal of oil directly from the pipeline can lead to injury or death.

Questions

1 Who are the stakeholders in Shell's activities in Nigeria?

2 Identify two groups of stakeholders in Shell Nigeria whose interests might clash. Explain how and why a clash might occur.

Oil spills and broken pipelines in Nigeria can have a devastating effect on the local environment

Key stakeholders

The following table summarises the different stakeholders in a business.

Internal stakeholders	External stakeholders
1 **Owners:** may be single owner in sole-trader business or partners in a partnership. In a company, shareholders are the owners. Without owners the business would not exist; they are the risk takers. They like to see their share of profit increasing, and the value of their business rising.	1 **Customers** want a company to produce high-quality, value-for-money products.
	2 **Suppliers** want steady orders and prompt payment; they also want to feel valued by the company that they supply.
	3 **Local and national communities**: actions of businesses can have major effects on communities: Shell's pipelines in Nigeria run through people's lands, can be dangerous and cause pollution. (Shell might argue that the dangers come from local people tampering with the pipelines to take fuel out of the pipeline for their own consumption or to sell on.) Community leaders are an important stakeholder group.
2 **Employees:** their stake is that the company provides them with a living. They want security of employment, promotion opportunities and good rewards. Ideally, they want to work for a company that they are proud of.	4 **Governments** want business to be successful – to create jobs and pay taxes. They want to see prosperous businesses that take full responsibility for looking after the welfare of society.
	5 **Pressure groups:** organised with particular interests and points of view. Examples are the environmental campaigning groups Greenpeace and Friends of the Earth, who see themselves as defending the environment. They will have an environmental stake in the business.
	6 **Trade unions:** represent interests of groups of employees; seek to secure high wages and better working conditions for their members.
	7 **Employers' associations:** employers' equivalent of trade unions; they represent the interests of groups of employers.

SUMMARY QUESTIONS

1 In each of the following cases, explain what the conflict of interest might be between the two stakeholder groups indicated.

Decision	Stakeholder group	Stakeholder group
To give employees a wage rise	Shareholders	Employees
To open a new factory next to a populated area	Shareholders	Local community
To close down a factory	Shareholders	Employees

2 What arguments would you put forward to support the view that shareholders are the most important stakeholder grouping in an organisation? What arguments would you present against this view?

3 Identify a business that is just moving to your local area, or a new business that has set up there. Make a list of all of the stakeholder groups and their stake in the business.

KEY POINTS

1 A stakeholder is an individual or group that has an interest in decisions taken by a business.

2 Sometimes stakeholders have the same interests, but their interests may also differ and conflict.

3 Owners are very important stakeholders. They play a key part in setting up and ensuring the continual success of a business.

4 Main stakeholders are owners, employees, customers, communities, government, pressure groups, trade unions and employers' associations.

Aims of the private and public sectors

LEARNING OUTCOMES

Demonstrate an awareness of the aims and objectives of enterprises in both private and public sectors.

- Describe and explain the different objectives of organisations in the different sectors in an economy.

In Unit 1.2 we saw that all organisations decide on broad aims (goals) to work towards and then break these down into more precise objectives.

The aims and objectives of businesses will be different depending on whether they are operating in the **private** or the **public sector**. Remember that private sector businesses are owned by individual risk takers, whereas in the public sector the government owns businesses on behalf of the nation.

Aims and objectives in the private sector

A major aim of businesses in the private sector is to survive. Businesses need to make a profit to survive and grow.

CASE STUDY | Virgin Trains

Virgin Trains provides rail transport between a number of major cities in the UK. It is a private sector business, jointly owned by the Virgin Group and the Stagecoach Group of companies, which in turn are owned by shareholders. The company states that its main objective is to maximise revenue. On the routes it operates, major competitors are coach companies and airlines. On longer routes, such as London to Glasgow (Scotland), it makes sure that the rate it charges passengers per mile is lower than for air travel.

Other important objectives for Virgin Trains are to ensure the safety and comfort of passengers and to provide rapid transport using high-speed trains.

Questions

1 Who will take the profits from Virgin Trains' rail operations?

2 How will the objective of maximising revenue enable Virgin Trains to make more profits?

EXAM TIP

Make sure that you understand that a public limited company is not in the public sector of an economy.

The Virgin Trains example indicates the way in which private sector businesses tend to focus on seeking to make high revenues and profits. By doing so, they are able to keep shareholders happy.

Other objectives of private sector businesses include:

- building a strong brand reputation
- winning customer loyalty
- coming up with exciting new ideas and innovations.

What other objectives can you think of for private sector businesses?

You can see that whatever these objectives are, they are usually related to enabling the company to make a profit.

ACTIVITY

Are the railways in your country run by a state-owned organisation or by the private sector? If your country has a rail service, how efficient is it? Does it give value for money? You could also look at the postal service, and national radio or television broadcasting organisations.

Aims and objectives in the public sector

Public sector organisations have wider responsibilities than just making a profit. They are expected to meet wider responsibilities to the community, such as providing a cheap and efficient train service for all members of society.

Public sector organisations therefore have broader aims than private sector organisations. They are expected to provide more of a public service. Today, they are increasingly required to combine public service with making a profit wherever possible. How possible do you think this is?

EXAM TIP

Make sure you can identify and explain the different objectives that private sector and public sector businesses set themselves.

CASE STUDY | Indian Railways

Indian Railways is the largest employer in India (over 1.6 million people) and operates the second-largest railway system in the world. The objectives of Indian Railways are to provide a modern, reliable, safe, customer-led and customer-focused service to the Indian nation. For a number of years, particularly between 2000 and 2005, the organisation made huge losses.

Railways in India were seen by the government as playing an important part in the life of the nation. The railway system provided a means of transport to remote parts of the country and an affordable means of transport to almost everyone. Trains enabled millions of people to get to work every day. The rail service was particularly important in times of national emergency, taking food to famine or flood victims. An important objective of Indian Railways is therefore to provide a public service.

Problems for Indian Railways have included safety, timekeeping and huge losses that had to be paid for by the government raising money

from taxpayers. More recently, the government has set profit goals for Indian Railways. Some of these have been achieved by putting more carriages on trains and providing special routes for carrying freight. The safety record has also improved.

Indian Railways is a state-owned railway company with a near-monopoly of the country's rail transport

Questions

1 Who takes the profit or pays for the losses made by Indian Railways?

2 How are the objectives of Indian Railways different from those of Virgin Trains?

SUMMARY QUESTIONS

1 In some countries, the postal service is run by a government-owned organisation. In other countries, post is carried by private companies that compete with each other. Make a list of possible objectives that would be set for a government-owned postal service. Make another list of possible objectives for a privately run postal service. How do the two lists differ, and why?

2 In what way are the aims of public sector organisations broader than those of private sector ones?

3 Describe the main objectives of Indian Railways.

KEY POINTS

1 Aims and objectives give organisations a direction to work towards.

2 Private sector organisations seek to make a profit, usually the main focus for their aims and objectives.

3 Public sector organisations may seek to make a profit but will focus on public service.

Practice exam questions

SECTION 1: Short-answer questions

1 Explain the difference between an 'aim' or 'goal' and an 'objective'. [2]

2 Why might a business include its aims in a 'mission statement'? [2]

3 What do the letters 'A' and the 'R' stand for in 'SMART', when it describes targets? [2]

4 Explain TWO reasons why a new business would set SMART objectives for sales. [4]

5 Explain TWO reasons why an established business would set SMART objectives for market share. [4]

6 Identify and explain THREE objectives for a named business in your city, town or village. [6]

7 Explain why the objectives 'increase profit by 10 per cent' and 'increase market share by 5 per cent' may be difficult to achieve at the same time. [4]

8 Explain the difference between 'stakeholders' and 'shareholders'. [4]

9 Use an example of a large national business in your country. Identify TWO external stakeholders and TWO internal stakeholders for this business. [4]

10 Using your answer to Question 9, identify TWO likely objectives for each of the stakeholder groups. [2]

11 Using your answers to Questions 9 and 10, explain TWO examples of conflict between stakeholder objectives. [4]

12 Identify and explain ONE reason why the aims of a public sector business may be different from those of a private sector organisation. [2]

13 Identify a public sector business in your country and explain TWO of its likely objectives. [4]

14 Identify and explain TWO ways in which the business you identified in Question 13 tries to meet its objectives. [4]

15 Identify and explain TWO factors which may stop the business in Questions 13 and 14 meeting its objectives. [4]

16 Identify a large multinational business which operates in your country and explain TWO of its likely objectives. [4]

17 Using a table like the one below, explain THREE factors in your country that may help the company in Question 16 meet its objectives, and THREE factors that may hold it back. [12]

Local factors that may help the company meet its objectives, and why	Local factors that may hold the company back from meeting its objectives, and why
Factor 1 Explanation	Factor 1 Explanation
Factor 2 Explanation	Factor 2 Explanation
Factor 3 Explanation	Factor 3 Explanation

SECTION 2: Longer-answer questions

The call centre

Sanjay runs a call centre in central Bangalore, India, on contract, for a large worldwide banking corporation. His 200 staff work in shift patterns covering the full 24-hour day, as they need to be available to answer the telephones and take queries from customers all around the world in different time zones. Each staff member is part of a team of eight, who are directly supervised by a team leader. Sanjay's company's aim is 'to provide the best possible customer service' for the customers of the big bank.

Sanjay is always looking for ways to cut costs and is considering moving his operation to a new business park on the outskirts of town, 20 kilometres from the present site.

1 Describe why it is important for Sanjay to break down his aim into clear SMART objectives for the company. [4]

2 Identify and explain TWO possible SMART objectives which Sanjay may set to try and achieve his overall aim for the business. [4]

3 Identify and explain THREE possible benefits to Sanjay of passing down objectives to his teams of workers on a weekly basis. [6]

4 Explain the likely view of THREE different stakeholders to the proposed business relocation. [6]

5 To what extent do you agree that Sanjay should relocate his business? [6]

The Handicraft Emporium

Sara is the manager of a government-owned shop in Delhi, which sells Indian handicraft products at fixed prices to local people and tourists. Carvings, textiles and other crafts come from small suppliers in country areas, who receive a fixed payment for each product, as well as the assurance that they will be able to sell all the items they produce.

The other local traders are unhappy at what they see as 'unfair competition' from Sara's shop. 'We have to pay our rents and are not subsidised by the government, yet our customers always try and knock down our prices by bargaining. How can we possibly survive?'

1 Identify and explain TWO external stakeholders in Sara's business. [4]

2 Identify and explain TWO objectives which the Indian government may be trying to meet by operating this business. [4]

3 Analyse ONE advantage and ONE disadvantage to local and tourist customers of the fixed price arrangement in Sara's shop. [6]

4 To what extent do you agree with the other local traders that Sara's shop is 'unfair competition'? [6]

5 Do you agree that the fixed-payment arrangement with the suppliers will lead to more choice and better quality for customers? [6]

A new hotel on Mahe

Mahe is the largest island in the Seychelles and home to most of the local population. There are already many beach hotels on the island, but one of the big multinational groups would like to build a big, new, all-inclusive resort near the capital, Victoria. The target market will be high-income tourists from US and Europe who will pay for their holiday, including all food and drinks, before they arrive, and spend most of their time in and around the hotel complex.

The proposed location is a beach area, beside the fishing harbour, which is popular with locals for swimming and other water sports. The local people have formed a pressure group and are trying to persuade the government to turn down the application, but the development does offer the prospect of jobs in the area, where unemployment is high.

1 Identify and explain TWO objectives the government of the Seychelles may consider when deciding whether to welcome this new development. [4]

2 Explain TWO internal stakeholder objectives of the multinational company, which may be met by this new development. [4]

3 Analyse ONE reason why the Mahe island traders may not benefit greatly from the proposed all-inclusive development. [4]

4 To what extent do you agree with the following statement? 'It is important for any business to consider the local community as an important stakeholder.' [6]

5 Should the Seychelles government let the development go ahead? Justify your answer. [6]

Government intervention

A **government** is a body with power to make and enforce laws within a state or over certain groups of people. In some countries, governments are chosen by the votes of citizens. In other countries, governments consist of groups who have established positions of power but have not been elected.

Governments intervene in the day-to-day life of societies. They make laws and carry out activities that affect business. The following paragraphs explain why governments intervene in the economy.

1 To protect individuals and groups from the actions of large powerful organisations. In the United States, the Sherman Act of 1890 was designed to break up the power of huge **monopoly** organisations that were limiting competition. (*Mono* means only: a monopoly is a company that controls a market and is the only supplier in a region or regions.) The act led to the breaking up of huge oil companies (such as Standard Oil) that dominated the US market. Today, most countries in the world have laws against monopolies and price fixing by large organisations. The Sherman Act is still at the heart of anti-trust legislation in the US.

Trusts

In a trust, a number of companies come together to control a market. A board of trustees is set up, with board members exchanging shares in the trust for shares in the individual companies. John D Rockefeller set up the first trust in the US. His board of trustees took control of 40 separate oil companies to create a monopoly that easily undercut prices charged by rivals, so that they were forced out of business.

2 To provide essential industries and services. Some industries, such as transport systems, energy and water supply, post and communications systems, are essential to the smooth running of a country's economy. In many countries, the government owns and runs key industries. In India, the government owns the railways, and in China telecommunications are dominated by three huge state-run companies: China Telecom, China Unicom and China Mobile. These are examples of public sector organisations.

Governments also play a major part in running a substantial part of services such as health and education. In most countries, the police, the legal system and the armed forces are also government-run. The money to pay for government services is obtained largely through taxation.

3 To help the economy to run smoothly and to protect employment. Governments are major employers and spenders. When businesses are laying off workers, the government can take action to protect jobs by increasing its own spending.

Governments should also try to ensure price stability. When prices are steady, business people can make business decisions with confidence because they know how much they will receive for goods sold on credit, or how much they will receive back when they lend money.

The impact of government intervention

Government intervention affects business decision making at local, national and international levels. Consider the following examples:

- Governments create laws about how goods can be produced. For example, health and safety laws determine safe ways of making goods that protect employees. Consumer protection laws aim to protect the end consumer by determining what materials and substances are allowed in goods.

- Government taxes and subsidies (see Unit 3.2) encourage certain methods of production, and may discourage others: in recent years, many governments have provided subsidies (see Unit 13.1) to farmers for growing crops in particular ways, such as using organic (i.e. not using any artificial fertiliser) farming methods. The Turkish government started subsidising organic farming of raisins, apricots and dried figs in 1985. The subsidies now cover more than 90 agricultural products. This benefits the environment and ensures steady supplies of healthy food.

- Government spending on defence, education and healthcare provides incentives for companies. Companies producing items such as military aircraft, tanks or school textbooks may supply only to governments.

- Government subsidies and taxes also determine what is produced: taxes and health warnings can discourage spending on tobacco, for example. (Tobacco smoking leads to poor health and high costs of medical care.) In recent years, many governments, including those of Japan, Germany and the United States, have provided subsidies for producers to make more environmentally friendly products, such as unleaded petrol, and electric and hybrid cars.

- Government import tariffs influence what is produced. The Indian government levies an import duty of 40 per cent on most imported electrical goods. These tariffs are designed to protect Indian manufacturers against cheaper imported goods, as well as protecting local jobs.

Government health warnings often use graphic images to show the risks and harmful impact of smoking to discourage consumers

EXAM TIP

Remember that interest rates are not a tax levied by the government. They represent the cost of borrowing money. In effect, they are the cost of money to the borrower.

ACTIVITY

Use newspaper reports to find out whether the interest rate is going up or down.

Write a short report explaining the impact of interest rate changes on two separate businesses.

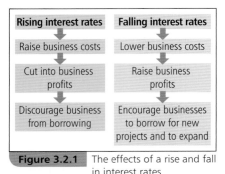

Rising interest rates	Falling interest rates
Raise business costs	Lower business costs
↓	↓
Cut into business profits	Raise business profits
↓	↓
Discourage business from borrowing	Encourage businesses to borrow for new projects and to expand

Figure 3.2.1 The effects of a rise and fall in interest rates

In August 2008, in an effort to reduce pollution and encourage car manufacturers to produce more small cars, the Chinese government raised its sales tax on large cars to as much as 40 per cent, while drastically reducing taxes on small cars

Taxes

Changes in tax and interest rates have a direct effect on business.

A tax is a compulsory financial charge imposed by a government. Taxes are levied mainly as a way of raising revenue to fund government activity. In addition, taxes are levied to discourage certain types of business behaviour, such as pollution or the creation of waste.

Interest rates

If you borrow money from a bank, you will have to repay what you borrow, as well as interest, a charge made by the bank for lending you the money.

The **interest rate** is the cost of borrowing money. It is charged by lenders to borrowers. It is expressed as a percentage (%). For example, if a business borrows $1,000 from a bank for a year at a 5 per cent interest rate, it would expect to pay back $1,050, usually in monthly payments.

$1,000 (the sum originally borrowed) + **$50** (the interest charge, 5 per cent of $1,000) = **$1,050**

Nearly all businesses have to borrow money. They hope that when they come to repay the money, the interest rate will be as low as possible. Rising interest rates harm business profits. Sometimes high interest rates can ruin a business. This is because they may have to pay a lot of interest on money they have borrowed and this adds to their costs. Usually the rate of interest is agreed at the start of a loan, except in cases where a 'variable rate' may change.

| Paying business taxes in Albania

The table below is based on data from the World Bank in 2009. It shows the main taxes a medium-sized company must pay in Albania, as well as the time spent in filling out tax forms and the number of payments that have to be made. The table shows that an Albanian business will spend 244 hours a year in preparing, filing and paying taxes and that these taxes take 44.9% of profits.

Number of payments per year	44
Hours spent by a business preparing, filing and paying taxes	244
Profit tax	8.0%
Labour tax and other contributions	31.9%
Other taxes	5.0%
Total tax rate (% profit)	44.9%

Questions

1 Why might businesses in Albania have been discouraged by the taxes that they have to pay and the time spent on form filling?

2 How would the taxes that businesses pay affect the costs of running a business and thus the profits that a business can share among the owners?

How tax rates affect business

For businesses, taxes are a cost. They are a deduction from profits and valuable time has to be spent administering them.

Changes in tax rules influence business decisions. For example, if businesses have to pay more in social security contributions, they may decide to employ fewer workers to save on some of these costs. When taxes on profits increase, businesses will be able to retain less profit to invest in new machinery.

The government may tax activities that it sees as harmful – for example, activities that create pollution and waste. Businesses may respond by developing new processes that reduce waste.

The government may also tax imports, goods and services brought in from overseas. These **tariff barriers** may be imposed to protect home businesses from lower-cost overseas competitors.

Subsidies are payments to a business to carry out certain activities. For example, the government subsidises certain types of agricultural production. The government also subsidises certain types of production, such as the production of organic fruit (i.e. fruit that is not sprayed with chemicals). Also subsidies are often given to firms to help them set up business in the first place.

DID YOU KNOW?

'Green' taxes discourage pollution and environmental damage. These might be taxes on the emission of greenhouse gases and pollution into water sources.

KEY POINTS

1 Taxes earn large revenues for governments; they also discourage certain types of activity.

2 A subsidy is a payment made by a government to encourage certain activities.

3 Rises in interest rates can reduce profits; a fall encourages borrowing and can lead to more spending.

SUMMARY QUESTIONS

1 What would be the impact on a small business of a rise in business taxes?

2 A business is considering building a new production line. How would a rise in interest rates affect its decision making?

3 A business is faced by rising labour costs and has large debts built up from the past. How would a fall in interest rates affect this business?

An example of new technology: the folding bicycle

Technology

Over time, people build more knowledge about the world around them and how things work. **Technology** involves applying (i.e. using) some of this new knowledge in a way that benefits people.

New technologies help us to do things better. Recent years have seen a rapid increase in the development of new technologies that have produced items such as fold-up bicycles, new medicines for combating disease and increasingly sophisticated robots in factory production lines.

The impact of new technologies

New technology has a range of different impacts on business.

1 **Enabling businesses to create new products and processes.** Today, increasing numbers of people have access to the internet, electronic banking services, mobile phones and many other innovations. These products are made in new ways, often requiring less labour input and more automated machine input.

2 **Damaging businesses that fail to develop new technologies.** Businesses need to be constantly alert to the development of new technologies. Although many people like shops, for example, for trying on clothes or shoes, or for checking the quality of goods, a lot of people want to buy clothes, jewellery and other items online. A retailer that fails to develop a trading website will quickly lose custom to rivals with a site that is strong and easy to use.

3 **The impact on costs.** New technologies create many different labour- and time-saving devices that help to cut costs. Think about internet searchability: the internet is a relatively new technology for businesses (mainly since 2000) that has enabled all sorts of web-based businesses to develop. At the same time, the development of powerful search engines such as Google has enabled quick access to information. Businesses can look for the cheapest suppliers, the lowest fares or the cheapest hotels.

4 **Changing labour requirements.** Many businesses are able to reduce their wage bill through applying new technologies. At one time, most of the world's population was involved in agriculture, for example. New machinery and equipment have replaced the need for human labour in this area (although in a large number of countries many farmers still use traditional, labour-intensive techniques). The same is true of manufacturing industries – for example, textiles, food processing and car manufacture. In service industries, computers and other forms of information technology mean that more work can be produced with the same number of workers.

5 **Methods of production.** Wherever products can be produced in a standardised way, machines have replaced human labour and been able to produce higher outputs at lower costs.

The table on page 29 summarises some of the changes in different industrial sectors.

Industrial sector	Example of new methods of production
Agriculture	Automatic dairy parlours for milking cows
	Automated harvesting machinery for harvesting corn and other cereal crops
Manufacturing	Non-stop automated production lines for the manufacture of bottled, boxed and packaged products
	Automatic checking for defects in products through electronic scanning devices
Services	Computerised warehouses for the packing and loading of goods
	Online banking: customers manage their own bank accounts

New technologies also make it possible to produce more sophisticated (often smaller) goods, such as the iPod®, MP4 players and mobile phones. In Japan there has been a trend towards 'miniaturisation' of all sorts of electrical goods, including computers and computer chips. Computer-aided manufacturing (CAM) systems can be programmed to produce goods from wedding dresses to bridges, using far more complex methods of production than is possible with human labour. Machines with sensitive sensors can be used to carry out complex operations, such as measuring and cutting, with a very low level of error. The impact of technological change on production methods is covered in more detail in Unit 8.

Marketing and technology

Developments in technology have enabled businesses to change the ways in which they conduct both market research and marketing of the finished products. Customers may complete online or phone questionnaires. Marketing information can be sent as emails, and as we have seen, via company websites to customers worldwide. Some people do not like unsolicited phone calls and emails, but technology now enables businesses to reach more consumers more cheaply than before. You will find more information on the role of technology in marketing in Unit 7.

EXAM TIP

If technology makes things better and more efficiently, why don't all companies invest in it? The answer is cost: a company has to spend money today in order to make money in the future. Many companies today do not have money to spend.

SUMMARY QUESTIONS

1 What do you understand by 'technology'? Give an example of a new type of production technology that has changed the way that an industry manufactures a particular product.

2 Toothpaste and soap are produced by large household goods manufacturers with modern production factories all over the world. How has the development of these high-tech plants affected:

• labour costs?

• labour requirements?

• methods of production in the household goods industry?

3 What are the advantages to a business of employing new technologies? What are the dangers of failing to apply new technologies?

KEY POINTS

1 Technology involves the application of new knowledge. Businesses apply new technologies to create new products.

2 New technologies can reduce business costs; they change the way in which goods are produced and often lead to the saving of labour.

3 New technologies can damage businesses that fail to adapt.

The internet and e-commerce

Interflora is an international firm selling flowers for delivery. Customers anywhere in the world can make purchases simply by logging on to the site, selecting items and paying for them electronically

The internet

The **internet** is an internationally linked set of computer networks with a common addressing scheme. The internet has been around since 1969, but was only widely used as a business tool in the mid 1990s, with the development of the first effective web browsers (the software required to navigate pages on the internet).

E-commerce (buying and selling over the internet) has changed the way that a lot of buying and selling is done in recent years.

There are two main types of e-commerce:

- **B2B** (business-to-business) buying and selling
- **B2C** (business-to-consumer) selling.

B2B buying and selling

Most large businesses recognise the importance of the internet in trading with other businesses. The internet has helped to cut the costs of ordering new components, parts and stocks of goods. Buyers can use databases for information about items for sale all over the world. Major companies such as car producers have pooled together to create databases of supplies and suppliers of car components. This procedure is estimated to have reduced car production costs by as much as 20 per cent.

B2C buying and selling

Electronic commerce is having its greatest impact in B2C links. Businesses have realised that the internet provides them with a way of developing a relationship with customers.

ACTIVITY

Carry out some research on an internet B2C site. Write a report that answers the following questions.

- How easy is the site to use?
- What are the benefits to consumers like you from using the site? What disadvantages are there?
- What are the advantages to the business of having only an internet presence?

A traditional shop may attract customers by displaying goods in its shop window. In e-commerce, the shop window is the company's **website**. As it can reach anyone in the world with internet access, it is obviously a much more powerful sales and marketing tool than the traditional shop window. If the website is well constructed, buying over the internet can be a time-saving and less expensive way of making a purchase. A customer wanting to buy farm equipment, for example, can search for sites selling the item. They can browse through the details of different types of equipment available and purchase directly over the internet, or by using phone or mail links.

It is important to develop a website that users will:

- want to visit
- make repeat visits to
- find exciting each time they visit.

The three main factors in a good website are content, community and commerce.

The following table sets out the benefits of a good website to providers and consumers.

Benefits to the provider	Benefits to the consumer
Low ongoing costs once the site has been established	Lower prices resulting from provider's low costs
The provider doesn't have to have a high street presence or other expensive location	Consumers can browse the website in the comfort of their own homes, or elsewhere
The provider can set out far more information about products or services on an easy-to-navigate site	Consumers can spend time navigating the website, finding out as much information as they need to before making a choice
The provider can access a wide market from a remote location	Consumers do not need to be near to the provider

There are some problems associated with the development of e-commerce.

- The cost and time taken to create a website that is attractive and easy to use: businesses usually employ specialist website designers to create the site and manage it for them. Once the site has been built, there will be enormous cost savings for the business.
- Payment: making payment over the internet requires users to provide details of their bank accounts. The risk of fraudsters stealing users' bank details can make buyers reluctant to make purchases over the internet, and businesses lose custom.
- Importance of relationship: internet buyers and sellers do not have face-to-face contact, which can be important in the purchasing process.
- Poor customer service has affected e-commerce development, for example, in India. Customers have found that deliveries are often late and they have been unable to contact customer service departments.
- There is limited or unreliable internet access in some countries, or deliveries may be unreliable.

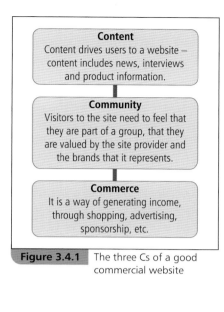

Figure 3.4.1   The three Cs of a good commercial website

SUMMARY QUESTIONS

1 Define the following terms:

Internet / website / e-commerce / B2B / B2C

2 What would be the benefit to a Pakistan-based clothes retailer of setting up a website to sell traditional regional clothes over the internet? What might be the drawbacks to the business of setting up this site?

3 What are the main ingredients of a good commercial website?

China is the world's largest producer of iron ore and steel, but it still has to buy additional steel on competitive world markets to meet all its needs

Consumer spending patterns

Consumer spending patterns are the typical goods and services bought by individuals and groups of consumers. Spending patterns are heavily dependent on income. The more income an individual has, the greater the proportion they are likely to save, and spend on luxuries.

As incomes rise, patterns of spending change. Increasing numbers of consumers are earning more. This is particularly so in huge countries like Brazil, Russia, India and China (the BRIC group of countries), and in other newly industrialised countries (NICs), which include a number of South East Asian countries, such as Indonesia, Malaysia and Vietnam, as well as rich oil states such as Kuwait and Dubai. Consumers here are spending more on internationally branded products – for example, Nike trainers rather than a cheaper pair made locally.

Spending patterns are also affected by **lifestyles** of groups of consumers. A lifestyle is a way of living and a pattern of buying associated with individuals. It is possible to have a unique personal lifestyle, but most people can be grouped with others.

'American lifestyles' or 'Western lifestyles' are associated with high levels of consumption and energy use. However, within these there are a number of separate groups. In the US there are 'lifestyle groups' – for example, 'affluent consumers', 'middle-income consumers', 'young families'. Each of these has its own distinct spending patterns.

More consumers are moving into the affluent lifestyle groups: they are more likely to consume a wider range of products, use more energy and create more waste.

> ### DID YOU KNOW?
>
> While the number of affluent consumers continues to rise, the vast majority of the world's population is still not able to afford modern lifestyles. United Nations statistics show that 80 per cent of the world's population lives on less than $1 per day.

Competitive markets

World markets have become more competitive for several reasons.

1 **The shrinking globe.** It is easier to transfer products and services across the world than ever before. Goods can be transported from Sydney, Australia to Nairobi, Kenya in hours rather than days. Services such as banking and insurance contracts can be supplied online almost instantly to large areas of the globe. The telecommunications and transport revolution has made this high level of competition possible.

2 **Access to overseas markets.** Over the last 30 years, international governments have made agreements to reduce taxes and other barriers that previously prevented imports from entering the home market; examples are in the trading of grain, steel and cars.

3 Low cost of setting up new businesses. Many small and medium-sized enterprises can be set up at relatively low cost. This is particularly the case with businesses that are prepared to inject the initial capital to create a simple website, selling goods and services, tickets, banking, insurance and other services.

4 Privatisation of industries. From the 1950s to the 1980s, many industries and businesses were government-owned. However, from the 1980s, a number of governments across the world have sold off some of these enterprises to private businesses. Instead of having a single government-owned business, there are now a number of competing companies in a range of industries. These include water supply, electricity, gas and transport networks such as private bus companies.

CASE STUDY | The global steel market

The global market for steel is very competitive. Steel is required as a material for building and manufacturing a range of products. In 2008 the main companies producing steel were as follows:

Company	Steel production [in million metric tonnes]	Country
Arcelor Mittal	103.3	Luxembourg
Nippon Steel	37.5	Japan
Baosteel	35.4	China
POSCO	34.7	South Korea
Hebei Steel	33.3	China

(Source: Reuters)

Each of these steel producers manufactures over 20 million tonnes of steel a year, but they each control only a limited share of the market. Purchasers of steel, such as construction companies, try to purchase from suppliers who can offer them the best deals. For purchasers, it is good to have so many suppliers because competition will help to cut prices. However, for suppliers, competition will restrict their profits, because they have to offer the best deals.

Questions

1 Who do you think benefits most from the competitive global steel market – producers or purchasers? Justify your answer.

2 Why do you think that the market for steel is so competitive?

In competitive markets, businesses mainly seek to win custom by:

• producing high-quality products (e.g. Rolls-Royce aircraft engines, Parker pens, Apple Macintosh portable computers).

• selling cheap products at lower prices than rivals (e.g. the German supermarket chain Lidl offers very cheap products in stores with basic layouts and the minimum of customer service).

KEY POINTS

1 Consumer spending patterns change in response to changes in income and lifestyle choices.

2 In competitive markets, businesses must aim to offer higher quality or lower prices than their rivals.

SUMMARY QUESTIONS

1 How is consumer spending likely to change as a result of:
   • rising incomes across the globe?
   • the development of 'lifestyles' common to groups of people worldwide?

2 Choose two of the following products and give two reasons that have led to their global market becoming more competitive.
   • Oil   • Computers   • Confectionery   • Books

3 Today consumers across the world can purchase CDs, books and films over the internet. How has this increased competition affected:
   • buyers?   • sellers of these items?

Unit 3   Practice exam questions

1 Explain the meaning of the phrase 'government intervention in the market'. *[2]*

2 Why might a government wish to intervene in the following situations?

   a Control of a very large supermarket company which is driving other companies out. *[2]*

   b Provision of a nationwide postal service. *[2]*

   c Setting up a free health service for all the country's citizens. *[2]*

3 Explain TWO reasons why a government would want to provide jobs for unemployed workers. *[4]*

4 Explain TWO reasons why price instability is bad for a country's economy. *[4]*

5 Identify and explain TWO ways in which consumers are protected in your country. *[4]*

6 Identify and explain TWO ways in which employees are protected in your country. *[4]*

7 Identify and explain TWO reasons why most governments try to discourage sales of cigarettes by putting health warnings on packets. *[4]*

8 Analyse ONE reason why governments want to encourage their citizens to become educated and learn skills, such as the ability to use information technology. *[3]*

9 Using your answer to Question 8, identify and explain TWO ways in which the government of your country tries to ensure that every child receives education. *[2]*

10 Identify and explain TWO reasons why governments need to raise money through taxation of individuals and businesses. *[4]*

11 Analyse why a business producing cars may pay more tax to your government than one producing essential agricultural foodstuffs. *[4]*

12 Analyse why rising interest rates in your country may be bad for consumers and business. *[4]*

13 Using the example of a business owner who wants to borrow $50,000 over 5 years, calculate the amount of interest that will be payable at a rate of:

   a 4 per cent per year. *[2]*

   b 7 per cent per year. *[2]*

14 Identify and explain TWO different ways in which a local business in your town uses new technology. *[4]*

15 Using your answers to Question 14, analyse the advantages to the business of new technology. Are there any disadvantages? *[5]*

16 Technology such as the internet has made the market for goods and services more competitive worldwide. Using a table like the one below, explain THREE advantages and THREE disadvantages to business and consumers of a more competitive environment. *[12]*

Advantages to business and consumers of a more competitive environment	Disadvantages to business and consumers of a more competitive environment
Advantage 1 Explanation	Disadvantage 1 Explanation
Advantage 2 Explanation	Disadvantage 2 Explanation
Advantage 3 Explanation	Disadvantage 3 Explanation

The city centre congestion taxation

Governments throughout the world are trying many schemes to reduce private car traffic congestion in their large cities. These include:

- flat-fee 'congestion charge' for driving into the city during peak hours
- very high fees for car parking and restricting the spaces available

- increasing numbers of dedicated 'bus and taxi' lanes, with fines for cars which use these
- high taxes on workplace parking spaces.

All of these regulations are stringently enforced, with the government declaring their aim to use the money collected to improve city public transport.

1 Describe why governments may decide to intervene to try to cut down city traffic congestion. [4]

2 Identify and explain TWO possible disadvantages to city centre businesses of these measures. [4]

3 Identify and explain TWO possible benefits to private city residents of these measures. [4]

4 Discuss the view that 'in the long run everyone will benefit from less traffic congestion'. [5]

5 To what extent do you agree that running public transport should continue to be the responsibility of government? [6]

The young fashion clothing company

Jessica Sung runs a very successful clothing business in Hong Kong. Her clothes are produced by a team of 10 sewing machine operators in a small workshop and sold to customers from a shop in the same building. Her market is mainly teenagers, who come to her to buy the latest styles at very low prices. Her busiest times are during weekends and holidays, when customers, mainly girls, come with their friends to choose new outfits. All Jessica's customers pay her in cash.

Jessica's brother Jack is trying to persuade her to install a computer system to help her with designs and to let him build a website for the company, so that she can communicate with customers and take orders over the internet. Jessica is worried, because she will need to borrow $40,000 from the bank.

1 Identify and explain TWO ways in which Jessica could use the internet to communicate with customers. [4]

2 Identify and explain TWO advantages of using a computer to design and make patterns for clothing. [4]

3 Analyse ONE advantage and ONE disadvantage to Jessica's current staff of the proposed new system. [6]

4 To what extent do you agree with Jessica's brother that she should start selling over the internet? [6]

5 Do you agree that 'new technology will always benefit business'? Justify your answer. [6]

The pure water bottling factory

A big multinational company wishes to build and operate a large factory for producing bottled water near Colombo on the island of Sri Lanka. The water produced here would meet the growing demand for safe bottled water throughout the area. The proposed location is an area of forest, owned by the government, but currently used for sustainable wood production and farmed by local workers, who also guide tourists on elephant safaris through the forest.

The factory would bring many jobs, but would also change the landscape of the area and cause pollution from the bottling process and the lorries undertaking deliveries.

1 Identify and explain TWO reasons why the government of Sri Lanka may allow this new development. [4]

2 Identify and explain TWO arguments which the local landowners may make against the new development, other than the damage to their own livelihood. [4]

3 Analyse ONE reason why hotel and restaurant owners in Sri Lanka may be in favour of the factory. [4]

4 To what extent should the government try to legislate to control the level of pollution from developments like this one? [6]

5 Should the Sri Lankan government let the development go ahead? Justify your answer. [6]

4 The economic environment

4.1 Mixed and market economies

Telephone users across Africa benefit from mobile phones supplied by the market

Businesses are part of a wider economic system that uses resources to make finished goods. The main groups involved in this system are consumers, the government, and other businesses. These groups make and buy goods and services. Economic activity takes place in what is described as the **market**.

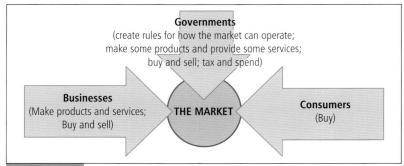

Figure 4.1.1 Groups in the economic system

The market brings together buyers and sellers. This might be in a traditional market, where buyers and sellers come together to trade for vegetables, meat, clothing and other items. The term 'market' also describes any other situation where buyers and sellers contact each other. They might do so over the telephone or by using the Internet for trading.

The price the seller sets helps buyers to decide what and how much they want to purchase. Buyers show what they prefer by 'voting' with their money for certain goods and services. This is **demand**.

Every day millions of buying and selling decisions are made. When you go shopping, you may make a decision (a choice) to buy a particular type of chocolate bar.

If many consumers decide to buy a new type of chocolate bar, then a chocolate manufacturer will benefit by switching resources (such as labour, machinery and materials) into making that type of bar. Making chocolate bars and other goods available to consumers is called **supply**.

A pure **market economy** would be one in which buyers and sellers make all their own trading decisions with no interference from government. However, there are about 200 countries in the world, and in all these the government interferes in the market.

The term **mixed economy** refers to a situation where decisions are made not only by businesses and citizens but also by government. The more decisions that are made by the government, the less free is the market. Today, decisions in all countries involve a mix of government decision-making and free decision-making by buyers and sellers. For example, in a number of countries in Africa the government owns landline telephone systems. However, these are only available to a small percentage of the population, usually in large cities. Mobile phone systems provided by private businesses have made telephone connections available to millions of new customers.

Figure 4.1.2 below gives some examples of countries and the different levels of government interference in the markets of these countries. At one extreme there is North Korea, where the government makes many of the decisions about what will be produced. At the other end of the spectrum, in the USA, the government leaves more decisions to firms and individuals. However, even in the USA the government is heavily involved in the economy, for example giving large subsidies to farmers and the motor industry to protect jobs.

Mixed economy with little government interference		Mixed economy with a lot of government interference	
USA	Japan	France	China	North Korea
United Kingdom		South Africa	Venezuela	

Figure 4.1.2   Levels of government involvement

Depending on the type of economic system in place, there will be different outcomes for consumers and businesses.

1 In a free market, customers are likely to have more choice. Because firms are competing, they will be providing a greater variety of brands to the market. For example, there may be rival bus companies operating on the same route. In contrast, if there is just one bus company, with a government licence to run on a certain route, customers have no choice if they want to travel by bus.

2 In a free market it is likely that prices will be lower. For example, rival bus companies would try to offer lower fares as well as better service. A single bus company does not have to be so competitive – provided that it can undercut prices for other types of transport.

3 In a free market suppliers will provide goods as long as there is enough demand to make a profit. However, where businesses can't make a profit, government interference can help. In a mixed economy the government can subsidise businesses to run loss-making services. For example, the government can subsidise bus routes to isolated villages to help villagers to get to work, to hospitals and to schools. The government can also provide essential services such as medical care and education for all citizens.

KEY POINTS

1   The market place is any situation in which buyers and sellers come into contact.

2   Producers and sellers supply the market provided they can make a profit.

3   In pure market economies governments do not interfere with buying and selling activities; in mixed economies governments make some of the economic decisions.

DID YOU KNOW?

Venezuela is a South American economy heavily dependent on selling oil. The government has set many price controls on foodstuffs. This limits the price that farmers can charge. Food prices are low, but there are often shortages.

ACTIVITY

Look at the provision of goods and services in your own country. To what extent are they provided by the government? Why does the government produce these goods and services? Interview some users of these services and find out if they believe they are getting value for money.

SUMMARY QUESTIONS

1 Give an example of a decision that each of the following groups might make in a mixed economy that would have an effect on other groups:

   a   consumers

   b   the government

   c   car manufacturers.

   In each case explain the effect that the decision would have on other groups.

2 How does the market help both consumers and producers/sellers?

3 A government runs its country's telephone service, but it will soon be opened up to competition. Private firms will set up mobile networks. How might this affect customer choice, the price of calls and the availability of a good service?

Show an appreciation of how international trade influences an economy and its business sector by creating opportunities for growth, increased competition and consumer choice.

• Explain how international trade creates opportunities and problems (threats) for business units.

EXAM TIP

It is a common error to think that countries only import goods that they cannot produce themselves. Make sure that you understand why customers sometimes buy imported goods, in preference to ones domestically produced.

DID YOU KNOW?

The Nigerian government is seeking to make the country less dependent on foreign food imports. It has set up an Agricultural Development Bank, which lends money to farmers for agricultural projects. Why do you think the government is supporting farmers in Nigeria in this way?

International trade: the benefits for economies

International trade allows countries to gain from specialisation. Nigeria, for example, is able to concentrate on producing its most saleable goods and services, such as petroleum products, cocoa and rubber. By trading these things on world markets, Nigeria is able to buy things which it finds it less easy to produce such as machinery (for example, oil drilling equipment), and transport equipment (for example, bus engines).

Countries trade in order to benefit from each other's resources and skills. For example, Nigeria is very good at producing oil because it has huge oil and gas reserves.

Overall Nigeria's biggest export earner is sales of oil and petroleum products. Nigeria is one of the world's major suppliers of oil and this helps the country to run a huge trade surplus. Much of the revenue from oil production goes to the government as well as to large overseas companies, such as Shell, that have set up operations in the country. In addition, Nigeria is a major producer of the agricultural cash crops cocoa and rubber. Cocoa is grown on small family farms.

Nigeria is not so good at producing some manufactured goods, like tractors and machinery, so it imports these from France and other European countries. It also imports agricultural machinery from India. In recent years Nigeria has not been able to produce enough food to meet demand in its home market. It therefore imports foodstuffs such as wheat and rice. Other reasons that countries trade include the following:

• to acquire items, such as scarce metals and minerals (for example, gold, diamonds, and bauxite), that can only be found in a small number of countries

• to achieve adequate supply for their markets of goods which they cannot produce in sufficient quantity; for example, the huge Chinese market requires imports of fresh food and vegetables, and minerals such as iron, silver and gold

• to provide greater customer choice; for example, customers in India can choose to buy an Indian car, or a German, French, or American one

• to earn foreign currency

• to introduce more competition through international trade; for example, Indian car manufacturers have to produce good quality, value-for-money cars, or Indian consumers will choose to buy foreign imports

• to foster good relations with other countries.

Importing and exporting: the benefits for business

An **import** involves the purchase of products or services from overseas.

An **export** is a sale of products or services to individuals or businesses overseas.

Through importing, businesses are able to acquire the best supplies. These might include supplies of raw materials, components, parts and semi-finished and finished products. For example, the German car manufacturer Volkswagen manufactures cars in a number of countries, including Germany, Brazil, India and South Africa. In India labour costs are lower than in Germany. Volkswagen therefore purchases 1 billion euros' worth of components each year for its European factories from factories in India. Each year Volkswagen purchases over 70 billion euros' worth of components for its global manufacturing plants from the best suppliers across the world.

Exporting makes it possible for firms to grow across the world. A good example of this is Massey Ferguson, the agricultural machinery brand. Originally Massey Ferguson's global headquarters was based in Canada. Today Massey Ferguson farm machinery is manufactured in many countries around the world, such as France, Denmark, Finland, USA and Brazil. From these countries farm machinery is exported throughout the world. AGCO Corporation was founded in 1990 and acquired Massey Ferguson in 1994, followed by other international farm machinery brands. Farming is a global activity and Massey Ferguson tractors are sold across the world (Figure 4.2.1).

International trade can also put businesses at risk. For example, Ford and Chrysler cars are very popular in the United States. However, through international trade there is strong competition from French cars like Peugeot and Renault, German cars produced by companies like Mercedes and Volkswagen and Japanese cars such as Toyota.

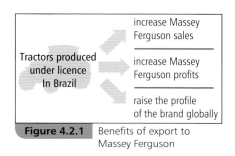

Oil is Nigeria's biggest export earner

SUMMARY QUESTIONS

1 Give examples of ways in which **a** businesses **b** consumers benefit from international trade with your country.

2 In 2008 the five largest imports into the United States from Malaysia were machinery ($12 billion), electrical machinery ($10.6 billion), palm oil ($1.2 billion), optical and medical instruments ($1.1 billion) and rubber ($1 billion). Which of these imports might American producers see as posing the greatest threats?

3 Explain how a large company based in your country can benefit from importing goods and services from other countries. How can it also benefit from exporting to other countries?

KEY POINTS

1 Trade gives countries access to resources and goods not available at home.

2 Trading enables countries to grow their economies.

3 Countries specialise in and sell abroad those items that they can make best.

4 A business benefits from importing raw materials, parts and finished products.

5 A business gains revenue and profit from exporting. This also enhances the brand internationally.

Illustrating the Beanz!

Merchants have traded goods for thousands of years. Traders selling goods such as nutmeg, pepper and silks were using the route known as The Silk Road between China, India and the Arabian peninsula over 2000 years ago. They travelled vast distances in the hope of selling at a profit in new markets.

However, it is not easy to enter a new market. There are a number of obstacles that create difficulty. A first major difficulty is that consumers in the market that you want to sell into may not be familiar with your brand or product.

This can be illustrated by the example of Heinz baked beans. The HJ Heinz company is a large American multinational producing many food products. One of its products is tinned beans. They are produced to different recipes in different countries, in different sized and shaped tins. Most commonly they are produced with a tomato sauce base. The variety of bean typically used is the haricot bean.

In the late 1990s the company started selling their beans in Eastern Europe, where beans are very popular. However, because customers were not sure what was inside the tin they were wary of buying the product. As a result the company changed its labelling to include pictures of the beans. This resulted in a large increase in sales. The company has also changed 'beans' to 'beanz' on the tin to support its advertising slogan of 'Beanz meanz Heinz'.

Other problems of entering new overseas markets include the following.

- **Lack of local knowledge**: businesses particularly want to find out about consumer tastes and preferences. They also need to know about rules and laws about what can be produced. For example, in Thailand a very popular drink for people working long hours was called 'Krating Daeng', which translates as 'Red Bull'. The drink helps to keep people awake because it contains substances called caffeine and taurine. It was sold in a brown bottle. Before it could be introduced to other markets, some of the ingredients needed to be changed because of health and safety laws in other countries. The drink has now been reformulated under the name 'Red Bull' and it sells across the globe.

- **Contacts**: it is very important to have contacts in overseas markets. These contacts may be with people who can help you to sell your product. They may be with government officials who can explain details of local laws.

- **Different cultures and tastes**: many products have to be altered for local conditions. This is particularly true in the food and drink market.

- **Language differences:** there can be challenges associated with setting up and operating in a foreign country. Without knowledge of a local languages lots of mistakes can be made.

Dealing with problems in overseas markets

One way of selling to overseas customers is to make sales visits to countries to sell your products. This could be supported by telephone links and the creation of a sales website (although unreliable web connections in some countries may make this unsuitable). This is a low-cost method, but has the disadvantage that the exporter only builds limited overseas contacts.

Another approach therefore could be to use an overseas sales agent or partner. The partner would share the profits from the sales.

On a larger scale, a business can open up an overseas production or sales operation. This is much more costly. Building an overseas operation helps a company to plan for the long-term. Customers will take the company much more seriously if it has a local base. For example, in South Africa, Volkswagen makes a range of cars for the African market from its base there. The company is sourcing an increasing number of components from local manufacturers. Another example is Oxford University Press, which has its own publication department in Africa – producing books for the East African market.

Another good way to enter an overseas market is to form a **joint venture** with a local partner. Here a joint business is set up between the two companies. Many Western companies have set up joint ventures in China and India. The local partner will have a lot of local contacts with government officials and business people in the home market. The local partner will also have a good knowledge of local tastes and preferences.

The table below gives examples of joint ventures in India.

Tata Motors and Fiat	The joint venture manufactures cars from Tata and Fiat. Tata motors buys diesel engines for its cars from Fiat. Fiat distributes Tata cars in Europe.
Mahindra and Renault	The venture will manufacture Renault's Logan cars in India. Renault gains access to the Indian market. Mahindra gains technical knowledge about car production.
Bharthi–Wal-Mart	The Indian government restricted the growth of foreign retailers in India. The joint venture therefore gave Wal-Mart access to the Indian market.

KEY POINTS

1 When entering a new overseas market companies are faced by a number of problems. These include language differences, lack of local contacts, lack of knowledge of the local market, and different rules and regulations.

2 There are cultural differences between different markets. As a result, customers in different countries have different tastes and preferences.

3 There are a number of ways of entering new markets that reduce the risk. These include working with local partners such as sales agents or setting up a joint venture.

4 It is possible to set up a new operation in an overseas market.

DID YOU KNOW?

McDonald's, the fast food restaurant, has introduced more spicy and vegetarian dishes in India to suit local tastes.

ACTIVITY

Visit a local shop. Can you identify one product that is produced in your own country that would need to be adapted if it were going to be sold in other countries? How would the product need to be altered, and why?

SUMMARY QUESTIONS

1 A Japanese company sells cameras in Europe through agents who deal directly with camera retailers. However, with the development of new digital camera technologies sales have started to increase substantially in Europe. The company wants to increase business in Europe. What methods would you recommend for increasing its presence in the European market?

2 What would be the main advantages to a Western company from creating a joint venture when seeking to increase sales in China?

3 In 2009 Tata Motors of India launched the Tata Nano – the world's smallest mass-market car. The car is designed to solve car-parking problems in cities and to have very low petrol consumption. Tata hopes to sell variations of the car in Western markets. What problems might Tata have in selling to these markets? How might Tata deal with these problems?

Appreciate the implications of tariff barriers, quotas and exchange rate changes for businesses that trade internationally.

- Gain awareness of how restrictions on trade impact on businesses that export and import.
- Understand the impact of exchange rate movements on competitiveness and profitability.

SPICED (Strong Pound – Imports Cheap – Exports Dear) can help you remember the effect of currency rises and falls.

EXAM TIP

When answering a question on the effects of a change in exchange rate, keep your analysis in the context of the 'home country', or where the business concerned is based. This way you are less likely to become confused!

Restrictions on trade

In mixed economies the government intervenes in the market for imports and exports. It usually does this to protect producers in its home market. Some good examples of this interference are tariff barriers and quotas. A **tariff** is a tax levied by the government on imported goods. A **quota** is a limitation on the number of goods that can be imported.

The government imposes these types of restrictions to protect businesses in its domestic market, usually from cheaper imports.

CASE STUDY	The ethanol tariff

A good example of a tariff is the import tax that the United States levied on imports of ethanol in 2002. The tariff had been levied to encourage the growth of ethanol production in the United States. Ethanol is a new type of fuel for cars that is produced from corn and other agricultural products. The United States is the biggest producer of ethanol and Brazil is second. In 2006 the American government decided to eliminate import taxes on ethanol, so that more ethanol would become available to power American cars. The corn growers in America were opposed to this action, because they said the competition would reduce the prices that they received for corn.

The effect of taking away the ethanol tariff was that American importers of ethanol were better off because they could import cheaper fuel. Brazilian exporters of ethanol were now able to sell more to the US market.

Questions

1 Why do you think that the United States initially imposed the tariff on ethanol imports?

2 What arguments would be put forward for reducing the ethanol tariff?

3 Who would be opposed to removing the tariff and why?

Quotas have a more direct effect than tariffs. An absolute quota limits the quantity of goods that can enter a country in a given period, for example, a year. This could be measured by weight, quantities imported or values of imports. Certain quotas will be filled shortly after the opening of the quota period. Faced by a quota to a country, exporters will compete with each other to sell as quickly as possible into a foreign market before the quota is complete.

The exchange rate

The term **'exchange rate'** refers to the rate at which two currencies will exchange for each other at a particular moment in time.

For example, the table opposite shows the exchange rate between the South African rand (ZAR) and the US dollar (US$) on 29 October 2008. You can see that the rate of exchange on that day was 10 rand to one dollar.

The daily value of the US dollar, South African rand and other currencies is determined in the foreign exchange markets (FOREX), where billions of US dollars' worth of currencies are traded every hour. The value is determined by the demand and supply. If lots of people want to buy South African rands for example, to buy South African goods, then this will raise the value of the rand.

When the South African rand increases in value, this will have an impact on South African trade. For example, if more people want to buy rand in order to buy South African goods, then the exchange rate against the dollar will rise – for example, to 9 rand to one dollar. In this scenario, a South African would only need to exchange 9 rand, rather than 10 rand, to get one dollar. South Africans will therefore find it cheaper than before to buy American goods.

A change in the exchange rate can affect the competitiveness of a business. This is because changes have an immediate effect on the prices at which products are sold in international markets. In the South African example given above, when the rand increases in value, South African goods become more expensive to foreigners. This would have an immediate effect of making South African goods less competitive.

When goods become more difficult to sell, profits are likely to be affected. With the rising rand, South African exporters will face falling sales and a knock-on effect can lead to reductions in profits. You will find out more about how changes in the exchange rate affect profits in Unit 13.8.

South African rand (ZAR)	US dollars (US$)
10	1
1,000	100
100,000	10,000
10,000,000	1,000,000

ACTIVITY

Look at a national newspaper in your country that shows the change in the exchange rate between your country's currency and that of its major trading partners. How is a change in the exchange rate likely to affect exporters in your home country?

The daily value of the South African rand (ZAR) is determined in the foreign exchange market

SUMMARY QUESTIONS

1 Describe the effect on international trade of tariffs and quotas.

2 In 2009 the value of the British pound sterling fell against the euro. It was more expensive for British people to buy goods when they visited Europe on business and on holiday. However, ASOS, one of Britain's best known internet-based retailers, found that its sales to Europe boomed.

Explain why British tourists lost out, while ASOS benefited from the fall in value of the pound.

3 A government is trying to encourage businesses in its home market to produce solar panels for heating homes and factories. Would it be better to impose quotas, tariffs, or tariff-rate quotas on imported solar panels? Give reasons to support your answer.

KEY POINTS

1 The government imposes tariffs and quotas to protect business in its own country.

2 Tariffs and quotas restrict trade. These restrictions make it more difficult for exporters to sell into foreign markets and for importers to import from overseas.

3 When the exchange value of a currency rises, exports from a particular country become less competitive. This may reduce profits for exporters.

Competition and business

LEARNING OUTCOMES

- Identify the impact of competition on business in terms of consumer choice and sales.
- Show awareness of the potential for consumer exploitation in uncompetitive markets.

DID YOU KNOW?

As well as facing direct competition, sellers also have indirect competitors. For example, while pineapple sellers are in direct competition with each other they also face indirect competition from sellers of other types of fruit. They are also indirectly in competition with other types of food sellers. The businesses are competing with each other to make sales, that is, to win the money that customers are willing to spend, see Figure 4.5.1.

EXAM TIP

It is often thought that an increase in competition is always of benefit to consumers. Try to understand why this might not always be true.

The impact of competition

Businesses compete with each other for customers. Read the following case study about how pineapple producers in Africa, South America and Asia, who are in **direct competition**, compete with each other to sell pineapples to buyers in the European Union.

CASE STUDY	Competition in world pineapple markets

At one time Africa was the main supplier of pineapple to Europe. In the 1980s, the 'Smooth Cayenne' variety, grown in Africa, dominated sales to Europe. However, in the 1990s a new variety of pineapple: the 'Sweet' or 'Extra Sweet' was introduced. This variety grows more quickly and is less prone to discolouration than the Cayenne. Huge plantations were set up in Costa Rica and some South American countries. Because the South American pineapples could be produced more cheaply, they were able to undercut Smooth Cayenne prices.

Pineapples for export

The massive influx of these mass-produced pineapples to Europe had a devastating effect on small and medium-sized African producers. In 2007 pineapple sales by Côte d'Ivoire in West Africa was one third of the level of the 1990s. Although the arrival of the Sweet pineapple created more choice for consumers, the impact of the competition was to make Smooth Cayenne pineapples less competitive and has led to a drop in sales for their growers.

Questions

1 How has the development of the 'Sweet' and 'Extra Sweet' pineapple affected customer choice and the sales of:

   a African producers
   b South American producers?

2 Who are the winners and who are the losers from this increase in competition?

The greater the level of competition the more choice customers have. For example, in a small town customers can usually buy petrol from more than one petrol station. They will choose to buy from sellers offering low prices or higher quality petrol. Sellers with lots of competitors will lose some sales to these rival businesses. In contrast, a petrol station in an isolated village may not have another competitor for many miles.

Direct competition	Indirect competition			
Pineapple seller	Pineapple seller	Other type of fruit seller	Food seller	Other goods which consumers could buy

Figure 4.5.1   Direct and indirect competition

Uncompetitive markets: risks for the customer

Because there is a lot of competition between sellers wanting to sell pineapples in the European Union, consumers get good quality at low prices. Where there is less competition, however, the seller is in a more powerful position than the consumer. For example, if there is only one petrol station or shop in an area, the seller can put up prices and may offer a poor quality service: in a remote location you might find that the shop does not always open on time. The goods might also not always be up-to-date.

Where there are only two or a small number of sellers they may get together to raise prices. This is called **price fixing**.

The term **uncompetitive practice** is used to describe situations where firms seek to limit competition.

In Jamaica and most other countries there are laws that restrict customer exploitation. The Jamaican law is called The Fair Competition Act. The Act seeks to create an environment in which all businesses can operate according to the same set of clearly defined rules. The law seeks to prevent restrictive practice like price fixing and 'marrying'.

ACTIVITY

Identify a company that is a major supplier of mobile phone services in your country. Who are the direct competitors for this company? Who are the indirect competitors? Set out your results on a chart like the one illustrated in Figure 4.5.1. What actions does the company you selected take to compete with its rivals?

DID YOU KNOW?

Another example of an uncompetitive practice is when a supplier will not provide a customer with a certain article unless he or she buys another one at the same time. In Jamaica this is called 'marrying'.

SUMMARY QUESTIONS

1 Copy and complete the following sentences using the words from the list.

Direct competition / indirect competition / consumer exploitation / uncompetitive markets / choice / sales / competitive market

Growers of a particular type of fruit such as bananas are in _____ with other growers of bananas. The fact that there are many growers working on small plantations across the world gives customers greater _____. The banana growers are also in _____ with other fruit growers such as those producing apples, pears, and pineapples. A _____ is one in which there are lots of competitors each seeking to win a share of consumer spending. Sometimes the government needs to step in where there are _____ and suppliers are restricting competition. In such markets _____ may be dominated by just a few firms. These firms are able to engage in _____ by limiting the choice available and by raising prices above levels expected in more competitive markets.

2 In what ways do consumers gain from competitive markets? How do consumers lose out if there is a less competitive market?

3 In Jamaica there is a Fair Competition Act. Why do you think that the Act was created? What will be the effect on business practice of having such an Act?

KEY POINTS

1 Businesses compete with each other to sell goods to customers.

2 Some of this competition is direct – where firms produce the same, or broadly similar, goods.

3 Firms are also in indirect competition with less closely related sellers to win a share of the consumer's spending.

4 The greater the level of competition, the more choice consumers have and the more businesses have to compete to win sales.

5 Where there is only one, two or a small number of sellers, consumers have less choice.

6 Consumers are more likely to be exploited in uncompetitive markets.

SECTION 1: Short-answer questions

1 Explain the difference between a 'market economy' and a 'mixed economy'. [2]

2 In a free market, what would be the result, in terms of use of resources, of a consumer trend towards buying 'low sugar' soft drinks? [2]

3 In a mixed economy, why might the government subsidise production of essential food crops such as maize or rice? [2]

4 In a mixed economy, why might the government control and run the public transport system in big cities? [3]

5 Identify THREE reasons why a big international company, such as Gap, might produce their clothing in countries such as Indonesia and China. [3]

6 Identify and explain TWO problems that Gap may have trying to export their jeans to areas of the world such as India, Asia and Africa. [4]

7 Using your answer to Question 6, suggest TWO ways in which Gap may ensure that their products are suitable for these particular overseas markets. [4]

8 On 29 October 2008, the exchange rate between the South African rand and the US dollar was ZAR10 = $1. Using this exchange rate, calculate the price in South African rand of an imported US-made computer which is priced at $299. [3]

9 Carry out research and complete a table such as the one below that shows details of your country's main exports and imports.

From your completed table, identify your country's main trading partners. [4]

10 Calculate the price of the computer in (8) above, following a 20 per cent appreciation of the South African rand. [2]

11 Calculate the price of the same computer, following a 15 per cent depreciation of the South African rand. [2]

12 Identify and explain ONE reason why the government of a country might impose an import tariff on products from abroad, such as cars and computers. [2]

13 Identify and explain ONE reason why the government of a country might impose an embargo (complete ban) on the import of meat products from abroad. [2]

14 Identify and explain TWO ways in which your country benefits from international trade as outlined in your answer to Question 9. [4]

15 Identify and explain TWO disadvantages to a country of heavy reliance on imported food products. [4]

16 Identify in your country ONE example of direct competition and ONE example of indirect competition to Coca-Cola. [2]

17 Identify and explain TWO benefits to consumers in countries where there is a high level of competition in the market for clothing. [4]

18 Identify and explain ONE advantage and ONE disadvantage to local fast food traders of the entry by big international companies, such as McDonald's, into their towns and cities. [4]

	Product or Service	Exported to	Product or Service	Imported from
Food and drinks				
Clothing				
Electrical				
Other				

The clothing company

Imran owns a clothing company in Lahore, Pakistan. In his factory, he produces cotton clothing which is exported to the USA and the UK. His employees work very long hours on noisy machines, with few breaks. He has built up his business due to the low prices and good quality of his goods.

1 What might be the effect on Imran's sales and profitability if the Pakistan rupee depreciates against the US dollar and the UK pound by 10 per cent? [4]

2 What might be the effect on Imran's business of the US government imposing an import tariff on clothing? [4]

3 Identify and explain THREE possible effects of a decision by the government of Pakistan to impose tougher laws on health and safety and limits on working hours in factories in Pakistan. [6]

4 Imran would like to try to sell his clothes in new European markets, such as France and Italy. Explain THREE difficulties that he may face in breaking into these areas. [6]

5 Do you think that Imran should try to sell his clothes in new European markets? Explain and justify your answer. [6]

Subway Sandwiches in Lusaka

Lusaka is the capital of Zambia, a sub-Saharan country in Africa. The country is mainly rural, with a mix of ethnicity and cultures among the population. Subway Sandwiches is a multi-national company that sells sandwiches and rolls with a range of fillings. The company already has successful shops in two of the new shopping centres in Lusaka, but would like to expand to other major towns throughout the country.

1 Explain TWO factors in connection with product choice, which Subway must consider when setting up in a new location. [4]

2 Identify and explain TWO ways in which an agent or local contact might be able to help Subway move into new markets like this. [4]

3 State and explain ONE advantage and ONE disadvantage to local fast-food shops if Subway Sandwiches set up in a new location. [6]

4 Identify and explain THREE factors which will be important to Subway when looking for new shop locations in other cities in Zambia. [6]

5 Do local consumers always benefit from this type of development? Explain your answer. [6]

The Maldives: paradise island tourism

The Maldives is a small country composed of many tropical islands, located in the Indian Ocean. The major industries are tourism and fishing. International visitors, mainly from Europe, come to the islands for luxury beach and diving holidays. The Maldivian government has fixed the currency, the rufiyaa, against the US dollar.

1 Explain TWO ways in which tourists help the economy of the Maldives. [4]

2 What might be TWO economic or cultural disadvantages of increased tourism to a small country such as the Maldives? [4]

3 The Maldivian government categorises tourism as an export for its country. Identify and explain why this might be. [4]

4 Identify and explain THREE changes to the economy of the Maldives if the US dollar (and therefore the rufiyaa) depreciates against the euro. [6]

5 The Maldivian government enforces strict laws against sea pollution and also charges a 'tourist tax' on hotel visitors on a 'per bed per night' basis. Explain reasons for this government involvement in the market. [6]

Types of business organisation – sole traders and partnerships

When setting up a business, one of the first decisions is 'what type of business to form'. The type of business chosen determines the legal status of the business and how easy it is to raise capital.

The sole trader

This unit looks at privately owned businesses – that is, ones that are owned by individuals or groups of owners rather than by the government.

Private businesses (private sector)	Public businesses (public sector)
Sole traders	Government-owned businesses
Partnership	
Companies (including multinationals)	

A **sole trader** is the most common form of business ownership and the easiest to set up. Examples include street-corner flowers or drinks sellers in cities, tailors and operators of shoeshine services. A sole trader is a business owned by one person – though it may still employ a large number of people.

The table below shows some of the advantages and disadvantages of setting up as a sole trader rather than as a larger business.

Advantages	Disadvantages
Easy to set up; no special paperwork is required	Having unlimited liability endangers personal possessions
Usually a small business; less capital is required	Finance can be difficult to raise
Speedy decisions can be made by the owner – few people involved	Small scale limits discounts and other benefits of large-scale production
Personal attention given to business affairs	Prices often higher than those of larger organisations
Special services can be offered to customers	Ill health, holidays, etc. may affect the running of the business
Can cater for the needs of local people; because the business is small, the owner comes into contact with the customers	Only one owner may mean narrow range of skills
Profits do not have to be shared	Mistakes possible, because no colleagues to consult for advice
Business affairs can be kept private	

Unlimited liability

When you set up a business you will need capital to run it. Sole traders have only their own resources to draw on. They will finance their business through savings, and borrowing from banks and on their credit card.

Any debt that a sole trader builds up has to be paid by the owner. They are personally responsible for all the debts of the business. This situation can be contrasted with larger companies. Owners of a company have legal protection known as **limited liability**: this limits the debts owed by an individual owner of a company to the sum of money they have put into their business. In contrast, sole traders' debts are unlimited. If sole traders find themselves in debt, they may have to sell off their house, car and other possessions in order to pay what they owe.

Partnerships

A **partnership** is a business association between two or more owners of an enterprise. Setting up a partnership usually involves creating a legal agreement between the partners. Partnerships usually have between 2 and 20 members, though this varies between countries. In some countries, legal restrictions allow a maximum of 20 partners.

Partnerships are common in many types of business – small shops as well as professional practices like vets, doctors, solicitors and dentists.

The table shows the advantages and disadvantages of setting up a partnership.

Advantages	Disadvantages
Capital from partners, so more capital available	Unlimited liability (except for 'sleeping partners', who put money into the business but do not get involved in its running)
Larger scale than sole trader	Disagreements between partners
Members of family can join	Limitation of number of partners (in many countries restricted by law to maximum of 20)
Affairs can be kept private	If partnership was set up by legal agreement, it will need to be re-formed if one partner dies
Risks and responsibilities spread among partners	

Most partnerships are not protected by limited liability.

SUMMARY QUESTIONS

1 Abdul is considering setting up a small business repairing broken windows and is not sure whether to set up as a partnership or a sole trader. What would be the benefits of forming a partnership in terms of the following?

Access to capital / liability / ease of setting up the business / access to skills

What other advantages might there be to setting up a partnership?

2 What is limited liability? How does not having limited liability disadvantage many sole traders and partnerships?

3 Set out a table showing the main differences between partnerships and sole traders.

Other types of business organisation

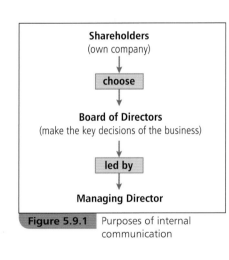

Shareholders
(own company)

↓

choose

↓

Board of Directors
(make the key decisions of the business)

↓

led by

↓

Managing Director

Figure 5.9.1 Purposes of internal communication

A company

'**Company**' suggests a group of companions who have come together to set up a business. The business they set up becomes a legal body, separate in law from the owners. To become a company, a business needs to become legally incorporated. This involves registering the company with the Registrar of Companies in the country in which the company has its head office.

The owners of a company are its shareholders. They appoint a **board of directors** to make the **strategic decisions**. The decisions they make include how much profit to distribute to shareholders, and what direction the business should take. The managing director is the senior director, with the lead role for managing the business.

The reasons for **incorporating** a business include:

- If the business gets into financial difficulty, shareholders risk losing only the value of their shareholding in the business. Their private possessions are protected by limited liability and only the assets of the business are at risk.
- An incorporated business is easier to sell than an unincorporated one, because all the complicated arrangements of setting up the business have already been done. Companies are expected to keep detailed accounts so that buyers can immediately see how the company is doing financially when they buy it.

The main disadvantages of a company concern the administration needed to register the company and the requirement to produce annual reports. Detailed accounts have to be kept.

The table shows the two types of **limited companies**.

Private companies (ltd)	Public companies (plc)
1 Shares can only be bought direct from the company with the permission of the board of directors.	**1** Shares can be bought and sold on a stock exchange. Anyone can buy them.
2 Usually has quite a small number of shareholders. May be a family-run business.	**2** Can have a large number of shareholders (may be millions) all over the world.
3 Has access to less capital than a public company.	**3** Has access to more capital.

The main advantage of being a **private company** is that the original owners can stop outsiders from buying up their company. Having a smaller number of people from whom to draw funds, however, may restrict growth. The main advantage of being a public company is access to large amounts of capital, which enables growth.

Franchises

A **franchise** business is made up of a franchisor and franchisees. The franchisor is an established enterprise (often a public limited company) with a well-known name and products or services. The franchisor grants a licence to a franchisee to produce a product, sell products or provide services in a given area. Examples of franchises include food franchises (e.g. a McDonald's franchise), a coffee shop franchise (e.g. Costa Coffee or Starbucks), and retail franchises such as United Colors of Benetton, operating in over 120 countries.

The franchisee pays for the franchise to trade in a given area, but will receive training and equipment from the franchisor. They will be expected to share the profit with the franchisor.

The main advantage to the franchisor is that they only have to invest a limited amount of capital in each franchise, but they take profits from the franchisee. The franchisee will work hard to make a success of the business, but in turn benefits from working with a proven business idea, trading under a well-known name and getting support and materials from the franchisor.

DID YOU KNOW?

Stock exchanges exist across the world where traders buy and sell shares in public companies on behalf of clients. Examples are the South African Stock Exchange in Johannesburg, the New Zealand Stock Exchange in Wellington, and the Jamaican Stock Exchange in Kingston. Companies whose stocks are listed on these exchanges can raise funds both within the home market and internationally.

ACTIVITY

Speak to a franchisee in your own country. Find out how they came to be in the business. What is the relationship with the franchisor? Share your findings with the class.

Joint ventures

A joint venture (JV) is formed when two independent businesses set up a new enterprise in which they jointly own a stake. It can take the form of an incorporated business or a partnership.

Joint ventures are commonly used when a business from one country wants to enter a new country, but prefers to do so with a local partner. The local partner will have a lot of contacts and know how to conduct business in that market. A lot of oil companies create joint ventures to search for and then exploit oil reserves. Many Western companies have created joint ventures when entering the Chinese, Indian and other South East Asian markets.

EXAM TIP

Joint ventures are often used as a means of avoiding tariff barriers and so gaining access to new markets. They reduce the amount of capital that a company needs, but they can also cause difficulties for that company, such as controlling the quality of the products or services provided.

SUMMARY QUESTIONS

1 Why might a group of friends setting up in business for the first time prefer to create an incorporated rather than an unincorporated business?

2 What benefits might a Western European manufacturer of chocolate and confectionery products gain from setting up a joint venture with an existing Chinese manufacturer rather than setting up its own independent plant there?

3 Fast-food franchises such as McDonald's are found in many countries. What would be the advantages to a local franchisee of working with McDonald's rather than setting up their own food business?

KEY POINTS

1 A company is owned by shareholders who are able to bring capital into a business.

2 Shareholders are protected by limited liability. The financial risk is limited to the value of the shares they hold.

3 Another way for a business to grow with less risk to its own capital is to sell franchises.

4 A good way of entering a foreign market is to create a joint venture with a local company.

Discuss the appropriateness of a given form of organisation (e.g. sole trader, partnership, company or franchise) in enabling a business to achieve its objectives.

• Recommend suitable forms of business organisation to the owners and management in a given situation.

Business objectives

We have seen that a key objective of businesses is to make a profit. However, how they make a profit varies with the type of business. Every big company began as a small company, often with just one or two enterprising individuals at its head. The person starting up the business may simply seek to earn a living and to support their family. They may prefer to work for themselves rather than for someone else.

A business that wants to remain small and to maintain control within a small group of owners will best operate as an unincorporated business. However, when businesses want to grow and purchase expensive capital, it makes sense to become incorporated and raise money from a large number of shareholders.

| CASE STUDY | Hero Cycles |

The Hero Group in India provides an excellent example of business growth. In the 1940s, Brij Mohan Munjal, in partnership with his three brothers, started supplying components to local bicycle businesses in Amritsar. In 1947, the family had to move to Ludhiana, which was a major centre for Indian bicycle manufacture. The Munjals expanded their business to become a major supplier of bicycle parts in India.

They then moved from just supplying parts to manufacturing them. They produced handlebars, front forks and bicycle chains. In the mid 1950s, the government in the Punjab was keen to encourage bicycle manufacture. The Munjals set up a company, Hero Cycles, and started to manufacture 7,500 bicycles a year.

Since then, the bicycles have become renowned throughout the world, offering sturdy, value-for-money cycles.

In the mid 1980s, the company joined together with Honda to manufacture motorcycles. Today, Hero is the largest producer of motorcycles in the world.

1940s	1950s	1980s	2000s
Partnership of four brothers – bicycle supplies	Company making bicycles – one of the largest in India	International venture producing motorcycles as well as bicycles	Global leader in bicycles and motorcycles

Questions

1 What objectives do you think the Munjal brothers would have had in the early days?

2 What would have been the advantages of running the business as a partnership?

Hero Cycles were able to profit from the popularity of bicycles in India

3 What objectives do you think Hero Cycles is likely to have today? How will these have changed from the early objectives?

4 How does the business benefit today from being a public company?

The partnership would have been appropriate when the brothers first set up because they only needed a little capital and they had enough skills to run a family business. However, when the company wanted to grow into a national, and then international, business, it was essential to become an incorporated business.

The table shows the key differences between various business forms.

Organisation	Objectives	Control	Sources of finance	Distribution of profits
Sole trader	To provide a living for the owner, profit, growth	By the one owner	Owner's capital, overdraft, credit card, loans, grants, mortgage, profit	All to the owner
Partnership	To provide a living for the owner, to run a professional service, profit, growth, increased market share	By the partners	Partner's capital, credit card, overdraft, loans, grants, mortgage, profit	Between partners
Incorporated business	Profit, growth, increased market share	By the board of directors, and managers working on their behalf	Share capital, overdraft, loans, mortgage, debentures, profits	Between shareholders
Franchise	For the franchisor – to expand business over a wider area and increase profits; for the franchisee – to set up a profitable enterprise using the support of the franchising organisation	By the franchisee, subject to limitations established when forming the franchise	Franchisees have to pay a fee to the franchisor to buy the franchise rights; they can then access other sources of finance, such as bank loans, to keep the business running	Franchisees pay a set % of their profits to the franchisor
Joint venture	To create a new venture based on an agreement between two existing companies; to make a profit in a new area of operations	The new venture becomes a distinct entity, with responsibility for running the venture	Funds provided by the companies that create the joint venture; the JV can then access other sources of funds	The joint venture distributes the profits to the companies that set it up

Business owners can also grow their business through setting up franchise outlets, which they can do when the business is sufficiently well known.

Creating a joint venture is particularly helpful in moving into overseas markets. Often there are restrictions involved in moving into new countries. Setting up a joint venture enables a business to make contacts and to take advantage of the local knowledge provided by a local partner.

SUMMARY QUESTIONS

1 What type of business would you form if you wanted to do each of the following? In each case, justify your choice.
   • Keep control of the business as the original owner.
   • Access a foreign market where there are many legal and cultural differences from your own country.
   • Expand quickly without risking your own capital.
   • Raise a lot of finance from a range of owners.

2 Identify a small business in your local area. How could this business change its form if it wanted to expand? What would be the advantages of doing so?

3 Who makes the decisions in a:
   • partnership?   • franchise?   • company?

KEY POINTS

1 Business objectives are best met when there is a suitable form of business organisation.

2 Sole traders and partnerships are a good way of setting up a small independent business.

3 If a firm wants to expand and grow, it may need to become a company, or it may set up a franchise.

4 Forming a joint venture can help a company expand into a new market.

Multinational companies

Identify reasons for the importance and growth of multinational business.

- Explain why multinational companies are created.
- Understand the potential impact of multinationals on the countries where they are located by looking at the advantages and disadvantages that they create.

Unilever owns 51 per cent of the shares of Hindustan Unilever – India's largest fast-moving consumer goods company, selling toothpaste, shampoo, ice cream and many other products. The company has 40 factories in India, which supply 6.3 million retailers

Multinational companies

A **multinational** is a company with its headquarters in one country but which produces and sells its products in other countries. Many of the goods and services that we consume are produced by multinationals.

You probably use a Unilever product in your home. Unilever is a British-Dutch company employing about a quarter of a million people worldwide. They have 300 local factories and own companies in 88 countries. In 2008, Unilever's top 13 products each had sales of over 1 billion euros. These included Knorr soups, Lipton tea and Omo and Surf washing powders. Some of Unilever's brands, such as Lipton tea or Magnum ice cream, are identical across the globe. Other brands are produced by Unilever specially for a particular country or area – for example, PG Tips in the UK, Home Cup in Nigeria and Ting Hua in China are all Unilever tea products.

Large multinationals

In July 2009, some of the world's largest multinationals in terms of sales were involved in banking and the oil industry. Many of the multinationals had their head offices in North America, Western Europe and Japan. The following table lists some of the largest companies. Their size is measured by the value of their sales.

Company	Sector	Country
Wal-Mart	Retailing	United States
Exxon Mobil	Oil	United States
Royal Dutch Shell	Oil	Netherlands
Toyota	Automobiles	Japan
AXA	Insurance	France
HSBC	Bank	UK
Lukoil	Oil	Russia
Indian Oil	Oil	India
National Australian Bank	Bank	Australia
Bank of China	Bank	China

Multinationals benefit from operating in a range of countries. Benefits include:

- the capacity to make use of natural resources in many countries. Oil companies like Shell and Exxon Mobil drill for oil in almost every continent, as well as on the ocean bed.
- making use of labour in other countries. The sportswear manufacturer Nike has many factories employing thousands of people in countries like Vietnam and Indonesia. These countries provide low-cost labour with the right skills.

- the opportunity to have a global market. In India and China there are over 1 billion potential consumers. Other huge markets include Brazil, Russia, Nigeria and Indonesia. The French multinational BIC, which produces biros, razors and other widely consumed products, has set up large factories which produce goods that are sold across wide geographical areas.

The impact of multinationals

Multinationals create employment in the countries in which they operate. For example, the Japanese multinationals Toyota and Honda are major providers of employment in the car industry in Britain, India, Thailand and many other countries. Multinationals often help to build up the infrastructure of a country – for example, by building road and railway links. They can also help to spread expertise in new technology to a country – for example, by training their employees.

However, multinationals can also have negative effects. Oil, gas and chemical multinationals often cause pollution and local environments are damaged, through chemical leaks and the destruction of forests. Because of their size, multinationals can often undercut local firms. Huge retailers such as Carrefour (France) and Wal-Mart (USA) do this in the various countries in which they operate. Multinationals also take profits out of the domestic economy and pay them to shareholders, who may live thousands of miles away.

ACTIVITY

Find out which companies are the largest multinationals. Use the keywords World's Biggest Companies to carry out an internet search. One of the top entries you will find is the *Forbes* list of companies. (*Forbes* is an American business magazine.) The homepage gives you the option to get a ranking list of the world's biggest companies. Produce a table, ranking these companies according to the size of their sales, profits and other indicators. Create a chart, showing the companies, the country in which their head office is located, the types of product they make and the number of employees they have. Why is it difficult to say which is the largest company?

EXAM TIP

Many people are concerned at the increase in importance of multinational companies. Multinationals potentially create benefits for the countries where they are situated, but they may also mean losses for smaller businesses and less choice for consumers.

SUMMARY QUESTIONS

1 How many countries does a business need to operate in before it is defined as a multinational? Can you give examples of a multinational company in the following industries: oil and petrol, retailing and clothing sales?

2 What are the advantages of being a multinational?

3 What arguments might be put forward for encouraging multinationals to operate in your country? What arguments might there be against this?

KEY POINTS

1 A multinational is a company that operates in several countries.

2 Companies become multinationals to benefit from wider market opportunities, to access scarce resources, and to take advantage of a new pool of labour.

3 Multinationals create employment and benefits, but they can also cause pollution and the withdrawal of profits from the host country.

DID YOU KNOW?

In rural India, Hindustan Unilever provides 'microcredit' to women – this refers to loans of very small sums of money or the supply of small quantities of goods on credit to set up small businesses. The loans enable women to sell products such as sachets of shampoo and soap to local people. The women benefit from the income; Unilever benefits from extending its sales into rural areas.

Nestlé produces many of the world's best-known food brands. It is a Swiss company with over 250,000 shareholders. The shareholders share in the profits made, but also take a risk that the company will not make a profit. Each shareholder has limited liability

Risk and ownership

One of the words most commonly associated with business is **risk**. The owners of a business risk the capital that they put into it. The capital may come from their life savings, from money they have received in redundancy pay, or even a loan secured against their house or other valuable possessions. More businesses fail than succeed, and the casualty rate of new businesses is particularly high in the first year of trading.

This principle of risking capital is the same for sole traders, partners, shareholders in a company, franchise operators and owners of joint ventures.

The owners of a business are liable for its debts. The amount of liability that sole traders and most partners are accountable for is not restricted to the sums that they have put into the company. They are required by law to meet all the liabilities of their business. As we have seen, this could mean having to sell their car, their house and other possessions to meet business debts (see Unit 5.1).

Limited liability

In the 1850s, the British and French governments passed laws that would allow individuals and groups to invest in companies. This was the principle of limited liability (See Unit 5.1). It limits the risk for a shareholder to the sum they have invested in a company.

Most large businesses are set up as limited companies (incorporated businesses). These companies have shareholders. A shareholder might be an individual, with only a small sum of money invested in, say, companies like Singapore Airlines, Nestlé or Tata. Alternatively, the shareholder might be a huge pension fund, investing the savings of millions of pensioners in these companies. These shareholders would not buy shares in companies if they were held liable for business debts.

Shareholders → invest money in → limited companies.

Shareholders may be individuals or other companies. They are not responsible for the company's debts unless they have given guarantees (e.g. of a bank loan). However, they may lose the money they have invested in the company if it fails.

The protection of limited liability therefore makes it possible for companies across the globe to raise large sums of money. The Swiss multinational company Nestlé is famous for its products such as Nescafé and Quality Street sweets. The company has over 250,000 shareholders and no single shareholder owns more than 3 per cent of the shares in the company. Each of the 250,000 shareholders is willing to invest in the company because they think that it has good prospects to make profits, and they know that because of limited liability, the maximum amount of capital that they are risking is the value of their shareholding.

SUMMARY QUESTIONS

1 Which of the following would have limited liability?

   An incorporated business / a sole trader / an ordinary partnership / a company / a limited partnership

2 Singapore Airlines is owned jointly by the government of Singapore and by private shareholders. The Singapore government has the majority shareholding in the airline. The airline is an incorporated business. How much would an individual shareholder be liable for in the event that the airline had to meet debts?

3 In what ways might it be more risky to set up a sole trader business than a small incorporated company?

DID YOU KNOW?

Some forms of business organisation are specific to particular countries. Indian law recognises the joint Hindu family form of business ownership: members of a family own a business and the eldest member manages it. Every member of the family gets a share in the profit, regardless of how much they participate. Apart from the eldest member, the liability of the partners is limited.

KEY POINTS

1 Limited liability is a legal protection that reduces the risks involved in business.

2 A shareholder or other owner of a business with limited liability is only liable for the value of their investment in a business.

3 There are certain types of partnerships that have limited liability status. However, in ordinary partnerships there is unlimited liability of partners.

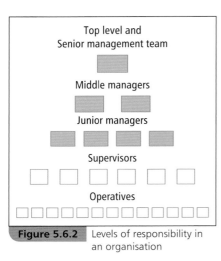

Figure 5.6.2 Levels of responsibility in an organisation

Organisation charts

An **organisation chart** shows the roles of people in an organisation and the relationship between them. For example, Figure 5.6.1 shows that a senior accountant in an organisation's accounts department has three junior accountants working for her.

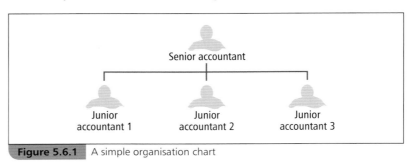

Figure 5.6.1 A simple organisation chart

Every organisation can be set out in this way, to show the departments, how they link together and the main lines of authority. It shows lines of decision making and levels of responsibility.

Role refers to what an individual does in an organisation. For example, a sales manager in Nigeria will be in charge of the company's sales team in that country. Their task will be to make sure that there is a clear sales plan and that the sales team receives the right level of training and support. The sales manager will be responsible for people and resources and for making sure that targets are achieved.

Levels within an organisation

An organisation chart usually indicates positions that have roughly equal amounts of responsibility on the same level. Figure 5.6.2 shows the **hierarchy** of an organisation – that is, how employees are arranged by rank or seniority. The managing director and the senior management team are at the top level. At the next level are the middle managers. Then there are junior managers, supervisors and, finally, operatives at the bottom level.

The diagram also illustrates a chain of command. Operatives are responsible to supervisors. Supervisors report to junior managers, and so on. The person that an individual reports to is often called their line manager.

Span of control

The span of control of an individual is the number of people he or she manages or supervises directly. Figure 5.6.3 shows an organisation with a narrow span of control.

Choosing the best span of control means finding a balance between having control over people below you (subordinates) and being able to trust them. There is a limit to the number of people who can be supervised well by one person. The diagram shows an organisation in which no one is directly responsible for more than two subordinates.

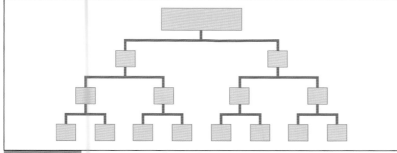

Figure 5.6.3 A narrow span of control

Tall and flat organisations

A narrow span of control makes it possible to control people and to communicate with them closely. However, the disadvantage is that this may lead to too many levels of management. This kind of tall organisation can be difficult to run.

In a flat organisation, managers delegate responsibility to subordinate staff. In this arrangement, managers need to have far more trust in their subordinates than in a tall organisation. Fewer managers are needed, and the hierarchy has fewer levels. Advertising agencies often give a lot of responsibility to their designers to come up with creative ideas. The designer will meet with the client and work on ideas themselves. This works well when the designer is comfortable with taking on responsibility and has good creative skills.

Some managers believe that the more senior an individual is, the fewer people he or she should have in their direct span of control. However, there are many examples of organisations that work well when senior managers have an extensive span of control. The best span in an organisation will depend on the skills of its managers.

When a business expands it may have to reorganise its structure. It may need to create a new hierarchy by adding extra layers of management.

Figure 5.6.4 A flat and a tall organisation

SUMMARY QUESTIONS

1 Define the following terms.

Span of control / hierarchy / chain of command / delegation

2 What are the benefits and disadvantages of having a large span of control within an organisation?

3 Some organisations are said to be 'too hierarchical'. What is meant by this and why is it a problem to be 'too hierarchical'?

EXAM TIP

Make sure that you understand what sort of tasks are delegated. A secretary in an office might be given the task of arranging business meetings with clients, but would not be allowed to decide how much money should be spent on promoting products.

Delegation means giving responsibility for carrying out a task to someone at a lower level. Delegation means that people at the top of an organisation do not have to make all the decisions themselves.

ACTIVITY

Draw a chart for an organisation that you are familiar with. This could be your school, a club that you are a member of or even your place of work. Comment on the structure of the organisation, using terms such as span of control and hierarchy.

KEY POINTS

1 Organisation charts show the roles of members of an organisation and shows the links of an organisation between its members.

2 There is a limit to an effective span of control.

3 Tall organisations are hierarchical and may be difficult to run.

Discuss the role of management.

- Knowledge of the functions of management.
- Understanding of the concept of ownership and control.

Managers need to look after resources efficiently. A key skill is to get on with people, particularly in an international setting

Management

Every organisation has objectives. **Managers** are people who help to steer the organisation towards meeting these objectives. Typical functions of management are shown in Figure 5.7.1.

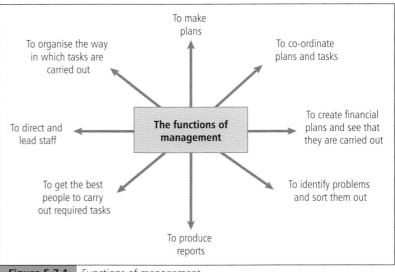

Figure 5.7.1 Functions of management

Managers are responsible for making sure that an organisation's resources are used efficiently. This means making best use of:

- people – employees
- finance – making sure that costs are adequately provided for sales and profit objectives to be met
- opportunities – making sure they are spotted and exploited
- materials – minimising waste and maximising output
- machinery and equipment – making sure that it is correctly maintained and replaced when necessary
- time – making sure that this is not wasted
- buildings – making sure that premises are safe and used efficiently
- information – making sure that the organisation has market knowledge, and that the right IT specialists are in place to provide high-quality information.

Managers are usually responsible for a specific area of work activity. This might be a particular business function, such as sales, marketing or production. A manager may be responsible for a particular geographical area. The sales manager for South East Asia, for example, will be responsible for meeting sales targets in that area. Project managers are appointed to oversee particular projects, such as the introduction of a new IT system across the organisation.

Ownership and control

The owners of a business – that is, the shareholders – invest their capital in the business, and in return take out profits. They do not, however, always control the business. They normally elect directors to do this and represent them. The directors, in turn, appoint managers to run the business on a day-to-day basis.

The directors therefore manage the business, but they do not own it. They are accountable to the owners for their managerial actions. The shareholders have the power to remove the board of directors at an **annual general meeting (AGM)**, but for much of the year the board is free to make decisions. In recent years, shareholders in a number of companies have not been happy about this. One area of disagreement has been the large salaries and bonuses that directors have paid themselves. Shareholders may decide not to approve pay packages awarded to directors. In some cases, they have voted to replace the board.

In a sole trader business, and partnerships, the owners are also the controllers of the business. The table summarises owners and controllers of different types of business.

Type of enterprise	Owned by	Controlled by
Sole trader	One owner	One owner
Partnership	Partners	Partners – although a senior partner may have more power to make decisions
Company	Shareholders	Directors and paid managers; shareholders can vote at an annual general meeting to replace the board
Franchise	Franchisee holds licence for a given time period	Franchisee makes day-to-day decisions within the rules set out by the franchisor
Joint venture	The businesses that set up the joint venture	Managers of the joint venture

ACTIVITY

Select an organisation that you are familiar with (e.g. your school, a club that you are a member of or another organisation that you belong to). What do you think are the most important tasks for the organisation? What role should managers take in ensuring that these tasks are carried out? How would you go about designing and managing tasks within the organisation to make sure that these tasks are carried out well?

DID YOU KNOW?

Shareholders may vote to replace boards of directors. In 2008, Google directors rejected a takeover bid from Microsoft. Some of the leading shareholders in Google did not agree with the decision and put themselves forward in an attempt to replace the board.

SUMMARY QUESTIONS

1 Explain the following functions of management.

   Making plans / coordinating activities / hiring and managing staff / organising activities / producing reports

2 How does the relationship between the ownership and the control of a business differ between a sole-trader business and a company?

3 What are the main types of resources that managers manage?

KEY POINTS

1 Management is the process of planning, organising, leading and controlling the efforts of organisation members.

2 Management involves the effective use of resources, such as people, finance and time, so that objectives are met.

3 Directors are appointed by shareholders to direct the organisation and make sure that it runs smoothly. Managers control day-to-day activities.

4 The owners of a business are responsible for controlling small organisations. In larger companies there is a separation of ownership and control.

EXAM TIP

Good communication is essential if a business is to be successful. Communications take place within a business (internally) and outside a business (externally), for example, with suppliers and customers. The methods used should reflect the nature and purpose of the message.

Communication

Communication – that is, passing on or exchanging information, ideas or feelings – is vital to a business. Instructions, orders, lists and specifications all need to be transmitted to others within the organisation. The organisation also needs to communicate externally – that is, to people outside it – to place orders, find things out and, very importantly, to promote and sell a brand and its related products.

Communication involves sending a message or messages to a receiver. The sender must select the best method of communication such as oral, written or electronic. The sender must then select the best medium to send the message, such as email or telephone.

Communication takes place both within a business and between the business and other organisations.

Effective communication depends upon:

- clearly defining the objective of the message
- taking account of the needs, attitude and knowledge of the receiver
- being aware of how distractions (noise) can distort the message
- selecting the best medium for communication

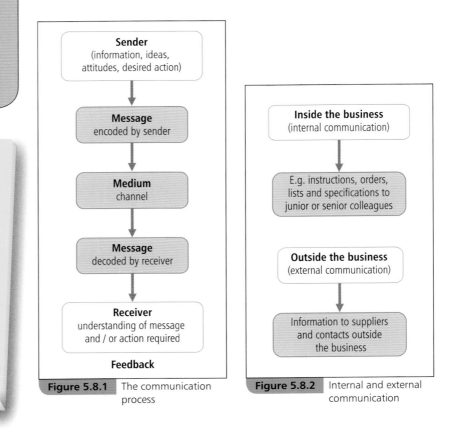

Figure 5.8.1 The communication process

Figure 5.8.2 Internal and external communication

- checking that the message has been understood through feedback
- listening to feedback and responding.

Common communication problems

There are a number of barriers to communication.

1 **Language**. The sender may not be a good user of language, or may use jargon, unfamiliar technical language or abbreviations. Problems may arise in international communication where a receiver's first language may be different from that of the sender. It is essential when creating a message to think about the needs of the receiver and be clear and direct.

2 **Emotional state**. The sender or receiver may be upset or angry and set out a message poorly or fail to listen carefully to a message. The receiver may read or hear what they want to hear rather than the message sent.

3 **Communication method**. The method chosen may be inappropriate for the receiver. For example, mobile phone communications may 'break up' or emails may not get through. Some topics may be better handled in person than by phone.

4 **Cultural differences**. The receiver's interpretation of the message may be different due to differing cultural experience and language. Organisations need to have a good understanding of the culture of countries that they communicate with.

Solutions to communication failure

All employees in an organisation need to be aware of the importance of effective communication. This involves making them aware of the problems of poor communication, and familiarising them with the best communication methods through training. For example, when making an order over the phone, numbers of items requested may easily be misheard. It is better to use written communication such as email or to fill in an order form.

Organisations need to have the right resources to enable effective communication. This involves investing in good communication technologies and making sure that employees know how and when to use different types of communication.

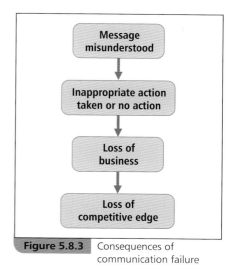

Figure 5.8.3   Consequences of communication failure

ACTIVITY

Identify some of the messages that you have received recently about your schoolwork. How were these messages communicated to you? Give examples of situations where 'noise' affected some of these messages. What could have been done to reduce this?

KEY POINTS

1 Communication involves exchanging ideas and messages with others.

2 Communication takes place within an organisation (internal) and with those outside the organisation (external).

3 Careful attention must be given to framing clear messages, and using an appropriate medium in a way that recipients find easy to understand.

SUMMARY QUESTIONS

1 Who are the main parties involved in the business communication process?

2 What is the difference between internal and external communication?

3 What are the main barriers to effective communication? Explain one method of dealing with one of these barriers.

Internal communication

Understanding of the methods of internal communication.

- Knowledge and understanding of different methods.

Comment on the appropriateness of different methods of internal communication.

- Understanding of when to use a given method of communication.

Video conferencing facilities enable face-to-face communication without travel costs

EXAM TIP

Make sure that you can evaluate the effectiveness of different communication methods in different situations. Effective communication is much more than just telling someone what to do. It involves the interchange of information, which is all about developing understanding of issues so that everyone appreciates what has to be done and what part they have to play.

Internal communication

Internal communications take place within an organisation. Figure 5.9.1 shows several purposes of internal communication.

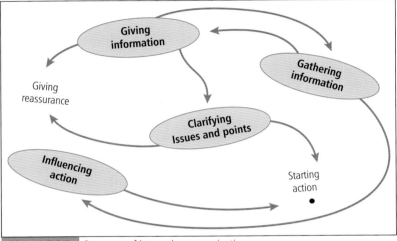

Figure 5.9.1 Purposes of internal communication

Types of communication

Formal communication takes place through the official channels in an organisation (e.g. in a formal meeting). In contrast, informal communication does not follow set guidelines (e.g. an informal online chat between two employees). Electronic communication takes place through email, telephone (including mobile phone), video conferencing and using a company website for employees, an **intranet**.

Formal written

Memo is a shortening of 'memorandum', a thing to be remembered. Memos are used to pass on information, instructions and enquiries. Today, this form of written communication has largely been replaced by email messages.

A report is a written communication from someone who has collected some facts or issues. A report is written for a particular purpose and is set out in a particular format:

1 Title page

2 List of contents

3 Terms of reference (why the report is being written)

4 Procedure (how the report has been put together)

5 Findings (what has been discovered that is of interest)

6 Conclusion (a summary of the findings)

Fax is short for 'facsimile'. A fax machine is connected to a telephone line. Documents such as drawings and notes can be fed into one machine, and are received and printed by another.

Businesses also communicate internally through posters (e.g. to convey messages about safe working) and through in-house magazines.

Formal verbal

Verbal communication takes place all the time within an organisation. This includes telling someone what to do (giving instructions) and giving feedback about their performance.

Meetings are held regularly in most businesses. Some of these are formal meetings, with a chairperson to conduct the meeting, an agenda (list of items to be discussed) and a minute taker (someone who keeps a written record of what has been said). Training sessions are organised to help employees to develop the skills and knowledge required to do their job well. **Appraisal** interviews are another form of two-way communication at which an employee is given targets to work towards (see page 156).

Informal

Much of the communication within a company takes place informally, using what is referred to as a grapevine. This helps to develop working relationships. An example of this might be senior business people having a round of golf together. Networking describes building informal contacts with others.

Electronic

Electronic links have transformed communication within businesses. Most companies have an intranet. This is a network of linked computers and databases of information. The intranet serves as an internal company website, providing lots of information about the company and its departments to people inside the organisation.

Telephone links are also important in maintaining external and internal relationships. Mobile phone links are particularly useful when employees are working away from the workplace. A company website created on the internet enables everyone involved with a business to find out more about its activities. **Video conferencing** enables visual link-ups between members of the same company at different locations.

(see page 156)

ACTIVITY

Identify different types of internal communication in your school. What types of information and instructions are given using these different types of communication? Identify one advantage and one drawback of each method when compared with an alternative method of internal communication.

DID YOU KNOW?

A **team** briefing is a formal method of verbal communication. The team leader will usually brief (inform) the team about the latest developments within a company and what is expected of the team in contributing to those developments.

KEY POINTS

1 Internal communications take place within an organisation.

2 Communication methods need to be appropriate to the type of audience to be reached and the messages to be sent.

3 Electronic communications, such as emails, fax, intranet, internet and video conferencing, have replaced many traditional methods.

4 Electronic communications enable immediate, relatively low-cost links in which a lot of information can be exchanged.

SUMMARY QUESTIONS

1 Which of the following forms of communication are most likely to involve an electronic element? Explain your answers in each case.

Fax / email / reports / meetings / memo / video conference / appraisal interview

2 VG Fashions is a manufacturer of cotton textiles in Pakistan in the process of introducing new advanced machinery for spinning cotton in some of its mills. This will require upgrading the skills of some of its existing employees. What methods of internal communication could it use to inform employees of the changes and to prepare them to upgrade their skills? Explain the benefits of each method selected.

Internal and external communication

We have seen in Unit 5.9 how the prime focus of internal communication is the people who work within an organisation – employees, managers and, in some cases, shareholders. Internal communication to these groups takes the form of organised information through a company intranet, employee magazines and newsletters, and shareholder reports, notices and letters.

External communication indicates how a business communicates with individuals and other businesses outside itself. It must be effective because it gives the outside world a view of the company, its brands and products. The table sets out the purposes of external communication.

Purpose	Example
1 Providing information and making sales	Most large companies have a website giving product details and inviting customers to make purchases. Bus, train and airline companies provide sites through which passengers can check timetables and purchase tickets. Sites also include terms and conditions of sale, costs of purchase, etc.
2 Giving instructions	Telling suppliers where to deliver goods or telling customers how to use products.
3 Confirming arrangements	May include confirming meetings or conferences or details of transactions.
4 Improving customer service	Helplines to deal with customer issues and complaints. Can help to reduce errors, provide customers with plenty of feedback and deal with enquiries. Customers view the communications they receive from a company as part of the service. For example, they expect to be communicated with on time and in a polite and helpful way.
5 Public relations (PR)	Brochures and advertising material. Effective PR projects a positive image, that a company is professional in its dealings with its stakeholders.

Kenya Airways is Kenya's best-known airline. Its website enables it to sell to international consumers as well as across Kenya

Methods of external communication

There are a number of different methods of external communication.

1. **Personal relationships** are the contacts and relationships that people in an organisation build up with others. They are vital to the success of the business.

2. **Business letters** are very important forms of formal written communication. A letter will usually contain the following features:
   - addresses of the recipient and sender
   - date
   - greeting (e.g. Dear Sir/Madam)
   - subject heading – the title of the topic the letter refers to (e.g. Price list request)
   - body of the letter
   - close (e.g. Yours sincerely)

   A business letter gives a good idea of how professional the business organisation is. It should look attractive and it should not contain any spelling or punctuation errors.

3. **Email** has become the most widely used form of communication and now has the same 'weight' as a traditional letter. Many companies today set out structures for emails that give them the official appearance of a traditional letter, with the company logo

and a particular layout and style. Writers need to take care with the contents of business emails.

4 **Company websites**. Most companies have a website for many forms of external communication. An effective site will have a distinctive name (e.g. lastminute.com, iwantoneofthose.com). The site should be welcoming, with interesting material to encourage the user to revisit. It should be easy to access and to navigate (i.e. to move around). It needs to be broken down into clear subsections, so that users can quickly access the part of the site that interests them. There should also be clear links to other parts of the site.

A successful site must be easy to use for purchasing: this includes order forms and credit card security measures. Many users are concerned about security – hackers may be able to access a company database and the credit card details of all their customers. Website designers need to find a ways of making purchasing safe, but not so cumbersome as to put off purchasers altogether.

5 **Customer newsletters**. The company can send mail directly to customers giving details of new developments (e.g. a store opening, forthcoming sale, products that are on offer in a particularly period).

6 **Advertisements**. Found in various media (e.g. television, newspapers and magazines).

7 **Telephone**. These links are important to businesses such as banking, insurance and utilities. These types of companies run call centres, which operate helplines to deal with customer queries, sell products over the phone or handle billing and other payment systems.

8 **File transfers**. Large quantities of data (e.g. in the form of pictures and statistics) can be sent electronically. File transfer involves sending 'bunches' of data from a sending to a receiving computer.

9 **Electronic data interchange (EDI)**. Many international food manufacturers and retailers set up large-scale systems of purchasing goods electronically. EDI is a network link that allows retailers to pay suppliers electronically, without using invoices and cheques. This reduces time, paperwork and costs.

10 **Video conferencing**. Workers at different locations can see and talk to each other on screen using electronic links. This avoids the expense and inconvenience of travel.

SUMMARY QUESTIONS

1 What is the difference between internal and external communication?

2 What arguments might a business put forward to justify setting up a company website?

3 What are the advantages of communicating with customers by business letter rather than through electronic communication?

DID YOU KNOW?

Payment systems today are usually encrypted. Purchasers' bank card details are put into code, making them very difficult to copy. Companies also protect their databases by making sure that only specified users with passwords are able to access them.

ACTIVITY

Compare three well-known commercial (selling) websites. Choose one that sells clothes, such as PPG or ASOS; another that sells books, such as Amazon; and a sportswear retailer, such as Nike or Reebok. Compare the sites in terms of the following criteria:

- quick to access
- easy to navigate
- easy to find information
- presents a good image of the company
- goods easy to order
- easy to make transactions
- other factors you consider important.

KEY POINTS

1 Internal communication takes place within a business; external communication is with individuals and businesses outside a given business.
2 Electronic communications such as emails are replacing traditional methods.
3 Company websites enable an organisation to present itself in a positive way to consumers all over the world.

SECTION 1: Short-answer questions

1 Explain, in terms of the number of owners of a business, the difference between a sole trader and a partnership. [2]

2 Why are most new businesses set up as sole traders? Explain your answer. [3]

3 Identify and explain ONE reason why a new sole trader may have difficulty in raising finance. [2]

4 Identify and explain TWO reasons why a sole trader may expand by taking on a partner. [4]

5 Explain TWO reasons why unlimited liability may be seen as a disadvantage in a partnership organisation. [4]

6 Identify and explain THREE advantages to members of a partnership of becoming an incorporated business or limited company. [6]

7 Explain why the result 'profits increase by 15 per cent' may lead to an increase in the stock exchange share price of a public company. [4]

8 Explain the difference between partners and shareholders. [4]

9 Use an example of a large national business which has set up a joint venture in your country. Identify and explain TWO advantages to the big company of the local contact. [4]

10 Look at this list of possible business objectives:

Growth / survival / increase in market share / increase in sales / personal service to customers / provide a living for owners

Identify and explain the most appropriate objectives for a business in the following situations.

• A new cake-making business set up by a young person who has just left school.

• A family textile business which is looking for new markets outside the local area.

• A large multinational company which is considering offering franchise agreements in your country. [6]

11 Identify TWO examples of multinational companies which are involved in production or selling in your country. [2]

12 Choose ONE of your answers to Question 11 and explain ONE positive and ONE negative effect that this company has on the economy of your country. [4]

13 Identify and explain TWO benefits of a hierarchical organisation structure in business. [4]

14 Identify and explain TWO ways in which the business you identified in Question 12 tries to meet its objectives. [4]

15 Identify and explain TWO differences between tall and flat organisations. [4]

16 Management means 'getting things done through people'. Explain this statement in terms of the role of managers. [4]

17 Identify and explain the most appropriate method(s) and type(s) of communication in the following situations.

• There is a fire in the building and everyone must leave.

• The managing director wants to tell staff about the company objectives for this year.

• The marketing manager wants to tell customers about a new product. [6]

SECTION 2: Longer-answer questions

The Vegetarian Treats Company

Ashok is a successful entrepreneur who has built his company up from a very small start. He now owns six shops in different areas of Mumbai and wants to expand into other Indian towns and cities. His sweet and savoury products are made in a central kitchen, to old family recipes, based on secret spice mixes which give the products their unique flavour. Ashok employs managers and teams of staff for each of his shops, and also a senior product manager and chefs for the kitchen. Other members of Ashok's family are keen to get involved in his success and are trying to persuade him to form a partnership with his brothers.

1 Draw an organisation chart for Ashok's business and describe the structure. [4]

2 Identify and describe TWO communication methods which Ashok may use when trying to communicate weekly sales targets to all his shops. [4]

3 Analyse TWO barriers to communication which Ashok may face if he opens new shops in other cities. [6]

4 Explain THREE objectives which Ashok may have in trying to expand his business. [6]

5 Do you agree with Ashok's family that he should form a partnership with his brothers? Explain your answer. [6]

The cellphone charger supplier

Nokia, one of the world's largest mobile telephone companies, outsources the production of charger units to a factory in rural China. Workers travel long distances to the factory to find work. They live in dormitories, split between males and females. The factory employs 3,000 staff and operates 24 hours a day. Workers are organised into teams of 12, supervised by a team leader. Orders from Nokia and other companies are increasing and the factory owner would like to expand.

1 Identify and explain TWO ways in which Nokia may communicate with its Chinese supplier. [4]

2 Identify and explain TWO barriers to communication which Nokia may experience when trying to communicate information to production line workers. [4]

3 Analyse ONE advantage and ONE disadvantage to the local area of the cellphone charger factory. [6]

4 To what extent do you agree with this view of one worker? 'The span of control is far too wide here, making it impossible to communicate effectively.' [6]

5 Do you agree that modern electronic methods of communication can solve all the problems which Nokia may experience due to the 'long-distance' supplier? Explain your answer. [6]

The cosmetics joint venture

Janet runs a successful company which makes and distributes 'natural' cosmetic and haircare products throughout Europe and North America. She is looking to grow the business and is interested in emerging markets in the African countries of Zambia, Uganda and Tanzania. Market research results seem to suggest great potential, as these types of products are becoming more popular. Janet is aware, however, that she has no local knowledge or experience, and is looking for a local company in each country to join her in a joint venture.

1 Identify and explain TWO reasons for Janet's proposed business expansion. [4]

2 Identify and explain TWO problems which Janet may face if she tries to enter these new markets without a local contact. [4]

3 Analyse TWO ways in which a local company may be able to help Janet solve the problems identified in Question 2. [4]

4 To what extent do you agree that the local companies will benefit from cooperation with Janet's business? Explain your answer. [6]

5 Evaluate the statement that 'multinational companies which form joint ventures with local contacts will always be successful'. Back up your answer with your own local examples. [6]

6 Financing business activity

6.1   The need for funds

Setting up an office requires funds for capital items such as office machinery, as well as staff salaries and rental charges

What are funds?

Funds are sums of money for use in a business, which are set aside for a particular purpose. The main purposes for funds in a business are:

1 setting up the business

2 running the business on a day-to-day basis

3 expanding the business.

CASE STUDY	Sanjay's market research

Setting up a new business is very costly. This is illustrated by the case of Sanjay, who has decided to set up a small market research business in a country in South East Asia. He has made out a list of payments that he will need to make just to set up in business. Costs are given in US dollars.

Start up costs	US$
Rental of 290 sq foot for the first 6 months (he has to pay 6 months in advance)	24,000
New office furniture and fittings	25,000
Laptops (Apple Macintosh x 4)	4,000
Printer (LaserJet x 1)	400
Fax machine	400
Telephones (2)	100
Electricity deposit	150
Telephone/fax connection (5 lines @ $20)	100
Internet access	50
Legal fees	500
Staff salaries for the first month (2 x $1,000)	2,000
Total start-up costs	**56,700**

You can see from the table that the start-up period for any new business is costly. When businesses start up they have to pay in advance for items like office rent. They will also often have to pay a deposit to cover things like damage and breakages.

Additional costs will include installing services such as telephone and electricity. Other start-up costs include capital items: these are durable items that remain in the business for several years, such as furniture and computer equipment. In a manufacturing company, capital items would include the machinery. Where a business buys buildings directly, these would be included in the start-up costs.

Sanjay and other new entrepreneurs need to have access to funds to see them through this difficult start-up phase. Some of these funds may come from Sanjay's own savings, and some from family loans. However, he will still need to acquire funds from other sources.

Questions

1 What are the main costs of setting up a business?

2 What sources of funds could Sanjay have used to finance the start-up of his business?

3 What capital items did Sanjay require? Can you suggest a way of financing the purchase or hire of these?

Day-to-day running of the business

Once a business is up and running it will need to have funds to cover day-to-day costs. These will include items like staff wages, costs of supplies and raw materials, and bills that will need to be paid from the beginning. For most businesses, therefore, costs in the first 12 months are normally higher than revenues. The business is unlikely to make a profit in this early period.

Expanding (growing) the business

At some stage, many businesses choose to expand or change direction. For example, Sanjay may set up other offices in different cities in his country, or in other countries.

It is often easier to acquire capital to expand than to start up: once a business has built up a reputation and has a steady stream of income, it becomes easier to raise funds from lenders.

Expanding businesses can also raise funds through asset-based finance: the borrower borrows funds on the understanding that if they fail to make repayments, the lender can take over particular assets (the items that the business owns that have value, such as buildings, vehicles or machinery). This is known as offering **security** for a loan.

SUMMARY QUESTIONS

1 What are funds? Why are they important in starting up a new business?

2 Yin Qiang is just about to start up an exporting business, selling rice from China to wholesalers in Europe. He is seeking to borrow funds from his bank. He has calculated that he will need US$10,000 to start up the business. He has told the bank that this is the only capital that he will require, because once the business has started, he will be able to finance all further funding requirements from profits made by the business. Why might the bank be reluctant to give him the start-up capital he has requested?

3 Explain the difference between start-up costs and day-to-day running costs of a business.

Sources of funds

Capital needs

Businesses need funds for both short- and long-term purposes. In the short term, funds are required to make regular payments: wages, costs of supplies, electricity and utility bills. These short-term funds are called **working capital**. They may also be needed to bridge the gap between, for example, buying ingredients or components, and the eventual payment for the finished goods that the business aims to sell.

In the long term, funds are required to purchase the major assets on which the business is based: land, buildings, machinery and other permanent assets.

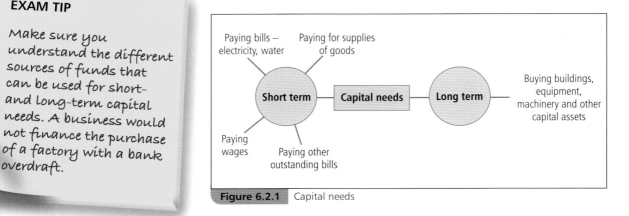

Figure 6.2.1 Capital needs

CASE STUDY | Dairy farming in Pakistan

Pakistan is the world's fifth largest producer of milk, and farmers need capital for all aspects of dairy farming

Pakistan is the world's fifth largest milk producer. About 35 million people in Pakistan keep two or three cows and small numbers of other livestock, such as sheep and goats, in their backyards. There are also larger commercial dairy farms, with herds of over 100 cows.

Farmers require capital for a range of short-term and long-term purposes: they need working capital to purchase new cows and supplies of feed for the animals. Large-scale farmers will need to purchase longer-term capital such as cow sheds and machinery to chill the milk. In some areas where water is in short supply farmers require capital to improve irrigation systems and to install wells and improve electricity supplies. They may also need funds to purchase large items such as refrigerator trucks to keep their milk frozen as it is transported to market.

Questions

1 Explain why farmers in Pakistan may require working capital.

2 What longer-term capital requirements are there in the dairy industry?

3 Where do you think farmers in Pakistan will acquire funds from for working capital and for longer-term capital?

There are a number of major sources of finance that a business can use to meet its capital needs.

1 Owner's funds. The owners of a business provide important finance. An owner investing capital in a business gives lenders more confidence in it. Additional **owner's funds (capital)** come from ongoing profits ploughed back into the business.

2 Loans. The bank provides the loan and the borrower repays the capital over time, with interest. Loans are typically taken out over a period of years rather than months. It is more difficult to secure a business loan from a bank at the start-up stage.

3 Mortgage. A **mortgage** is a method of long-term finance: it is a loan for the purchase of property that is secured on the property. If the borrower fails to make repayments, the lender can take them to court and, if necessary, take over ownership of the property. The size of the mortgage depends on the value of the property and how much is borrowed.

4 Short-term finance. Trade credit is an important form of short-term finance. The supplier does not expect immediate payment for goods or services. There is a period of trade credit – for example, one month, three months or longer. Many small businesses use a credit card for short-term bills. (Credit cards are not available in all countries.) Payment is made for goods with a credit card provided by a finance company. The business can then pay the credit card company at the end of the month, or later. The longer the business takes to repay the credit, the more interest they will have to pay. Another form of short-term finance is an overdraft (see page 74).

5 Microcredit. For some very small businesses, particularly in rural areas, it is almost impossible to get credit. Professor Mohammad Yunus started the Grameen Bank in Bangladesh. This is called microcredit and provides small amounts of funds to set up microbusinesses, to help people who would otherwise have no means of earning an income.

SUMMARY QUESTIONS

1 What is working capital? Give two examples of sources of funds for working capital.

2 Businesses have short- and long-term capital needs. Provide three examples of fund sources that could be used to meet short-term capital needs, and three examples of types of finance that could be used to meet long-term needs.

3 Explain the main difference between:
  • a mortgage and a loan.
  • trade credit and credit card finance.

KEY POINTS

1 Businesses need short-term finance to provide working capital.

2 Typical sources of short-term finance include trade credit and credit card payments.

3 Businesses need long-term finance for substantial capital expenditures.

4 Long-term finance may be in the form of a mortgage to help finance property purchases.

Finance

Millions of businesses have been set up worldwide during the last 10 years. None of them would have progressed beyond the ideas stage if they had not been able to get hold of a basic ingredient of business – finance!

A company that has hit headlines in recent years is India's Tata Motors. This is a public company (see page 50). The company has recently launched the world's smallest and cheapest car, the Tata Nano, priced at about US$2,000. Two of the principal sources of finance to build the car were:

• selling shares to shareholders. The shareholders are the owners of the Tata corporation, and so part of the business. This capital is therefore internal capital, raised inside the business.

• borrowing from the banks. Tata borrowed considerable sums of money in loans to build the production plant to manufacture the cars. This is external finance, raised outside the business.

Internal finance

We have seen that internal finance is the capital provided by the owners. A sole trader business provides internal finance from a single owner. Sole traders frequently expand by taking in partners who bring in more capital to the business.

Companies raise capital by selling shares. The shareholder buys shares and so provides capital for the business. Another source of internal finance for a business is the profit that it generates.

Businesses can also raise funds by selling some of their assets, such as a piece of land, a factory or a machine. Sometimes they do this and then lease (hire) the item they have sold from the buyer. They lose the asset, but gain cash to run the business.

The world's smallest car, the Tata Nano, required internal and external funding

External finance

The following table summarises the several sources of external finance available to a business.

Source or finance	Explanation
Trade credit	The time between receiving the good or service and having to pay for it.
Overdraft	Most frequently used form of short-term finance, used to ease cash-flow problems. Arrangements are made between the customer and the bank on an agreed drawing limit on an account. Interest is calculated on the level of the overdraft on a daily basis.
Leasing and hire purchase	Major banks have links with finance houses which provide a variety of schemes so that the customer receives goods and makes payments over time. Goods on hire purchase remain the property of the finance company until all the payments have been made. Leasing enables a company to use an asset without having to pay for it. The lessee uses the asset and makes regular payments to the owner, the lessor.

Loan	Sums of money typically lent for a specific purpose (e.g. to buy an asset). Interest is charged on the amount owed.
Mortgages	Loan secured on property.
Government grant	Important source of finance for many businesses: the government provides funds for the business for particular purposes (e.g. to update machinery).
Venture capital	Venture capital companies provide finance in return for a shareholding in the organisation, and some control.

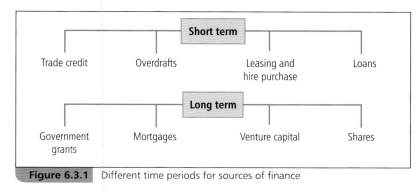

Figure 6.3.1   Different time periods for sources of finance

EXAM TIP

A company with a high gearing ratio relies heavily on borrowed capital to finance its activities. It is taking a financial risk, as it has to make a return on this capital which is greater than the rate of interest on the loans. If the gearing ratio is very low, it often means that a business is short of capital, because it does not borrow money. So too high or low a gearing ratio can be 'bad'.

The ratio of external to internal finance

When a business raises internal finance, it owes money to the owners. When it makes a profit, it can give the owners a good return on their investment by paying a high dividend to shareholders; in poor years it can limit the amount it pays.

However, a business is legally bound to pay providers of external finance. For example, with a loan or mortgage, it is required by law to make repayments. Similarly, it must pay for goods received on credit and money borrowed on a credit card.

A business must therefore maintain a good balance between funds raised internally and externally. If it raises too much capital externally, it may build debts for itself that it is unable to pay back in years when profits are low.

The ratio between capital raised internally (owners' funds) and capital raised externally (external finance) is called the **gearing ratio**.

If a high percentage of funds is borrowed, this is referred to as a high gearing ratio.

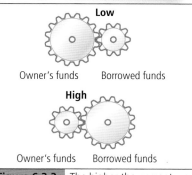

Figure 6.3.2   The higher the percentage of funds that are borrowed (i.e. the higher the gearing), the bigger the risk that the company will not be able to pay the interest in years when profits are low

KEY POINTS

1   Internal finance is raised within a business. It may be owner's capital or profits. In a company it will be share capital.

2   External capital is raised outside the business; sources may be mortgages, loans or hire purchase.

3   The gearing ratio describes the relationship between internal and external capital.

4   Where profits fluctuate, it is risky to have a high gearing ratio.

SUMMARY QUESTIONS

1 What is the difference between internal and external sources of funds? Give an example of who might provide these funds.

2 What sources of funds would you recommend when businesses have the following needs for funds, giving reasons for your choices?

• A start-up business wishes to have 20 new computers available for use.

• A farmer requires seeds and fertiliser, which he will pay for at harvest time.

3 What are the risks of high gearing?

TOYOTA

Large international businesses like Toyota are able to raise capital from shareholders, as well as loan money at preferential rates of interest

Choosing a source of funds

In seeking funds, businesses need to consider the following factors.

- **The sum required.** The amount of capital required can range from just a few dollars to pay an outstanding bill, to a huge investment in a new factory. When a business requires a large sum of money, it will have to borrow from a large financial institution, or ask shareholders to provide more share capital.
- **The cost of borrowing.** Most sources of investment require interest payments, or that the lender receives a share of future profits.
- **Risk.** The more risk the lender is taking, the more interest payment they will expect. Some forms of borrowing, such as from a credit card company, can be very expensive.
- **Permanent or temporary.** Some forms of funding are permanent (e.g. when a company sells shares, it does not have to repay the money to the shareholders). Other types of borrowing are for a fixed period (e.g. a 25-year mortgage, a 3-year loan).
- **The size of the business.** Large businesses usually have access to a wider range of sources of funds. They can also often borrow at lower interest rates because their custom is valued more by the lender than the custom of a small business.
- **Influence and control.** Some lenders, such as venture capitalists and banks, will only provide capital in return for some input into the running of the business.
- **Advice.** Some providers of capital offer advice in addition to the capital. This can be particularly helpful for a business person, although they may have to pay for the advice.

Matching

Businesses need to match their need for finance with a suitable source. We have seen that key points to consider are:

- Should we raise finance internally or externally? If the business relies on external finance, it can build debts which are difficult to meet when cash flow is low.
- Should we raise finance for a short or long period? The longer the period that capital is raised, the higher the interest rate is likely to be.
- When are we going to be able to repay? If a business is unable to repay borrowings in the short term, it should seek longer-term finance.
- Are we willing to lose some of the control of our business? If a business raises finance from borrowing, then it risks losing some control of what it does to outsiders.

The idea of matching is best illustrated by looking at two examples.

1 A food shop is just about to open up. The shopkeeper has bought the premises and the fittings, but now needs to purchase a stock of food to sell. She needs a fast injection of cash to make these purchases, knowing that she will be able to make payments once the stock has been sold.

Possible solutions:

- She could take out an overdraft with her bank to pay for the stock. She would only have to pay interest for each day that she is overdrawn. However, the bank may not grant her an overdraft if she does not have enough money coming into her bank account.

- She could pay using her credit card. Many small businesses finance cash purchases in this way. However, the interest charged on outstanding credit on credit cards is high.

- She could buy stock by taking trade credit. The supplier would give her credit until a set date. However, this might limit her suppliers, so that she loses some control of her business.

2 A large international business wishes to set up a new factory in an overseas market. How could it raise the capital?

Possible solutions:

- Funds could be raised internally by selling more shares in the business. A relatively cheap way of doing this would be to invite existing shareholders to buy more shares. It would be much more expensive to advertise the shares for sale to a wider public.

- The business could borrow money in the form of loans from investors. It would take time to attract investors, however, and they may want a stake in the business.

- The business could create a joint venture with a partner in the overseas market. The factory would then become part of a new business that would be jointly owned by the two partners.

- The business might be able to receive a grant and tax breaks from the host country.

EXAM TIP

Candidates often think that it is easy for a business to raise extra capital by issuing more shares. For a small unincorporated business this is not an option. Even for large companies it may not be easy if potential shareholders have doubts about the future of a company.

ACTIVITY

Look in local and national newspapers to find a story about a business that is expanding. Suggest suitable sources of finance that would finance the expansion.

SUMMARY QUESTIONS

1 What are the main considerations when choosing a suitable form of finance?

2 What forms of short-term finance would you recommend to a business that continually finds that it is short of cash at the end of each month?

3 A business has a seasonal sales pattern. For the first 3 months of the year, its sales revenues are high and easily cover costs. For the next 6 months, revenues fluctuate: sometimes they are higher than costs; at other times they are lower. In the final 3 months, sales revenues are always below costs. What sources of funds would you recommend that the company employs in each of these periods?

KEY POINTS

1 Businesses need to consider several factors when choosing sources of finance.

2 The greater the loan, and the longer the loan period, the greater the likely rate of interest.

3 Large businesses generally have access to a wider range of sources at lower cost.

4 Taking outside finance into a business risks losing some control over decision making.

5 The need for finance needs to be matched to the sources available.

SECTION 1: Short-answer questions

1 State FOUR examples of likely start-up costs for a bakery business. [4]

2 Using the bakery business example, explain what is meant by 'capital items' and give an example. [3]

3 Identify and explain TWO possible sources of funds for a new business, other than an individual's own savings. [4]

4 Identify and explain TWO reasons why a new business may not make a profit in the first year of trading. [4]

5 Using a retail clothing business as an example, explain the difference between working capital and long-term capital. [4]

6 Analyse TWO reasons why it may be easier to obtain funds for expansion than for a new business start-up. [6]

7 Explain, with examples, the difference between internal and external sources of funds. [4]

8 Identify and explain TWO differences between trade credit and a bank loan. [4]

9 Using the following example of financing a small sole trader bakery business, calculate, and comment on, its gearing ratio.

Owner's savings: $10,000
Mortgage: $5,000
Bank loan: $2,000
Government grant: $5,000 [6]

10 Look at this list of possible sources of finance.

Shareholders' funds / Owner's savings / Loan from family / Bank loan / Overdraft / Mortgage / Trade credit / Retained profit / Leasing / Sale of assets

Identify and explain the most appropriate source(s) of finance for a business in the following situations:

- A new hairdressing business set up by a young person who has just left school.
- A family textile business which is buying a new shop in order to expand.
- A large multinational company which wants to buy a competing business. [6]

11 Explain what is meant by 'a rate of interest of 5 per cent per year'. [2]

12 Calculate the total interest payable over five years on a bank loan of $15,000 at:
- 3 per cent per year
- 6 per cent per year. [4]

13 Identify and explain TWO benefits to a business of using retained profit to help finance expansion plans. [4]

14 Identify and explain TWO benefits to a limited company of raising funds by selling more shares. [4]

15 Analyse why an established business with a low gearing ratio may not be making the best of its opportunities in the market. [4]

16 Identify and explain TWO reasons why a lender may not be willing to provide a loan, repayable over 10 years, for the purchase of a company van. [4]

SECTION 2: Longer-answer questions

The business start-up

Joyce has just left school and wants to start her own small business. She has always loved sewing and has made clothes for herself and her family since she was very young. The school uniform shirts and dresses she made for her brothers and sisters have attracted the attention of the school principal, who has asked her whether she would be prepared to supply uniforms for other children. Parents will buy the uniforms from Joyce once she has completed them, and demand will depend on the number of new children at the school and the ability of parents to pay. Joyce has worked out that she will need to buy a new sewing machine and materials for both boys' and girls' clothing. Joyce has a small amount of savings ($200) and her family have offered to help her with a loan of $300, but she will need a small bank loan ($300) to help her buy the sewing machine.

1 Identify and explain ONE item for which Joyce will need short-term finance and ONE item for which she will need long-term finance. *[4]*

2 Identify and explain the proposed internal and external methods of finance for Joyce's business. *[4]*

3 Analyse TWO reasons why a lender may consider Joyce to be a high-risk borrower. *[6]*

4 Identify and explain THREE factors which may determine whether Joyce makes a profit in her first year. *[6]*

5 Do you agree that the local bank manager should give Joyce the loan? Justify your answer. *[6]*

The rescue package

The Tikka Takeaway is a fast-food restaurant in a busy residential area of Bangalore, India. It has always been very busy and successful, but over the past 2 years trade has decreased and the owner, Prakesh, is worried. The problem seems to be that customers, particularly young people, do not want traditional food these days, but prefer the modern, multinational approach of companies such as KFC and McDonald's. Prakesh has carried out some market research and these results seem to support this view. Prakesh is not willing to see his business fail, however, and has spotted a gap in the local market for pizzas, including a home delivery service. He will need to buy a pizza oven and one or two motor-scooters as delivery vehicles. He has some profit retained

from previous years, and is trying to find a way to borrow the rest of the money in order to save his business.

1 Explain the term 'retained profit'. *[2]*

2 Identify and explain TWO external sources of finance which Prakesh could use. *[4]*

3 Analyse ONE advantage and ONE disadvantage to a lender of providing the money to try to save Prakesh's business. *[6]*

4 To what extent do you agree with Prakesh that a long-term loan, repayable over five years, will be suitable? *[6]*

5 As a lender, would you classify Prakesh as a high-, medium- or low-risk borrower? Explain your answer. *[6]*

The expansion plan

Felix is the general manager and major shareholder in an advertising consultancy, which specialises in advising companies who want to launch their products in overseas markets. At present, the company, based in Johannesburg, South Africa, is an incorporated business, but only sells shares to a small group of designated owners. Felix feels that the business has great potential and he would like to open new offices in Europe, the US and Asia. This expansion will be very costly, so Felix is trying to persuade the other shareholders to launch the company on the stock exchange and open up the shares to be bought by the general public. The other shareholders are not so optimistic and are worried about losing control of the company.

1 Identify and explain TWO possible sources of finance that Felix may consider, apart from selling shares. *[4]*

2 Identify and explain TWO advantages of selling shares to raise large amounts of capital for expansion. *[4]*

3 Explain how shareholders will be protected by limited liability in this proposed expansion. *[4]*

4 To what extent do you agree with the other shareholders that control of the business could be lost? *[6]*

5 As an investor, would you buy shares in Felix's business expansion deal? Explain your answer. *[6]*

7 Marketing

7.1 The role of marketing in a business

LEARNING OUTCOMES

Describe the role of marketing.

• Understand the role of marketing in a business.

EXAM TIP

Remember that marketing is much more than simply **selling**. Students often think that they are the same thing.

ACTIVITY

Write down five questions that could be used to find out what benefits people look for in a washing powder.

A product sold in several countries needs to adapt to different uses

The role of marketing

Businesses would not exist without customers. It is essential, therefore, to find out what customers want and need. A business then needs to satisfy these needs by providing what can be memorised as the four Ps:

• **product:** the right goods and services
• **price:** at the right price
• **place:** where customers want it
• **promotion:** by providing the right sort of encouragement.

The four Ps summarise the role of **marketing** and the marketing department in a company: anticipating and identifying consumer wants and needs and then planning the means to meet these requirements. You will learn more about the four Ps in Unit 7.6, *The marketing mix*.

When customers buy products they are looking for particular benefits – that is, what a product will actually do for them. A benefit of a particular brand of washing powder might be that it washes clothes clean, smells nice or is inexpensive. Customers may be interested in 'features' – physical qualities of the product, such as what it looks like – but it is the benefits that will persuade them to keep purchasing.

CASE STUDY | Bonux, Romania and Nigeria

Marketing seeks to find out what customers want and then to provide it. In October 1995, Procter and Gamble (P&G), one of the world's largest producers of washing powder, took over a well-known Romanian company that produced washing powder and soap. One of its brands, Perlan, was particularly popular. Customers liked it because it provided a clean wash at an economical price. P&G invested a lot of money on improving the production plant in Romania. The washing powder was rebranded as Bonux. It came in two varieties: one for hand-washing and the other for washing machines. P&G spent a lot of time interviewing customers to find out ways to improve the product. They introduced a number of improvements, so that Bonux can now offer consumers a threefold benefit: cleaning, a pleasant scent and savings.

P&G market researchers have found through questionnaires and field tests that this formula is what consumers are looking for in other countries as well. In 2006, they opened a detergent factory producing Bonux in Nigeria. The product is produced using

Market research carried out by P&G for Bonux washing powder revealed that global consumers want: cleaning, pleasant smell and saving

a special formula which improves cleaning in dusty conditions. The product is exported from Nigeria to other parts of West Africa, South Africa and East Africa. More customer interviews showed that they liked to purchase the powder in larger packets. Customer questionnaire answers indicated that although this is initially more expensive, it works out cheaper over time. More larger packs are now supplied to the market.

Questions

1 What particular benefits does Bonux offer customers?

2 How was P&G able to find out the sorts of benefits that Bonux customers were looking for?

3 Why do you think that P&G has set up a factory in Nigeria? How would knowledge of the market have enabled P&G to decide to set up there?

Businesses are most likely to make a profit when they provide the benefits and products that customers want. Finding out what customers require involves careful research and analysis of the findings. Think of a product that is successful and you can be certain that the company that produces it has a very good marketing department.

You will find more information on market research in Unit 7.2. Other aspects of marketing covered later in this unit include advertising, promotion and pricing.

ACTIVITY

Choose three of the products from the list below. Using your own knowledge, state what sorts of benefits customers would look for from each product.

- BIC razors
- BIC biros
- Mercedes-Benz motor cars
- A bar of soap that you use in your home
- A bottle or can of drink that is popular in your country

KEY POINTS

1 Consumers look for particular benefits when purchasing goods and services.

2 Marketing involves finding out what customers want and expect in order to provide them with appropriate goods and services.

3 Businesses are most likely to make a profit when they meet customer requirements.

SUMMARY QUESTIONS

1 Chad has come up with a brilliant idea for a new energy-saving device that can be used in the home. He has tried it out in his own house and it works well. He now wants to borrow some money from the bank so that he can produce and sell these devices on a larger scale. However, a friend has suggested that he should first investigate the market. Do you agree with the friend? What would be the advantage of finding out information about the market? What sorts of information should he find out?

2 In the Bonux case study, you read how P&G decided to invest in the Romanian factory and change the name of the product. They also altered the formula of the washing powder and started selling it in different containers. How do you think market research would have helped them to decide to make all these changes?

3 Identify a product that your family or friends use that in your view might benefit from some changes. What sorts of questions would marketers need to ask in order to find out what changes they should make to this product?

Kenya provides 30 per cent of all flowers imported in Europe. Kenyan flower growers have carried out market research to identify which types of flowers are most popular in which European countries, and at what times of the year

Market orientation

Without customers, a business would not exist. Businesses need to ask themselves: 'What would I, as my own customer, expect from my firm?' This focus on customer needs is market orientation. To orientate means to find your direction. A marketing-orientated company takes its direction from what customers want. For example, Kenyan flower growers provide 30 per cent of all fresh-cut flower imports in Europe. The Kenya Flower Council carries out marketing on behalf of all flower growers to find out what the market wants (which varieties of flowers, in what condition), when flowers are required and how to price the flowers competitively.

Market-oriented firms succeed because they listen to customers and give them what they want. For example, some sportswear manufacturers talk to top athletes to find out what sort of clothing they would like to enable them to perform better. In contrast, product-oriented firms concentrate on providing a good product, but without finding out first whether customers want to buy it. Product-oriented companies might include hi-tech businesses experimenting with very new technologies of which customers are not yet aware.

Market research

Market research means carefully gathering, making a record of and then analysing data about the market for goods and services.

Some typical market research questions are set out below. Answers to these questions provide market information.

- Who are our customers?
- What do they want?
- When do they buy/use?
- How much will they pay?
- Can we improve it for them?

Market research methods involve the collection of primary and secondary data. Primary data is new data collected by the company (or by researchers acting on its behalf). Secondary data has already been gathered and been published by someone else. Primary research can be focused on the types of questions that are specific to the business carrying out the research. However, it can be costly.

Primary data is obtained by interviewing a sample of the targeted market (expected customers). A sample is a group that is representative of the overall market. Primary data may be collected through a questionnaire, consisting of a sequence of questions. The questions should be clear and simple, and wherever possible tested on a few people in a pilot survey. It is often easier to analyse results if you ask **closed**, not **open questions**. Closed questions ask for an answer to be chosen from alternatives, for example:

How often do you shop here?

a Every day   **b** Once a week   **c** Once a fortnight   **d** Hardly ever

Questions can be asked in person (often best because it involves face-to-face interaction and the interviewee is likely to elaborate on their answer), through the post (can be slow and produce a poor response), by telephone (quick and easy, but not always very reliable – some people do not like being called for this purpose) or via a website. Another approach is to use e-mail marketing, but this may give a low response rate. To increase rates, it can be helpful to offer a reward for completing a questionnaire (e.g. a $10 gift voucher for an 'on-the-spot' street interview, or a discount on online purchases).

Observation involves looking at how customers behave when shopping. For example, supermarket planners may observe the route that customers take round a store.

A group of customers may be brought together to talk about a product and the choices they make. This consumer panel might also be asked to discuss a list of topics, or test products and give their reactions. Researchers watch and listen to the customers for ideas about what products will and will not be successful. A customer panel is sometimes called a focus group.

Secondary research

Secondary research, as noted earlier, is carried out by someone else. It can be in the form of published research on set topics by market research organisations. It may appear in government statistics, or in books and magazines. It may indicate, for example, what households spend their money on, or numbers of women in part-time work.

Published reports can be expensive, but secondary research is often cheaper to conduct – the research is already published. However, it may be out of date and may not be closely related to a particular organisation and its targeted customers.

Both primary and secondary data may be inaccurate because:

- only a small percentage of the target market is researched
- a consumer panel may not be representative of typical consumers
- a survey may not be given to (or answered by) enough people, or may be given to the wrong people
- the data may go out of date quickly
- questions may be badly worded and misunderstood.

EXAM TIP

Market research results are not always accurate: there may be weaknesses in the way the data was collected. Researchers need to make sure, for example, that there is no bias in the samples used.

KEY POINTS

1 Market research is a systematic process designed to find out about customer needs.

2 A market-oriented company uses market research to find out about customer wants and expectations.

3 Primary research involves finding out data first-hand; secondary research is the use of data generated by others for research purposes.

SUMMARY QUESTIONS

1 Which of the following are primary and which are secondary market research sources?

- Conducting a survey of every fifth person in the street.
- Asking each of your classmates 20 questions.
- Copying out information from a magazine article.
- Interviewing people through a phone survey.
- Sending a questionnaire through the post.

2 A national radio station has carried out research to find out what types of programmes its listeners are interested in. It interviewed 1,000 people in the south of the country and held a consumer panel of 10 listeners in the north. Why might the results be inaccurate?

3 You want to find out whether there is demand for a new type of ice-cold drink. What types of primary research and secondary research could you carry out? What would be the benefits of using primary rather than secondary research?

Presentation and use of results

ACTIVITY

Carry out some primary market research to find out customers' views on two competing household products (e.g. brands of matches or canned drink). Questions you could ask might include:

- How often do you purchase the product?
- Which brands do you prefer?
- What quantities do you buy?
- How much do you pay?
- Does the product offer good value for money?

Set out your findings in a market research report. For each of the questions you ask, set out the data using an appropriate chart or graph.

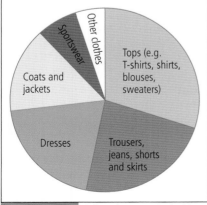

Figure 7.3.2 Sales of women's clothing in the US (% of items sold)

Graphs and charts

Presenting information in a visual way makes it easy to understand and helps to break up text. Graphs and charts are a useful way of presenting key points of market research information. The following table shows the sales of different types of women's clothing from clothes shops in the United States in 2008. The charts that follow the table show ways of presenting this information in a more visual way.

Type of clothes item	Sales of these items as a % of all sales in clothes shops
Tops (e.g. T-shirts, shirts, blouses, sweaters)	30
Trousers, jeans, shorts and skirts	23
Dresses	20
Coats and jackets	15
Sportswear	7
Other clothes	5

A pictogram

A pictogram is a type of bar chart that uses pictures of the items it is connected with. Figure 7.3.1 presents the data in the table as a pictogram.

Figure 7.3.1 Sales of women's clothing in the US (% of items sold)

The advantage of pictograms is that they are easy to understand because the picture represents the actual items. However, they take time to draw to scale.

Pie charts

Pie charts show a total figure split into various categories. Figure 7.3.2 presents the clothes sales data in the form of a pie chart.

Advantages of pie charts are that they immediately show the relative size of items (by the size of the slices of the pie). However, they are not very clear when showing the size of items which only take up a small part of the pie.

Bar charts

In a bar chart, a series of horizontal or vertical bars represent the values of particular items. The reader can quickly make comparisons.

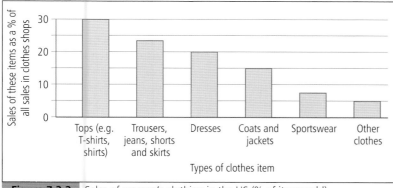

Figure 7.3.3 Sales of women's clothing in the US (% of items sold)

Figure 7.3.3 sets out the sales of different types of women's clothes in the form of a bar chart.

The height of the bar makes it easy to compare one item with another – for example, figures for different years. They are less useful, however, if figures vary considerably from year to year.

Line graphs

A line graph can be used to illustrate how particular figures change over time. They show the size and speed of an increase, so that comparisons can be made. Figure 7.3.4 shows the number of women's clothes stores in the United States compared with the number of enterprises selling women's clothes. (A particular business enterprise may own just one store, two stores or a chain of stores.) The vertical axis of the chart shows the number of stores and enterprises. The horizontal axis shows the dates from 1995 to 2010.

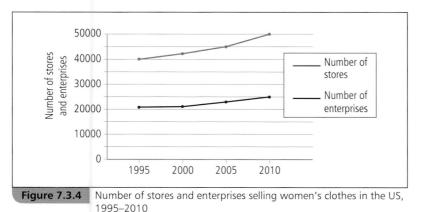

Figure 7.3.4 Number of stores and enterprises selling women's clothes in the US, 1995–2010

The figure shows that the number of stores is rising at a faster rate than the number of enterprises. For example, in 2010 there were twice as many stores as enterprises. On average, each enterprise owned two stores. If we go back to 1995, we can see that there were 40,000 stores and 21,500 enterprises – roughly 1.8 stores per enterprise.

KEY POINTS

1 Market research information can be displayed in graphs, charts and diagrams.

2 Line graphs may be used to show changes over time to specific variables.

3 Pie charts show how a total figure is split into various categories.

4 Bar charts are used to compare relative sizes of items and changes over time.

SUMMARY QUESTIONS

1 What types of graphs and charts would you use to illustrate the following?
   - The percentage market share a company has at a particular moment in time.
   - The rise in the market share of the company over time.
   - How total company sales are split between the various products that it sells.

2 What is a pictogram? Give an example of the sort of market data that a pictogram would be helpful in illustrating.

3 Why is it important to carefully select the scale of the axis used in a graph?

Segmentation

Groups of customers with similar characteristics can be divided into separate groups known as segments. It is useful for marketers to identify groups with similar buying patterns. They can then target their products, promotions and advertising. The different ways of segmenting markets are summarised in the following diagram.

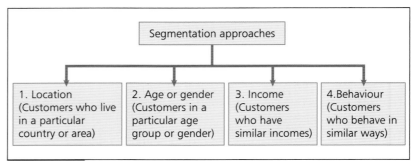

Figure 7.4.1   Approaches to market segmentation

Location

People in certain countries and regions have common characteristics which influence buying attitudes. In marketing to different countries, it is important to look at aspects such as income per person and the culture and tastes of people. For example, in Egypt, green beans are very popular in many food dishes; in the north of France, butter is widely used in cooking. Electrical products sometimes require different technical specifications for sale in different countries (e.g. they may be required to be fitted with a different plug). Different languages are spoken in different parts of the world, requiring the use of different labelling and product instructions to meet local consumer requirements.

Age and gender segmentation

Customers may be divided into discrete segments either by age (e.g. for clothes retailing) or by gender (e.g. for the sale of cosmetics and magazines). It is very important to understand how population patterns can create groups of similar customers. Consumers in similar age groups often have broadly similar interests. For example, in Saudi Arabia, more than 41 per cent of the population is under 14 years old, and a further 18 per cent between 15 and 24 years old. Many of these young people have broadly similar tastes, although there is a significant difference between the products that young males and young females want to purchase. Marketers therefore target this group by finding out what sorts of toys and books appeal to the under-14s, and the types of clothes and music favoured by young people aged 15–24.

Customers in the same location may have similar purchasing patterns, but other differences, such as age, may put them into different segments of the market

Income and social class segmentation

Income is a major factor influencing purchasing decisions. Rising incomes across the world over the last 10 years, particularly among younger people, has led to a boom in demand for branded products, including many high-status clothing items (e.g. expensive trainers and designer-label shirts and sweaters). Products such as cars, jewellery and perfume are targeted at particular income groups. For example, some perfume is sold at very low prices, while other perfume is much more expensive and is designed to appeal to more sophisticated tastes and richer consumers. Many societies are also divided by occupations (e.g. manual workers, who work with their hands, and professional workers, who work in offices or in a profession like a doctor, lawyer, etc.). The type of occupation a person does influences their income and thus their likely buying patterns. Richer people will be able to afford to buy cars, washing machines and televisions, whereas poorer people may only be able to afford a bicycle and radio.

Behavioural segmentation

It is also possible to classify customers by **behavioural segmentation** – for example, how often they buy a product and how loyal they are. Some people may buy a newspaper every day, others only when they want to read about an interesting event. Some people will always buy the same brand of washing powder, while others will compare prices and other aspects before making a choice. Items that people are loyal to include a particular newspaper (because of the quality of the way it presents the news, e.g. *The Times of India*, or *The Daily Gleaner*, Jamaica) or a type of soap.

EXAM TIP

You should be able to explain how and why a business needs to segment a market if it is to market its products successfully.

ACTIVITY

To what extent are there different geographical markets for clothing in your country? For example, is there a difference between the fashions of young people living in cities and those living in rural areas? How have producers and marketers adjusted their product and advertising to appeal to different segments?

SUMMARY QUESTIONS

1 Procter and Gamble is a global company that produces soap powders and other detergents. They have developed washing powders specifically for the Nigerian market because of the higher levels of dust in rural areas. What type of segmentation is this? How does this segmentation help Procter and Gamble?

2 What is the difference between segmentation by age and segmentation by income? What products can you think of where it would be helpful to use these types of segmentation? Explain your answer.

3 In many countries in Africa, the Middle East, South East Asia and South America, a very high percentage of the population is under 21. Identify products that will typically be bought by this age group in these countries. How can producers make sure that these products are targeted at this age group?

KEY POINTS

1 Market segmentation is the process of dividing up a market into different groups of customers by identifying common characteristics of these groups.

2 Segmentation involves identifying customers in the same location, the same age group, of the same gender or with the same behaviour patterns.

3 Knowledge of these segments enables a business to target its products and marketing activities accurately and cost-effectively at distinct segments.

Mass marketing

Most markets can be divided into a number of separate segments. For example, the tea market is divided into a cheap, low-cost segment, a speciality tea segment, a high-quality premium segment, and other segments such as fruit and herbal teas. A **mass marketing** strategy ignores this segmentation and seeks to appeal to all of the customers within different segments. Marketing is to the widest audience. Advertising and promotional messages are designed to appeal to a broad audience. Hopefully this will lead to a large number of sales. Products are designed to appeal to the whole market. Another product that is mass marketed is a standard type of family toothpaste such as Colgate. Colgate was the first type of toothpaste to appear in a tube, over a hundred years ago. Today, it is still one of the best-selling brand names across the globe. It may be advertised on television, with the hope of attracting buyers of all ages, genders, ethnic backgrounds and income groups.

Niche marketing

Niche marketing is the opposite of mass marketing. A niche market is a relatively small segment of a larger market. Marketers will focus their marketing activity on the characteristics of consumers that make up a particular niche. The nature of the niche determines the type of product. For example, toothpaste may be designed to appeal to children. Children's toothpaste tends to come in a smaller tube, and to have some attractive packaging, such as an illustration of a children's cartoon character on the tube.

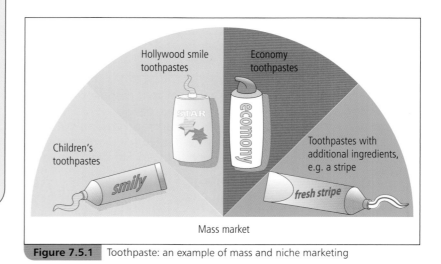

Figure 7.5.1 Toothpaste: an example of mass and niche marketing

| Niche marketing of tourism in Jordan

Tourism is the largest productive sector of the economy in Jordan. Jordan has four main tourist sites – Petra Nabatean City, which is set in rocks; the Dead Sea; the River Jordan; and the Wadi Rum desert. Tourists visit Jordan for a number of reasons, including:

- health and wellness tourism – for their health
- cultural and religious tourism – to visit historical and religious sites
- ecotourism – to see deserts
- sports tourism.

Rather than targeting marketing activity at the mass market of all tourists, the Jordanian tourist board is focusing on market niches. This involves identifying groups of tourists who are very similar in what they are looking for. For example, in the health and wellness niche, tourists want to relax and get well. They want to visit spas where there are waters with healing properties and stay in quality hotels. In the ecotourism sector, tourists are looking for wilderness and desert adventures, and to meet local people.

The tourist board in Jordan is therefore targeting its marketing mix (including advertising) and its products (e.g. types of hotel facility) at specific customers who fit into these niches. At the same time, it is developing its main tourist sites to appeal to these customers.

Questions

1 What is the mass market and what are the niche markets described in the case study?

2 How can identifying the niche markets help the Jordanian tourist board to attract visitors to Jordan? Why is this likely to be more effective than mass marketing?

The Nabatean City of Petra – one of the main tourist sites in Jordan. The Nabateans were an ancient Arab people who built this magnificent city in the rocks. Religious and cultural tourism to sites like Petra provides one segment in the overall Jordanian tourist market

1 In a mass marketing strategy, a business ignores differences between customers and aims to cover the whole market.

2 Niche marketing involves creating marketing activities designed for a segment of a larger market.

1 What is the difference between a niche and a mass market? Illustrate your answer by reference to specific products (e.g. motor cars, cosmetics).

2 Who are the customers that make up a mass market that you are familiar with? How do they differ from customers in specific niches of the overall market that you identified?

3 In what ways does a business have to modify the marketing mix for niche markets? Give examples to illustrate your answer.

Identify and explain the terms of the marketing mix.

- Show knowledge and awareness of the four main elements of the marketing mix (product, price, place and promotion).

The correct marketing mix is all about getting the right balance between the factors that influence sales. Think about the consequences of getting this balance 'wrong'.

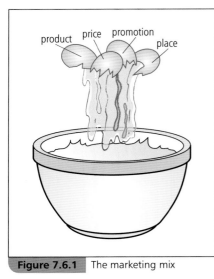

Figure 7.6.1 The marketing mix

The four Ps

As we saw in Unit 7.1, the ingredients of the **marketing mix** are often referred to as the four Ps: product, price, place and **promotion**.

A mix is made up of ingredients that are blended together for a purpose. Think of the ingredients used to make a cake: no ingredient will work on its own. They have to be blended together to make a successful cake. In the same way that there are many cakes to suit all tastes, a marketing mix can be designed to suit the precise requirements of the market.

To create the right marketing mix, businesses have to meet the following conditions.

- The product has to have the right features (e.g. it must look good and work well).
- The price must be right. Consumers will need to buy in sufficient numbers to cover costs.
- The goods must be in the right place at the right time. Making sure that the goods arrive when and where they are wanted is an important operation. The method of selling must be suitable for the customers (e.g. through a small corner shop or a large supermarket).
- The target group needs to be made aware of the existence and availability of the product through promotion. Successful promotion helps a firm to spread costs over a larger output.

Think of a product that you spend money on regularly – perhaps a type of sweet or a visit to the cinema. How effective is the marketing mix for this product? Before you start, make sure you know, with your teacher's advice, who the product is supposed to sell to (the target market). Is the product aimed at young people? Male or female? Choose a sample of 30 people to interview from the appropriate group (e.g. females in the age range 14–18). Ask your sample to compare the marketing mix of your selected product with three other rival products. Compare their views of the marketing mix of these products.

An up-market product is one with a high price and of high quality: it tends to be sold from exclusive locations with expensive advertising and promotion. A down-market product is a cheap product with little or no advertising, sold from down-market locations. Can you identify some up-market and down-market products in the same product category?

CASE STUDY | The Tata Nano

The Tata Nano provides an excellent case study of the marketing mix in action. The car is designed to meet the mass market in India and other similar markets. It is the smallest and cheapest new car in the world. The captions in the diagram show how the *product* has been designed for simplicity. The car can be ordered direct from dealers in India, although it is hoped to launch a more expensive version in the European and American markets (*place*). The car has been *promoted* through a worldwide press launch and a lottery in India (which is the main market): the first million customers drawn in the lottery were to be first in line for the new car. The car was launched at a *price* of 100,000 rupees (about US$2,000). This made it the world's most affordable new car.

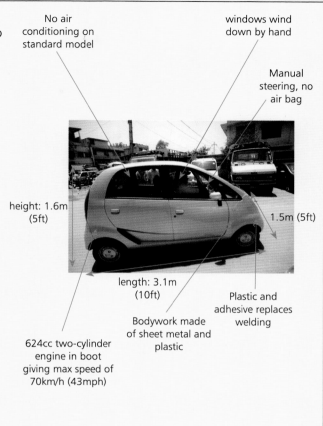

No air conditioning on standard model

windows wind down by hand

Manual steering, no air bag

height: 1.6m (5ft)

1.5m (5ft)

length: 3.1m (10ft)

Plastic and adhesive replaces welding

Bodywork made of sheet metal and plastic

624cc two-cylinder engine in boot giving max speed of 70km/h (43mph)

Questions

1 Do you think that the marketing mix for the Nano is likely to lead to high sales? Explain your answer.

2 How would you expect the marketing mix for the Nano to compare with the mix for an expensive car?

3 Is it going to be possible to sell this car in other markets (e.g. in the US and Europe)?

SUMMARY QUESTIONS

1 Match the following terms with the definitions below.

Product / promotion / place / price / marketing mix

- Advertising and other means of enticing customers to buy a product.
- Getting the product to where customers want to buy it.
- A combination of the four Ps.
- The good or service that is being sold.
- The amount charged for a good or service.

2 Choose a product that you have recently bought. What aspects of the marketing mix encouraged you to buy that product?

3 How is the marketing mix different for an exclusive type of tea such as Earl Grey tea when compared with a standard, cheap variety of tea?

KEY POINTS

1 A well-chosen marketing mix is required to attract the targeted customers to make purchases.

2 The marketing mix consists of getting the right product in the right place at the right price and supported by appropriate promotions.

3 The four Ps need to be blended together in the most appropriate way.

The product

Demonstrate an understanding of the product life cycle.

- Knowledge and understanding of the importance of packaging.
- Awareness of the concept of a brand name in influencing sales.
- Knowledge of the stages of the product life cycle.
- Draw and interpret a product life cycle diagram.
- Understanding of the four main stages of the product life cycle.
- Show awareness of extension strategies.

ACTIVITY

Look at the items shown in Figure 7.7.2. In your country, where is each of these in the product life cycle?

Identify products that your classmates purchase that are at different stages of the product life cycle.

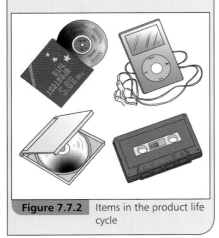

Figure 7.7.2 Items in the product life cycle

Products

The most important part of the marketing mix is the product. It must meet an identified consumer need.

We like products because they provide us with **benefits**. A bicycle is not just something that sits outside our house; it provides the benefit of transporting us to school or to the sports club, or to meet friends.

Products have a number of features. For example, your bicycle has:

- shape • design • colour • size • packaging (when first bought).

In addition, there may be other benefits associated with your bicycle, after-sales service (repairs to the chain, replacement of the tyres by the seller) such as a guarantee (in some cases).

Starting with the packaging

The first time a customer sees many modern products is in the packaging. Figure 7.7.1 gives some of the many reasons that products are packaged.

Packaging adds value to products for all of the reasons shown in the diagram. However, there are some negative aspects: packaging can raise the cost and, as a result, the price of a product. It also creates pollution and waste.

Figure 7.7.1 The purposes of packaging

Branding

A **brand** is a product or group of products with a unique, consistent and easily recognisable character. For example, we all recognise the Coca-Cola brand, not only by its logo, but by the shape of the bottle, the colour of the can, the taste of the product and other features.

The product life cycle

The life of a product is the period over which it appeals to customers. At the *introduction* stage, sales growth is slow. Only a small number of people know about a product or realise its benefits. Profits start to rise in the *growth* phase. More and more people find out about the product and want to purchase it. Competitors are coming into the market. In the *maturity* phase, most of the potential customers have been reached. However, there may be lots of repeat purchases. Competition from rival producers is strong. In the *decline* stage, the product becomes 'old' and sales start to fall. An updated or replacement product may have entered the market.

Giving new life

To prolong the life cycle, new life needs to be injected to the marketing mix. There are various ways of doing this.

1 **Modify the product.** In the 19th century, Lifebuoy soap was introduced to India with the promise of 'health and hygiene' to millions of rural customers. The product was sold as a basic red bar of soap. The brand went through a period of steady growth and eventual maturity in the 20th century. At the start of the 21st century, sales were falling by 15 per cent a year. The company then relaunched the soap in 2002, in a new shape, with a new, high-lather formula and attractive advertising. This has won back customer loyalty. Sales of Lifebuoy increased by 10 per cent per year in India. (Today, over 3 billion bars of Lifebuoy are sold per year in Asia and Africa.)

2 **Altering distribution patterns** to create more attractive retail outlets for consumers. For example, Hindustan Unilever, the makers of Lifebuoy, has created networks of women with business skills in rural villages to sell their products. There are over 25,000 of these women, selling in 100,000 villages and reaching 1 billion customers. Many other businesses have injected new life into their products by creating new channels, such as attractive websites, where customers can buy products online.

3 **Changing prices.** Prices can be lowered or raised to become more attractive to customers. Lower prices make goods more affordable, while higher ones make them appear more exclusive.

4 **Promotional campaigns.** Advertising, 'buy one get one free' offers and other promotions encourage new customers to try out a product and reward existing customers for their loyalty.

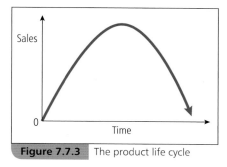

Figure 7.7.3 The product life cycle

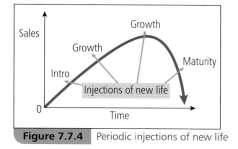

Figure 7.7.4 Periodic injections of new life

SUMMARY QUESTIONS

1 Draw a product life cycle for each of the following products.
- A new product that has recently become popular in your country.
- A product that has been available in your country for a long time, but has now become less popular.

Explain your answer in each case.

2 List four products that are well-known brands. In each case, explain how packaging helps, or fails, to make the product more attractive.

3 How can a product's life cycle be extended?

KEY POINTS

1 Products have life cycles that can extend from just a few weeks to hundreds of years.

2 Sales and profits increase during the growth and maturity phases of the cycle.

3 Businesses employ a range of extension strategies to inject new life into the product life cycle.

7.8 Price

Price

The price a business charges will depend on the percentage of the market – that is, the number of customers – that they are trying to attract. The main decision, therefore, is whether to charge:

- a *low price* in order to attract sales by undercutting the competition. This makes it possible to sell large quantities at a low cost per unit.
- an *average price*. If you charge an average price, you will need to compete with your rivals by other means (e.g. better packaging, advertising and promotion).
- a *higher price*. Firms can charge a *high* or *premium price* if they are seen as being better than their rivals in meeting the needs of customers.

Figure 7.8.1 Different pricing positions

Price elasticity of demand – a measure of responsiveness of demand to a change in price

It is useful to find out how customers will react to a change in price. Price elasticity is used to measure this: this measures how much the quantity demanded changes following a change in price. Demand is *elastic* when the change in the number of goods demanded is high when compared with the change in price. For example, Ramesh sells fruit and vegetables from a cart. One week he lowered the price of his mangoes by 5 per cent (undercutting his competitors) and demand increased by 20 per cent. Demand for his mangoes in this case was elastic.

However, when the change in numbers of goods demanded is lower than the change in price, demand is said to be *inelastic*. For example, Ramesh sells oranges that are sweeter and contain fewer pips than those of his competitors. He decided to raise his price by 5 per cent. When he did so, sales of his oranges only dropped by 2 per cent. Demand for his oranges was inelastic. Knowledge of how elastic demand is helps sellers decide how much to charge for a product, and whether they will increase sales revenue from lowering or raising prices.

LEARNING OUTCOMES

Understand how pricing decisions are made.

- Understand the main methods of pricing: cost plus, competitive, psychological, penetration, price skimming.
- Show awareness of the implications of the methods.

Understand the significance of price elasticity of demand.

- Appreciate the difference between a price elastic demand and a price inelastic demand.
- Understand the importance of the concept in pricing decisions.

Our glasses

		Glasses Direct	Spec-savers	D&A	Vision Express	Saving-Glasses Direct
Fully rimmed		From £24	From £25	From £29	From £25	£1
Rimless		From £24	From £99	-	From £99	£75
Semi-rimmed		From £89	From £169	-	From £169	£80
Bendable		From £39	From £125	-	From £125	£86
Titanium		From £89	From £125	-	From £125	£36
Designer		From £69	From £125	From £109	From £125	£56

Table comparing prices of spectacles. This advertisement is designed to attract customers to an online spectacle seller, Glasses Direct, by showing how prices are lower than those of rivals (competitive pricing)

ACTIVITY

Visit a local retail store and look at the prices displayed for different products. What examples can you find of penetration pricing, psychological pricing, skimming and competitive pricing?

The main methods of pricing

Cost-plus pricing

A common way to make pricing decisions is to calculate how much it costs to do a particular job or activity, and then add on a given percentage as a profit for the job or activity. This is sometimes known as a mark-up. For example, a business may calculate that it will cost $100 to do a small repair job on a car, including parts, labour and equipment. The business also wants to make a profit, so may decide to add on another 20 per cent as profit. It therefore charges the customer $120. This **cost-plus pricing** is a simple and easy way to price which makes sure that costs are covered.

Psychological pricing

Psychological pricing is based on the idea that certain prices encourage buyers to make purchases. These are prices that are just under a round number (e.g. $9.99 or $19.95). Sellers use psychological pricing to encourage buyers to think that items are cheaper than they are.

Competitive pricing

Competitive pricing involves undercutting the price of rival products. A business may price its products lower than those of rivals. Businesses may make a loss in the short term by doing this, perhaps to force a competitor out of business.

Penetration pricing

When a firm brings out a new product into a new or existing market, it may feel that it needs to make a lot of sales very quickly in order to establish itself and to make it possible to produce larger quantities. It may therefore start off by offering the product at quite a low price. A loss may be made until the new product has penetrated the market. When market penetration has been achieved, prices can be raised.

Skimming

When you bring out a new product, you may be able to start off by charging quite a high price. Some customers may want to be the first to buy your product because of the prestige of being seen with it. The word **skimming** comes from the idea of skimming off the top layer of cream, allowing the cream to build up again, skimming off the second layer, and so on. For example, you could sell an exclusive dress at an exclusive price to wealthier customers. The next season, you could lower the price, making it accessible to a less wealthy group of customers.

SUMMARY QUESTIONS

1 A local clothing business is considering lowering its prices (to increase sales and profits). An advisor carries out some research and reports back that there is elastic demand for the type of clothes being offered by the shop and that local consumers are highly influenced by psychological pricing. How might this affect the pricing decisions made by the business?

2 A sign-writing business that produces shop signs uses a cost-plus pricing method. It marks up prices by 20 per cent on the costs of painting shop signs. The owner has calculated that it will cost $50 to produce a sign for a restaurant. What price should the business charge for the job?

3 A new book has just been published by a best-selling author. Initially, the book is to be produced in hardback and will cost $100. Next year, it will be relaunched in paperback form and sell for $50. What pricing technique is being used, and why?

KEY POINTS

1 The simplest method of pricing is to add a percentage mark-up on costs.

2 Psychological pricing involves setting prices at an odd number like 9 or 5. Competitive pricing involves undercutting rivals. Skimming pricing involves starting at high prices and then gradually lowering prices over time.

Distribution channels

Appreciate the importance of distribution channels and the factors that determine the selection of them.

- Knowledge and understanding of a distribution channel.
- Recommend and justify an appropriate channel in a given situation.

Coca-Cola has shortened its distribution channels to China by setting up joint ventures with the Chinese government and other Chinese partners to build bottling plants in China

Distribution

Supply, or *distribution* as it is commonly called, makes products available to customers where and when they want them. This is an aspect of place, a very important part of the marketing mix.

Something like 20 per cent of the total production cost of a product is taken up with freight charges. These are the costs of moving raw materials to the producer and then transporting finished products to the end-user.

Channels of distribution

A **distribution channel** is the means by which an organisation and its customers are brought together at a particular place and time to buy and sell goods. This may be in a shop, via a computer link or by television shopping.

The organisations that are involved in the distribution chain are:

- **Manufacturers** – firms that make the products.
- **Wholesalers** – firms that store goods in bulk which they purchase from manufacturers and then sell on to retailers.
- **Retailers** – the firms that sell goods to the final consumers.
- In Channel A, the manufacture sells direct to the customer by mail order. The customer selects goods from a catalogue and purchases through the post.
- In Channel B, the manufacturer distributes direct to their own warehouses and company shops, which supply customers. Examples are products that are produced directly by large supermarket chains in their own factories. The manufacturer is responsible for distribution.

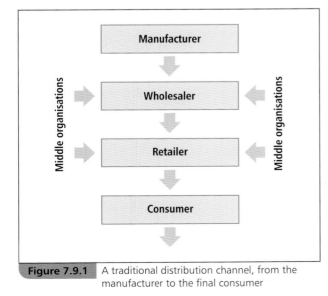

Figure 7.9.1 A traditional distribution channel, from the manufacturer to the final consumer

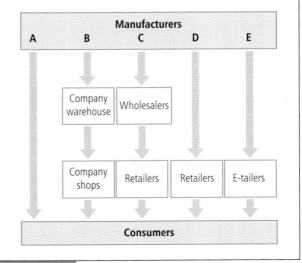

Figure 7.9.2 Different types of distribution channel

- In Channel C, sometimes referred to as the 'traditional channel', a manufacturer makes goods; a wholesaler buys lots of different goods from several manufacturers. The wholesaler sells on to retailers. The manufacturer, wholesaler and retailer are all independent. (The term wholesaler refers to a business that stocks items in bulk until they are required by retailers.)
- In Channel D, retailers buy directly from manufacturers. This is easiest when the retailers have a very large storage area, or when goods can be bought in bulk.
- Channel E has become particularly important as more and more households become linked to the internet through computers and mobile phones. The e-tailer is the organisation that deals with customers through an interactive website, which enables customers to buy goods online.

ACTIVITY

Interview the owner of a local shop to find out what channels of distribution they use for the various items they stock. (You will normally find that they use more than one channel of distribution.)

CASE STUDY | Coca-Cola in China

Distribution can become more expensive when it takes place internationally: the longer the supply chain, the greater the cost. The American company Coca-Cola's fourth biggest market is China. Eventually it could become the largest market.

In the 1970s, China had only one brand of soft drink, distributed nationally. It was difficult for foreign companies to enter the market. Coca-Cola started out by exporting Coca-Cola to China and selling it to retail outlets such as hotels. Over time, the company developed a relationship with the Chinese government. Bottling plants were set up that were owned by the Chinese government. The next stage was to set up a joint venture (see page 51) bottling plant, owned jointly by Coca-Cola and the government. Eventually, Coca-Cola was

allowed to set up its own bottling plants. In this way, the company was able to produce cheaply using local supplies or raw materials. By 2008, Coca-Cola had 40 bottling factories in the country. It now produces tea, coffee and bottled water, as well as Coca-Cola itself and many other soda drinks.

Questions

1 Why would Coca-Cola want to set up bottling plants in China rather than exporting bottles of Coca-Cola to China?

2 Illustrate how the supply chain was shortened when Coca-Cola set up its own bottling plants in China.

KEY POINTS

1 Distribution is the process through which goods are made available to consumers.

2 Channels of distribution are the series of stages involved in bringing goods to the end-consumer.

3 There are many different channels of distribution, depending on the type of product and the market. Increasingly, goods are distributed through shortened channels, often involving electronic selling.

4 The purpose of simplifying distribution channels is to reduce costs.

SUMMARY QUESTIONS

1 What is a distribution channel? How is a product that you are familiar with distributed? What are the various stages of distribution?

2 In what ways does e-tailing help to shorten the distribution channel?

3 Define the following terms.

Distribution / manufacturer / wholesaler / retailer / e-tailer

Promotion

LEARNING OUTCOMES

Understand the role of promotion.

- Understand the aims of promotion.
- Identify, explain and give examples of different forms of promotion.
- Understand how promotions influence sales.
- Justify an appropriate method of promotion in a given situation.

Advertising in Kenya includes simple billboards, advertisements on buses, radio, television and leading newspapers, as well as in the cinema

Promotion

Promotion refers to ways of spreading information about a product, brand or company.

Promotion can be carried out in many different ways (e.g. advertising on television, radio, cinema, newspapers and, nowadays, using the internet and even mobile phones to get messages across).

Other forms of promotion include the sponsorship of events, sales promotion, merchandising (making products look attractive, e.g. in a shop window), trade shows and public relations.

The combination of different types of promotion is referred to as the promotional mix.

A distinction is made between promotions 'into the pipeline' and 'promotions out of the pipeline' (see Figure 7.10.1).

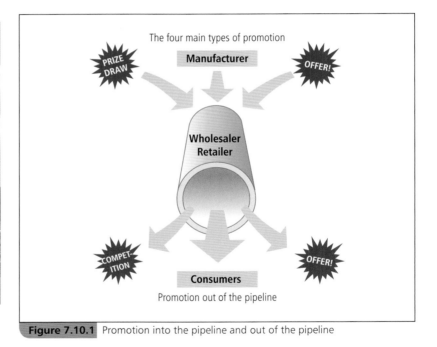

Figure 7.10.1 Promotion into the pipeline and out of the pipeline

Promotions into the pipeline are methods that are used to sell more products into the distribution system – that is, they are aimed at wholesalers and retailers rather than final consumers. Examples are 'dealer loaders', such as 20 for the price of 10, display units, dealer competitions, extended credit to dealers, sale-or-return, and so on.

Promotions out of the pipeline help in promoting and selling products to the final consumer. These include free samples, trial packs, coupon offers, price reductions, competitions, demonstrations and point-of-sale materials.

Different forms of promotion

Advertising

Advertising is a widely used form of above-the-line promotion. For example, in Kenya, advertising includes outdoor billboard advertising on street poles along major traffic routes, and advertising on the side of buses. In addition, there are around 50 radio stations with over 6 million radio-set users. Adverts can be placed in English and Swahili, as well as 17 other languages. There are eight television broadcast stations. Television covers the main centres of population. Television ownership tends to be among wealthier people, but there are televisions in most community and village centres. Leading newspapers are the *Daily Nation*, *East African Standard*, *The People* and *Kenya Times*. Stills and film clips are used extensively to advertise products in Kenya, including in mobile cinemas touring rural areas.

Advertising can increase sales by making consumers aware of new products, demonstrating how good products are and reminding consumers about products. Cinema and television advertising is highly visual and can build an image.

Sales promotions

Sales promotions take place through media and non-media promotion for a limited time to increase consumer demand. Examples include:

- competitions
- point-of-purchase displays
- special price offers for a limited period
- free gifts.

Personal selling

Personal selling is oral communication with potential buyers of a product in the hope of making a sale. Initially, the seller will try to build a relationship with the buyer before going on to try to 'close' the sale.

Public relations

Public relations involves managing the flow of information from an organisation to its 'publics' in order to build the reputation of a company and its brands. Any form of activity which does this is termed *PR*. PR might involve publicising a charity, informing consumers about a brand or producing advertisements that show the company and its products in a positive light.

The purpose of each of the promotion methods described above is to increase the sales of the business.

Figure 7.10.2 The four main types of promotion

EXAM TIP

Price reduction is only seen as promotion if it is for a limited period of time. Permanently lower prices are part of the pricing strategy of the business.

DID YOU KNOW?

A good example of sales promotions are those offered by budget airlines such as India's Spice Jet. To attract new customers to the route, the airline will offer flights to new destinations at very low prices for a limited period of time. This has been very successful in winning new customers.

SUMMARY QUESTIONS

1 What type of promotion is involved in the following?
  - Giving out free samples of a new type of shampoo
  - Publicity surrounding a major charity event
  - Publicising a product on television or in a newspaper

2 What is the difference between promotions into the pipeline and promotions out of the pipeline?

3 What is the purpose of promotion? Illustrate your answer by reference to a promotion that you are familiar with.

KEY POINTS

1 Promotion is the process of making consumers aware – that is, communicating information about a product or company.

2 There are four main types of promotion: advertising, sales promotion, direct selling and PR.

3 The ultimate purpose of promotion is to increase awareness, and therefore sales, of products and brands.

Marketing strategy

A marketing strategy is a plan of the marketing activities for a range of products, or for a single product. In effect, this means choosing the right combination of marketing mix elements to support the product/s.

The best possible mix will depend on the stage of the product life cycle.

The elements of a marketing strategy

The table shows the four key elements of the marketing strategy. The case study that follows gives an example of a marketing strategy used by a supermarket chain in the UK to enter a new market in the US.

Product	Price	Place	Promotion
What product are we selling to our target customers? What does the product look like? What benefits does it provide?	What is an appropriate price for our product and the relevant target audience?	Where should we sell it? What are the most suitable channels of distribution?	How do we promote the product in a way that fits with the product image and the type of customers?

CASE STUDY | Tesco's Fresh & Easy

Tesco is the UK's biggest supermarket chain. The company devised a strategy for entering the US market, which was dominated by huge hypermarkets. The new product concept was a chain of stores called Fresh & Easy. The Fresh & Easy stores stock locally produced, fresh products, such as green vegetables and salads. The first few stores were set up on the West Coast of the US, including California, a centre for growing fresh fruit and vegetables. Tesco created a huge distribution centre at a central location close to a large number of the stores. It covered this with solar panels for energy, stressing its 'green' image. It also used a polar bear as its corporate symbol, to indicate its concern with global warming. Tesco's ambition is to have Fresh & Easy stores providing fresh produce locally everywhere in the United States over the next 10 years.

The three key elements of the Tesco strategy are affordability, convenience and freshness – in other words, good healthy products at discount prices. The launch of the stores came with a wide advertising campaign, using television, press and radio advertisements, as well as a public relations campaign to promote the green image of the company. It is too early to say whether this strategy will be a success, but initial signs show that consumers have taken to the concept in large numbers.

Questions

1 Identify the elements of price, place, promotion and product mentioned in the case study.

2 How do you think that the marketing strategy outlined in the case study will enable the business to be competitive with the huge US supermarket chains?

In the mid 1990s, Unilever had gained 81 per cent of the Brazilian washing powder market. The only sector it had not captured was that of the very lowest income households. The company therefore set out an 'Everyman' campaign to win even this sector of the market. Market research showed that washing in the poorer areas was typically carried out by hand, using washboards and bars of laundry soap. Washing was a major social event, with people coming together to talk at the river and taking pride in their work. Though many people owned television sets, many could not read or write, so it would be difficult to convince them to change washing habits with a 30-second TV commercial. Typically, this group of consumers shopped at local, family-owned stores, which manufacturers find difficult to reach through large wholesalers.

Questions

1 What marketing strategy would you suggest to reach the low-income sector of the Brazilian market for soap powders?

2 How would this involve blending each of the elements of marketing into a consistent mix?

The changing marketing mix

Over time, it may be necessary to change a marketing strategy. This involves changing the marketing mix. For example, we saw earlier (see page 93) how Lifebuoy soap was successfully relaunched in India with a new advertising campaign and strategy.

At the start of a product life cycle, the emphasis is on gaining a hold in the market. This may involve promotional activity and promotional pricing. Distribution may be through a small number of outlets. Over time, the business will adopt new promotional activities, alter its product and employ different distribution channels.

Tesco's Fresh & Easy stores combine cheap, fresh, locally sourced produce with an environmentally friendly image at convenient locations

ACTIVITY

Identify a product and create a marketing strategy for it in your domestic market. Your marketing strategy should include a description of the product, its benefits and its target customers. Justify the pricing strategy, the locations for selling the product and the channels of distribution. You will also need to justify promotions to support each of the other elements.

ACTIVITY

Recommend a strategy for the relaunch of a product of your choice. Choose a product that is widely used in your country that has been losing popularity in recent times.

SUMMARY QUESTIONS

1 What is meant by the term 'marketing strategy'? Illustrate your answer by using the example of a product or brand that you are familiar with.

2 How is the marketing strategy different for a low-price, low-specification product, compared with one for a high-price, high-specification product? Use examples of products from the same market segment to illustrate your answer.

3 Why is the marketing strategy for a product likely to change over the course of its life cycle? Explain with reference to a specific product.

KEY POINTS

1 A marketing strategy is a plan setting out approaches that will be used to market a product or range of products.

2 The strategy covers each element of the marketing mix and how the elements fit together.

3 Marketing strategies need to be adjusted over the course of time.

Marketing budgets

A marketing budget shows how much a company plans to spend on marketing activities in a given period of time – for example, the coming year. It will look like the following table.

The sum of money in the budget will depend on the type of industry and the product. In some industries it can be very high. For example, companies selling washing powder, mobile phones and popular motor cars will have a large advertising and promotional budget. Spending will be much lower in companies selling non-branded products (e.g. fish, fresh fruit and vegetables) or products (e.g. matches and drawing pins) which sell by reputation and customer familiarity.

	Jan	Feb	Mar	Apr	May	Jun	Jul	Aug	Sep	Oct	Nov	Dec
Marketing staff salaries												
Market research activity												
Advertising												
Press relations												
Direct marketing												
Sales promotions												
Events												
Sponsorship												
Total												

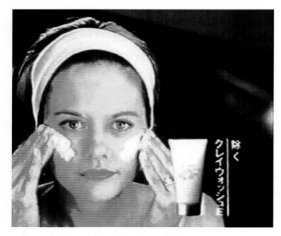

When television advertising is used for promotion, this takes up a sizeable chunk of the marketing budget. However, the impact of these adverts is enormous

Business people sometimes see marketing expenditure as a cost. It is better, however, to consider how effective the marketing activity is. How much will it return in sales revenue? A low-cost marketing budget may have a poor return in terms of impact.

The following table illustrates some appropriate sizes of budgets for different-sized companies. You can see that large companies can afford more than small ones. This has a tremendous impact on the markets they can reach, leading to much higher sales and profits.

Sales revenue of company	Marketing budget as % of income
Under $5 million	7–8%
$5–10 million	6–7%
$10–50 million	5–6%
$50–100 million	4–5%
Over $100 million	2–3%

Cost-effectiveness

Cost effectiveness describes the relationship between the cost of an activity and the returns from it. A cost-effective marketing activity is one that yields a high return compared with the budget allocated to it, as is shown below.

High cost, high impact = Cost-effective

High cost, poor impact = Cost-ineffective

Low cost, high impact = Cost-effective

Low cost, low impact = Cost-ineffective

The best way of judging the effectiveness of any form of marketing activity is to calculate the extra sales revenue for each additional dollar spent on marketing. This is the ROI – return on investment.

ACTIVITY

Working in a small group, identify a product that you would like to promote in your own region.

You have been allocated $5,000 for advertising the product.

A television advert will cost you $800 for each time the advert is shown. It will cost you $1,000 to have an agency prepare the advert. A newspaper advertisement will cost you $400 for a regional newspaper and $200 for a local newspaper for each time the advert appears in the paper. A graphic designer will prepare the advert for a further $200. A cinema advert will cost you $250 to screen and $500 to make the advert. You can advertise on the side of bus shelters for $100 per shelter for a week, but the posters will cost you $250 to design.

Decide how you will allocate the budget between advertising and other promotional activities. Which of these activities do you think would be the most cost-effective in terms of having a high impact relative to cost?

KEY POINTS

1 A marketing budget is money allocated for marketing expenditure in a given period.

2 The budget is usually set out in a plan showing the costs of different marketing activities.

3 A wise business will seek to create a cost-effective marketing budget. This involves making sure that there is a high impact compared with the costs of the marketing activity.

SUMMARY QUESTIONS

1 Explain two possible uses of the term 'marketing budget'.

2 What sorts of items would you expect to appear in a marketing budget?

3 A company has a high marketing budget compared to that of its competitors. Why might this be beneficial? Explain your answer in terms of cost-effectiveness.

SECTION 1: Short-answer questions

1 Identify and explain TWO objectives of the marketing department within a business. *[4]*

2 Using a mobile phone or laptop computer as an example, explain the difference between 'features' and 'benefits' of a product. *[3]*

3 Identify and explain TWO reasons why a business might carry out market research. *[4]*

4 Explain the statement 'the consumer is king in a market economy'. *[4]*

5 Explain why primary research may be known as 'field' research and secondary research may be known as 'desk' research. *[4]*

6 Analyse TWO reasons why primary market research results may be inaccurate. *[6]*

7 Explain, with examples, the difference between a consumer survey and a focus group. *[4]*

8 State and explain ONE example of data that would be best presented using a pie chart and ONE example of data that would be best presented as a line graph. *[4]*

9 Explain, using examples, the following approaches to market segmentation:
   • geographical
   • gender
   • socioeconomic group. *[6]*

10 For each of your answers to Question 9, explain a market for which this method of segmentation would be appropriate. *[6]*

11 Identify and explain a niche market within the market for food in your country. *[4]*

12 Identify and explain TWO benefits to a small business of aiming its product at a niche market. *[4]*

13 Analyse why it is important for a business to get all the elements of the marketing mix right. *[4]*

14 Analyse why an established business may aim to sell a range of products at different stages of their life cycle. *[4]*

15 Analyse ONE example of a product for which a skimming pricing strategy may be appropriate and ONE example where penetration pricing may be more successful. *[4]*

16 Explain, with examples other than advertising, THREE examples of promotion. *[6]*

SECTION 2: Longer-answer questions

The pizza delivery company

Prakesh has managed to borrow the money to relaunch his traditional fast-food business, The Tikka Takeaway, in Bangalore, India, as a pizza restaurant and takeaway, including a home-delivery service. He has put together a menu, including 12 different pizza recipes in three different sizes, and he now needs to make as many people as possible aware of his new products and service. Due to overspending on the redecoration of his shop, however, Prakesh has had to set a low marketing budget.

1 Identify and explain TWO changes in Prakesh's marketing mix. *[4]*

2 Identify and explain TWO ways in which Prakesh's target market may change due to the switch from traditional food to pizzas. *[4]*

3 Analyse TWO possible pricing methods you would recommend Prakesh to consider for his pizzas when he launches the new business idea. *[6]*

4 Identify and explain THREE marketing methods you would recommend to Prakesh for the launch. *[6]*

5 Due to his local reputation and loyal customers, Prakesh does not want to change the name of his business. Do you agree with him? Justify your answer. *[6]*

The Maldives Reef holiday company

The Maldives Reef holiday company operates in a niche market. The target customers are high-income, young professionals, mainly from Europe, who are interested in combining taking a holiday with obtaining an advanced diving qualification. Guests are accommodated on one of the smallest, most exclusive resort islands, where all the chalets have their own private beach areas. The diving instructors are highly qualified and the company has good knowledge of the best underwater locations. The company spends very little on marketing, as most guests are regular travellers and recommendations come through word of mouth. Fiona, the marketing director, is keen to seek out new markets, due to a worldwide economic downturn. 'Maybe,' she says, 'we should explore a new market segment of more budget-conscious travellers, who still want to dive but are quite happy with basic accommodation and therefore a lower price'.

1 Explain the term 'niche market' in this case. [6]

2 Analyse how the unique selling point of the Maldives Reef holiday company enables high prices to be charged to current customers. [6]

3 Analyse ONE advantage and ONE disadvantage to the Maldives Reef holiday company of relying on the business from their loyal customers. [6]

4 To what extent do you agree with Fiona that the company should be looking for new markets? [6]

5 Suggest a market research strategy for Fiona to find out what budget-conscious customers want from a diving holiday. [6]

Zigzag: the school enterprise company

The Zigzag enterprise company at Good Start School in Livingstone, Zambia, has decided on two events to launch its enterprise this year: a school talent show and a doughnut sale during lunchtimes. They have carried out primary market research on pupils in school and have found out the following information about predicted sales.

- **Talent show:** at $5 they will sell 250 tickets, but if they drop the price to $3, they will sell 275 tickets.

- **Doughnuts:** at 50 cents they will sell 300 doughnuts, but if they drop the price to 30 cents, they will sell 500.

1 Identify and explain TWO possible reasons why Zigzag's market research may be inaccurate. [4]

2 Identify and explain TWO reasons why Zigzag's current target market may limit their success. [6]

3 Calculate the price elasticity of demand (PED) for each product, when the price is reduced, using the formula:

$$\text{PED} = \frac{\text{\% change in quantity demanded}}{\text{\% change in price}}$$ [6]

4 Using the information on price elasticity and the figures, recommend what price should be charged for each product. Explain your answer. [6]

5 The members of Zigzag have decided to try to extend their market to include selling wooden souvenirs to tourists in a local craft market. Analyse TWO ways in which their marketing strategy will need to change for these customers. [6]

6 Evaluate the extent to which personal selling in the craft market may lead to high sales of souvenirs for the Zigzag company. [6]

8 Production (operations management)

8.1 Using resources

LEARNING OUTCOMES

Understand how resources can be used and managed to help organisations achieve their objectives.

• Understand the difference between production and productivity.

• Identify factors that increase productivity.

A very productive system. In a Japanese sushi bar, the chef converts the rice, fish and vegetables into rice parcels which go round a moving belt for diners to choose from

EXAM TIP

It is a common error to confuse increasing production with increasing productivity. Make sure you understand the difference between these two concepts.

ACTIVITY

Choose two businesses from the following: shoe manufacturer, hotel chain/hotel reception desk, cycle repair shop owner, hairdresser. Suggest ways each could increase productivity.

Inputs and outputs

Businesses convert inputs into more valuable outputs. This is referred to as adding value (see page 2). Production involves making resources more valuable. Figure 8.1.1 shows how various business inputs are made into more valuable outputs.

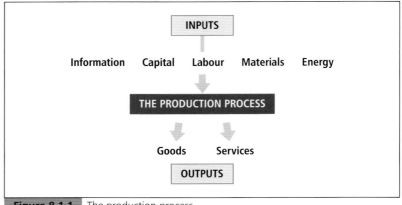

Figure 8.1.1 The production process

A number of **operations** (organised work tasks) are usually carried out to add value when managing resources. Operations management is therefore the term that describes the process of managing these activities. An example is a Japanese sushi restaurant, where fish, rice and vegetables are brought into the restaurant as the main raw materials; other ingredients such as ginger and soy sauce will be added. Chefs then work with these materials to produce the sushi – parcels of rice containing the fish and vegetables. The chefs carry out operations such as taking the ingredients out of the stores, cutting up the fish and vegetables, rolling the rice parcels, and putting the prepared sushi on plates. The plates pass round a moving conveyor belt and customers choose which dishes they would like. The production process therefore involves converting the food materials into the finished sushi products.

Production and labour productivity

Production means making goods or services. **Productivity** refers to how effective resources are in producing goods. Productivity rises when resources are used well. The diners in the sushi bar receive quicker service than in an ordinary restaurant because they help themselves to food from the moving line produced by the chef – they do not have to wait to be served. More output is produced with given quantities of inputs. In a sushi restaurant, considerable output is achieved by a small staff.

The productivity of a company can be measured by the following calculation.

$$\text{Productivity} = \frac{\text{Quantity of output}}{\text{Quantity of inputs}}$$

Measurements are often carried out to measure the productivity of particular resource inputs. This is often the case with labour. For example, if a Toyota car plant produces 500 cars per hour with 1,000 employees, then the labour productivity would be 0.5 cars per hour. (The figure indicates the amount produced by one worker.) If the number of cars increased to 600 per hour with the same number of workers, then labour productivity could be said to have risen to 0.6 cars per hour.

Labour productivity $= \dfrac{500 \text{ cars per hour}}{1,000 \text{ employees}} = 0.5$ cars per hour

There are a number of ways of increasing productivity. These include:

- organising work more efficiently (e.g. the layout of machines in a factory might be improved to reduce wasted time)
- using more productive resources (e.g. by using more modern machinery and equipment or training employees to work more efficiently)
- automation and computerisation: many factories today employ robots and automatic machinery (e.g. electronic eyes that check on the quantity of fluid in containers and stop the filling process when the containers are full)
- using approaches that motivate staff to work harder (e.g. offering bonuses, job rotation and job enrichment).

In some areas of work, particularly service jobs, it is not easy to increase productivity in a measurable way. Services often involve care and attention to customers. Examples are the work of dentists, doctors, teachers and accountants. In these cases, productivity should be measured not just by the quantity of work done, but also by its quality.

ACTIVITY

Identify four operations involved in each of the following.

1 Running a cinema.

2 Making a loaf of bread in a bakery.

3 Serving a customer with petrol at a filling station.

DID YOU KNOW?

Many service jobs are involved with leisure industries. The development of tourism in countries across the world has opened up opportunities for service jobs such as hotel receptionists, cleaners, restaurant workers, tour guides and sports instructors.

KEY POINTS

1 Businesses convert inputs into outputs through transforming resources.

2 Operations management is the process of managing resources in an efficient way.

3 Productivity is a measure of the quantity of output produced in relation to the input of resources.

4 Labour productivity measures output in relation to the number of employees (or labour hours) input in a particular period of time.

5 Productivity can be increased by improving the quality and the organisation of resources.

SUMMARY QUESTIONS

1 Explain how the production process involves converting inputs into finished outputs. Illustrate your answer with an example from a particular business. Show the various inputs and outputs, as well as the operations that take place in the business.

2 The following table shows the number of loaves baked per day in a bakery. The table shows that the number of loaves baked per day is increasing. What is happening to productivity?

Year	Number of loaves (per week)	Number of workers	Labour productivity (output per employee)
2010	10,000	20	
2011	12,000	25	
2012	21,000	30	

3 Using the examples of farming, construction and nursing, explain the difference between productivity and production. In which of these occupations would it be most difficult to measure productivity? Why?

An example of job production. The fan of cables design on Angchuanzhou Bridge in Hong Kong was specified to help resist typhoon winds. At 1,596m it is also the longest bridge in the world

Different methods of production

Some products are produced one at a time, with great attention to detail. Others are **mass-produced**, when hundreds of thousands of identical items flow off a production line. There are three main types of production methods, outlined below.

Job production

Job-produced items are produced individually to meet the requirements of a specific customer. They are typically expensive because of the amount of work needed to go into them. They may need to be altered if they do not meet the customer's specification the first time. The Angchuanzhou bridge that spans the mouth of the container port in Hong Kong is an example of **job production**. Like every bridge, it had to be designed and manufactured individually to meet local conditions – in this case, the length required and an ability to withstand typhoons.

Other examples of job production are designer-made clothes, suits and wedding dresses. The tailor will produce garments that are individually measured and designed to fit a particular customer. Job-produced items are sometimes produced on the premises of the producer: parts of a bridge may be constructed before being transported to the construction site. Shop and café signs are also job-produced, as are passenger ships and wedding cakes.

Batch production

In **batch production**, a number of identical, or similar, items are produced in a set or batch. The items need not be for any specific customer, but are made at regular intervals in specific quantities. Batch production involves work being passed from one stage to another. Each stage of production is highly planned.

We saw in Unit 8.1 how a sushi restaurant is an example of high productivity. The process also illustrates batch production. A chef in a sushi restaurant makes a number of different types of sushi. For example, he or she may make a batch of 20 nigirizushi (hand-formed rice parcels with a fish topping). These will then be placed on the moving belt in the restaurant. The chef will then make 20 makizushi (circular rolls of rice surrounded by seaweed). The chef may then make 20 sweet dishes. The chef may then go on to produce another batch of 20 nigirizushi, and so on. Each time he places the fresh food on the belt. By producing batches, the chef can concentrate on one type of item at a time, whilst still supplying a steady supply of fresh food.

A key feature of batch production is that every now and then you have to stop the production process and change over to a new type of production using similar equipment. Many manufacturing and service organisations operate in this way. For example, in an electronics factory, the production line may be set to produce one type of electronic circuit board for the first two hours of the day. Then the machine may be reprogrammed to produce another type of circuit board for the next two hours, and so on.

Flow production

Flow production involves products or services passing down a **line of production**. The production process is a repeating one, with identical products going through the same sequence of operations; car production, chocolate bar manufacture and bottled drink manufacture are examples. Lifebuoy soap and cans of Coca-Cola are also produced in this way. Continuous flow involves producing for 24 hours a day, using automatic equipment in a standardised way. An oil refinery, for example, works on a continuous flow basis, with petrol being refined around the clock. While this production method may be ideal for the examples given here, a disadvantage is that there are many products that consumers prefer to be customised rather than mass-produced.

Figure 8.2.1 Providing a steady supply of sushi to the belt

Figure 8.2.2 Types of production

SUMMARY QUESTIONS

1 Think of three items that you or members of your family have purchased lately. Which are likely to have been produced by:
   • job production?
   • batch production?
   • flow production?

   Why do you think they were produced in the way you identified?

2 What would be the advantages and disadvantages of producing the following products by job production or flow production?
   • T-shirts
   • Suits
   • Running shoes

3 A confectionery company is producing a well-known chocolate bar for international markets. It needs to consider factors in different countries, such as languages, customer tastes, etc. How should it produce the bars? Explain your choice of method or methods.

ACTIVITY

The illustrations above show workers in several types of jobs. Identify an example of job production, flow production and batch production.

KEY POINTS

1 Different types of work have different methods of production.

2 Job production is suitable for products that need care and attention for each item.

3 Similar items produced in large quantities are more suited to batch production.

4 Identical products produced on a large scale benefit from line production.

5 New technology is changing these divisions.

Scale of production

Large greenhouses like these have been built in the Philippines for growing flowers. These are expensive to erect, but enable large-scale production at lower costs

From a small start...

Most of the giant businesses that we know today began on a small scale, as homemade efforts. Coca-Cola was originally brewed up on a kitchen stove, and many mechanical goods, like bicycles and tractors, were first hammered together in an inventor's backyard.

Many businesses prosper as they become larger. An advantage of growth is **economies of scale**. Economies of scale occur when large businesses produce larger outputs at lower unit costs.

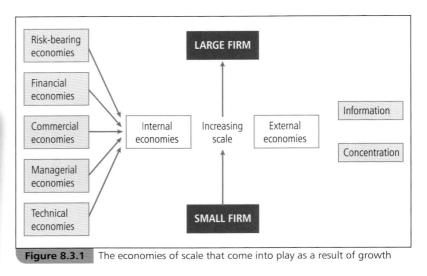

Figure 8.3.1 The economies of scale that come into play as a result of growth

It is helpful to distinguish between:

- internal economies of scale – that result from the growth of a business
- external economies of scale – that result from the growth of the industry of which the business is part.

Internal economies of scale

The most obvious benefit of growth is the ability to produce units of output more cheaply. In the Philippines, there has been an increase in fresh flower production using large-scale greenhouses. The greenhouses are expensive to set up: to benefit from large-scale economies, the structures need to be at least 1,000 square metres in size. Once they have been installed, however, they enable growers to produce large quantities of flowers with fewer chemicals, water and fertiliser. Other economies from large-scale production are outlined below.

Labour and management economies

Large organisations can employ specialist staff, such as accountants and researchers, who can relieve general managers of responsibility for these areas.

Buying and selling economies

As firms grow larger, they can buy their inputs, such as raw materials or finished goods, in bulk. When you buy in bulk, you can negotiate discounts. The cost of transport per unit will be much lower with larger loads. Larger firms are also better able to organise the selling of their products. For example, if a business can sell all its output to one or a few buyers, the cost of making each sale will be considerably lower than if it deals with thousands of separate customers.

Financial economies

Large firms can borrow more cheaply than smaller ones. This is because they are usually regarded as a safer investment.

Risk-bearing economies

Large firms can spread risks over a number of products or markets. This is diversification. For example, Cadbury, the British chocolate manufacturer, produces a range of chocolate products that appeal to different people, including Dairy Milk and Creme Eggs. The company spreads its risk by operating in many countries across the globe.

Diseconomies of scale

There are some disadvantages to being large. These are **diseconomies of scale**. One of the most important disadvantages is managing an organisation that gets too big. An organisation that takes on too many activities may not have the resources to carry out all of them efficiently. It may be less able to react to market needs as quickly as a small organisation. Communications within a large organisation may also deteriorate because of the numbers of people involved.

External economies of scale

External economies of scale are those shared by a number of firms in the same industry in a particular area. Examples are explored below.

Economies of concentration

As firms within an industry grow larger, more numerous, special services (e.g. a skilled workforce) may develop. Businesses in that area may gain an improved reputation. Suppliers of parts and services may move to the same area. For example, there are many hairdressers in large cities. This may lead to the setting up of local businesses supplying hairdressing supplies, such as hair products, scissors, mirrors or basins.

Economies of information

Larger industries can set up special information services to benefit all companies. These might be a specialist research organisation jointly owned by a number of firms, or specialist magazines and publications about a particular industry.

Of course, external diseconomies of scale may also arise. These might include pollution and congestion in a particular area where too many similar businesses have set up, and too much competition, which drives down prices.

ACTIVITY

Working with a partner, decide whether the following are internal or external economies of scale. In each case, explain how the economies would drive down costs for a firm or firms in the industry.

- A fish-canning factory makes use of a new automated production line.
- A food-processing firm in Accra, Ghana, is able to sell all of its supplies to one supermarket chain.
- A firm develops new carbon-capture technology that will enable other companies to reduce their greenhouse gas emissions from production.

SUMMARY QUESTIONS

1 Define economies of scale. List and explain five major types of economy of scale that a large hotel might benefit from.

2 Huge sporting stadiums are required for major sporting events, such as the 2008 Olympic Games in Beijing, the 2012 Games in London and the 2010 Commonwealth Games in Delhi. What diseconomies of scale might result from running such huge stadiums?

3 What are external economies of scale?

KEY POINTS

1 Economies of scale enable firms to produce more at lower cost per unit.

2 Economies of scale can be internal or external.

3 Firms can grow too large and become difficult to organise, so that unit costs go up; the result is diseconomies of scale.

Lean production

Lean production means doing more with less. It is based on the idea that any use of resources that does not create value for the consumer is 'waste'. A lean company will make best use of resources by cutting out waste.

CASE STUDY | The Toyota production system

A Toyota continuous-flow production line is designed to eliminate waste. Note the robots carrying out the production processes

The Toyota production system was designed by the Toyota car company to cut waste and focus activity on the elements that add value for the customer. Through lean production, Toyota has cut the following seven wastes almost to zero.

1 **Overproduction:** producing goods before customers demand them. This leads to high storage costs and possible damage to items waiting to be sold.

2 **Waiting:** whenever goods are not moving or being processed, the waste of waiting occurs.

3 **Transporting:** transporting goods is a waste that adds no value to a product. Too much handling can also cause damage.

4 **Unnecessary inventory:** having too much stock uses up space and gets in the way of productive activity.

5 **Motion:** employees involved in unnecessary bending, stretching and other body movements wastes time. It is also a health and safety risk.

6 **Over-processing:** using complex equipment to carry out simple tasks can be wasteful.

7 **Defects:** products that are poorly made have to be rejected, and time is wasted on inspecting for faults.

Questions

1 Identify an activity that you are involved in (e.g. queuing in a shop or a fast-food outlet, cooking food, making something). Identify examples of the 'seven wastes' that are associated with carrying out this activity. How could these wastes be eliminated?

2 Give examples of the ways in which Toyota is able to produce more with less.

Acting lean

Japanese companies have been particularly associated with lean production. However, most other major companies are now using these techniques. The important thing is to identify those activities that add value for customers, and then try to cut out non-value-adding activities. There are some simple practical steps that can be taken to achieve this.

1 **Keeping work areas tidy and organised.** Time is not wasted on finding things or moving them around.

2 Just in time (JIT). JIT is another key element in the success of Japanese companies. Costs are cut simply by reducing the amount of goods and materials a firm holds in stock. Goods must be produced and delivered **just in time** to be sold, partly finished goods must be assembled just in time into finished goods, components to go into partly finished goods are prepared just in time, and materials are made into parts just in time. At the centre of a JIT system is the heartbeat of a factory: this is the speed at which the production line runs. A JIT system is sometimes termed an advanced manufacturing system. Figure 8.4.1 illustrates the process.

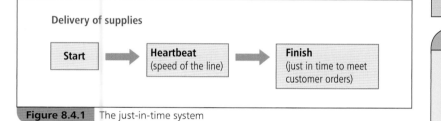

Delivery of supplies

Start → **Heartbeat** (speed of the line) → **Finish** (just in time to meet customer orders)

Figure 8.4.1   The just-in-time system

3 Kaizen. Another important part of the process is **kaizen**, or continuous improvement. Everybody in a company is given responsibility for identifying and suggesting ways of improving production. It does not matter how small the change is, provided that it cuts out waste. In this way, a better product or service is provided for the end-customer.

SUMMARY QUESTIONS

1 Copy and complete the paragraph below using the following words.

   Lean / value-adding activities / just in time / waste / overproduction

   Customer satisfaction can be increased by cutting out and eliminating _____. For example, this could involve eliminating _____ that occurs when products are made before customers have demanded them. The important thing is to concentrate on _____. The concept of _____ production was first developed in Japan by employees of the Toyota company. Another important idea stemming from Japan is that of _____ where products and parts are made to be delivered at the time they are required, but not before.

2 What are the benefits of creating a lean product (or service):
   • for the product/service provider?
   • for the customer/clients of the provider?

3 How do the processes of kaizen and just in time contribute to lean production?

Quality

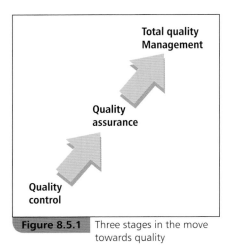

Figure 8.5.1 Three stages in the move towards quality

Quality

Today, we use the term **quality** to mean 'producing a good or service to customer requirements'. There are three main steps that international companies have taken in moving towards quality: quality control, **quality assurance** and, more recently, **total quality management (TQM)**.

Quality control

Quality control has long been part of business practice. It involves inspectors checking finished goods, and detecting and cutting out components or final products that do not meet the required standard. It can involve considerable waste, as substandard products have to be scrapped.

Quality assurance

This is less wasteful than quality control. Quality assurance occurs both during and after production, and seeks to stop faults happening in the first place. Quality assurance aims to make sure that products are produced to the required standard. It is the responsibility of the workforce working in teams, rather than of inspectors.

Total quality management (TQM)

This is the most complete form of operations management. Everyone in the workplace is encouraged to think about quality in everything they do. Every employee places customers at the heart of the production process. Quality management is the process of managing quality at every stage within an organisation and in every aspect of operations within a company. It will be set out in clear documents, and employees in the company will be trained to operate using the highest quality standards.

Total quality management involves creating small groups of employees called **quality circles**. These employees meet regularly to discuss ways they can improve the quality of their work. They are encouraged to suggest new ideas to cut out waste. The result of fewer defects and getting it right first time may actually be a decrease in costs.

International quality standards

It is important for consumers that all products and services meet certain standards. A standard is a published document that sets out precise criteria, or rules, designed to be used consistently when producing a good or managing a process.

Various bodies have been set up by governments working with industries to set these standards. The world's first standards body was the British Standards Institution (BSI). The standards it set out are based on best practice and cover processes applicable to, for example, manufacturing footballs, handling waste or meeting safety standards. BSI provides certificates to show that the standards have been met. BSI inspectors monitor companies to check that they are applying the standards.

Businesses worldwide seek to meet BSI standards. An engineering company in Kenya or Indonesia will seek BSI certification for its components and finished items, to show that their products meet a highly regarded international standard. This would then raise their company's reputation.

Modern quality standards are set at a number of levels. They relate to thousands of products, services and processes:

- internationally (e.g. ISO indicating standards agreed by bodies worldwide)
- in a particular part of the world (e.g. EN indicating standards agreed in Europe)
- national standards (e.g. BS indicating British standards).

Products like this plug which are stamped with the BSI mark give consumers a reassurance of quality

DID YOU KNOW?

The international governing body for football competitions, FIFA, licenses manufacturers to produce footballs. The balls must pass six tests – for weight, circumference, shape, loss of air pressure, water absorption and rebound. Manufacturers whose balls meet the standards can have the official marking stamped on their balls – 'FIFA APPROVED' or 'FIFA INSPECTED'.

ACTIVITY

Use the web page www.fifa.com and carry out a search for Football Test Criteria to find out more about the test criteria applied by FIFA.

SUMMARY QUESTIONS

1 Match the following terms with the definitions below.

Quality product / quality control / total quality management / standards / international standards

- Detecting and cutting out faults after they have happened.
- Creating a system that cuts out waste in every element of production.
- Published documents setting out criteria on which rules can be based about how to produce goods.
- A good that meets customer requirements.
- Agreed criteria for producing goods and services that are agreed across the world.

2 The British Standards Institute (BSI) works with industry specialists to identify best practice. BSI has over 30,000 standards. What would be the advantage to manufacturers in a small country seeking to export goods, of applying BSI standards to production processes in their company?

3 A company currently has a system of quality control. It uses careful inspection at the end of its production line for motorcycle helmets to check for faults. Any rejects are discarded. Explain why this company might be better moving on to developing quality assurance or total quality management.

KEY POINTS

1 Customers expect to be provided with products and services that meet the required standards.

2 Quality control involves checking for quality at the end of the production line.

3 Quality assurance occurs both during and after production to check for faults.

4 Total quality management takes place at every stage of production. Quality circles suggest ways of cutting out waste.

Costs and classifications of costs

The importance of costs

All business production involves **cost**. For example, in book production, costs include the fee paid to the author, editor and designer, and, later in the process, the paper used for printing and the energy to drive the printing presses. In business, it is essential to keep costs of production as low as possible. Businesses with lower costs have an advantage over rivals.

Fixed and variable costs

To help managers decide how to produce and how much to produce, costs may be split into two types: fixed costs and variable costs.

Fixed costs do not increase as output increases – for example, rent, heating bills, mortgage repayments, rates and salaries. These costs remain the same whether the firm produces 0 units of output, 100 units of output or 10,000 units of output. They remain fixed because the business is obliged to pay them, regardless of how much it produces.

Fixed costs can be drawn as a straight line. For example, if a book publisher has three types of fixed costs – rent $500 per week, salaries $2,000 per week and heating/air-conditioning bills $100 per week – then the fixed costs will be $2,600 per week (Figure 8.6.1).

Variable costs increase as output increases. As output increases, more of these costs are incurred. For example, if you produce more books, you need more paper and more energy to run the machines for longer.

Variable cost starts at 0. It then rises, depending on the variable cost for producing each unit of production. For example, if the variable cost of producing 1 book is $1, then the variable cost of producing 2 books will be $2, 10 books = $10, 100 books = $100, 1,000 books = $1,000 and so on (Figure 8.6.2).

Total cost

The total cost of producing different levels of output is found by adding the fixed and variable costs. It simply involves combining the fixed and the variable cost curves at different levels of output. The total cost curve should therefore start at zero level of output. At this point, total cost is simply made up of fixed cost. Then the variable cost is added to the fixed cost for each level of output (Figure 8.6.3).

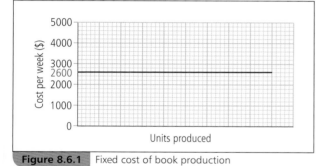

Figure 8.6.1 Fixed cost of book production

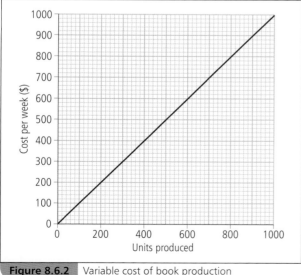

Figure 8.6.2 Variable cost of book production

Direct and indirect costs

It is very important to know how much it costs to produce each unit of production. This information helps managers to decide on how to price each unit.

The cost of an individual product consists of two elements: direct and indirect costs.

Direct costs are costs that can easily be identified and related to the production of a product or service. For example, it is easy to calculate how much cotton goes into producing a T-shirt and what the cost is. It is also possible to work out much labour it takes to produce the T-shirt and what the labour cost is.

Indirect costs are less easy to relate to the production of a particular unit of production, hence the label 'indirect'. For example, a factory may produce goods made of different types of textiles, such as wool and cotton. The cost of a worker handling cotton goods could be related to the costs of cotton production, but the factory also has costs such as lighting and rent, necessary whatever is being produced. These indirect costs are sometimes called **overheads**. Managers have the task of deciding how these indirect costs should be shared out, or allocated, between the various items that the factory produces.

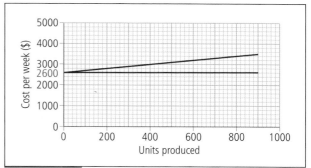

Figure 8.6.3 Total cost (the fixed costs and the variable costs added together for each unit of output)

Cost of producing = Direct cost of producing + Indirect costs
an item   that item   allocated to
                                    that item

SUMMARY QUESTIONS

1 Which of the following describes variable costs, fixed costs and total costs?
   • Costs that do not change with the level of output that is produced.
   • All the costs of production.
   • Costs linked to the quantity produced.

2 A small taxi business has 10 taxis and employs taxi drivers to work for the firm. Explain which of the following would be included as fixed costs of running the taxi service and which would be the variable costs. Explain your answers.
   • The cost of renting the premises from which the business runs.
   • The petrol cost of each taxi journey. (calculated per kilometre or mile).
   • The cost of maintaining a radio-controlled booking service in the office of the taxi business.

3 A business selling flowers has the following cost structure:
   • Rent per month: $300
   • Salaries per month: $1,000
   • Cost per bunch of flowers prepared for sale: $1
   • Telephone (line rental, calls) per month: $100

   Illustrate this information in the form of a diagram showing the fixed costs per month. Draw another diagram to illustrate the variable costs per month.

ACTIVITY

Using the example of a local farm or small manufacturing business in your area, identify what items are likely to be the fixed costs of the business and what the variable costs will be.

KEY POINTS

1 Calculating costs is an important part of managing production.

2 Fixed costs do not alter with the number of units produced or sold.

3 Variable costs increase as production levels increase.

4 Total cost is the combination of fixed and variable cost at each level of output.

Break-even analysis and cost-based decision making

Explain, interpret and use a simple break-even chart.

• Construct a simple break-even chart.

• Interpret a given chart and use it to analyse a situation.

• Show understanding of the limitations of break-even chart.

EXAM TIP

Remember that the sales revenue line always starts at the origin; the total cost line starts from the point where the fixed costs intersect with the y axis.

DID YOU KNOW?

Break-even for a period of time (e.g. a month) can be calculated by a simple formula:

$$\frac{\text{Average month's fixed costs}}{\text{Unit selling price} - \text{variable cost per unit}}$$

$$=$$

Number of units needing to be sold to break even

Break-even

Break-even is the point at which an organisation covers its costs with the money it makes through sales. If sales go beyond the break-even point, profits are made. If sales do not reach the break-even point, losses are made.

A **break-even chart** is prepared in advance to see how much the business needs to sell at a particular price.

Producing a break-even chart

A break-even chart shows the point at which a business breaks even, and the profits and losses it will make at various levels of activity. It is constructed by:

1 labelling the horizontal axis to show different levels of production (or sales)

2 labelling the vertical axis to represent the value of costs and the value of sales

3 plotting fixed cost – this will be a straight horizontal line which starts at the value of all the fixed costs

4 plotting total costs – the total cost line is found by adding the fixed cost and the variable cost for each level of output

5 sales are plotted by showing the total value of money received from selling the product – this is calculated by: Number of items sold x Price per unit.

ACTIVITY

Draw the break-even chart for each of the following businesses and calculate the break-even number of sales needed.

• A taxi driver who charges an average price of $10 per customer for a cost per trip of $5; the driver has fixed costs of $25,000 per year.

• A hairdresser who charges an average of $12.50 per customer for a cost per visit of $5; the hairdresser has fixed costs of $100,000 per year.

Limitations of the break-even chart

A break-even chart is only a rough guide. One of the problems is that it is not easy to estimate costs. Variable costs can change quickly – for example, if the price of labour or raw materials increases. The variable cost may also alter with the scale of production – the more that is produced, the lower the unit cost will be. However, break-even charts are helpful in indicating to business owners roughly how much they need to make or sell in order to break into profit.

A business produces business studies textbooks which it sells directly to schools. The business has fixed costs of $80,000, made up of rent on its premises, salaries for staff and some other overhead costs. However many books it produces, it will therefore have this fixed cost to pay.

In book production, variable costs include the paper and card that go into the book; fixed costs might include the rental of the factory space

It has been calculated that the variable cost of producing books is $8 per book. This $8 includes the cost of paper, ink and of running the printing presses. The business will sell the books for $12 each.

The managers have set out the information above in the form of a table, showing costs and revenues at three different levels of output.

	10,000 units ($)	20,000 units ($)	30,000 units ($)
Fixed costs	80,000	80,000	80,000
Variable cost = $8 per unit	80,000	160,000	240,000
Total costs	160,000	240,000	320,000
Sales $12 per unit	120,000	240,000	360,000

When this information is shown in a chart form, it immediately becomes clear where the break-even point is.

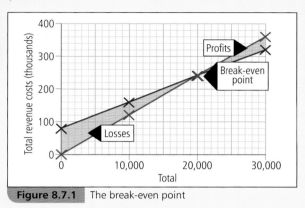

Figure 8.7.1 The break-even point

When 20,000 books are sold at $12 each, total sales revenues are $240,000. The total cost of producing these books is $240,000 ($80,000 of fixed costs and $160,000 of variable costs). If the firm is able to produce and sell higher levels, then its profits will increase. For example, if it can sell 30,000 units, its profit will be $40,000 (total cost $360,000 and total revenue £320,000).

Questions

1 How much profit, or loss, will the business make if it sells 10,000 books?

2 How much profit, or loss, will the business make if it sells 25,000 books?

SUMMARY QUESTIONS

1 What two figures are equal at the break-even point? Explain the meaning of fixed and variable costs? Which of these types of costs does a business need to cover to break even?

2 An ice-cream shop sells luxury ice creams at $5 each. Variable costs per ice cream are $3. The owners of the ice-cream shop have fixed costs of $5,000 per month, including the lease. How many ice creams need to be sold to break even?

3 Seema Patel plans to set up a busy restaurant in a smart business location. This will immediately incur a fixed cost of $100,000 for the first year of trading. Market research indicates that a typical customer will pay $8 for a meal, and variable costs (such as cooking ingredients and the costs of serving customers) will amount to $3. How many customers will need to be served in the first year for Seema to break even? Show how you calculated this.

KEY POINTS

1 The break-even point is the point at which a business just covers its total costs with sales revenues.

2 The break-even point is expressed in terms of the quantity of items made or sold.

3 An alternative method for calculating break-even is to divide the total fixed cost by the contribution from selling each unit.

In recent years, many North American and European companies have set up operations in India and China, where a highly skilled labour force is available at a lower wage cost

ACTIVITY

These are some of the factors that influence the location of a large supermarket:

- plenty of land available, including car parking
- ease of access to labour
- close to transport links for supplies
- near to customers.

Produce a list showing the factors that might influence the location of:

- a service business
- a manufacturing business.

Location and relocation

An important consideration for a new business is **location** – that is, where to site it. Considerations involve being close to the market, or on sites where costs are low, perhaps because labour is plentiful and wages are cheap. Later on, a firm may choose to relocate, often because costs have become too high at the original location. In the first decade of the 21st century, many Western companies relocated manufacturing and other functions to India and South East Asia, where production costs were lower.

Distance to markets

Many businesses need to be located close to their market (i.e. their customers). Many manufacturing industries locate close to markets, particularly if they produce bulky or fragile items that are expensive to transport. Service industries, such as hairdressing, restaurants and entertainment, need to be near to customers. Other services, such as banking and insurance, sometimes need to be near to customers (although many transactions are now carried out online).

Availability of raw materials

Some manufacturing businesses use a lot of heavy, bulky raw materials to make their products, even though the end-product is smaller and lighter. For example, finished steel is a lot lighter than the ore, limestone and other materials of which it consists. If the raw materials are bulky and expensive to transport, it makes sense to locate near their source.

Transport costs

Two major influences on transport costs are the raw materials and how near the market is. These depend on whether the industry is 'bulk increasing' or 'bulk decreasing' (i.e. whether the goods become larger and heavier or smaller and lighter as they are assembled). Many businesses (e.g. hotels, factories) set up close to good transport links – for example, near a major road junction, rail station or airport.

Availability of land

Land costs vary considerably. Firms such as large automobile production plants that need a wide area to make their goods, or giant supermarkets that need a large selling area, will choose sites that are out of town where costs are lower.

Availability of labour

The right sorts of labour and skills are easier to find in some areas than others. If businesses want a large pool of cheap labour, they might set up in centres of population where there are not many employers. If they want skilled labour they will set up where they are most likely to find those skills. In recent years, many Western companies have set up call centres in India, where there are large numbers of highly educated people with information technology skills and where wage costs are relatively low.

Safety

Some industries (e.g. nuclear power stations, munitions factories and some chemical companies) will be wise to locate their premises well away from heavily populated areas, to avoid danger to the public.

Utilities

A business must consider five standard utilities: gas, electricity, water, disposal of waste and drainage. Industries such as food preparation and paper production use large quantities of water. Food processing creates waste and the cost of waste disposal will affect location.

Communications

Many businesses need a strong core of IT communications systems. It is therefore important to set up in areas where communications are clear and reliable. This might exclude some mountainous or highland areas, or countries where the links do not exist. Cities with excellent wireless and broadband facilities are a strong attraction for new businesses.

Regional factors

Locating in the same area as similar business, suppliers and markets may be considered an advantage. The quality of local schools, housing and leisure facilities can also help to encourage high-quality staff to join and stay with the business.

Government incentives

The government provides financial support to businesses to set up in some regions. These will usually be areas of higher unemployment.

Deciding in which country to locate

In the modern global economy, companies will consider a range of countries to locate in or to relocate to. Key considerations will be having access to larger markets, and the possibility of reducing costs in new locations. For example, many American IT-based companies have transferred jobs to India and China. American companies like Microsoft®, Accenture and IBM have set up offices employing thousands of people in large Indian cities, where there are a lot of highly skilled employees available at lower wages than in the United States. By setting up these new units, the US companies also benefit from having access to the new, huge, growing markets of India and China.

Another consideration that will be important for a business is the stability of the government and the exchange rate in the host country. If exchange rates fluctuate often, this causes difficulties in planning and predicting the value of sales and costs such as wages.

KEY POINTS

1 Important location considerations for manufacturing companies are access to raw materials, good transport links, access to a workforce and to the market. Low costs are important.

2 Important considerations for some service industries are to be close to the market and to recruit skilled employees.

3 Important location considerations when choosing a country are costs, the quality of labour and the stability of government and the exchange rate.

SUMMARY QUESTIONS

1 Which three factors do you think are most important in locating the following? In each case, justify your answer.
   • Gold mining
   • Nuclear power plant
   • International call centre

2 What factors do you think a supermarket business should first consider before deciding to branch out into a new country?

3 Explain why a Japanese motor manufacturer like Toyota might want to set up a car plant in Western Europe.

Improving efficiency

Understand the concept of productivity.

- The concept of turning resource inputs into an output.

Awareness of methods of improving efficiency, e.g. automation, new technology.

- Show awareness of the impact of the implication of change for production methods and labour skills.

EXAM TIP

Improvements in efficiency reduce unit costs because resources are used more effectively.

DID YOU KNOW?

New technologies can be rapidly transferred around the world: a new automated factory system, such as a bottling or canning factory, can be set up wherever there is available land and labour. This makes it possible for large international firms to set up in low-cost locations, where government taxes and labour costs are low.

Efficiency

Inputs are people, money, raw materials and assets such as factories or offices. *Outputs* are goods and services. Efficiency involves turning inputs into outputs for maximum impact on productivity.

An organisation, or a process that an organisation carries out, can be more efficient and productive if it produces:

- the same output with fewer inputs
- more or better outputs from the same inputs.

An efficient organisation can provide its customers with better value for money and build a reputation for quality, which then leads to customer loyalty. Adopting new production methods often involves a substantial investment in new equipment – for example, the purchase of a new automatic production line. Although investment is costly, it should lead to increased profits in the long term.

Some people see new technology as providing a threat to jobs. For example, in agriculture, many farm workers have been replaced by tractors, and harvesting and sowing machines. However, in other industries, new technology has created work, or at least kept people in work. In the oil industry, for example, advanced technology enables oil to be drilled at greater depths. Workers may need to be retrained to work with the new equipment, but often their wages increase as the business prospers.

Methods to increase efficiency

A technique is a way of making something, using available resources such as human labour or machines. Technological change occurs when new techniques of production are applied. Technology has been a major driving force in enabling efficiency in the modern world. This is particularly true with the development of the internet and the use of computers in production. These are some of the computer-based innovations now used in industry.

- **Computer-aided design (CAD)** is a system that works like an electronic drawing board, allowing complex two- and three-dimensional shapes to be modelled quickly and accurately on screen, stored conveniently and copied when needed. Engineers in Nigeria design oil platforms using computers networked with qualified draughtsmen and draughtswomen in India. CAD has improved the reliability and speed with which complex structures such as aeroplanes, cars and bridges can be designed.

- **CADCAM (computer-aided design/computer-aided manufacturing)** refers to the use of data from a CAD system to drive machines as part of the manufacturing process. A bridge designer can design part of the structure on a computer and the design can be sent instantly to the factory computer, so that the parts can be cut to size.

- **CIM (computer-integrated manufacturing)** involves the computer-controlled manufacturing system driving machine tools. These tools, or robots, are multipurpose machines that can be programmed and reprogrammed to perform physical tasks. An industrial robot in a car factory may be programmed to paint and then reprogrammed to weld pieces together or to assemble parts.

- **Computer-based stock control.** Stock-control systems are used in manufacturing and retailing to ensure the arrival of stocks just in time for purchase by the end-customer. For example, it is essential that retailers of fresh fish, vegetables or fruit, provide customers with the latest stock. By ordering just the right levels needed, waste is minimised. For tinned and packaged goods, electronic barcodes make it possible to manage a computer-based stock-control system.

- An **EPOS (electronic point-of-sale system)** works in the following way: items for sale carry barcodes. When new stock arrives, the numbers are registered in the stock system. At the checkout, the barcodes of sold items are scanned in. The cash till adds up and records the sales. The cash till automatically creates the bill, which is a record of transactions with an individual customer. The customer then pays and receives a record of their payment. At the same time, a record is made on the back-office system showing items sold. The back-office computer will then automatically reorder new stock to replace the products that have been sold.

Other ways of improving efficiency include:

- changes in working methods (e.g. cutting out wasteful activities that take up time)

- total quality management – ensuring quality is focused on at every stage of production

- people simply working harder – perhaps because there is some form of bonus or other motivating factor.

An EPOS system increases efficiency in a hotel, restaurant or supermarket by speeding up operations

Automation

Automation is the use of machines in a series of tasks. Each machine is linked to another, without human intervention. Computers can be programmed to start, finish, shut down and speed up operations, as well as detect flaws in a system, without human intervention. Investing in automation is costly, but will lead to high levels of accuracy at very low cost.

KEY POINTS

1 In the modern world, new technology enables business to become more productive.

2 Computer-driven technologies have played a major part in increasing productivity across the globe.

3 New technologies can replace as well as create jobs.

SUMMARY QUESTIONS

1 What is automation? Give an example of how automation has been used to improve manufacturing.

2 Give two examples of how efficiency can be increased in manufacturing.

3 How do computers improve efficiency in production?

Practice exam questions

SECTION 1: Short-answer questions

1 Identify and explain TWO objectives of the production department. [4]

2 Using the example of a McDonald's burger, identify the inputs, production process and output. [3]

3 Identify and explain TWO ways in which productivity may be increased in a clothing factory. [4]

4 Calculate labour productivity in a factory that employs 200 workers and produces 500 shirts every hour. [3]

5 Identify and explain TWO differences between batch and flow production. [4]

6 Analyse TWO reasons why a car production line that produces the same model, but with each car altered according to customer orders, may be categorised as both flow and job production. [6]

7 Explain, with examples, economies of scale that may be enjoyed by a very large clothing company, such as Levi Strauss & Co. Jeans. [4]

8 Identify and explain TWO reasons why communication difficulties in a large organisation may lead to diseconomies of scale. [4]

9 Explain, using examples from a bread production factory, the following examples of waste in the context of lean production:
   • defects
   • overproduction
   • waiting. [6]

10 Explain how just-in-time production methods could cut down the areas of waste you have identified in Question 9. [6]

11 Explain why it may be said that under kaizen 'everyone in the organisation has two jobs'. [4]

12 Identify and explain TWO differences between quality control and quality assurance. [4]

13 Analyse why quality assurance does not simply mean producing the best quality. [4]

14 Analyse why a total quality management approach may lead to lower costs as well as better quality. [4]

15 Analyse why labour costs may be fixed or variable in a production business. [4]

16 Identify and explain THREE factors that will be important when deciding the location of:
   • a vegetable canning factory
   • a firm of solicitors. [6]

SECTION 2: Longer-answer questions

Daisy Fresh Cleaning

Flora runs a successful business from her home in Islamabad, laundering and dry cleaning clothes for local customers and business people who stay in nearby international hotels. She has built up an excellent reputation due to the speed and quality of her service. Flora collects the clothes twice a day from the hotels and returns them within 12 hours, fully washed, or dry-cleaned, and ironed. She uses large industrial machines and makes sure that similar colours are washed together. All items are pressed individually. Delicate items, such as silk dresses and suits, are kept separate and treated with extra care. Flora is so busy that she is looking for new premises for her business.

1 Identify and explain TWO methods of production used by Flora. [4]

2 Identify and explain TWO ways in which the quality of Flora's service may be measured. [4]

3 State TWO examples of fixed costs and TWO examples of variable costs for Flora's business. [6]

4 Identify and explain THREE factors that Flora will need to take into account when looking for new premises. *[6]*

5 To what extent may a break-even chart help Flora decide on a suitable location? Explain your answer. *[6]*

Amrita's fair trade spices

Amrita runs a production company, based on the outskirts of Delhi, India. The company produces large packs of Indian spice mixes, in a range of flavours, mainly for the export market. The packs are bought in bulk by overseas companies who use them to give authentic flavour to Indian ready meals for the Western market. The spices come into the factory directly from the growers in their dried form, and are ground up together, depending on the mix required, then packaged and labelled. Amrita's monthly costs are as follows:

- Factory rent: $1,000
- Business rates: $200
- Power: $300
- Amrita's wage: $200
- Production workers' wages: $0.50 per pack
- Raw materials (herbs per pack): $3 (growers are paid a fair-trade price, which is 50 per cent higher than the usual market price)

- Packaging and labelling per pack: $1

The packs sell for an average price of $10, on the wholesale market.

1 Explain the term 'fixed costs' and calculate Amrita's total fixed costs. *[3]*

2 Explain the term 'variable costs' and calculate the variable cost per pack of herbs. *[3]*

3 Analyse ONE advantage and ONE disadvantage to Amrita's company of the fair-trade price paid to herb growers. *[6]*

4 Using graph paper, draw a break-even chart and work out the break-even monthly sales for Amrita's business. *[6]*

5 Evaluate the advantages and limitations of the use of break-even analysis to plan in a business like Amrita's. *[6]*

The market research call centre

Jim runs a telephone market research company based in the UK, on the outskirts of Manchester. He employs 100 staff at the call centre; their job is to contact consumers by telephone and ask their opinions on everything from views on new products to which party they will vote for in the parliamentary elections. He is paid by the companies who employ him to carry out this research and produce reports. Jim would like to expand the call centre, but land is expensive and staff wages are rising by the day. He also finds that his staff productivity rate is very variable, as staff change jobs and leave the company frequently, and some workers are often late or unwell. Jim is investigating the possibility of

moving the call-centre part of his business to India.

1 Identify and explain TWO possible ways that Jim may measure his staff productivity. *[4]*

2 Identify and explain TWO reasons why staff absence and frequent replacement may lead to low productivity. *[4]*

3 Identify and explain THREE factors that Jim will need to take into account if he is relocating his call centre to India. *[4]*

4 Evaluate the view that 'relocating to India will save money on land and labour costs'. *[6]*

5 Evaluate whether the call-centre move to India will benefit Jim's business customers. *[6]*

Any type of business needs cash to keep running. For example, a street vendor needs cash to purchase new stocks of fruit to sell and to service their vending cart. Without this cash, their business would close

EXAM TIP

It is a common mistake to assume that sales and cash are the same. If a business sells on credit, it has to wait for the debtors to pay cash. This then affects the cash flow of the business.

The importance of cash

Businesses need to have a steady flow of **cash** to survive. Without cash, a business cannot make payments and would soon have to close.

Businesses use a **cash-flow forecast** chart to keep a record of the movement of cash they expect to have coming in and going out. Receipts represent cash flowing into the business; payments represent cash flowing out of the business. The balance is the amount of cash that the business will have at a particular moment in time (see case study, *Pritesh*, opposite).

CASE STUDY	Calculating cash flow for Tarun

Tarun owns a small sole-trader business as a street vendor of fresh fruit. At the end of December, he has a cash balance of 1,000 rupees. His only outgoing is the purchase of fresh fruit from gardens at the edge of the city. He makes purchases of fresh fruit costing 5,000 rupees a month. He then transports the fruit to his vending stall in the city centre. This costs him a further 1,000 rupees a month. He has forecast that the value of his sales receipts will be as follows: January 8,000 rupees, February 7,000 rupees, March 6,000 rupees, April 7,000 rupees, May 10,000 rupees, June 11,000 rupees.

Questions

1 Set out a cash-flow statement for Tarun's business.

2 In which month will his cash balance be lowest?

DID YOU KNOW?

A new business's sales estimates for the first few months of trading are often too high. Cost forecasts are often too low. This means that after a few months of trading, when bank loans have been used up, the new business faces cash-flow difficulties. Cash-flow management is one of the main problems facing start-up businesses.

Many small businesses use a credit card to help them survive cash-flow difficulties. The business purchases goods on credit and makes the payment after receiving the credit card statement.

Pritesh is the owner of a small clothes shop selling T-shirts and jeans. His business has been in existence for 3 years, and he finds it quite easy to predict the income (receipts) coming into the business and the expenses (payments). He has set out a chart to illustrate payment and receipts for the first 6 months of the year.

All figures in dollars	Jan	Feb	Mar	Apr	May	Jun
Balance B/F	1,000	2,000	1,750	1,750	1,250	750

Income

Sales	3,000	2,250	2,500	2,500	2,000	2,000
Total receipts	3,000	2,250	2,500	2,500	2,000	2,000
Total cash available	4,000	4,250	4,250	4,250	3,250	2,750

Expenses

Purchases	1,000	1,250	1,250	1,500	1,250	1,250
Wages	1,000	1,250	1,250	1,500	1,250	1,250
Total payments	2,000	2,500	2,500	3,000	2,500	2,500
Balance C/F	2,000	1,750	1,750	1,250	750	250

To understand how the chart is set out, look at the column for January. The first item that appears is Balance B/F. B/F stands for brought forward. So $1,000 is the sum of cash that the business had at the end of December in the previous year.

The next heading is **Income**. Pritesh has only one type of income: sales of clothes. In January he sold $3,000 of clothes for cash. Total receipts (income) for January are therefore $3,000. This should be added to the cash that was brought forward from December.

If we add $3,000 (cash receipts) to $1,000 (cash brought forward), we can see that the total cash available to the business in January is $4,000.

This cash can be used to make payments. Pritesh makes two types of payments:

• purchases of clothes that he buys to resell – he pays $1,000 for these

• wages – he has to pay out wages of $1,000.

So his total payments amount to $2,000 ($1,000 purchases + $1,000 wages).

Remember that in January Pritesh expects to have total cash available of $4,000. If he has to pay $2,000 out of this for expenses, his balance at the end of the month will be $2,000. This is shown in the bottom left-hand corner of the chart as $2,000 Balance C/F. C/F means that this sum will be carried forward into February.

The same process can be carried out for each month of the forecast.

The closing balance figure is very important. If it is negative (i.e. if the business has no cash of its own and has to borrow to finance the shortfall), the business cannot automatically meet its debts and could be in trouble.

Questions

1 Working with a partner, take it in turns to explain each of the columns to each other.

2 When does Pritesh have least cash available?

3 Why is timing important in working out cash flows to the business?

SUMMARY QUESTIONS

1 What is the purpose of the cash-flow statement?

2 Define the following terms.

Opening balance / closing balance / income / expenses / receipts / sales

3 Why is timing so important in managing cash flow in a business? What are the dangers of not having enough cash to meet outgoings?

KEY POINTS

1 Failure to manage cash flow is one of the main reasons why businesses fail.

2 Businesses need to check their cash flow on a regular basis.

3 A cash-flow forecast estimates the incoming and outgoing of cash to a business.

4 Income in the form of receipts needs to be greater than outgoings in the form of spending.

Profit

Explain the concept of profit.

- Show understanding of why profit matters to a private sector business.
- Show an awareness of the difference between retained and distributed profit.

Profit

A private sector business exists to make money for the owners. The money they are interested in is not the money that the company makes from sales, but the money that ends up in their pocket, purse or bank account – in other words, the **profit**. Profit is the final amount of money that a business makes, once all the costs have been subtracted from sales **revenue**.

The notes that follow explain how the end profit figure is reached.

Gross profit

The **gross profit** of a business is the profit less all the costs of the things that it had to do to earn that profit. For example, a firm selling computers might buy them for $400 and sell them for $600. It sells 10 computers per day. To work out the daily gross profit, we would need to do the following:

1 Work out sales revenue: 10 computers x $600 = $6,000

2 Subtract the costs: 10 computers x $400 = $4,000

Daily gross profit = Sales – Costs incurred in making those sales
$2,000 = $6,000 – $4,000

Calculating gross profit

Gross profit is a good indicator of the efficiency of the selling activities of a business. A trading business buys in goods which it then sells to the customer for a higher price. Cost of sales can be reduced by buying from a cheaper supplier or by arranging discounts for bulk buying. It is then important to price the items in such a way as to make a healthy gross profit from selling activities.

Gross profit = Sales revenue – Cost of sales

Net profit

If the business wants a clearer indication of how much profit it is making, it will calculate its **net profit**, by deducting the overhead costs from the gross profit. (You read about overheads in Unit 8.6.) These are indirect costs, such as the rent of the building, the salaries of the senior directors, interest payments on loans, and heating and lighting.

Net profit = Gross profit – All expenses associated with
the normal running
of a business

A business has calculated that its annual overhead costs amount to $100,000. The business consists of three separate teams. Their sales and cost figures are shown in the table below.

Team A	Team B	Team C
Sales revenue $50,000	Sales revenue $200,000	Sales revenue $150,000
Cost to make sales $10,000	Cost to make sales $100,000	Cost to make sales $100,000

1 Calculate the gross profit of each of the teams.

2 Calculate the net profit of the business as a whole.

Retained and distributed profit

A business has a choice about what to do with its profit. One alternative is to retain, or keep back, as much profit as possible in the business. This *retained profit* can be used to expand and improve the business. This will help the business to become more competitive, by giving customers better value for money.

The alternative is to distribute the profit to the owners. Owners will want to receive some of the profit in the form of a **dividend**. If they do not receive what they consider to be a good dividend, they might sell their shares.

Retained profit is therefore the profit left over after the shareholders have been paid their dividends.

1 Two students are having an argument about what they understand profit to be. Thaksin says that profit is the sum of money that a business makes when you add together all the sales it makes in a given period of time. Meena disagrees; she thinks that profit is the difference between sales revenues and all the costs that a business incurs in making those sales.

Which of these students do you agree with, and why?

2 What problems would arise from a business:
• retaining all its profit in a given year?
• distributing all its profits in a given year?

3 Which of the following would you expect to be higher in a profitable business? Explain why.
• Net profit or gross profit?
• Sales revenues or direct costs?

A business manufactures perfume which it sells at $10 per bottle. It sells 1,000 bottles in a month. Its manufacturing cost per bottle is $1. Calculate the gross profit of the business per month.

EXAM TIP

Remember that profit is not the same as cash. You need to be able to explain why this is the case.

1 Profit is the final amount remaining after all costs have been paid from revenue.

2 Revenue is the money charged to customers for buying goods and services.

3 Costs are the total money it takes to provide products or services.

4 Gross profit is the difference between revenue and the cost of making sales.

5 Net profit is the true profit when overheads are deducted from gross profit.

The profit and loss account

Profit and loss accounts

Business owners need to know what their costs are, and what money is coming in. The financial statement that helps them to do this is called a **profit and loss account (P&L)**. This account shows owners how well the business is being run. It is also helpful if the owner needs new funds, such as a bank loan, because it gives an idea of how big a risk a lender will be taking. *Actual P&L accounts* can be produced at the end of a trading period. This might be each year, or over a much shorter period, such as one month.

Businesses can also create *forecast P&L accounts* to show how much they expect to make in a future period.

An actual profit and loss account shows how much a firm has earned from selling its product or service, and how much it has paid out in costs. The difference between sales and costs is the profit earned.

A typical profit and loss account will look like the following.

	$ million
Sales revenue	1,000
less Cost of goods sold	(400)
Gross profit	600
less Overhead costs	(200)
Trading/operating profit	400
Profit for shareholders (dividends paid)	150
Retained profit	250

Reading the profit and loss account

In the account shown above, the firm has sold $1,000 million worth of goods. All the expenditures involved in making these sales accounted for $400 million.

So if a chain of bookshops had paid $400 million for all the books that it sold in a year, and sold these books for $1,000 million, this would give a gross profit of $600 million.

It is then necessary to take off the $200 million in overheads that it cost to run the bookshops during the year: rent, salaries, advertising, and so on. The bookshop thus makes a trading profit of $400 million.

It then needs to decide how to share this $400 million between the shareholders and retain profit to improve the business. In this case, the business distributed $150 million to shareholders and retained $250 million.

A profit and loss account gives an immediate indication of how well a business has done over a period of time. If an investor has put money into the business, they will want to see that sales more than cover costs. If the cost of making sales is almost as high as the sales revenue figure, the business will not have much scope for making a profit.

Cooking Pots is a public limited company that sells cooking containers to the catering industry. It has set out its profit and loss account for 2011.

Profit/loss account for Cooking Pots 2011

	$m
Sales	?
Cost of making sales	700
Gross profit	300
Overheads	?
Net profit	100

Questions

1 Why is it important for Cooking Pots to make a profit? Give two reasons.

2 Some of the figures are missing in the table. Calculate what they should be.

A small business has an annual sales revenue of $150,000. It has a number of overhead costs, including $3,000 for insurance, $80,000 for staff salaries, $2,000 interest on loans and energy bills of $5,000. During the year it has bought $50,000 worth of stock for resale.

Set out the profit and loss account for this business for the year's trading.

It is also important to look at the overheads in relation to sales. If overheads cut into profits, it might be sensible for the business to move to a cheaper location, or to look at other ways of reducing overheads (e.g. cutting energy bills or staff salaries).

SUMMARY QUESTIONS

1 Ping Yung has kept records of the sales and costs involved in running his bicycle shop.
   • Purchases of bicycles to resell: $80,000
   • Energy costs of running the business: $10,000
   • Advertising: $2,000
   • Wages: $10,000
   • Sales of bicycles: $150,000
   • Rent on premises: $10,000

   Can you organise these figures into a profit and loss account for him?

2 Explain the difference between the following terms.
   • Sales and cost of making sales
   • Gross profit and net profit

3 Seema Singh is puzzled by the way that entries are presented in her profit and loss account. Her accountant has set it out using the following figures.

	$
Sales	2,000
Cost of sales	(1,000)

   Explain why the accountant has put the cost of sales figure in brackets.

KEY POINTS

1 The P&L account shows how a business has generated a profit or loss in a particular period of trading.

2 The top part of the account shows the sales a business has made and the costs involved in making the sales. The difference is 'gross profit'.

3 The account then goes on to deduct the overhead costs of running the business to arrive at net profit.

4 Some of the net profit will be retained in the business. The remainder can be distributed to the owners of the business.

The function of profit

Explain the function of profit.

- Explain the importance of profit as a reward for enterprise and risk taking.

Distinguish between cash and profit.

- Show awareness of why cash and profit differ.

Hiroshi Yamauchi, who transformed Nintendo – in 2009 he was Japan's richest man

ACTIVITY

Study the headlines in the financial pages of a newspaper. Find out a headline related to a company making a profit. Does the paper suggest that the profit is large or small? How has the profit been made? Does it state how much of the profit will be distributed to shareholders?

DID YOU KNOW?

A business should hold enough cash to service its regular day-to-day needs and unforeseen cash requirements. Too much cash, however, is money that is not being used profitably. Cash that simply sits in the tills does not earn any interest.

The function of profit

Profit is a reward for owners of a business. It also provides an important source of investment funds. With profit, a business is able to buy more stock, buy machinery and buildings, train its staff to higher standards and engage in other improvement activities.

Profit is also important for the business owners. In setting up and running it, the owners are taking a risk with their money. They make nothing if the business does not generate a profit. There would be little point in starting a business if there were no opportunity to make a profit.

If a business fails to make a profit for a long period, it will probably have to close down. This could be disastrous for employees, suppliers and the local community.

CASE STUDY	Nintendo

Hiroshi Yamauchi transformed Nintendo from being a maker of card games into a multibillion dollar video-game giant. Even during the global economic recession in 2008/9, the company made record profits. For the financial year ending 21 March 2009, the company profit was 279.1bn yen (95 yen = US$1). The company was able to weather the economic crisis better than its rivals, mainly due to the success of its Wii console. This sold 10.17 million in 2008/9, and its portable DS device made over 9.95 million sales. Nintendo announced these profits at a time when its main rivals, Sony (maker of the PlayStation systems) and Microsoft (which produces the Xbox 360 console), were making job cuts.

Questions

1 Why do you think that Nintendo was able to make such large profits?

2 Hiroshi Yamauchi owns 10 per cent of the shares in Nintendo. He became Japan's richest man in 2008/9. How has he been able to benefit from being an entrepreneur? Do you think that entrepreneurs like Hiroshi Yamauchi deserve the rewards that they receive?

The difference between cash and profit

It is very important to understand the difference between cash and profit. A business needs both. Cash is the money that a business has in its tills and its bank accounts at a particular moment in time. Cash is required to pay bills. It is needed when creditors (people to whom the business owes money) demand payment. If creditors are not paid, they can take the business to court. The court can decide that a business should be closed down and its assets sold off to pay pressing debts. So it is essential to have cash.

However, cash is not profit. Cash is simply money that is available to the business. It might come from profit, but it could just as easily be borrowed from someone else.

Profit is earned from running a business well. A business earns a profit when the money that it makes from sales is higher than the cost of running the business. Profit is earned over a period of time.

Profit as a reward

People who put money into a business – that is, shareholders – take a risk. They could invest in other things, such as lending money to the government. They may make less money from holding shares than they would lending to the government. Buying shares in a company therefore needs to be rewarded. Profit acts as an incentive to take risks. The greater the chance of making a profit, the more likely that people will be willing to take a risk.

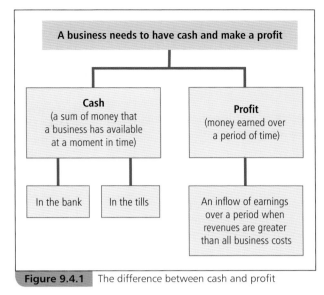

A business needs to have cash and make a profit

Cash (a sum of money that a business has available at a moment in time)

Profit (money earned over a period of time)

In the bank | In the tills

An inflow of earnings over a period when revenues are greater than all business costs

Figure 9.4.1 The difference between cash and profit

DID YOU KNOW?

There are two types of shares: *ordinary* for investors prepared to take a higher risk, and *preference*, with a smaller risk. When a company distributes its profits, preference shareholders, as its name suggests, are paid before ordinary shareholders.

SUMMARY QUESTIONS

1 Which of the following refers to cash, and which to profit?
   - It is a sum of money that exists at a given moment in time.
   - It is earned by a business over a period of time.
   - It is held in the bank or the tills.
   - It needs to be available to pay off debts.
   - It is the difference between revenues and costs.

2 Who receives the distributed profit of a business in:
   - a sole-trader business?
   - a company?

3 What problems might arise when:
   - a business makes a large profit but has no cash?
   - a business has a large amount of cash but does not make a profit?

KEY POINTS

1 Profit is a reward for taking a risk. Shareholders take risks, as do the other owners of a business.

2 A business needs to make a profit over a period of time. This profit can be ploughed into improving the business.

3 A business also needs to have cash to cover day-to-day costs and to meet pressing bills.

4 Businesses need to make a profit and at the same time have an appropriate cash balance.

LEARNING OUTCOMES

Understand the main elements of a balance sheet.

- Understand the difference between assets and liabilities.
- Interpret a balance sheet and deduce simple conclusions, such as to determine how a business is financing its activities and what assets it owns.

ACTIVITY

Choose a business that you are familiar with, such as a local factory or large shop. Make a list of the types of fixed assets and current assets that the business will have. For example, a fixed asset for a newspaper might be the computers journalists use to write their stories on. A restaurant's fixed assets might include the tables and chairs, as well as the oven.

EXAM TIP

Stakeholders find the data in a balance sheet very valuable. Banks will look at the financial stability of the business; suppliers might assess the probability of being paid what they are owed.

Balance sheets

A **balance sheet** is a statement showing the financial health of a business at a particular moment in time. It is usually drawn up at the end of the financial year, but can also be created at other times (e.g. halfway through the year).

Assets and liabilities

Information in a balance sheet enables you to compare immediately how much a business owns and how much it owes to lenders (e.g. banks).

Assets are items that are owned by a business. There are two main types of assets: *fixed* assets and *current* assets. Fixed assets are items used continuously by the business, such as buildings, machinery and vehicles. Current assets are also owned by the business, but they are more easily turned into cash (and include cash).

The three main types of current assets are:

- stock waiting to be sold by the business
- debtors – money owed to the business by debtors
- cash.

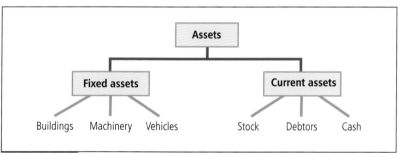

Figure 9.5.1 Fixed assets and current assets

Liability is money that a business owes. It is the money that the business is responsible for paying to others. **Long-term** liabilities are debts that a business has to pay over a number of years. Some of them may be very long-term, such as repayment of a 25-year mortgage. Short-term liabilities are debts that a business has to pay in less than a year.

The assets and liabilities can now be shown in a balance sheet. Figure 9.5.2 shows the balance sheet for Fresh Sandwiches, a company that manufactures and supplies fresh sandwiches to small retail outlets.

Fixed assets amounted to $100,000. This figure represents the value of the small kitchen that is owned by Fresh Sandwiches, and the work benches and kitchen tools it owns.

The **current assets** are $110,000. These include stocks of filling ingredients to be made up into sandwiches (e.g. stocks of fresh meat and other ingredients that might need to be kept refrigerated). These are worth $50,000.

```
Balance sheet for Fresh Sandwiches as at 31/12/00

                                                        $000s
Assets that are tied up        ──────────▸ Fixed assets          100
Assets that can quickly be     ──────────▸ Current assets:
   turned into cash                        Stocks                 50
                                           Debtors                50
                                           Cash                   10
Debts or loans that must be                                      110
   repaid quickly
                               ──────────▸ Current liabilities   (30)
The difference between current ──────────▸ Net current assets     80
   assets and current liabilities
Loans that must be repaid in   ──────────▸ Long-term liabilities (20)
   over a year
Assets – liabilities           ──────────▸ Total net assets      160
How total net assets are       ──────────▸ Financed by:
   financed                                Share capital         140
                                           Profit                 20
```

Figure 9.5.2   A balance sheet

Debtors are calculated as $50,000. This is the total sum owed by retailers who have bought sandwiches on credit. Additionally, Fresh Sandwiches holds $10,000 in cash (some of this will be held at the bank).

Current liabilities represent the sum of money that Fresh Sandwiches owes that needs to be paid back in the short term. For example, it may have bought its meat and bread on credit.

The next heading shown is net current assets. This is the difference between current assets and current liabilities. (The importance of this figure is explained in Unit 9.7 on page 140.)

Fresh Sandwiches has also borrowed some money for a longer period. This is shown as $20,000 long-term liabilities.

When all the liabilities have been subtracted from all of the assets, we arrive at an important figure – total net assets. This is a good measure of the value of the business because it shows the value of everything that the business owns, less money owed to people outside the business.

The final section of the balance sheet shows how the business is financed.

This part of the balance sheet shows where the finance has come from to account for the total net assets of $160,000. In the case of Fresh Sandwiches, it comes from $140,000 put into the business by shareholders and $20,000 of profit that it made in the year.

Reading the balance sheet tells you important information about the assets and liabilities of Fresh Sandwiches and how the business is financed.

SUMMARY QUESTIONS

1 Which of the following are fixed and which are current assets of a business?

Stock / machinery / factory buildings / debtors / vehicles / cash

2 A business has the following assets and liabilities:
   • Fixed assets: $100,000
   • Current liabilities: $20,000
   • Current assets: $30,000
   • Long-term liabilities: $30,000

Using these figures, create a simple balance sheet. Work out the total net assets of the business and explain how the business is financed. Assume that profit is $10,000. Calculate the figure for share capital.

3 A food-processing company manufactures canned fruit using a modern production line. It then sells the cans to large supermarket chains. What items would you expect to appear in the balance sheet for the company?

Financial statements

Gross and net profit, return on capital employed (ROCE).

Alternative ways that businesses can judge their success (e.g. ROCE, market share).

Interpret the performance of a business by using simple accounting ratios (return on capital, gross and net profit margin).

- Using accounting ratios, make evaluative comments on the success and performance of a business.
- Use a balance sheet to aid decision making.

Profit and profit margin

The account below shows the profit calculation for The Honey Shop, a specialist retailer of honey in a major city. It shows how much was spent on buying honey (purchases) and the total revenue received from selling that honey (sales). It also shows the expenses of running the business.

P&L account for The Honey Shop for the year ended 31/12/00

	$	$
Sales		30,000
Cost of sales (purchases)		(15,000)
Gross profit		15,000
Less Expenses		
Electricity	500	
Insurance	300	
Wages	4,200	5,000
Net profit		10,000

Summarising the account we can see that:

Sales = $30,000
Gross profit = $15,000
Net profit = $10,000

From these figures we can make calculations which indicate how well the business is being run. It is important to find out how much profit the company is making for every $1 of sales.

The *gross profit margin* shows how much gross profit is made for each $1 of sales.

The *net profit margin* shows how much net profit the business makes for each $1 of sales.

The calculation is easy:

$$\text{Gross profit margin} = \frac{\text{Gross profit}}{\text{Sales}}$$

$$\text{Net profit margin} = \frac{\text{Net profit}}{\text{Sales}}$$

For example, for The Honey Shop:

$$\text{Gross profit margin} = \frac{15,000}{30,000} = \frac{1}{2} = \text{50 cents profit for every } \$1 \text{ of sales}$$

$$\text{Net profit margin} = \frac{10,000}{30,000} = \frac{1}{3} = \text{33.3 cents profit for every } \$1 \text{ of sales}$$

When gross profit margins for a business fall, this tends to indicate that either:

- the firm's prices are wrong: prices are either too high or too low
- the firm is paying too much for the items that it is buying for resale
- some of the items the firm is selling are being damaged or stolen.

When net profit margins fall, this tends to indicate that:

- the cost of one or more of the overhead costs has risen. The firm will need to look at ways of cutting these costs or of raising its own prices.

ACTIVITY

The profit and loss account shown below is for a small clothes shop. Examine the account and then calculate the gross profit margin and the net profit margin for the business.

Fashion Clothes Ltd P&L as at 31/12/00

	$	$
Sales turnover		150,000
Purchases		(50,000)
Gross profit		?
Less expenses		
Rent and business rates	(15,000)	
Advertising	(1,000)	
Wages and salaries	(28,000)	
Administration	(2,000)	
Interest	(1,000)	
Legal fees	(3,000)	
Net profit		?

Return on capital employed

Comparing how well businesses are being run

It is always helpful to know how well a business is being run. Comparisons can be made with previous years' performance and the performance of similar companies. This is easier if the companies are the same size or in a similar industry.

One way of comparing businesses is to look at market share. This is the percentage of sales in a particular market that a particular business makes.

However, another useful comparison can be made using financial information. A good indicator of business performance is **return on capital employed (ROCE)**. ROCE is a calculation of how much net profit a business makes as a percentage of the amount of money used.

$$\text{ROCE} = \frac{\text{Net profit} \times 100}{\text{Capital employed}}$$

As noted above, to illustrate this point it is helpful to compare two businesses of similar size operating in the same market.

Firm A uses $100,000 worth of capital and generates a profit of $10,000. Firm B also uses $100,000 of capital and generates a profit of $5,000.

Firm A's ROCE is $\dfrac{10\,000 \times 100}{100,000} = 10\%$

Firm B's ROCE is $\dfrac{5\,000 \times 100}{100,000} = 5\%$

CONTINUED

EXAM TIP

Ratios are more useful than absolute figures. When calculating ratios, think about whether a high figure is better than a low figure. For example, a high ROCE is better than a low figure, but a low gearing ratio is probably better than a high one.

ACTIVITY

The following table shows the net profit and capital employed by three businesses.

Business	Capital employed ($)	Net profit ($)
Fresh vegetable store	15,000	5,000
New vegetable store	14,000	7,000
Traditional vegetable store	16,000	4,000

Which business is using its capital best to generate profits?

Interpreting figures from the balance sheet

The balance sheet shows the financial affairs of the business at a specified moment in time. It provides information concerning:

• the nature and value of assets employed in the business
• the nature and value of liabilities to others
• how the business has been funded.

The outline format of a balance sheet is:

	$
Assets	50,000
Less liabilities	20,000
	30,000
Financed by	
Owner's capital	30,000

The net assets of the business (total assets less total liabilities) represents the owners' investment in the business.

Assets are presented according to their **liquidity** (how easily they can be turned into cash), starting with the least liquid items:

• Fixed assets
• Current assets.

Liabilities are presented the other way round, starting with the most pressing liabilities:

• Current liabilities
• Long-term liabilities.

KEY POINTS

1 The profit and loss account shows how profit is reached.

2 From the P&L, profit calculations can be made for each $1 of sales. These calculations give profit margins.

3 Comparing the net profit with the amount of capital used gives ROCE, an indicator of how well the capital is being used.

4 The balance sheet can indicate the value of a business's assets and liabilities and how the net assets are financed.

Study the balance sheet below and answer the questions that follow.

Pina Mistry balance sheet as at 31 December 00

	$000s	$000s
Fixed assets		
Land and buildings	300	
Motor vehicles	10	
		310
Current assets		
Stock	60	
Debtors	5	
Cash	5	
	70	
Current liabilities	(50)	
Net Current Assets		20
Long term liabilities		(30)
Total net assets		300
Financed by		
Profits		30
Owner's capital		270

Questions

1 What types of assets does the business have?

2 What is the value of:
   • all the fixed assets?
   • all the current assets?
   • all the assets?

3 What is the difference between current liabilities and long-term liabilities?

4 What does 'net current assets' mean? Why is it important for this to be a positive rather than a negative figure?

5 What is the value of the current ratio of the business? What is the value of the quick ratio?

6 What does 'total net assets' mean? What is the value of total net assets in this business?

7 Explain how the net assets of this business are financed.

SUMMARY QUESTIONS

1 The following table gives financial information about two businesses.

Business	Turnover ($)	Gross profit ($)	Net profit ($)	Capital employed ($)
Engineering Supplies	240,000	60,000	30,000	300,000
Superior Engineering	300,000	75,000	30,000	200,000

Which of the businesses is the most profitable? Which has the highest return on capital employed?

2 Here is the middle part of the balance sheet for Superior Engineering:

Current assets	
Stock	6,000
Debtors	3,000
Cash	3,000
Current liabilities	6,000

• Calculate the current ratio for Superior Engineering. Is this ratio high enough?

• Calculate the acid test ratio. Is this high enough?

• Why may the balance sheet figures not give an accurate representation of the liquidity of this business?

3 Define the following terms.
   • Asset
   • Liability
   • Net current assets
   • Net assets
   • Financed by

Identify and calculate working capital.

- Understand the concept and importance of working capital.
- Understand the concept of liquidity.
- Understand simple accounting ratios – current and acid test ratio.

Clothes shops need to have plenty of working capital to finance the purchase of new stock and to pay wages and other bills. Stock therefore needs to be sold quickly to generate more cash

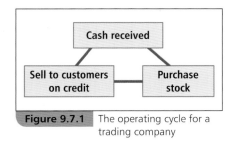

Figure 9.7.1 The operating cycle for a trading company

The operating cycle

Every business has an operating cycle. For a manufacturing business, this starts with the purchase of materials, which are then made into a product. The cycle finishes with the receipt of cash from customers.

In a trading company (e.g. a wholesaler), the cycle involves the purchase of stock, selling the goods on to customers, usually on credit, and then, after a short period, receiving a cash payment.

Incurring liabilities

In both of these operating cycles (for manufacturing and trading companies), a business will create liabilities. For example:

- the manufacturing company will buy raw materials and supplies on credit
- the trading company will buy stocks of goods on credit to resell.

Current liabilities are debts that the company must pay within a year.

The importance of current assets

In order to meet these ongoing liabilities, such as pressing payments or wages, a business will need to have access to cash and other **liquid assets**. These are assets that can be turned quickly into cash to make payments. These assets are also referred to as *current* assets. They are ranked in order of liquidity:

1 Stocks (least liquid)

2 Debtors

3 Cash (most liquid).

Current assets – current liabilities

The amount of working capital in a business is calculated by subtracting current (short-term) liabilities from current assets:

Working capital = Current assets – Current liabilities

Working capital is also commonly set out as a **ratio**. The ratio will show how many dollars of current assets a business has for each dollar of current liabilities.

The ratio should be at least: 1:1.

Ideally, it should be between 1.5:1 and 2:1.

The middle part of a balance sheet

You can read the working capital ratio from the middle part of a balance sheet.

For example, in Unit 9.5 we set out the balance sheet for Fresh Sandwiches. The middle part was set out in the following way:

Current assets: Stocks   50
                      Debtors 50
                      Cash   10
                               110
Current liabilities: **30**

In this case, the working capital ratio is 110:30, which can be simplified to 3.66:1.

In other words, the company had $3.66 of short-term assets for every $1 worth of short-term liabilities.

The acid test (quick) ratio

Businesses also use another ratio to check whether they have enough working capital. This is the **acid test ratio**.

This liquidity ratio does not include stock. This is because if a business has to sell its stock in a hurry, it will normally have to sell at a loss.

The acid test ratio is therefore: Debtors + Cash:Current liabilities.

In the example we showed for Fresh Sandwiches, this is: 50 + 10:30, which is 2:1.

This shows that for every $1 of liabilities that the business has, it has $2 of assets that can be turned quickly into cash.

The quick ratio should be at least 1:1.

Liquidity ratios only have a limited use. The balance sheet of a company is created on a particular day of the year, but the value of current assets and current liabilities changes every day as payments are made, new stock ordered and new liabilities incurred. It is important, however, to have liquid assets, particularly in the form of cash. For example, a clothes shop will need working capital to pay for its stock. To get this, it must make sure it stocks items that sell well, to keep the cash turning over in the business.

SUMMARY QUESTIONS

1 The following table shows the current assets and current liabilities of three businesses. Work out the current ratio and acid test ratio for each of the businesses. Which of the businesses has the best working capital position?

Name of business	Current assets (Stock + debtors + cash) $	Stock $	Current liabilities $
Shankar Kumar (shawl merchant)	40,000	30,000	10,000
Shi Fang Fang (photography)	100,000	80,000	70,000
Peter Burden (cake shop)	50,000	20,000	30,000

2 At the end of the year, a business has fixed assets of $200,000, stocks worth $80,000, debtors of $60,000, cash of $20,000 and current liabilities of $100,000. What is its working capital ratio? What is its quick ratio?

3 Why does a business need to have working capital? What are the dangers of having:

• too little working capital?
• too much working capital?

Financial budgets

Creating a budget for factory expenditure enables managers to control costs through analysis of variances from budgeted figures

What is a budget?

A **budget** is a plan set out in numbers. As 'plan' suggests, it is made out before spending occurs. For example, a company may create a budget in December 2010 for the year starting in January 2011 and ending in December 2011.

The main purpose of creating budgets is to *control* business spending and to indicate to employees what money is available in a given period.

Budgets are created in such a way that *budgeted figures* can be compared with *actual figures*.

An expenditure budget

An expenditure budget sets out how much an organisation plans to spend on particular headings in a period. For example, a manufacturing company may identify its main expenditures as being wages, raw materials, energy, packaging materials and 'other'. It can set these out in a spreadsheet for the coming 12 months.

Expenditure type	Jan	Feb	Mar	Apr	May	Jun	Jul	Aug	Sep	Oct	Nov	Dec
Wages	1,000	1,000	1,000	1,000	1,000	1,000	1,000	1,000	1,000	1,000	1,000	1,000
Raw materials	9,000	9,000	9,000	8,000	8,000	9,000	9,000	10,000	9,000	9,000	9,000	9,000
Energy	500	500	500	500	500	500	500	550	500	500	500	500
Packaging	450	450	450	400	400	450	450	500	450	450	450	450
Other	200	200	200	200	200	200	200	200	200	200	200	200

Note that in the budget there are two columns for each of the months. The first column is for the budgeted (planned) expenditure. The second column is for the actual expenditure.

To keep control of the business, the managers meet every month to compare the budgeted expenditure with the actual expenditure. When the actual expenditure is higher or lower than the budgeted amount, this is described as a variance. This can be illustrated by taking the examples of January, February and March.

Type of expenditure	January Budget	January Actual	January Variance	February Budget	February Actual	February Variance	March Budget	March Actual	March Variance
Wages	1,000	1,000	0	1,000	1,200	−200	1,000		
Raw materials	9,000	9,000	0	9,000	9,500	−500	9,000		
Energy	500	500	0	500	600	−100	500		
Packaging	450	450	0	450	500	−50	450		
Other	200	200	0	200	200	0	200		

The budget chart above was presented to managers at the end of February. It shows that in January the factory managed to keep exactly to budget, and no variances are shown. However, in February there was overspending on wages (–200), raw materials (–500), energy (–100) and packaging (–50). In total, the factory is now $850 over budget.

Managers now have to decide whether this is a problem. If it is, decisions will need to be made to get spending under control and make sure that the budget is put back on track. This shows how budgeting and identifying variances can give managers control over the business.

ACTIVITY

Create a budget showing what you intend to spend over the next month. Set this out for 4 weeks. Remember that your budget is a plan. Break the budget down into main categories (e.g. food, clothing, entertainment). At the end of each week, total up how much you have actually spent. Work out the variance. Use the budget to control your spending.

EXAM TIP

Unfavourable variances can be put right if they're spotted in time!

SUMMARY QUESTIONS

1 Simon owns a restaurant. Diners in the restaurant pay on average $20 for a meal. He has created a sales budget for next year. In January he expects to have 2,000 customers, in February 1,800, March 2,200 and April 1,800. Set out a table to illustrate these figures. In the event, his actual figures are January 1,800, February 1,600, March 2,000 and April 1,800. Illustrate these figures by creating a budget table to show budgeted figures, actual figures and variances for the first 4 months of the year.

2 What is the difference between budgeted figures and actual figures?

3 How does budgeting give managers greater control over their business?

KEY POINTS

1 A budget is a plan set out in numbers.

2 A budgeted figure shows what is planned; actual figures show what happened. Variances are used to calculate the difference.

3 Budgeting gives managers greater control over their business.

4 Budgets are typically used to control expenditure.

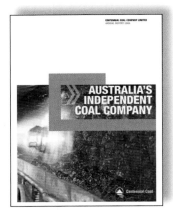

The front cover of the Annual Report produced by an Australian mining company – Centennial Coal, containing financial statements such as the profit and loss account and the balance sheet

'Who reads the accounts?'

Different groups of people read company accounts. The information provides important useful details. The accounts give a picture of the past, present position of a business and some idea of its future prospects.

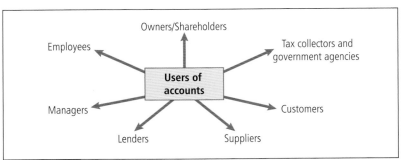

Figure 9.9.1 Different users of accounts

Owners/shareholders

In a small business, the owners may be a sole trader or group of partners. In companies, the owners are the shareholders. As the principal risk takers, owners want to know that their investment in the business is being looked after. They can always decide to take their money out and invest elsewhere. To help them decide, they will be interested in:

- profitability (from the P&L account) – is the business making enough profit?
- liquidity – does the business have enough cash to meet pressing bills and debts?
- the financial position of the business (from the balance sheet) – what is the state of the business's assets and liabilities?

Lenders

Lenders want to know that the business is able to pay interest and eventually repay any loans. Banks will ask to see the accounts of a business to check whether they should risk lending to the business. They will want to look at figures for past profits, and also budgeted figures for future profits. They will want to check that a business has enough income to cover outgoing expenditures. In particular, lenders will be interested in the cash-flow position of a business. This relates to the timing of incomings and outgoings of cash.

Managers

Managers need to check on the profitability of their business, whether it has enough cash and whether it is investing in suitable assets.

Suppliers

Before they make supplies available on credit terms, suppliers will want their customers' accounts to indicate whether or not the business is financially sound, and whether it generates enough cash to pay for supplies.

Customers

Customers who have a long-term relationship with a company will want to make sure that the business is financially sound enough to keep supplying them. If the business they buy from is making excessive profits, this might suggest that they are being charged too much.

Employees

Employees are concerned about job security. They will want to make sure that their company can pay its debts and is profitable enough to pay the wages.

Tax collectors

The government collects a number of different taxes from businesses. One of the most important of these is a tax on profits. This should be shown in the profit and loss account. Businesses also are likely to have to pay sales taxes – often in the form of a tax on value added by the business.

The government also uses business accounts to create national statistics, which can help it plan its national economic policy.

Annual reports

Small businesses, such as sole traders and partnerships, are expected to produce accounting information for the government tax collection department.

Companies are expected to produce an annual report. Public companies produce an annual report for shareholders. This annual report contains a statement from the chairperson of the company, giving a review of how the company has performed in the previous year and its plans for the coming year. The profit and loss account and the balance sheet will be presented, along with another chart which shows the cash position of the business.

KEY POINTS

1 Users of accounts are groups and individuals that read accounts for specific purposes.

2 Shareholders (and other owners) use a business's accounts to check on the safety of their investment.

3 Other users of accounts include employees, managers, suppliers, customers, tax authorities and lenders; the accounts provide useful information on which to base important decisions.

SUMMARY QUESTIONS

1 What information will Shareholders try to find in a company report?

2 Choose a well-known company that operates in your country. Identify five different groups of people in your country who would use the accounts of this business to find out financial information about the business. What information would they be looking at? How would this be of use to them?

3 What sorts of decisions do the following groups make that result from reading accounts and other information?
   • Lenders   • Suppliers   • Shareholders

SECTION 1: Short-answer questions

1 Explain the purpose of a cash-flow forecast. *[4]*

2 Using the example of a bakery stall, explain why it is important to have cash available on a daily basis. *[3]*

3 Identify and explain TWO reasons why a new business may face higher payments than receipts in the first few months of trading. *[4]*

4 Explain how a small business owner may use a credit card to help with short-term cash shortages. *[3]*

5 State the formula for working out profit at the end of a trading year. *[2]*

6 Analyse TWO reasons why a business that has cash to pay for things on a daily basis may not make a profit at the end of the year. *[6]*

7 Explain, with examples from a small local business, the difference between gross and net profit. *[4]*

8 Explain why major shareholders may face a difficult decision over the amount of profit to be retained by a firm. *[4]*

9 Explain how the following figures are calculated on a profit and loss account:
   - trading/operating profit.
   - retained profit. *[4]*

10 Identify and explain TWO reasons why profit is 'an important reward to business owners'. *[4]*

11 Explain why a successful business needs to retain profit as well as pay it out to shareholders. *[4]*

12 Explain, with examples, TWO differences between fixed and current assets in a business. *[4]*

13 Analyse why a prospective lender to a business will be interested in its balance sheet. *[4]*

14 Using the example of a clothes shop, analyse why the acid test ratio is a better test of liquidity than the current ratio. *[4]*

15 Identify and explain TWO reasons why managers prepare cost budgets for each department of the business. *[4]*

16 Calculate the variances, including favourable (F) or adverse (A), and comment on the following:
   - Budgeted sales of $20,000, actual sales of $18,000.
   - Budgeted wages of $4,000, actual wages of $5,000.
   - Budgeted advertising of $3,000, actual advertising of $2,000. *[6]*

SECTION 2: Longer-answer questions

Blooms – Flowers for all Occasions

Grace's flower display business is based in Gaborone, Botswana. She supplies arrangements for special occasions such as festivals and weddings, and also has contracts with many of the local hotels. Demand is seasonal, but as she has been operating for 5 years, it is reasonably predictable. Grace employs one trainee assistant, but does much of the artistic work herself. Grace holds a large stock of flowers and plants on a daily basis, but needs to make sure that she matches supply with demand as far as possible, because of the short life of cut flowers.

Grace's financial documents are shown opposite.

Cash-flow forecast for the first half of next year

All figures in dollars	January	February	March	April	May	June
Balance brought forward	1,000					
Income						
Sales	1,500	1,000	3,000	4,000	5,000	4,000
Total receipts	1,500	1,000				
Total cash available	2,500	1,350				
Outgoings						
Rent	400	400	400	400	400	400
Purchases (average 50% of sales figure)	750	500				
Wages	1,500	1,500	1,500	1,500	1,500	1,500
Total payments	2,650					
Balance carried forward	(150)					

Profit and loss account for Blooms 2011

	$
Sales	48,000
Cost of making sales	24,000
Gross profit	
Overheads	20,000
Net profit	

Figures taken from the balance sheet for Blooms 2011:

• Current assets: $10,000

• Stock: $6,000

• Current liabilities: $8,000

Use the financial information above to answer the following questions.

1 Fill in the missing figures for Grace's cash-flow forecast. [4]

2 Identify TWO months where Grace is forecasting a cash-flow problem. [2]

3 Do you agree that the bank should lend Grace the money to solve her cash-flow problem? Explain your answer. [5]

4 Identify and explain TWO ways in which Grace could improve her cash flow in the months when she may face problems. [4]

5 Calculate and fill in the gross and net profit figures on Grace's profit and loss account. [4]

6 Calculate the gross and net profit margins, using the figures from Grace's profit and loss account. [4]

7 Calculate the new margins if Grace's supplier increases the price of the flowers and plants she sells to Blooms by 10 per cent. [6]

8 Explain the following terms, with examples from the Blooms business:
   • Current assets
   • Stock
   • Current liabilities [6]

9 Calculate Grace's net current assets. [2]

10 Calculate Grace's current ratio. [3]

11 Calculate Grace's acid test ratio. [4]

12 Analyse your answers to Questions 9 and 10. What does this show about the liquidity of Grace's business? [4]

13 To what extent might the acid test ratio be a more accurate measure of liquidity for this type of business? Justify your answer. [6]

14 Grace's budgeted and actual figures for last month are as follows:

	Budget	Actual
Sales	$4,000	$4,500
Costs	$3,000	$3,250

Work out the variances and indicate whether adverse or favourable. [4]

15 Comment on your answer to Question 14. Should Grace be happy with this result? Explain your answer. [5]

10 Human needs and rewards

10.1 Why people work

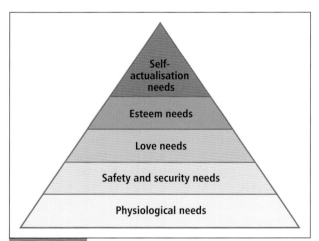

Figure 10.1.1 Maslow's hierarchy of needs. People are motivated to move up the pyramid (see Unit 10.4)

Time spent at work

To some people, work is a great pleasure that gives them a sense of personal fulfilment. For others, it is more of a necessity, a way to make a living.

Working hours

Many people spend a large part of their lives at work. Statistics from national household surveys in different countries show that the annual hours worked by employees vary considerably. For example, in the following Asian economies in 2007, people worked on average more than 42 hours a week:

- South Korea
- Bangladesh
- Sri Lanka
- Hong Kong
- Malaysia
- Thailand.

This contrasts with Western European countries – for example, Germany 41.2 hours per week, Belgium 38.6 hours per week. Workers in France are only required to work 35 hours per week, but in practice some work longer.

A major reason for these lower working hours is the existence of laws that prohibit employees from working more than a maximum number of hours in a week. In France, for example, employees work only 35 hours a week. This contrasts with Mexico (40 hours) and South Korea (45 hours).

Work satisfies human needs

Through work, we are able to satisfy our needs. At a basic level, we need food, shelter and clothing to survive. These are physiological needs and are associated with biological well-being. Hopefully, a job of work will provide us with the income to meet these needs. However, because we spend 35 hours or more a week at work, it is desirable that work does more than meet just these basic biological needs.

Abraham **Maslow** set out what he referred to as a **hierarchy of needs** (see Figure 10.1.1).

The following table sets out the needs identified by Maslow.

Need	Description
Physiological needs	Life essentials, such as food, shelter and clothing; must be met in order to keep the body functioning. There are many people in the world who struggle to meet their physiological needs.
Safety and security needs	In order to be safe from danger, people need to be able to live work in a clean and orderly space. Work needs to be secure, and employees should have the right to take part in pension and sick-pay schemes.
Love and social needs	Humans need to be able to give and receive love and friendship. This involves building up good relationships and a feeling of belonging. In the workplace, these needs can be satisfied by the companionship of fellow employees, the pleasure of working in a group or team and company social activities.
Esteem needs	Based on our desire for self-respect and the respect of others. Employees have a need to be recognised as individuals, to have a job title or some form of status or prestige, and to have their efforts noticed.
Self-actualisation needs	Humans need to develop skills and creativity and achieve full potential as individuals. Employees need the chance to progress and develop through training and use creative talents and abilities to the full.

Fewer people achieve the top levels in the hierarchy than the lower levels. Barack Obama, the President of the United States, not only earns a top income, but also does a job where he has a direct influence on the lives of people across the globe. This is likely to give him a lot of personal satisfaction. In a similar way, footballers like Cristiano Ronaldo and the tennis stars Venus and Serena Williams not only earn high salaries, but are also able to express themselves through their sport, which for them is their work.

Barack Obama: someone who is likely to self-actualise from his work as President of the United States

SUMMARY QUESTIONS

1 Which levels of satisfaction in the hierarchy of needs would the following jobs provide for you?
 • Street seller of cheap toys
 • International footballer
 • Market research analyst
 • Managing director of the international company of your choice
 • Production line operative in a large company
 • Owner of your own retailing business

2 What jobs can you identify that would enable you personally to fulfil all the elements of the hierarchy of needs?

3 In South Korea, employees work longer hours than in France. Does this mean that South Koreans are likely to have more of their needs met than employees working in France? Explain your answer.

KEY POINTS

1 Human needs range from basic physiological needs to the need for personal fulfilment through work.

2 A job can fulfil human needs by providing money, a safe environment, a sense of belonging, self-esteem and the opportunity to develop skills.

Financial rewards

In some parts of the world, diamonds are found close to the earth's surface and are literally washed out of riverbeds or from the earth with high-pressure hoses. What would be a suitable payment system for people working in these conditions?

Payment systems

The payment for a normal working week is the basic wage or salary. Many employees receive extra benefits on top of their basic wage, either as money or in some other form. Payment systems may include some form of bonus, or incentive, to encourage employees. The bonus payment might be for high-quality work, or for completing a task ahead of schedule.

Not all employees receive a wage or salary. Salespeople may be paid on a commission basis – that is, a percentage of the revenue, or profit, that they make for the company by selling the firm's products.

The main ways of calculating pay are described below.

Flat rate

This is a set rate of pay, based on a set number of hours – for example, $200 for a 40-hour week. This is easy to calculate and administer, but it does not give the employee any incentive to work harder.

Time rate

Under this scheme, the worker receives a set rate per hour. Any hours worked above a set number are paid at an overtime rate. The overtime rate may be time and a half (i.e. 150 per cent of the normal rate) or double time (i.e. 200 per cent of the normal rate).

Piece rate

This system is sometimes used in the textile and electronics industries, for example. Payment is made for each item produced that meets a given quality standard. The advantage of such a scheme is that it encourages effort. However, it is not suitable for jobs that require time and care. Also, the output of many jobs in service industries is impossible to measure accurately. For example, how could you measure the output of a teacher, bus driver or doctor?

Bonus

A bonus is paid as an additional encouragement to employees. It can be paid out of additional profits earned by the company as a result of employees' efforts and hard work. Bonuses may also be used as an incentive to workers just before the firm closes down for a holiday period. The bonus incentive encourages employees to keep up a high work rate.

Commission

This is a payment made as a percentage of the sales a salesperson has made. For example, in a retail store, an employee might receive 10 per cent of each sale made, or may be paid an hourly rate plus 5 per cent commission on every sale made. The commission thus acts as an incentive to sell more.

Performance rates

Performance rates are a good way of encouraging high performance. An employee will be set targets to achieve, based on some form of work measurement. For example, a standard time may be set to do a particular task. An employee who meets the standard will receive a set rate of pay. For exceeding the target, the employee will receive additional payments. The higher the target reached, the higher the level of pay.

Profit sharing

Under profit sharing, pay varies with the level of profit a company makes. The organisation sets a target for profit. If profit reaches this target, or exceeds it, the organisation will pay either a set sum for each employee, or will calculate the pay as a percentage of each employee's salary. Schemes such as this recognise the importance of hard-working employees in helping companies to make higher profits. The profit-sharing reward will usually be in addition to other payment schemes. The table summarises the benefits of different payment schemes.

Payment scheme	Key benefit
Flat rate	Easy to calculate, cheap to run.
Time rate	A good way of encouraging employees to work longer hours.
Piece rate	Acts as an incentive to employees to produce higher levels of output.
Bonus	Rewards high levels of performance and can be targeted at high performers.
Commission	Directly relates pay to sales made or other measures of output.
Performance rate	Directly links pay to meeting or exceeding targets.
Profit sharing	Enables employees to see the direct link between their efforts and company profits.

EXAM TIP

Make sure that you understand the difference between a bonus and time rates. Bonuses are usually paid for performance in excess of an agreed target. Time rates are always linked to hours worked.

KEY POINTS

1 Payment systems reward effort and should act as incentives.

2 Time rates are based on the numbers of hours worked; piece rates vary with the number of units produced.

3 Bonuses, commission, performance rates and profit sharing systems create incentives for meeting or exceeding targets.

SUMMARY QUESTIONS

1 What types of financial reward systems would be suitable in the following situations? Briefly justify your choice.
   - Firefighters (i.e. employees with responsibility for putting out fires and attending other emergencies).
   - Professional footballers playing in a knockout cup, where it is hoped that they will reach the final.
   - Homeworkers who are producing textile garments for a supplier who provides them with equipment and materials to produce high-quality textiles.
   - Shopworkers whose job it is to put new goods onto the shelves.

2 A company specialises in making handmade furniture using skilled craft workers. Each item of furniture is unique. The company is keen to make high profits and believes that the craft workers play an important part in the success of the business. Suggest a payment system, or combination of payment systems, that would enable the company to be successful and its employees to receive appropriate rewards for their efforts. Explain the reason for your choice.

3 A call centre sells insurance over the phone. The employees have been making several mistakes and there is a high turnover of staff. The current payment system is flat rate. Suggest alternative payment systems that might encourage higher levels of employee performance. Explain the reasons for your suggestions.

Non-financial rewards

Understand the significance of different methods.

- Show understanding of non-financial methods such as fringe benefits.
- Understand when benefits such as discounts on products, free accommodation, use of company car might be used.

Fringe benefits

Fringe benefits are non-financial incentives given to employees. They can act as a real incentive to attract employees into a particular job and then to retain them in the company.

In designing fringe benefits, it is important to consider factors that are likely to be attractive. Subsidised or free housing is a strong incentive in city areas where accommodation is expensive and there are long waiting lists for houses. Some jobs may have accommodation provided – for example, a dormitory or hostel for workers at a mine or factory. Some hotel workers are provided with accommodation at their place of work.

Fringe benefits are a useful way of meeting employee needs. The table shows how fringe benefits relate to Maslow's hierarchy.

Level in the hierarchy of needs	Example of fringe benefit
Physiological needs	Housing provides shelter. Subsidised canteen meals provide cheap food.
Safety and security needs	Insurance and health care benefits (e.g. the company pays the health insurance of its employees).
Love needs	Sports clubs or social activities where employees can meet and enjoy recreation together.
Esteem needs	Company cars, laptop computers and other status items.
Self-actualisation needs	The company pays for employees to go on training and development courses, which enable them to develop their skills and master their line of work. These might include courses in higher education.

One fringe benefit that is an important incentive is payment of school fees. In most countries in the developing world, education is highly regarded because it enables children to go on to get better jobs. However, school fees can be high for low-income families. An offer to pay all or part of children's school fees can be a powerful incentive. For example, the oil company Shell provides 2,600 scholarships a year to help with school fees for post-secondary school pupils in the areas of Nigeria where Shell is operating (Shell Secondary School Scholarship Scheme). Fringe benefits related to education and health insurance are powerful tools for winning employee loyalty.

It makes sense for a company to identify the sorts of fringe benefits that will provide the greatest incentive.

Companies need to design fringe benefits to give the greatest possible benefit to their employees. For example, in a rural area, it may be sensible to offer employees the use of company cars. In a congested urban area, the employees may be more interested in subsidised use of public transport.

Some fringe benefits will be relatively low-cost to a company and may be related to the company activity. Purchases of company products

A company may build a school or a clinic as a fringe benefit to encourage loyalty

may be subsidised. Many transport companies allow employees and their families to travel for free or at very low prices.

Some fringe benefits are intended to make employees feel good about working for their company: tickets may be provided to sports events and concerts, and company away-days or short holidays to attractive locations may be offered. Fringe benefits may relate directly to unsocial hours that some employees are expected to work – for example, a free evening meal and taxi home for those working after a certain time. Some employees, such as sales representatives, may benefit from a petrol or car allowance.

SUMMARY QUESTIONS

1 From the following list of fringe benefits, identify the ones that would be most attractive to employees in the situations listed below. In each case, justify your choices.

   Subsidised school fees / subsidised public transport / subsidised canteen services / car petrol allowance / low-cost company goods / free accommodation

   • Employees live a long way from their place of work.
   • There is a shortage of housing and what is available is very expensive.
   • Employees do not have access to cooking facilities and have to travel a long way to work.
   • Education is expensive and there is a strong emphasis placed on educational qualifications.

2 A large international confectionery company (producing sweets and chocolate) is seeking to develop rewards systems that encourage high performance. What sorts of fringe benefits could it create that would act as an incentive for high-performing employees?

3 In what circumstances are fringe benefits likely to act as stronger incentives to motivate employees than alternative financial rewards?

KEY POINTS

1 A fringe benefit is a property or service provided in addition to financial reward.

2 Fringe benefits act as incentives for an employee to join a company, stay with the company and work hard for the company.

3 Fringe benefits should be designed to best meet employee needs.

4 Health, education and housing benefits are good non-financial incentives.

5 Subsidised products and petrol and car allowances also help to subsidise an employee's income.

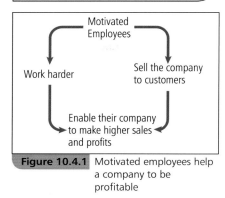

Figure 10.4.1 Motivated employees help a company to be profitable

Motivation

Motivation is what causes people to act or do something in a positive way. By understanding why people behave in the way they do, managers can make work more fulfilling for people, and thus motivate them. A well-motivated workforce will work harder and contribute more to the success of a business.

Many people believe that real motivation comes from inside an individual. This is intrinsic motivation. It is associated with meeting higher-level needs. For example, an individual will take pride in completing a task or project if this makes them feel good about themselves and they have the opportunity to use their talents and skills.

The other form of motivation is extrinsic. This occurs when some form of reward or punishment is given. A bonus or commission can be positive extrinsic motivators. Fear of losing a job can be seen as a negative extrinsic motivator.

The importance of motivation to a business

Motivated employees work harder. They also feel proud to work for their employer. This is particularly important where they come into contact with customers. In these situations they are much more likely to be positive and present the company and its products in a positive way.

Motivation of employees is closely related to Maslow's hierarchy of needs. The higher the level of needs that can be fulfilled, the more likely employees are to be motivated.

Factors influencing motivation

There are a number of factors that can increase motivation, outlined in the following paragraphs.

Job satisfaction

The happier people are with their jobs, the more satisfied they will be. Jobs should be designed to increase this satisfaction. Employers will often measure job satisfaction by using rating scales for employees to report their reaction to their jobs. A rating scale could be set out from 1 to 5 (where 1 represents 'not at all satisfied' and 5 represents 'extremely satisfied').

A number of factors influence job satisfaction, including:

• the nature of the work, including how interesting it is

• variety of work tasks

• encouragement from others

• suitable rewards

• feelings of being treated fairly

• good relationships with colleagues and managers.

Each year, the American business magazine *Fortune* carries out a survey of employees to find out America's best company to work for. The 2009 survey contains 57

Google staff: Google employees report some of the highest levels of job satisfaction – with high pay and interesting jobs

questions, given to a sample of 400 employees. Questions relate to views about management, job satisfaction and friendship among the workforce. In 2009, the top 10 companies included a number of internet-based companies, such as Google, where pay and fringe benefits were still high, in spite of a global slowdown in economic activity.

Questions

1 Write down five questions to include in a survey to find out about the best companies to work for. Why would you choose these questions?

2 In the survey outlined above, employees were asked about their opinions on their current level of job satisfaction and the effectiveness of management. How would studying the answers to these questions have aided managers to make changes that would enhance motivation?

3 Carry out an internet search to find the most recent report on America's 100 best companies to work for. What are the top three companies? Why do employees rate them so highly?

Job rotation

Job rotation widens employees' experience and increases motivation by moving them through a range of jobs. Variety and change provide greater interest, and the experience gives employees a better understanding of how the jobs fit together. They are also more likely to feel that they are being challenged and thus meeting higher-order needs.

Job enrichment

While job rotation involves increasing the variety of tasks, job enrichment involves increasing the challenge involved. Work activities become more complex and demand a greater range of skills. In job enrichment, it is important to clarify the objectives of the tasks to be carried out and to give the employees clear feedback on their performance.

SUMMARY QUESTIONS

1 Explain how job rotation and job enrichment are likely to motivate employees.

2 What are the differences between intrinsic and extrinsic motivation?

  Which of these is likely to lead to true motivation?

3 Think of a job that you know something about (e.g. a job done by a member of your family). How could the design of that job be improved to make job holders more motivated?

KEY POINTS

1 Motivation involves wanting to do something rather than having to do it.

2 Intrinsic motivation is a drive from within an individual. Extrinsic motivation comes from external rewards and punishments.

3 Businesses can encourage motivation by making work more interesting and thus satisfying.

Management styles

LEARNING OUTCOMES

Appreciate the role of management in motivating employees.

- Understand the importance of the role of management in motivating employees.

Explain the different styles of management.

- Know and understand management styles, such as autocratic, democratic and laissez-faire.

Have an awareness of their appropriateness in different situations.

- Recommend and justify an appropriate management style in a given situation.

DID YOU KNOW?

Managers need to be able to delegate, that is give responsibility to another person for carrying out a task.

EXAM TIP

If you find it difficult to understand the issues in this unit (Motivation), think about your own experience. How does your teacher or your school try to motivate you? Are their methods effective?

Managers as motivators

People are the essential resource in an organisation that helps it to achieve its objectives. Managers help to steer the organisation towards meeting these objectives. As people work best when they are motivated, an important task for management is to motivate employees. This is often referred to as human resource management or people management.

Appraisal involves managers sitting down with employees to discuss and agree targets and training plans

Good human resource managers listen to their employees and use approaches such as job rotation and job enrichment to create job satisfaction. They realise that employees are all human beings, with their own hopes and fears.

Many companies use an annual appraisal interview as a way of motivating employees. The employee meets with his or her manager to set targets to identify performance strengths and weaknesses over the past year. A training and development plan can then be created for the employee which sets out ways for improving work performance and enjoyment of work. Suitable training may also be identified.

Management styles

Management style refers to a manager's pattern of behaviour. There are three main styles: autocratic, democratic and laissez-faire.

- **Autocratic** means taking decisions by oneself. Autocratic managers make decisions on their own and then tell staff what they will do and how to do it. This tightly controlled approach may be called 'tell and do'. The autocratic manager may provide clear instructions, but staff may be demotivated because there is little opportunity for their own ideas.

- **Democratic** means decision making by people, after considering everyone's ideas. Persuasive democratic management usually means that the leader makes the decisions, and persuades the followers that these are the right decisions. In consultative democratic management, the group will have a lot of input into the discussion – that is, they are 'consulted' – even if the leader still makes the final decision.

- **Laissez-faire** is a French phrase that means 'let [them] do [it]' and it is used to describe a loose management style. Managers create guidelines and objectives, but then leave staff to carry out the tasks for themselves. This can be successful if the employees are motivated and good decision makers. However, it can lead to chaos if staff need strong direction from the manager and are unable, for various reasons, to make decisions themselves. The table summarises the three styles.

Management style	Advantages	Disadvantages
Autocratic	Rapid decision making. Good for armed forces, fire and other emergency services.	Can lead to dissatisfaction. Motivation can drop.
Democratic	Makes use of many ideas. Involves consultation about decision making.	Can be slow in making decisions. May lead to disagreement and arguments.
Laissez-faire	Employees have freedom to manage their own work within given guidelines.	Lack of clarity can lead to low motivation and disagreement.

Some organisations are more suited to particular styles. In an advertising agency, it is helpful to share ideas between lots of people, so democratic or laissez-faire styles are helpful. Where decisions have to be made quickly and to a set pattern, a more autocratic style may be useful.

KEY POINTS

1 Human resource management involves treating people as an organisation's most important resource.

2 Good managers make employees feel valued and identify their needs at work.

3 Autocratic managers direct others by making most, or all, decisions.

4 Democratic managers listen to others and share responsibility for decision making.

5 Laissez-faire managers create guidelines but leave their staff to carry out the tasks.

ACTIVITY

Working in a small group, decide on the most suitable management style to use in the following scenarios. Explain how the style you recommend would be suitable.

1 A business has received a large order for goods from a new customer. These goods need to be produced within a very short timeframe.

2 A fault has occurred on the production line in a car-producing plant. It is not clear what is causing the fault, so the views of everyone working on that line are to be taken into consideration.

SUMMARY QUESTIONS

1 Copy and complete the paragraph below using the following words.

Laissez-faire / autocratic / democratic / management style / human resource management

It is important to match _____ with the situation and the type of organisation. For example, _____ management may be most suitable when it is important to consider the views of a range of people with specialist knowledge in an organisation. In contrast, when decisions need to be made quickly and with clarity, an _____ style may be more appropriate. A third approach, referred to as _____, gives greater freedom to individuals within the organisation to make their own decisions. People are the most important resource in the organisation. Looking after their individual interests is referred to as _____.

2 With which type of management styles would you associate the following potential problems?

• Employees are demotivated because they feel that there is little room for them to think for themselves.

• Employees are demotivated because they feel that they are not being led or directed properly.

• Employees are demotivated because it is taking too long to arrive at decisions.

3 Suggest ways in which a manager can make his or her staff feel more valued in the workplace.

SECTION 1: Short-answer questions

1 Identify and explain TWO reasons why people work. [4]

2 Explain what is meant by 'maximum weekly working hours'. [3]

3 Identify and explain TWO types of human needs from Maslow's hierarchy. [4]

4 With reference to Maslow's hierarchy, analyse the levels of need satisfied by a teacher compared to a worker in a fast-food outlet. [4]

5 With reference to Maslow's hierarchy, analyse why working in teams may act as a motivator for workers. [4]

6 Explain the difference between overtime pay and bonus pay. [4]

7 Analyse TWO reasons why piece rate may not be a suitable method of pay for machine operators producing clothing according to individual customer orders and designs. [6]

8 Identify and explain TWO reasons why big companies frequently offer profit sharing schemes to their employees. [4]

9 State and explain ONE example of a fringe benefit that may be suitable in the following occupations:
   • shop or supermarket worker
   • car factory worker
   • airline stewardess. [6]

10 Analyse why a company vehicle, offered as a fringe benefit, may help an individual meet one of Maslow's higher-level needs. [4]

11 Identify and explain TWO reasons why every business aims to have a well-motivated workforce. [4]

12 Identify and explain TWO factors that could increase job satisfaction for workers in a telephone call centre. [4]

13 Identify and explain TWO benefits to owners of a business of introducing job rotation for employees. [4]

14 Analyse how a well-conducted yearly appraisal interview may motivate an employee. [4]

15 Good managers use different styles according to the situation. Using the example of a large restaurant business, identify and explain which management style you would recommend in each of these scenarios.
   • There is a fire and the manager needs his staff to take all the customers out of the building.
   • The restaurant manager wants to find out staff ideas on new menu items.
   • The restaurant manager wants all staff to comply with health and safety rules, such as hand-washing and tying back long hair. [6]

16 Analyse ONE reason why employees may be demotivated under a laissez-faire leader. [4]

SECTION 2: Longer-answer questions

The Sea Breeze Hotel

Jon is the newly appointed manager of the Sea Breeze Hotel and restaurant, which has been acquired by a new owner. The hotel has become run down in recent years, partly due to a poor manager, who was absent much of the time and failed to give staff direction and leadership. When he was present he was overpowering, shouting orders at the staff and keeping for himself any extra gratuities left by guests. Jon has a major job on his hands and knows he must start by winning the respect of the hotel workers. His first move on taking over was to call a staff meeting and explain that he would be consulting his staff over proposed changes and emphasising a new focus on 'excellent' customer service.

1 Describe the management style of the previous manager of the Sea Breeze Hotel. [4]

2 Identify and explain TWO reasons for the current low staff morale. [4]

3 Analyse TWO ways in which Jon can win the respect of the hotel staff. [6]

4 Do you agree that Jon's consultative management style will lead to an improvement in the guests' experience at the Sea Breeze? Explain your answer. [6]

5 Jon is proposing to offer workers an hourly rate of pay, plus a performance-related bonus, based on comments from guests and his own observations of customer service standards. To what extent will this help to raise standards? [6]

The Rickshaw Taxi Company

The Rickshaw Taxi Company's vehicles are a common sight on the streets of Bangkok, Thailand. The drivers lease their cars or rickshaws from the company, making a monthly payment, which includes the right to trade using the company name. Drivers of the company must give 3 months' notice to end the arrangement, except in the case of customer complaints, when drivers may be dismissed instantly. Drivers choose their own hours, driving around the streets waiting to be flagged down by passengers or waiting in popular locations such as outside hotels and railway stations. Passenger fares are set by the company and displayed inside the rickshaws so that customers can see how much they should pay. The company keeps the vehicles in good working order and offers training to new drivers. The Rickshaw Taxi Company enjoys a good reputation, due to its cheerful and helpful drivers.

1 Explain why it would be difficult for the government to regulate maximum working hours for the rickshaw drivers. [4]

2 Identify and explain TWO factors that determine how much income the drivers earn in a week. [4]

3 Analyse ONE advantage and ONE disadvantage to the Rickshaw Taxi Company drivers of the leasing scheme. [6]

4 To what extent do you agree that the Rickshaw Taxi Company helps its drivers to reach higher-level needs in Maslow's hierarchy? [6]

5 Do you think that the motivation of the drivers is mainly extrinsic or mainly intrinsic? Explain your answer. [6]

The factory boss

Michael Chung runs an electronics factory for a large multinational corporation near Shanghai, China. His large workforce is low-skilled, as jobs in the factory are mainly routine production-line tasks. The production lines are housed in a large building with artificial light, and progress against daily targets is displayed on screens, visible to all workers. Breaks are regulated and one meal is provided to each worker during each 10-hour shift.

Michael passes down orders via senior managers, but allows no discussion about business issues. Michael says, 'I pay all my staff above the average piece rate for this type of job and they do as I tell them. It is the best way to run this business.'

1 Identify and explain TWO reasons why piece rate payment is suitable for this type of business. [4]

2 Identify and explain TWO factors that may motivate workers to continue their employment at the factory. [4]

3 Describe Michael's management style. [4]

4 To what extent do you agree with Michael that this is the best way to manage his staff? [6]

5 Analyse TWO ways in which Michael could improve the motivation of his senior managers. [6]

11 The workforce

11.1

The recruitment and selection process

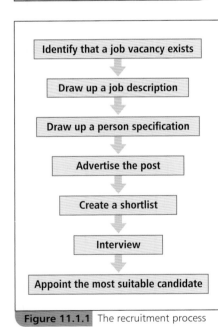

Identify that a job vacancy exists

Draw up a job description

Draw up a person specification

Advertise the post

Create a shortlist

Interview

Appoint the most suitable candidate

Figure 11.1.1 The recruitment process

Recruitment

Recruitment involves attracting the right standard of applicants to apply for vacancies. Figure 11.1.1 summarises the typical stages in the recruitment process.

Recruiting may be *internal* or *external*. Internal recruiting means employing someone already working for the organisation: this may mean promotion. External recruitment involves appointing someone from outside the organisation.

The table shows the advantages of the two types of recruitment.

Advantages of internal recruitment	Advantages of external recruitment
There is less risk because the employer already knows the person and their capabilities.	New ideas are brought into the organisation from outside.
The cost of advertising is saved, so the recruitment process is cheaper. (In some countries and organisations, however, equal opportunities legislation means that all positions have to be advertised.)	Advertising externally may reach more widely into the business community (e.g. a teacher might be attracted to an educational publishing company and bring useful experience and knowledge to the job).
The opportunity for promotion within the organisation encourages people to work hard.	Internal jealousies are avoided from promotion.
Induction costs are saved.	

Advertising the job

Once a business is clear about the job it is offering, it can draw up an advertisement for the post. How this is set out depends on:

- who the business is trying to attract
- where the advert is going to be placed – that is, what media will be used (newspaper, radio, TV, website, etc.).

A good job advertisement will include the following features:

Feature	Description
Job description	The major requirements of the job, setting out the key responsibilities and tasks involved
What the business does	A brief description of the business and its activities
Location	Where the job will be based
Salary expectation	Figures are not always necessary, but an indication of salary level should be given
Address and contact	How to contact the recruiter (e.g. e-mail address)
Closing date	This gives candidates the time limit for applications
Qualifications	Certain jobs require a minimum entrance qualification
Experience	Experience that candidates should have
Fringe benefits	Mention additional benefits (e.g. company car)
Organisational identity	A logo or badge associated with the company

Selection

Selection involves choosing the most suitable applicant for a vacancy. Screening applicants is a very important part of this process. Figure 11.1.2 illustrates the various stages in screening applicants.

The recruiters put together a shortlist of candidates who most closely meet the person specification for the job. These candidates will be invited for interview. This may involve a panel of interviewers, who will ask questions and score candidates on the extent to which they meet the specification.

The interview process may take one or two days. As well as being interviewed, the candidates may be asked to take tests and perform tasks: these are considered good indicators of a person's ability to carry out the job, and of whether a person will fit into an organisation. An aptitude test might be set; this is a practical test to assess suitability for a post. For example, a prospective airline pilot might be tested for reaction time to moving objects. Another test might be a psychometric test, used widely for management posts and some jobs with international companies. This is a personality test in which candidates are asked for their views on a particular subject, or to indicate how they would act in a given situation. The test may be carried out with pencil and paper or online.

The recruiting process for jobs at a lower grade may simply involve a short interview of candidates.

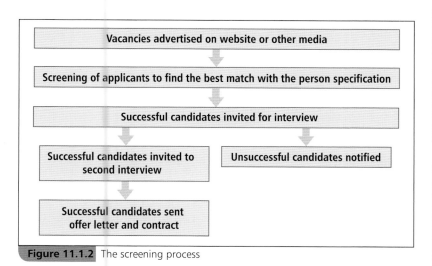

Figure 11.1.2 The screening process

DID YOU KNOW?

In most countries, equal opportunities laws govern recruitment and selection. All candidates should be asked the same questions and not be favoured on the grounds of, for example, sex, race, ethnic group, disability or being an existing employee of the company.

ACTIVITY

Identify the main stages that were involved in the recruitment of a friend or relative who has recently started a job. How closely do these stages mirror the stages outlined in this chapter?

KEY POINTS

1 Recruitment is the process of identifying the need for a new employee, defining the job, and finding and selecting the right person to do that job.

2 Recruitment may be internal or external.

3 Creating a well-structured job advertisement is important for attracting good candidates.

4 Companies also create a person specification and job description for recruitment purposes.

SUMMARY QUESTIONS

1 What are the most important steps in recruiting and selecting a new employee to join an organisation?

2 Why does an organisation shortlist candidates?

3 Outline the difference between external and internal recruitment. For a food-exporting company, what would be the benefits of recruiting a new sales manager:
   • internally?   • externally?

The job description

When a business starts to grow, it may need to employ new staff. From time to time, it will need to replace existing staff who leave or retire. Whenever a business recruits, it is essential to set out a clear description of what the job entails. The table sets out the information that should be included in a **job description**.

Title of the job	Indication of what the job involves and the level of responsibility (e.g. sales manager, South East Asia)
Department and location of the job	Organisational department and its location (e.g. marketing and sales department, Beijing, China)
General terms of what is involved in carrying out the job	Indication of what is involved in the post (Many job vacancies describe the job in fairly general terms, particularly if these might change over time.)
Responsible to whom	Who the employee will report to, their line manager
Responsible for whom	Other employees for whom the employee will be responsible and manage
Other responsibilities	Resources for which the employee will be responsible
Scope of the post	Sets out the level of the post (e.g. managerial)
Education and qualifications	The level of education required to carry out the post
Name of compiler and approver and date of issue	The person who designed the job description and the date on which the description was written

Here is an example of a simple job description for the role of a market researcher.

	ABC Markets, plc Job description
Job title	Senior Market Researcher
Department	Marketing, Accra, Ghana
Responsible to	Kojo Agyeman
Responsible for	Junior and part-time market researchers
Scope of the post	The market researcher's main role is to conduct interviews in line with guidance provided by the Head of Market Research
Responsibilities	The post holder is expected to: arrange interviews ask questions of interviewees record interviews on forms, on computer or on video carry out interviewing over the telephone keep accurate and detailed records.
Compiled by	Akwesi Sarpong (Market Research Manager)
Date	12 June 2010

ABC Markets Accra plc, Ghana
Person specification

Post title: Senior Market Researcher

Criteria	Essential	Desirable
Qualifications/ knowledge	A business studies university-level qualification (The successful candidate will have successfully completed at least 3 years of study at university.) Information technology qualification – including information processing and presentation	
Work-related experience	1 year's experience of working in a market research role	Experience of having managed a small market research team
Skills/abilities and special attributes	Good planning and organisation skills Ability to prioritise tasks Excellent communication skills Team-working skills	Team-leadership skills Advanced mathematics skills

Job or person specification

A **job specification** (sometimes referred to as a person specification) sets out the skills, characteristics and attributes needed for a particular job. Job descriptions and person specifications then provide the basis for job advertisements. They help job applicants and post holders know what is expected of them. As they are sent to anyone applying for jobs, they should:

- contain enough information to attract suitable people
- act as a checking device for the business to make sure that applicants with the right skills are chosen for interview.

The job specification gives a list of requirements related to the person doing the job. It will include an introduction, giving details of the job title, post reference number and management responsibilities. It will then set out the attributes that the organisation wants that person to have – for example, their type of personality or educational level. Typically, there will be two columns. One column will set out the essential requirements, and the other the desirable requirements. In selecting for the job, the interview panel will choose someone who has all the essential requirements. If they have to choose between two or more candidates who fit all the essential requirements, they will use the desirable requirements.

Different media for advertising jobs

Jobs can be advertised in various media:

- Websites can target local, national and international job seekers.
- Newspapers and magazines are useful for targeting applicants. National newspapers often advertise certain types of jobs on particular days. Magazines are often targeted at special interest groups e.g. accountants or marketers who may be looking for jobs.
- Local radio can attract local recruits, particularly in urban areas.
- Vacancy boards/noticeboards in prominent locations such as supermarkets are useful for recruitment.
- Other suitable media include adverts on the sides of trains, buses and in bus and train stations.

KEY POINTS

1 A job description should set out clearly what a job entails.

2 A job specification sets out the skills, characteristics and attributes needed for a specific job.

3 The job description and job specification can be used as a basis for framing interview questions and suitable tests.

SUMMARY QUESTIONS

1 Explain the differences between a job description and a job specification.

2 Draw up a job description and a person specification for a business studies teacher.

3 What would be the most suitable media for advertising a senior marketing post in an international company?

The main types of training

Training is the process through which the employees learn the knowledge and skills needed to do their job well. Because modern jobs are continually changing, employees usually need to receive training throughout their working lives. For example, they may need new training to keep up to date with technological developments, or with new laws that affect the business. Figure 11.3.1 shows the two main types of training.

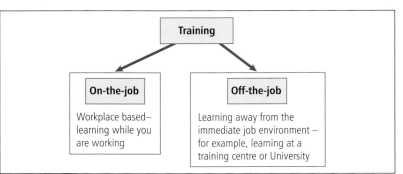

Figure 11.3.1 Two main types of training: on-the-job and off-the-job

The main purposes of training

Training is important for both employees and managers. Through training, individuals are better prepared to carry out their work tasks. The main purposes of training are explored below.

- **Induction:** this introduces an employee to a new job and to the company and/or the workplace. It will usually include an overview of the company, but there will be information specific to certain industries, such as health and safety training for employees involved in the manual handling of goods or driving forklift trucks. Another important part of induction is getting to know other people and being introduced to company procedures.

- **Understanding the job requirements:** initial training should focus on making sure that an employee is able to fulfil the basic requirements of the job.

- **Development of job skills:** specialist skills will need to be developed to enable an employee to do a job well. These might be interacting with customers or using important IT applications.

- **Broadening knowledge of the business:** the more trainees know about the wider activities of the business and the nature of its work, the more they will be able to help the organisation meet its objectives.

- **Changing attitudes and skills:** organisations frequently have to make changes. Training needs to be designed to help individuals adapt to new attitudes which move the organisation forward.

In Australia, there is a network of 150 group training organisations. These employ over 40,000 apprentices. (An apprenticeship is a structured process for training in a set of skills that is recognised by a particular industry.)

Apprenticeships enable young people to learn a skill, working for a company for a short or long period of time

There are group training organisations for most industries in Australia, including automotive, construction, electrical, plumbing, engineering, horticulture, community service, retail and hospitality. The group training organisations carry out preliminary training at the apprentices' premises. The Master Plumbers Group Training Organisation runs workshops for apprentice plumbers. When the apprentices are sufficiently skilled, they are taken on by plumbing businesses. The apprentices will then work for the employer for a set period of time. This may be for just a week or for several years. Trainees can work towards particular qualifications. The employer pays a part of their wage, with the government topping this up. The group training organisation handles all the paperwork and payment of the apprentices. They only provide apprentices to companies that they feel are competent to carry out work-based training.

Questions

1 In what ways do the group training schemes involve on-the-job training?

2 How do they additionally involve off-the-job training?

3 How do employers and apprentices in Australia benefit from the group training schemes?

Training is important for employees at every level in the organisation and at every stage of their career. New employees will learn how to fit into the organisation and how to develop the skills they need. Experienced employees can upgrade their knowledge and skills.

Management training is also important. Managers need to learn how to manage and motivate others. They also need to learn complex job skills and keep up to date with the latest developments in their field. A new manager will often work for a few months in a number of departments in a company to gain an understanding of how the various parts of the organisation fit together.

SUMMARY QUESTIONS

1 Martha completed a university degree in business studies and then went to work as an accountant for 2 years. She now wants to become a business studies teacher. What types of on-the-job and off-the-job training would be helpful to Martha in preparing her to become a skilled business studies teacher?

2 Prakesh is about to start a job at a supermarket involving a range of general duties that include shelf stacking and managing a cash till. What sort of induction activities should Prakesh be given in his first week at work? Explain why you have suggested these activities.

3 What sort of training would you expect to receive for a job that you are currently interested in doing once you leave school? Where is this training likely to take place?

KEY POINTS

1 Training improves employee knowledge and skills and helps an organisation to have effective workers with the right skills.

2 On-the-job training takes place internally within an organisation. Off-the-job training takes place externally.

3 Induction training enables new employees to settle in quickly and learn their responsibilities.

4 Ongoing training keeps employees up to date with new developments and enables them to learn new skills.

5 Management training enables motivation and effective management of employees.

Dismissal and redundancy

Explain the difference between dismissal and redundancy.

- Use examples to illustrate the difference.

Appreciate why the workforce of a business may need to be reduced.

- Understand the circumstances when downsizing a workforce occurs (e.g. automation, closure of a factory).

The global economic crisis in 2008–9 led to many companies creating redundancies by closing down plants and cutting their workforces

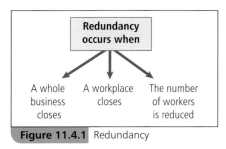

Figure 11.4.1 Redundancy

Employers cannot guarantee everyone a job for life. There are times when a company has to close down all or part of its operations because they are not profitable; in these situations, jobs will have to be cut.

At other times, an employer may have to dismiss an employee – for example, because he or she is not competent in their job, or because they have behaved in an unacceptable way. In all countries, there are laws with which employers must comply when they dismiss employees. A distinction is made between fair and unfair dismissal.

Dismissal

Dismissal occurs when an employer terminates a worker's employment contract. There are many reasons for dismissal, which may be fair or unfair. Employees can be fairly dismissed for, say, poor timekeeping, stealing company property, bullying and harassing other workers or criminal damage to the workplace. The exact legal requirements vary from country to country. There are instances, however, when law courts decide that unfair dismissal has occurred. A worker might prove, for example, that the true cause for dismissal was some form of prejudice, which would be unfair.

Redundancy

Redundancy occurs when a job role is no longer required. The person in that role therefore loses their job.

Redundancy involves either the closure of a business as a whole, closure of a particular workplace where the employee was employed, or a reduction in the workforce. As a result of redundancy, employees are no longer required to perform particular job roles.

It is important that managers handle redundancy very carefully. Poor handling can lead to bad feelings among those made redundant, as well as among remaining workers and in the community as a whole. At the least, managers must make sure that they comply with employment law, particularly in relation to fairness. Typically, the law will set out requirements for a redundancy payment; this is related to how long the employee has worked for a company.

Why do redundancies occur?

Redundancy may occur when a business downsizes and reduces its labour force. This happened in most countries across the world in 2008 and 2009. A world economic crisis resulted from poor decisions in the banking industry (see Unit 13.9) and millions of people worldwide lost their jobs. Some businesses shut down, others closed down some of the plant, while many others made some of their workforce redundant. In manufacturing, many factories, particularly in the automotive industries, were closed. At the same time, many services jobs were cut – for example, there were many bank closures. In some cases, this involved the closure of branches of a bank; in others, the whole bank was closed. The American bank Lehman Brothers was a famous example.

Retrenchment means cutting down expenditure to become more financially stable. In many companies, the wage bill accounts for 70 per cent of costs, so this is often the easiest area to reduce. Retrenchment, therefore, often refers to reducing the labour force, and the word was seen several times in newspapers in 2009.

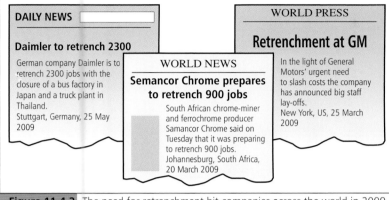

DAILY NEWS

Daimler to retrench 2300

German company Daimler is to retrench 2300 jobs with the closure of a bus factory in Japan and a truck plant in Thailand.
Stuttgart, Germany, 25 May 2009

WORLD NEWS

Semancor Chrome prepares to retrench 900 jobs

South African chrome-miner and ferrochrome producer Samancor Chrome said on Tuesday that it was preparing to retrench 900 jobs.
Johannesburg, South Africa, 20 March 2009

WORLD PRESS

Retrenchment at GM

In the light of General Motors' urgent need to slash costs the company has announced big staff lay-offs.
New York, US, 25 March 2009

Figure 11.4.2 The need for retrenchment hit companies across the world in 2009

Other causes of redundancies are:

- Focus: sometimes, directors of a company believe that it has grown too large, is trying to do too many things and, as a result, is not performing well. The directors will then seek to focus the business on what it does best and announce redundancies in 'non-core activities' or 'non-core markets'. So a company that has retail outlets in India, China, the United States and Norway might decide that the Norwegian market is too small and decide to focus on the other three areas.

- Automation: machinery may take over work previously carried out by people. Computer systems often reduce numbers of staff. Most banks, for example, offer phone services so that a customer can call the bank and hear a message giving details of their accounts. Phone messages are automatically generated by computer rather than a human operator.

EXAM TIP

Understand the difference between redundancy and dismissal: a worker is made redundant because their job has disappeared. Workers made redundant may get financial help, while those who are dismissed do not.

ACTIVITY

Find out about the law covering dismissal from work in your country. For what reasons can an employee be fairly dismissed? In what situations would the law courts decide that the dismissal was unfair? What does an employer need to do before they can 'fairly' dismiss an employee? Does an employee need to be warned before they can be dismissed?

KEY POINTS

1 A business cannot guarantee a job for life. At times, it may need to reduce the number of employees.

2 Dismissal takes place when an employee's contract of employment is terminated (ended). There are legal requirements relating to dismissal.

3 Redundancy results when a business shuts down, closes part of its operations or cuts down the workforce. There are legal requirements relating to redundancies.

SUMMARY QUESTIONS

1 Write down definitions of the following terms: redundancy, dismissal, retrenchment, downsizing.

2 Provide two examples of situations in which an employee might be made redundant. Then provide an example of a situation where an employee might be dismissed for reasons other than redundancy.

3 In your view, would the following examples illustrate fair or unfair dismissal? Justify your answers.

- A business sustains losses for several years and is forced to close one of its factories. In consultation with the trade union, it agrees which of these factories to close. In line with legal requirements, it provides redundancy pay, depending on how long employees have worked for the company.

- A company needs to make cutbacks because it has lost a major order. It informs the employees that those who have been working the longest will be made redundant because their wages are too high.

Unit 11 — Practice exam questions

SECTION 1: Short-answer questions

1 Identify and explain TWO reasons why a business may need to recruit employees. [4]

2 What is the difference between internal and external recruitment? [3]

3 Using the example of a call centre business, identify and explain TWO reasons why a team leader's position may be recruited internally. [4]

4 Using the example of a market research company, identify why a new researcher may be recruited externally. [4]

5 Explain why a business may create a shortlist for candidates to interview. [4]

6 Analyse TWO reasons why a business may fail to recruit a suitable candidate for a senior manager position. [6]

7 Explain, with examples, the difference between a job description and a person specification. [4]

8 State FOUR important pieces of information that must be included in a job advertisement. [4]

9 Identify and explain appropriate places where the following jobs might be advertised.

- A bakery shop assistant
- A senior accountant
- A city taxi driver [6]

10 For each of your answers to Question 9, explain a test, other than a face-to-face interview, that would be appropriate to help in the selection process. [6]

11 Explain why 'employees in the modern world need training throughout their working lives'. [4]

12 Explain the difference between on-the-job and off-the-job training. [4]

13 Explain why apprenticeships are a popular method of training in occupations such as electricians and plumbers. [4]

14 Analyse why induction training is so important for new factory employees. [4]

15 Analyse ONE possible disadvantage to a business of gaining a reputation for offering the best training in the industry. [4]

16 Explain, with examples, TWO differences between redundancy and dismissal. [4]

17 Analyse ONE objective a business may be trying to achieve by making some middle-management roles redundant. [4]

SECTION 2: Longer-answer questions

The new low-cost airline

Skyways is a new privately owned airline, based in Malaysia. The company has a growing fleet of Airbus planes and is expanding its network of routes on a weekly basis. Fares are low, which is encouraging new air travellers. Skyways is finding it difficult to recruit suitable cabin crew staff, as there is a shortage of trained personnel available, so the airline is now looking abroad for pilots and senior crew. Skyways have also introduced their own staff training programme for more junior customer service agents and ground staff.

1 Identify and explain TWO reasons why Skyways needs to recruit trained staff. [4]

2 Identify TWO items that may appear in the job description and TWO items from a likely person specification for a Skyways cabin crew vacancy. [4]

3 Analyse TWO possible business problems that may occur as a result of Skyways recruiting air crew from other countries. [6]

4 Identify and explain THREE tests, other than a face-to-face interview, that Skyways might use to screen job applicants. [6]

5 Skyways' general manager has expressed the view: 'If we spend a lot of money on staff training it will be wasted, as staff will leave for jobs with other airlines'. Do you agree with him? Justify your answer. [6]

Crisis at the Orange Grove Drinks Company

The Orange Grove Drinks Company is a major employer in a small Spanish town. Orange juice and other soft drinks are processed and bottled by machine, before being stored in warehouses and sent for sale throughout Europe. However, the company has been losing market share to big multinational companies and the modern taste for smoothie fruit drinks, which at present the company does not provide. There has also been a problem of contamination at the factory, as a result of a group of workers failing to sterilise equipment – fortunately, a quality check picked up this mistake before the contaminated juice was bottled. The business is now in bad financial trouble and the banks are threatening to withdraw support. Management has calculated that they will need to cut the workforce by 20 per cent to save on costs.

1 Explain the term 'major employer' in this case. [2]

2 Analyse why Orange Grove may consider dismissing those individuals who caused the factory contamination. [4]

3 Analyse TWO possible ways that the management of Orange Grove could select jobs for redundancy. [6]

4 To what extent do you agree that all employees should receive regular training in health and safety? [6]

5 Orange Grove is trying to get a local government grant to help it retain all the existing staff and develop new production techniques. Do you agree that the company should receive money from local taxpayers? [6]

The ICT skills training company

The TeachIT company is a privately owned enterprise in Kenya. It provides business with staff ICT training at their own training centre in Nairobi. The company also receives money from the local Ministry of Education to advise on ICT education in schools. The company is successful, but is also becoming a victim of its success, as children are leaving school and starting work with good ICT skills, so there is therefore less need for TeachIT's services. The company is now trying to diversify into training in leadership skills, as their market research indicates that this is a growing area of need in business.

1 Identify and explain TWO possible reasons why businesses may outsource their ICT training to companies such as TeachIT. [4]

2 Identify and explain TWO reasons why ICT training in schools may be a priority for many governments around the world. [4]

3 Analyse ONE advantage and ONE disadvantage for business of this type of off-the-job training in ICT skills. [4]

4 Evaluate the view that 'all managers will benefit from training in leadership and team-building skills'. [6]

5 TeachIT's managing director tells his customers that 'good staff training is one sure way to business success'. To what extent do you agree with him? [6]

12 Reasons for regulations

12.1 The impact of unregulated business activity

The growth of air travel in the 21st century brings in revenues to the airline businesses. However, this is also at a cost, as planes release harmful toxic greenhouse gases close to the ozone layer

Costs and benefits

We have seen how businesses need to spend money to set up – in other words, they have costs. Their owners hope, however, that these costs will bring benefits, both **private** – that is, to them – and social – that is, to their customers and others in the community. Look at the case study to find out more about this.

CASE STUDY	Sylvia Simms' laundry

Sylvia Simms has recently set up a street-corner laundry, washing clothes for local people in her neighbourhood. She charges low prices and offers customers a 24-hour wash, dry, iron and return of their clothes.

Sylvia has made a list of the costs and benefits of her laundry.

Private costs (to Sylvia)	Private benefits (to Sylvia)
The financial costs (paying staff, buying equipment and materials)	The revenues (sums of money paid for having clothes washed) from customers
Social costs (to other members of society)	**Social benefits (to other members of society)**
Traffic congestion from people delivering clothes	Employment for people working in the laundry
The smell of the laundry and pollution caused by pouring a lot of soapy water into the drains	Extra income for other local shopkeepers
	The availability of a convenient laundry

Questions

1 What is the difference between a social cost and a private cost?

2 What is the difference between a social benefit and a private benefit?

3 Can you suggest other social costs and benefits that could be added to the table?

Externalities

An **externality** is the result of business activity that is not taken into account in normal business decision making. In other words, it is the external, or 'outside', effect of a decision. For example, a new local shop may be very convenient for a lot of people, but it may also put another one nearby out of business. The favourable effect is a *positive* externality. The effect on the rival shop is a *negative* externality. Here are some other negative externalities.

- pollution, accidents and congestion from too many vehicles on the roads
- obesity and lack of fitness from eating too much of the wrong type of food
- drug dependence on certain medicines
- greenhouse gas production and noise pollution from air transport
- exploitation – that is, businesses paying low wages (or using child labour) in order to increase their profits.

In the case study, Sylvia's laundry may produce both positive and negative externalities:

- (negative) on the environment (e.g. water polluted with detergents entering the drains)
- (positive) for people (e.g. customers who benefit from a laundry service)
- (positive and negative) on the community (i.e. people who live near to the laundry have the social cost of traffic pollution, but there is also the social benefit of extra custom for other local shopkeepers).

Business activities also result in positive externalities: shops and restaurants in busy cities create attractive sites and encourage visitors. Business advertisements in newspapers and on television help television companies to pay for interesting programmes and provide news stories. These business activities thus have positive spillover effects.

Government action is required at a local, national and international level to make sure that a fairer system exists to prevent, or at least reduce, negative externalities. In Unit 13, we look at ways in which government can intervene to create rules covering what is acceptable business behaviour. Governments also encourage activities with positive externalities – for example, by partially subsidising local carnivals, or encouraging farmers to use techniques that make the local environment more attractive.

ACTIVITY

Working in groups of two or three, identify an example of negative externalities caused by a business or businesses in your region. Make a presentation to the rest of your class, describing the impact of the business activity on people, society and the environment. Is the government or anyone else doing anything to try to control the harmful effect that the business is having?

KEY POINTS

1 Businesses often make decisions that have an effect on others, including society, the environment and people with whom the business comes into contact.

2 Some of these effects are positive externalities; others create negative externalities.

3 An important role of government is to make sure that businesses are made accountable for their negative externalities.

SUMMARY QUESTIONS

1 Give an example of a business decision that might have a harmful effect on the environment and specific groups of people. Explain what these negative effects might be.

2 What do you think that the role of the government should be in dealing with negative externalities?

3 Why do businesses create negative externalities? Illustrate your answer by providing two examples.

The impact of business decisions on people, the economy and the environment

Explain why intervention in business activity is required so that social and economic objectives of the state can be achieved.

- Give examples of intervention to support and control the impact of business activity on people, the economy and the environment.
- Use the examples to show how outcomes differ (following intervention) and are more in line with the objectives of the state (e.g. to create employment and minimise resource depletion).

In many countries, government legislation controls industrial waste and pollution. Some waste is buried in landfill sites and businesses pay a tax to have it processed

Intervention in business activity

A government intervenes when it takes actions or makes decisions that affect businesses and other members of society.

In some countries, the government intervenes in nearly every aspect of business life, whereas in other countries, it rarely gets involved (see Unit 4.1).

Social and economic objectives

In many countries, the government is chosen by the people in elections. People vote for a particular organised group (a political party) to represent them. The government then establishes social and economic objectives. In about 20 per cent of countries, there is a lot of freedom in the election of the government. In a further 50 per cent, there is some freedom. In the remaining 30 per cent, there are no elections.

The table below gives some examples of objectives.

Economic objectives	Social objectives
To make sure that more people have jobs	To make sure that all children are educated in schools
To make sure that the economy grows from year to year, so that citizens become better-off	To look after the health and well-being of citizens
To protect consumers and business from unfair practices by other businesses	To protect the local, national and international environment

To achieve these objectives, the government intervenes in some way in business activity.

Types of government intervention

The government intervenes in three main ways: public provision of goods and services; creating rules and laws; and taxing and subsidising activities.

Public provision of goods and services

In many countries, governments own and run essential industries like rail (e.g. Indian Railways) and utilities (e.g. gas, electricity and water supply in China). In addition, they may run their own international airline (e.g. Singapore Airways) and parts of the telecommunications network, as well as funding a radio and television broadcasting service (e.g. the British Broadcasting Corporation). Government provision creates jobs for millions of people and ensures that a country's essential industries are financed and maintained. In some countries, the state education (schools and universities) and health service (hospitals, surgeries and clinics) provide these essential services to people who would not be able to afford to pay for them.

When a government takes over a company or all the companies in an industry, this is **nationalisation**. When it sells off a state-run industry to shareholders, this is **privatisation**. Services such as education and health run by a government are public services.

Figure 12.2.1 Privatisation and nationalisation

Creating rules and laws

Governments create laws at local and national levels, and take part in creating international law. **Regulation** refers to the creation of these rules; deregulation refers to reductions in the number of rules.

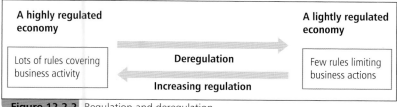

Figure 12.2.2 Regulation and deregulation

Too much regulation limits the freedom of business to make decisions: businesses become anxious in case they unknowingly break the law. Too little regulation can lead to abuse – for example, of employees, other businesses and customers, and the environment.

Taxing and subsidising activities

The main purpose of raising taxes is to create revenue for the government. The government can then use this money for social and economic objectives. For example, business and income taxes can be used to finance healthcare, education and building roads. Governments can raise taxes to discourage antisocial behaviour such as smoking, and then use that money for hospital care. Governments also subsidise some businesses, usually to encourage positive externalities. This involves providing funds, or subsidies, to encourage certain activities. This might be growing important agricultural crops or introducing environmentally friendly technology (see page 25).

(see page 25)

KEY POINTS

1 Intervention refers to governments becoming involved in economic and social activity.

2 Governments intervene in order to pursue their economic and social objectives.

3 Increasing intervention can make it easier to run a business; too much interference can make it more difficult.

EXAM TIP

A private business has different objectives from one owned and run by the government. Sometimes the profit motive puts a business in conflict with the social and economic objectives of the government.

SUMMARY QUESTIONS

1 Explain what is meant by government intervention, using a specific local example to illustrate your point.

2 Explain whether the following actions would lead to increasing or decreasing government intervention in an economy.
   • Nationalisation of the oil industry
   • Decreasing the number of rules affecting business
   • Increasing subsidies
   • Raising taxes
   • Increasing deregulation

3 Identify and outline:
   • two economic objectives of government.
   • two social objectives of government.

Who intervenes and how

Friends of the Earth helped to organise 'waste pickers' to protest in South Africa. Their action led to the South African government passing laws supporting the rights of such groups to earn a living from picking waste from waste tips

DID YOU KNOW?

Throughout the 1970s and 1980s, anti-apartheid campaigners put pressure on customers to stop using Barclays Bank. The bank had many branches in South Africa, where the system of apartheid treated people well or badly depending on their race. This pressure finally influenced Barclays, in 1986, to sell off its South African business.

The main methods of government intervention

In Unit 12.2 we saw that one of the main methods of government intervention is through regulation. The main way that government does this is through legislation – that is, creating laws. In every country, many laws affect business. Examples include:

- who can set up a company, and the steps required to set one up
- what accounts a company is required to present to shareholders, and when
- what type of products and services it is legal to produce
- laws governing how production can be carried out (e.g. covering health and safety at work)
- how a company should manage its waste and pollution
- how much packaging is acceptable
- what constitutes reasonable and fair advertising
- how firms are allowed to compete with each other.

Laws covering these areas are usually national laws. However, if a country is part of a larger political group, such as the European Union, companies within member countries will also have to comply with laws that are created centrally to govern all the member states.

Governments also work together to create intergovernmental treaties, with laws that may apply worldwide. Most countries have agreed on environmental legislation, that carbon emissions from industrial and other activities should be limited. International agreements have been created to set limits and targets for individual countries.

Other examples of intergovernmental treaties that affect business relate to:

- intellectual property rights –to prevent copying someone else's ideas, such as in films or music, or a well-known brand name or logo
- the movement of goods and services: the World Trade Organization (WTO) has encouraged countries to agree to cut tariffs and quotas (see Unit 4.4) on internationally traded goods; the WTO takes action against countries imposing restrictions that have not been internationally agreed.

Implementing legislation

Governments create laws, but it is up to the courts and policing bodies to make sure that the laws are upheld. Figure 12.3.1 shows some of this policing activity.

Here is an example of intervention: in all countries there are laws against resale price maintenance, which occurs if manufacturers insist that sellers agree on prices for their products. This stops competition between retailers. If officials discover that a manufacturer is trying to do this, the courts will impose heavy fines and may imprison company directors. Breaking the law in this way causes bad publicity for a business in the country's newspapers, and on radio and television.

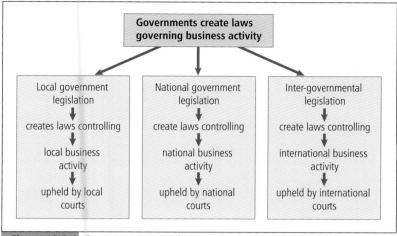

Figure 12.3.1 Governments create laws governing business activity

The sportswear company Nike was in the news for working with local factories in South East Asia that employed underage child labour.

Intervention by other agencies

As well as government and the courts, other organised bodies intervene to stop social and environmental harm by businesses.

- Trade unions are organisations set up to represent employees (see Unit 13.2). They put pressure on business to provide fair and decent conditions for workers.
- **Pressure groups** try to influence the government and business. They may be a few people complaining about noise from a local factory, or a large environmental group like Greenpeace, campaigning on environmental issues worldwide.

Well-known pressure groups like Greenpeace and Friends of the Earth have had a major impact on the activities of governments and multinational companies. They draw attention to actions that threaten the environment and people's general well-being. Other pressure groups campaign for consumer rights, or against the low pay of poor workers in developing countries. Friends of the Earth has successfully helped the microbusiness of waste pickers in South Africa and India, to defend their rights to recycle waste from refuse tips.

ACTIVITY

Identify a pressure group that is active in your own country. What are the objectives of this pressure group? Who do they put pressure on: governments, business or both? What are the results of their actions?

KEY POINTS

1 Government intervention affects business through local, national and international laws.

2 Laws are implemented through the courts and other policing authorities.

3 Failure to comply with laws can lead to fines and public shame for a business.

4 Business also needs to pay attention to groups such as trade unions and pressure groups.

SUMMARY QUESTIONS

1 What is legislation? Provide examples of three types of legislation that affect business.

2 How are laws that affect business implemented? What sorts of penalties can be imposed on business for failing to comply with legislation?

3 What is a pressure group? Why is it important for businesses to pay attention to suggestions put forward by pressure groups?

SECTION 1: Short-answer questions

1 Identify and explain TWO objectives that a government may try to achieve by regulating business activity. [4]

2 Explain the difference between private costs and social costs in the context of business activity. [3]

3 Explain the difference between private benefits and social benefits in the context of business activity. [3]

4 Identify and explain ONE social cost and ONE social benefit that might result from a new shopping centre on the outskirts of town. [4]

5 Explain why externalities are also sometimes called 'spillover effects'. [3]

6 Analyse TWO reasons why it may be difficult to calculate a figure for externalities caused by business. [6]

7 Explain, with examples, the part that organisations such as Greenpeace may play in cutting down negative externalities caused by large business organisations. [4]

8 Identify and explain TWO reasons why communication difficulties in a large organisation may lead to diseconomies of scale. [4]

9 Explain how the following organisations may give rise to positive externalities.
   • a government recycling scheme
   • a new school in a rural area
   • a vaccination programme against malaria. [6]

10 Analyse, with examples, why working towards an economic objective may help the government of your country meet a social objective. [6]

11 Explain why governments in many countries undertake the provision of public transport services. [4]

12 Identify and explain TWO reasons why organisations in the government sector may not aim to make a profit. [4]

13 Explain, with examples, the difference between regulation and deregulation in an industry of your choice in your country. [4]

14 Analyse why firms in a highly regulated industry may face higher costs of production. [4]

15 Analyse why many governments around the world impose high taxation on the sale of cigarettes. [4]

16 Identify and explain THREE ways in which the government in your country intervenes to protect:
   • workers
   • consumers. [12]

SECTION 2: Longer-answer questions

The Olympic sports facilities

The government in Brazil is set to build a number of new sporting facilities to host the Olympic Games in 2016. Cities such as Rio de Janeiro have been identifying suitable locations, which will involve the use of land that is currently occupied by low-quality housing. There are no plans to rehouse the residents, as the buildings have been put up without permission.

Merchandising has also been discussed, as there is a large industry in Brazil producing imitation products. The government is determined that only licensed products will be allowed for sale as souvenirs of the games.

1 Identify and explain TWO social costs that may arise from the construction of the new sports facilities. [4]

2 Identify and explain TWO social benefits that may arise from the construction of the new sports facilities. [4]

3 Identify and explain THREE reasons why the government of Brazil wants to regulate the production of Olympic Games merchandise. *[6]*

4 To what extent do you agree that the Olympic games in Brazil may lead to long-term social benefits to the population? *[6]*

5 Charity campaigners are trying to persuade the government to give financial help to the previous residents whose homes are due to be demolished. To what extent do you agree that this should be considered? *[6]*

The textiles factory

Jing runs a fabric-dying factory by a river, close to Jakarta, Indonesia. Cotton cloth arrives in bulk and is then dyed in batches to a selection of traditional patterns. The work is unpleasant and hours are very long. Jing sometimes finds it difficult to find staff, so she often employees young workers, without checking if they are old enough to be employed. The factory is unpopular locally, due to several incidents where dye has spilled into the river, making the water undrinkable for cattle and killing the fish.

Jing has recently received a letter from the local government inspector, saying that he will be visiting in the near future to check that the business is complying with regulations about employment, pollution and health and safety. Jing is worried and thinks the factory may have to close.

1 Identify and explain TWO reasons why production processes in a business such as Jing's factory may be regulated by the government. *[4]*

2 Analyse why many governments legislate to prevent young children gaining employment in factories. *[4]*

3 Analyse ONE advantage and ONE disadvantage to Jing's employees of regulations about maximum working hours permitted. *[6]*

4 Jing has said: 'All these regulations will add to my costs and we will not gain any benefits'. To what extent do you agree? *[6]*

5 Evaluate the extent to which regulation against pollution can be used successfully against businesses such as Jing's. *[6]*

The new metro system

Bangalore residents are looking forward to the completion of their new metro system, which is due to revolutionise public transport in the city. The metro, which has cost many millions of rupees of public money, should cut down road traffic and reduce journey times in the city. As a result, pollution caused by traffic congestion should also reduce, making the city a much more pleasant place in which to live and work.

However, the disruption to traffic while the building project is going on has been great, and many residents are complaining about what they see as the slow progress of the work.

1 Identify and explain TWO objectives that the metro project may help the Bangalore government to achieve. *[4]*

2 Identify and explain TWO reasons why governments often fund public transport provision. *[4]*

3 Identify and explain ONE private cost and ONE private benefit that may arise from the metro project. *[4]*

4 Evaluate the extent to which the fares to be charged on the metro should reflect the construction costs. *[6]*

5 Analyse TWO other ways that traffic congestion and pollution may be reduced in big cities. *[4]*

Government planning regulations set out areas where shopping malls and other business premises can or cannot be set up

The government and location decisions

In 2006, the Indian government asked the Supreme Court to order businesses in the residential areas of Delhi to close. The government argued that businesses should be set up in business parks and shopping malls, away from residential areas. Initially, this involved closing down a number of businesses that had set up in residential areas. The ruling eventually proved to be unworkable, because many businesses continued to operate, but it shows how a government may try to affect the location of business.

In this case, the government was seeking to improve traffic flow and reduce traffic noise. However, it failed to realise that access to shops can be important for local people. In Delhi, there is a zoning system. A zone is an area where only certain types of activity can take place. There are zones for housing, zones for industry, retail zones and mixed zones. The city planning authorities decide where these zones are. Planning regulations are therefore very important in determining the location of industry. There are rules about:

- where different types of buildings and businesses can be located
- the size and acceptable structure of these buildings
- what types of building fit in with the local environment.

Grants and subsidies

A grant is money given by the government to a business for a particular purpose. It is a single payment and repayment is not expected. The grant might be for exporting, investment in machinery, or to encourage relocation. Often, a condition of receiving the grant is that the business has to contribute some funds as well.

One area where governments give grants is in the European Union countries. Certain areas are designated as needing additional support – usually because there is high unemployment. In parts of southern Italy, there are particularly high levels of unemployment and grants are given to businesses that choose to set up there.

A subsidy is money provided for firms over a longer term, to prevent decline and job losses in a certain industry. Subsidies to agricultural businesses in Europe and the US, for example, keep farmers in business and help to keep prices down. Subsidies might be in the form of tax breaks, loan guarantees or cheap land.

Figure 13.1.1 shows how grants, subsidies and planning regulations can work individually or collectively to encourage firms to locate, relocate or stay in a particular area.

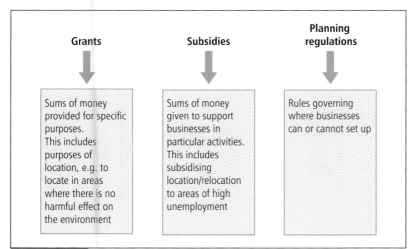

Figure 13.1.1 Grants, subsidies and planning regulations

ACTIVITY

Can you identify examples in your own country where the government has used grants, subsidies and planning regulations to influence where a business is set up? Make a presentation in a group of three students, explaining how, and why, the government has intervened in this way.

KEY POINTS

1 Governments encourage industry location in particular areas and away from other areas.

2 Grants and subsidies provide financial incentives. This helps to protect jobs.

3 Planning regulations set out where businesses can and cannot set up.

SUMMARY QUESTIONS

1 How are grants and subsidies:
   • similar?
   • different?

   How can the government use subsidies and grants to influence where businesses are located?

2 How do planning regulations affect where a business locates? Give an example to illustrate your answer.

3 Why is it important for government to intervene in the location and relocation of business?

Trade unions

Describe the work of trade unions.

- Understand the concept of a trade union.
- Show awareness of the benefits that union membership can provide for employees.

Show an awareness of how trade unions can influence business behaviour.

- Use examples to show how business behaviour might be modified in terms of levels of pay and treatment of employees.

French workers taking strike action and protesting to protect their jobs and their right to only work a maximum of 35 hours per week

Trade unions

A **trade union** is an association of the employees formed to protect and promote the interests of its members, and to achieve other jointly agreed aims. Trade unions are formed, financed and run by their members, who pay an annual subscription. The unions try to influence some of the decisions made by the owners and managers of a business.

In the UK, the National Union of Teachers (NUT) seeks to improve pay and conditions for teachers. In some countries, such as Germany, there are very large trade unions that represent all the workers in the same industry. In India, there are 11 major trade union groups representing workers in a range of industries, and many smaller unions representing sometimes only a few hundred people in a particular area.

Figure 13.2.1 shows some of the aims of trade unions. You can see that the main aim is to secure the best possible conditions of work for members. Unions know that the decisions a firm makes will affect the livelihoods of workers and their families.

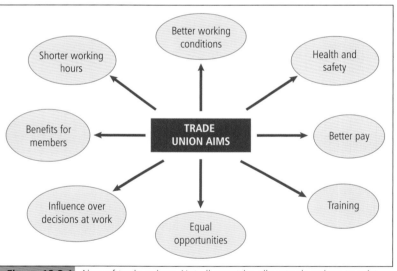

Figure 13.2.1 Aims of trade unions. Not all countries allow trade unions to exist

Negotiation

One of the purposes of a trade union is to negotiate – that is, discuss – with employers. Talks take place between representatives of the employees (union officials) and representatives of the employer. Both sides try to reach agreement on issues such as conditions of employment (e.g. hours worked, safety of the workplace) or wage levels. This negotiation can take place at a local level (e.g. within a factory) or at national level, where the union represents all the members of the trade union in the country.

The benefits of trade union membership to individuals

Typical benefits of belonging to a trade union include:

- knowing that you are not alone in the workplace; you are part of a group that represents you and your fellow workers
- belonging to a body that is negotiating better terms and conditions (e.g. pay increase, improved conditions) for you
- direct benefits (e.g. sickness benefit) for employees
- support for members if there is a grievance or disciplinary procedure (a grievance occurs when a member of a trade union feels they have been treated badly at work; a disciplinary procedure occurs when a union member has been disciplined for, say, poor timekeeping)
- direct action to support members (e.g. if negotiations over pay break down with employees, union officials may call a strike; this means that union members stop work).

The ability to strike gives unions a lot of power: if airline or railway workers go on strike, their companies lose money, profit and their reputation for reliability. Other actions that unions can take include working more slowly (a go-slow) and working to rule – only doing things which fit with the rules set out in a contract of employment.

The impact of trade unions

Strong trade unions can impact on business behaviour. In France, the trade unions are very strong. They were influential in setting a 35-hour working week in the European Union. Unions in France have often succeeded in creating national strikes: workers from many trade unions stop work for a day, or longer, to put pressure on employers and the government.

Over time, union action, or the threat of it, can influence businesses to:

- increase pay
- provide better conditions, such as cleaner washrooms, healthier working environments, longer holidays, safer workplaces.

ACTIVITY

Find out about some of the trade unions in your own or a neighbouring country. Use the search terms List of Trade Unions to search on the internet. Compare your findings with those of a partner. What is the purpose of these unions? Can you find a news story which illustrates the activities of a union? (In some countries, the government does not allow trade unions.)

EXAM TIP

Remember that trade unions do not pass laws. They can put pressure on employers, but not force them, to pay higher wages or improve working conditions.

SUMMARY QUESTIONS

1 What is a trade union? Who are its members?

2 Provide examples of two issues that trade unions become involved in, and explain why.

3 What benefits would an individual worker gain from being a member of a trade union?

KEY POINTS

1 A trade union is an association of employees, set up to protect their interests.

2 The nature of trade unions varies between countries; essentially, all unions are created to negotiate wages and conditions of employment.

Show an awareness of ethical considerations in business activity.

• Show an awareness of the possible conflict between the profit motive and ethical considerations, such as exploitation of employees (e.g. using child labour).

Many people think that it is unethical business behaviour to use child labour. The children may be prevented from going to school and playing with their peers. Wages may be very low and working conditions dangerous

EXAM TIP

Make sure that you understand the difference between acting unethically and acting illegally. Acting illegally always means breaking the law; acting unethically means acting in a way that puts profit above morals. The action may not break the law, even if many people disapprove of it.

Ethics

Ethics are the values and principles that influence how individuals, groups and society behave. Business ethics are therefore the values and principles that operate in the world of business. It is possible to carry out many practices that are not strictly ethical, but are still legal.

Ethical decisions

Whether business owners and managers recognise it or not, all business decisions have an ethical dimension. Here are some ethical questions that a business might have to face.

• Should products which might damage the health of consumers (e.g. cigarettes, petrol) be withdrawn from the market?
• Should a firm make sure that its business activities (e.g. making furniture from mahogany and other rare woods) do not harm the environment?
• Should money be spent to create lifts and ramps that allow wheelchair access to workplaces and retail outlets?
• Should a firm refuse to offer money to individuals in a business to help secure an overseas contract?

A firm that answers yes to these questions might be described as operating in an ethical way. Remember, though, that acting in an ethical way may increase business costs, and some customers may be lost. Profits may then decrease.

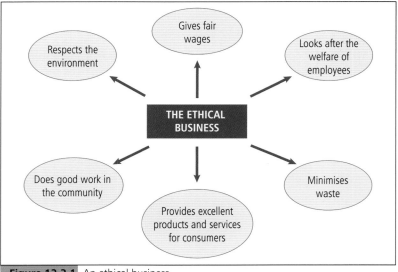

Figure 13.3.1 An ethical business

Figure 13.3.1 outlines some of the most important aspects of an ethical business.

What else can you think of?

The following illustrations provide examples of business practices that sometimes occur.

- Style Clothing is an international supplier of branded goods which carry the 'S' logo. The international buyer for the company has agreed a deal to buy low-cost T-shirts from a supplier in an overseas country where wages are low.

- Workers in the factory in the country are paid $1 per day to sew the T-shirts. Many are under the age of 13. They work in hot and unpleasant conditions, from 8 in the morning to 6 at night. They do not go to school.

- The shirts that they make are then sold to wealthy consumers, usually in cities like Paris, London, New York, Beijing, Delhi, Moscow and Rio de Janeiro.

- A typical consumer will buy a Style T-shirt at a price which is 10 times the amount that the worker who sewed the shirt together makes in a day.

Questions

1 In what ways does this case study represent unethical behaviour?

2 What could be done to improve this situation? Who should take this action?

Social responsibility

Corporate social responsibility (CSR) describes the way in which an ethical business contributes to society. A firm which behaves ethically towards the local community and society as a whole is socially responsible. Examples of social responsibility include:

- making sure that your business does not use child labour or buy from suppliers that use child labour
- providing fair wages for employees
- giving a fair price to suppliers, particularly in poorer parts of the world – this is sometimes referred to as fair trade
- minimising waste and eliminating or reducing pollution.

Health and safety

Demonstrate an understanding of the importance of health and safety requirements.

- Use examples to show how businesses might have to change their behaviour to conform to legislation regarding conditions at work.

International conventions provide guidance for creating health and safety laws to protect workers such as miners

Health and safety requirements

Health and safety at work is a very important issue, which includes:

- protecting workers from dangerous machinery
- requirements to wear safety equipment and clothing
- hygienic conditions for employees to work in
- number of hours worked.

The International Labour Organization (ILO) creates international labour standards. It has created over 70 conventions and recommendations dealing with health and safety. *Conventions* are the equivalent of international treaties drawn up by a number of governments. A state that ratifies (signs up to) a convention is expected to build its requirements into the national laws. The ILO then checks that businesses around the world comply with these laws.

Recommendations are guidelines for action by member states of the ILO.

The conventions and recommendations relate to:

- particular industries (e.g. agriculture, mining, dock working and the building industry)
- specific risks (e.g. safety of workers working with chemicals, night working, underground working, noise and vibration).

DID YOU KNOW?

In Mexico, the law states that employees should work for a maximum of 44 hours per week. However, in the private sector, this is often ignored. In France, the law sets a 35-hour (maximum) working week. Legislation was passed in South Korea in 2004; before then, employees were expected to work 6 days a week, Monday to Saturday.

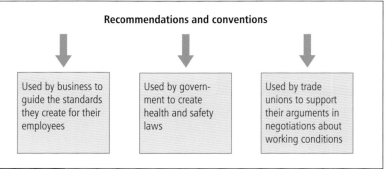

Recommendations and conventions

| Used by business to guide the standards they create for their employees | Used by government to create health and safety laws | Used by trade unions to support their arguments in negotiations about working conditions |

Figure 13.4.1 Recommendations and conventions

Changing business behaviour

Health and safety laws and requirements are intended to make sure that businesses behave responsibly. Enforcement varies among countries and in some there may be incentives to encourage businesses, or penalties if regulations are not enforced.

Examples of requirements include:

- **protection from dangerous machinery:** this may mean providing shields on cutting equipment, or requiring employees to complete a training course before working with dangerous machinery such as cranes. Providing safe facilities involves a cost in the short term, but protects businesses from **negligence** claims (i.e. being sued for failure to provide a safe environment).

- **safety equipment and clothing:** in the construction or the chemical industry, workers may be required to wear safety helmets and protective suits, gloves and boots.

- **hygienic conditions:** in food preparation, employees may be required to wear hairnets. Employees may also be required to undertake tough medical screening to ensure that they are not passing on infections to consumers or each other.

- **hours of work:** in some industries, working long hours is particularly dangerous, as levels of concentration are likely to fall. Long hours may also harm the long-term welfare of the employees. Many countries therefore set a maximum number of hours that can be worked. In some countries, this is between 35 and 45 hours per week, with between 2 and 5 weeks' holiday a year.

In most countries, there is an organisation responsible for checking that companies are implementing health and safety requirements. Failure to operate in a safe way or to look after the health of employees can lead to fines and other punishments (including imprisonment) for a business and its owners.

ACTIVITY

Carry out an internet search using the terms Working Time, to find any working-time regulations in your own country, and to compare regulations in different countries. Produce a table showing the regulations in different countries. Compare the results from your own country with the results from other countries. What conclusions can you draw from this research?

EXAM TIP

Spending money on improving health and safety increases the costs of a business. In the short term, this will mean decreased profits. It is easy to see why businesses will not spend this money unless required to by law. In the long run, such spending might produce a 'payback' through fewer accidents, higher employee morale and improved motivation. However, businesses do not always think long-term!

SUMMARY QUESTIONS

1 Give an example to show how a business might have to change its behaviour to keep to the laws regarding conditions at work.

2 How do international conventions and guidelines relating to health and safety influence international governments and employers?

3 Who benefits from health and safety legislation?

KEY POINTS

1 Businesses have a responsibility for ensuring the health and safety of their employees.

2 Governments create health and safety laws, some of which comply with international standards created by the ILO.

3 Businesses have to conform to requirements. Failure can lead to fines. A poor health and safety record can harm the public image of a business.

4 Regulations may exist but not be enforced.

Employment legislation

Understand the main features of employment contracts and employment legislation.

• Describe the main features of an employment contract.

• Understand why employees need protection against discrimination and unfair dismissal.

• Use examples to demonstrate such protection in terms of racial and gender discrimination.

An important aspect of employment legislation is making sure that all groups in the labour force are paid the same wage for doing work of equal value

EXAM TIP

Remember that dismissal is different from redundancy. If employees are dismissed, they are removed from the job usually because of some misconduct. If they are made redundant, the job no longer exists, so the employee is no longer needed.

Employment legislation

Employment legislation is intended to protect employees in the workplace. Laws cover areas such as health and safety (as we saw in Unit 13.4), as well as areas such as employment contracts and protection from unfair dismissal, and racial, sexual or age discrimination.

Employment contracts

A contract is an agreement between people or organisations to deliver goods or services, or to do something on jointly agreed terms.

A **contract of employment** sets out the relationship between the employer and the employee who has been contracted to work for them.

A contract of employment is usually set out in writing and typically includes the following details:

• the names of the employer and the employee
• the job title
• the date when the employment began
• the scale or rate of pay and method of calculating pay and bonuses
• when payment will be made
• the hours to be worked
• holiday entitlement and holiday pay
• sick pay and injury arrangements
• entitlement to a pension scheme
• the conditions of termination (length of notice that the employer must give).

Protection of employees against discrimination and unfair dismissal

In most countries, there are rules about the dismissal of employees. As we read in Unit 11.4, at the heart of this issue is the difference between what is described as **fair** and **unfair** dismissal.

When employees are dismissed unfairly, they may have grounds for taking the case to court to receive compensation or to be reinstated in their job.

Grounds for fair dismissal might include the employee:

• deliberately destroying company property
• harassing another worker, either verbally or physically
• continually being late
• being unable or unwilling to do the job
• continually taking time off.

However, in some instances, employees may claim that dismissal has been unfair, on the grounds that they have been discriminated against because:

- of their race or religion
- they have joined a trade union
- they are a woman, or too old.

Protection against discrimination

National legislation is required to make sure that individual workers are not discriminated against at work. **Discrimination** is treating one person or group less favourably than others. This may be because of, for example, race, religion, gender, age or disability.

| CASE STUDY | The Employment Equity Act, South Africa |

South Africa has passed an Employment Equity Act, which applies to all employers and workers and protects workers and job seekers from unfair discrimination. It also provides a framework for implementing affirmative action. This involves making sure that everyone who is suitably qualified for a particular job has equal opportunities.

In the past, certain groups have found it difficult to get jobs. The new legislation aims to ensure that the different groups of people in the country are treated equally and with respect and dignity. All levels of jobs should be open to everyone who is qualified to do them. This may mean that companies have had to make changes to their employment procedures.

Questions

1 What examples of recruitment, selection and training practices can you think of that might discriminate against designated groups? What practical steps could an employer take to remove these obstacles?

2 How could an employer make sure that designated groups are equally represented in all job categories and levels in the workplace?

SUMMARY QUESTIONS

1 Describe the main features of an employment contract.

2 In what ways can employees be discriminated against in the workplace? Give two examples of groups that may be discriminated against in the workplace in your country. How can employees be protected against discrimination?

3 Briefly explain how the following types of legislation can protect workers.
- Fair pay legislation
- Legislation against unfair dismissal
- Race equality legislation

ACTIVITY

Carry out some research to find out about protection that employees in your own country have against discrimination at work. You could carry out an internet search using the keywords [Name of your country], Employment Legislation, Discrimination. Alternatively, your teacher may provide you with sources to research this information. Present your findings in the form of a report headed 'Employment discrimination in [Name of your country]'.

DID YOU KNOW?

Equal opportunities exist when everyone is given the same opportunity with regard to being interviewed for a job, stands an equal chance of being selected, is given equal access to training, promotion, etc., regardless of gender, racial group, age, physical characteristics or other features.

KEY POINTS

1 Employees need protection against unfair treatment.

2 Certain groups need additional protection against discrimination.

3 There may be specific encouragement for businesses to support these groups.

4 Legislation may exist, but not be enforced.

Meeting standards

Businesses supply goods or services for consumers in return for payment. Every good or service that is bought or sold, however, must meet certain standards. Some of these standards are laid down in law (legislation), and some in voluntary codes of practice within an industry, while others are set by individual businesses. The legal system will set out a fair framework for trading, and to help settle disputes that may arise.

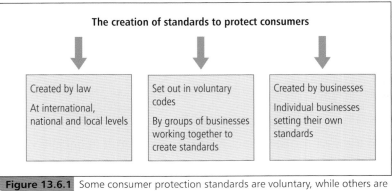

Figure 13.6.1 Some consumer protection standards are voluntary, while others are enforced by law

Protection when buying goods

In most countries, consumers are given protection when buying goods. This protection covers the following areas.

How goods are sold

Goods should be *fit for the purpose* for which they are sold. For example, when you buy a bicycle, you expect to be able to cycle on it. You would have a justifiable complaint if, for example, some spokes were broken or the wheel was bent.

Goods should also *fit the description* given of them. This is particularly important for goods sold in packets. The pictures or descriptions on the packet should accurately fit the products inside. Goods should also match the description of their quality. In addition, buyers should be given the correct weight or quantity of goods that they have paid for.

Dangerous products

Consumers are usually protected against dangerous or harmful products. For example, children's toys should not have sharp edges. Electrical goods should be safe to use. Food products should contain edible and safe ingredients.

Buying a service

When you buy a service – for example, from a hairdresser, bank worker or taxi driver – you are entitled to certain standards.

A service should be carried out with reasonable care and skill. It should also be provided within a reasonable time. For example, if you have asked a repair business to repair a radio for you, it would be unreasonable to have to wait for months for the repair to be completed. The service should also be provided at a reasonable charge.

CASE STUDY	Consumer protection in Jamaica

Like most countries today, Jamaica has developed a range of laws to protect consumers.

- Physical safety laws (e.g. relating to how food is made and stored).
- Promotion and protection of consumers' economic interests (e.g. relating to how goods are sold and the rights of consumers when they buy goods on credit – i.e. buy now and pay later arrangements).
- Standards for safety and quality of goods and services.
- Laws setting out ways in which consumers can make complaints and receive compensation through the courts.

Questions

1 Can you identify a consumer protection law in your own country that fits into each of the headings listed above? Briefly describe the nature of that law.

2 Do you have the equivalent of a Consumer Affairs Commission in your country? Find out what it does.

Consumer protection laws in Jamaica cover the ways in which food is made and stored

SUMMARY QUESTIONS

1 What do you understand by the term 'consumer protection'? Why do consumers need protection?

2 Government legislation sets out the rules of consumer protection. How are consumers protected in addition to the law?

3 Give an example of one way in which consumers are protected by the law. How do they benefit from this protection?

KEY POINTS

1 Consumers are given some measure of protection by the law, by voluntary codes and by businesses themselves.

2 Examples of consumer protection laws include protection against dangerous products and misleading selling.

External costs and benefits

A new toll road: as well as the financial costs and benefits to the builders, it was necessary to consider wider social benefits, such as the creation of jobs, as well as the social costs, such as extra noise and pollution, caused by the new road

Financial costs and benefits

Businesses need to look at the **financial costs** and **benefits** of carrying out a decision. For example, the decision might be taken to build a new factory in Malaysia. The table shows some of the financial considerations of this decision.

Financial costs of building and operating factory in Malaysia	Financial benefits of building and operating factory in Malaysia
Cost of borrowing necessary finance to build the factory	The revenues earned from the factory
Cost of building the factory and equipping it with machinery	The saving to the business resulting from operating in Malaysia rather than at a higher-cost location
Cost of labour	
Cost of raw materials	

To work out the profit from running the factory, accountants will calculate the net financial return in the following way:

Financial revenues – Financial costs = Net financial return

The net financial return is called profit.

This is a very narrow view of looking at the impact of a business. There are other costs and benefits, which are outlined below.

Social costs and social benefits

As we saw in Unit 12.1, **social benefits** include the financial benefits to a company and other positive benefits that result from a particular business activity or decision. **Social costs** are the financial costs to the company of building the factory, plus all the other costs resulting from the factory. These external costs might include the traffic noise to people living near the factory. Social costs and benefits might be visualised as follows:

All benefits – All costs = Net benefit

The table illustrates some of the major costs and benefits to a large supermarket chain of setting up a new store in a large city. You can see that different stakeholders are affected in different ways.

Financial costs to the business	Financial revenues to the business
Costs of borrowing finance	Revenues received from the goods sold in the supermarket
Wages paid to supermarket employees	
Costs of buying products to resell in the supermarket	
Additional social costs (external costs)	**Additional social revenues (external benefits)**
Traffic congestion and pollution from shoppers travelling to the supermarket and lorries delivering supplies	Convenience to shoppers of buying a range of goods in one shop
Small shops have to close down because they are unable to compete with the large supermarket	Wages earned by employees who work in the supermarket

In this example, the owners of a business and its managers are most interested in the financial costs and revenue. Other stakeholders, such as employees, local residents and shoppers, are interested in the social costs and benefits that affect them directly.

CASE STUDY | The Marrakesh–Agadir motorway

In 2006, work began to construct the 233.5 km motorway between Marrakesh and Agadir in Morocco. Costs involved in the project included:

- construction of the road and the interchanges with other roads
- construction of the toll gates
- putting up the signs on the motorway
- paying compensation to people on whose land the motorway was built.

The benefits of constructing the road were to improve the standard of living of communities in Morocco and to create jobs, particularly in the construction and tourist industries. The new motorway was designed to reduce travel time for motorists, reduce accidents and create jobs in constructing and then running and maintaining the motorway.

Questions

1 What were the financial costs and benefits of building the Marrakesh–Agadir motorway?

2 What are the social costs and benefits of the motorway?

3 Which stakeholders will benefit most, and who will experience social costs?

Activities should only be carried out if the social benefits are greater than the social costs. It is not always easy to calculate social costs and benefits and give a monetary value to factors such as noise pollution or the benefit of reduced journey times. Specialists are trained in techniques to attach values to these factors. Cost-benefit analysis (CBA) is used as part of the decision-making process, especially for government projects.

Any decision that a business makes affects stakeholders – shareholders, employees, suppliers, customers, the government or the local community. Each of these groups will experience costs and benefits in different ways.

SUMMARY QUESTIONS

1 What is the difference between a financial cost of an activity and the social cost of that activity?

2 Give an example of an activity that involves financial costs and benefits and social costs and benefits. Give examples of these costs and benefits.

3 An independent report has calculated that the social cost of building a new factory in a given location is a lot higher than the financial cost. Should the local planning authority allow the factory to be built there – or should it take into consideration other things?

ACTIVITY

Imagine that a large retail outlet or factory is to be built close to your school. New access roads will need to be built. Which stakeholder groups will be most affected? In each case, outline one social cost and one social benefit to each of the stakeholder groups of the new outlet.

KEY POINTS

1 Financial costs and benefits are monetary calculations of the effects of a business project.

2 Financial costs and benefits are only one part of wider social costs and benefits.

3 Businesses need to use cost-benefit analysis to take into account social costs and benefits, as well as financial ones.

Exchange rates

The yuan is the national currency of China. The strength of the yuan depends on how many people worldwide want to purchase this currency to trade with China (although Chinese exporters will be quite happy to be paid in dollars and other strong currencies, such as the euro)

The exchange rate

When international trade takes place between businesses in countries that use different currencies, at least one of the businesses will need foreign exchange.

A country's foreign **exchange rate** is the price at which its own currency exchanges for that of others. For example, the Japanese yen can be compared with the US dollar (US$), the European Union's euro, or the Chinese yuan (RMB). (The Chinese currency is called *renminbi*, which means 'the people's money'.)

The importance of the exchange rate to business

There are two main ways in which the exchange rate may influence business activities.

- It may affect the price of goods and services that businesses buy in international markets.
- It may affect the price at which businesses sell goods and services in international markets.

If a business imports good or services, the exchange rate will influence the price of their purchases, and any changes will make pricing more difficult. On the other hand, if they sell goods or services abroad, changes in the exchange rate will affect the amount of foreign currency coming in, and this will change the amount they earn. Changes in exchange rates will therefore affect profit margins. Figure 13.8.1 shows how changes in the exchange rate can cause uncertainty in both situations.

Figure 13.8.1 Buying and selling in international markets

The table below shows the effect of rises and falls in the value of a currency.

Home currency appreciates (gets stronger) External value of the currency goes up	Exports from home country become more expensive to customers from other countries, therefore more difficult to sell. Exporters will sell less/make less profit. Value of exports decreases.	Imports from other countries become cheaper, including raw materials and finished goods. Importers will find goods from other countries cheaper to buy, so they can sell more in the home country, enabling them to make more profit. Value of imports increases.
Home currency depreciates (gets weaker) External value of the currency goes down	Exports from home country become less expensive to customers from other countries, therefore easier to sell. Exporter will sell more/make more profit. Value of exports increases.	Imports from other countries become more expensive, including raw materials and finished goods. Importers will find goods from other countries more expensive to buy, so they can sell less in the home country/make less profit. Value of imports increases.

A Chinese importer wishing to buy American goods will usually buy dollars with which to purchase them. In 2009, US $1 was worth about 7 yuan (RMB), the currency of China. So if the Chinese importer wanted to buy a tractor from the United States for a price of $50,000, he or she would have to exchange RMB 350,000 to buy the US dollars. However, exchange rates change over time. A currency can become stronger (appreciate) or weaker (depreciate). If, for example, the yuan appreciated against the dollar to US$1 = 5 yuan, the American tractor would become much cheaper for the Chinese importer. Instead of having to give RMB 350,000 for it, the importer would only have to give 250,000.

The result of this would mean that the importer can show an improved profit margin or invest the money saved in other parts of the business.

Questions

1 Find out the most recent exchange rate – how has it changed since 2009?

2 Has the yuan appreciated or depreciated against the dollar since 2009? What will be the effect on Chinese exports to the United States?

ACTIVITY

Look in a newspaper or on the internet to find out the most recent exchange rate between the yuan (RMB) and the US$. Has the yuan been rising or falling in value against the dollar? What are the implications for Chinese importers and exporters?

CASE STUDY | Single currencies

Some countries are grouped into an area that uses a single currency. The European Union consists of 27 countries, including Germany, Ireland, Italy, Spain and Greece. The single common currency is the euro. A small number of countries in the Union are not members of the eurozone. This includes the UK, which still uses the pound sterling (£). There are other trading zones that use a common currency, such as countries in the eastern Caribbean.

When businesses import and export within a common currency zone, they do not have to worry about fluctuations in exchange rates.

Questions

1 What is the advantage of many countries using a single currency?

2 What other EU countries apart from the UK are not part of the eurozone? Try to find out why they have decided to retain their existing currency.

EXAM TIP

When answering a question on the effects of a change in exchange rate, keep your analysis in the context of the home country, or where the business is based. This way you are less likely to become confused.

KEY POINTS

1 The exchange rate is the price at which one currency exchanges for that of other currencies.

2 An appreciation in the currency involves an increase in the price against other named currencies; a depreciation involves a fall against other currencies.

3 Businesses need to be aware of any changes in their currency level.

SUMMARY QUESTIONS

1 What is the difference between the appreciation and the depreciation of a currency?

2 How does the appreciation or depreciation of a currency affect a business that exports goods overseas? Use the example of a business that exports from your own country.

The business cycle

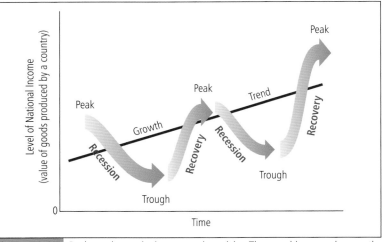

Figure 13.9.1 Peaks and troughs in economic activity. The trend is towards growth over time, with a series of recessions and recoveries

An economic recession such as that of 2008–9 causes many businesses to shut down. As incomes fall, people have less to spend on bicycles and other goods

The business, or trade, cycle

Unfortunately, economies do not grow in a steady pattern. Instead, there are periods in which the economy grows for a few years, followed by periods in which growth starts to fall. This is known as a **business**, or **trade cycle**.

Recession describes a period in which national income (the total value of goods produced in the economy) falls for at least two quarters of the year – that is, over a 6-month period. When the recession lasts for a much longer period – say, 3 or 4 years or more – this is a slump.

Recovery would be used to describe a period in which national income rises for at least two quarters after a recession or slump. A boom is a period of prolonged increase in national income.

Figure 13.9.1 shows that most economies go through a series of recessions and recoveries. When these are maintained over a period of time, they lead to booms and slumps in economic activity.

In a boom:

• output of goods rises
• firms take on more employees
• wages and prices rise
• prosperity rises for many people
• businesses boom.

In a slump:

• output falls
• firms lay off workers
• wages and prices fall
• prosperity falls
• businesses do badly (some cease trading).

Businesses and the business cycle

Business favours a boom period in the business cycle. This is the time when order books are most likely to be full and when it is easiest to sell goods.

However, as the boom reaches its peak, costs are likely to rise. At the top of the boom, it will become more difficult to recruit labour, and wages and other costs will rise. Businesses will be far more cautious in the downturn in the cycle and will tend to make cutbacks, such as reducing the size of the labour force and postponing the purchase of new machinery.

Business managers should understand the stages of the cycle and what is likely to happen in the near future. In a period of recession, businesses should be cautious about taking out loans and taking on additional fixed costs. However, in a period of recovery and boom, businesses are prepared to take more risks: they can expand by borrowing more, increasing the number of employees, expanding into new markets or producing a wider range of products.

The downturn of 2008

In 2008–9, the global economy experienced a long-term financial crisis that led to a slump in economic activity. The downturn initially started in the United States and spread across the world's economies. The price of oil, coal, and other minerals collapsed; house prices fell in many countries. The volume of world trade decreased. Millions of people across the world lost their jobs, in industries ranging from construction to car manufacture and banking.

EXAM TIP

Not all cycles are the same! In a business cycle, the economy as a whole goes through phases; a product life cycle refers to changes over time in the level of sales of a particular product for a particular business. Sales of a product may be falling because it is in the decline phase of its cycle, while the economy as a whole is expanding (booming).

SUMMARY QUESTIONS

1 What problems are caused for business by recessions? How might businesses react in a period of recession?

2 What is the difference between recession and recovery? How are businesses likely to respond in a period of recovery?

3 State, and explain, the main stages of a business cycle.

KEY POINTS

1 The economy rarely grows at a steady rate; it is characterised by periods of recovery and recession.

2 Businesses need to be aware of the current stage and likely future stages of the business cycle.

3 In a recession, businesses cut costs and are cautious about borrowing. In a recovery, they can expand by taking on more finance and increasing their labour force.

DID YOU KNOW?

During the recession of 2008–9, many governments encouraged banks to lend more money, particularly to business. They also nationalised a range of industries and businesses that were in danger of collapsing.

SECTION 1: Short-answer questions

1 Identify and explain TWO reasons why governments may want to influence business location decisions. [4]

2 Explain the difference between a grant and a subsidy in the context of business activity. [3]

3 Explain how planning laws may influence existing businesses to move to a new location. [3]

4 Identify and explain ONE social cost and ONE social benefit that may result from moving a steel factory to a rural location. [4]

5 Explain the role of trade unions. [3]

6 Analyse TWO benefits of trade union membership to workers in a factory. [6]

7 Explain, with examples, the part that trade unions may play in disputes between employers and employees. [4]

8 Explain, with examples, what is meant by ethical behaviour. [4]

9 Explain how the following organisations may behave in an ethical manner.
   • A fast-food company that causes street litter.
   • A company offering tourist boat tours on a lake.
   • An individual who is awarding government contracts to business. [6]

10 Analyse, with examples, why an ethical business, working in a socially responsible manner, may suffer from higher costs, but gain customers. [6]

11 Explain why governments in many countries have introduced laws to ensure that workers' health and safety at work are protected. [4]

12 Identify and explain TWO problems a business may face if it is found to have breached health and safety laws in your country. [4]

13 Identify and explain TWO benefits to workers of being given a contract of employment. [4]

14 Explain TWO reasons why the phrase 'Young woman worker wanted' in a job advertisement may breach employment law. [4]

15 Explain, with examples, THREE ways in which consumers in your country are protected by legislation. [4]

16 Identify and explain how sales and profits of a company which exports goods from your country may be affected by:
   • home currency strengthening
   • home currency weakening. [4]

17 What are the likely effects of a recession on a company producing:
   • essential food?
   • cars? [4]

SECTION 2: Longer-answer questions

The fair-trade souvenir shop

Ethical Gifts is a business selling African souvenirs in Livingstone, Zambia. Customers are mainly foreign tourists who are visiting the Victoria Falls, who come to buy jewellery, ceramics, wood carvings and textiles. Ethical Gifts' unique selling point is that all its products are sourced from suppliers who pay fair prices to the makers of the products. Non-renewable hardwood objects are not sold and nor are animal skin products. Ethical Gifts' prices are higher than the competition, but customers, mainly from developed Western countries, are happy to pay them, secure in the knowledge that they are buying ethically produced goods.

1 Explain what is meant by 'ethically produced goods' in this context. [4]

2 Analyse how Ethical Gifts' unique selling point helps the company add value to the souvenirs. [4]

3 Analyse TWO difficulties Ethical Gifts may have in ensuring that the goods they sell are 'ethically produced'. [6]

4 Analyse TWO social benefits that may arise from the trade in ethical products. [6]

5 To what extent is the willingness to pay more for ethically produced products 'a luxury which only benefits rich tourists'? [6]

The factory location problem

It is not proving easy for a food-processing factory to find a new location in Kerala, India. The problem is that although the production unit will provide many jobs, much needed in the area, the process uses a lot of water and produces a high volume of waste. The multinational company that wants to build the factory has promised that health and safety regulations will be treated as the highest priority. However, planning permission has been turned down on two different sites due to:

- closeness to a tourist beach and wildlife park
- closeness to residential housing
- closeness to a river where water is the main source for drinking for a large number of people and animals.

At last, Amit, the manager, thinks he may have found the ideal location. It is in an area well out of town, in an area occupied by one other factory, which produces soft drinks.

1 Explain what is meant by 'planning permission' in this context. [3]

2 Explain why planning permission for the factory may have been turned down due to 'closeness to residential housing'. [3]

3 Analyse TWO business benefits to the company of following health and safety regulations. [6]

4 Identify and explain THREE important factors that Amit may have taken into account when choosing the proposed locations for the food-processing factory. [6]

5 Evaluate the advantages and disadvantages to the local population if the factory is allowed to locate in the new proposed out-of-town location. [6]

The Shop 'n' Save supermarket

The Shop 'n' Save supermarket is having a hard time due to the economic recession. A major business has closed down in the town and there are very few employment opportunities for those made redundant. Customers therefore have little money to spend and are looking for basic necessities at bargain prices. Many of the company's competitors have ceased trading, but Abdul, the owner of Shop 'n' Save, is determined to try to weather the storm.

1 Identify and explain TWO ways in which consumers may be affected in a recession. [4]

2 Analyse, with an example, why some businesses may cease trading in a recession. [4]

3 Explain why Abdul may believe it is worth weathering the storm during the recession. [4]

4 Identify and explain THREE types of product that Abdul should stock to help him increase sales during a recession. [6]

5 Do you agree that the local government in Abdul's town should offer him some support during the recession? Explain your answer. [6]

CASE STUDY	Leila's new bakeshop

The opportunity

Leila had always enjoyed cooking and making treats and cakes for her friends. She loved to make cakes for special occasions such as birthdays and other celebrations, as well as small bags of homemade sweets, beautifully wrapped, as presents. When she was old enough, Leila found a part-time job helping out in a local cake shop. The owner encouraged her to try out some of her own ideas and designs for special-occasion cakes and treats. To her surprise, Leila's products became popular with customers, who would come back regularly to buy her products and also told their friends and relatives about her.

This gave Leila the idea that after leaving college she would start her own business. She would need to rent a small shop and there would be other start-up expenses, such as an oven and other cooking equipment, not to mention stocks of essential ingredients and materials. Leila was also keen to widen her product range and start making cakes for 'everyday' use, perhaps with fruit, chocolate or honey flavourings. Leila had already saved $1,500, but would need to take a loan for her business start-up. She made an appointment to see her local bank manager, full of enthusiasm.

The bank manager was impressed with her idea, but told her she would have to produce a proper business plan.

How would Leila go about putting her plan together? She started to collect information about her customers' tastes, business costs and proposed prices.

Business plan sections

Introduction and mission statement	An outline of the opportunity and aims of the company Long-term and short-term objectives, including a time plan
Human resources	Details of personnel, experience and skills
Marketing	Details of market research and results Outline of marketing mix (product, price, promotion, place) and strategy
Finance	Sources of finance and predictions, including cash flow and 'contribution' from each product
Production/operations	Production plans, including resources, skills needed, materials and timescale
Executive summary	A short summary of the whole document which appears at the front of the plan

Market research results

Questionnaire

Leila managed to question a sample of 100 local customers to try to predict sales for her new shop. The results were as follows:

1 Do you ever buy your cakes and sweets 'ready-made' from shops?

   Yes: 75   No: 25

(People who replied 'Yes' then answered the rest of the questions.)

2 How many times each year do you buy a 'celebration' cake?

   Never: 20

1–3 times: 45
4 or more times: 10

3 How many times each year do you buy wrapped sweets?

   Never: 5
   1–3 times: 10
   4 or more times: 60

(Questions 4 and 5 refer to Leila's proposed new products.)

4 Which of the following cakes would you prefer for everyday use?

   Fruit: 35
   Chocolate: 25
   Honey: 15

5 How much would you pay for an 'everyday' cake (500 grams)?

Up to $5: 30
$5–$7: 35
More than $7: 10

Leila's revenue and costs

Leila's prices

Celebration cakes: $10
Wrapped sweets: $6
Everyday cakes (fruit, chocolate or honey): $7

Leila's production costs

Ingredients, decoration and wrapping:
Celebration cakes: $3
Wrapped sweets: $1
Everyday cakes (fruit, chocolate or honey): $1.50

Leila's other costs (all figures are monthly)

Rent of shop: $300
Leila's own wage: $200
Assistant's wage: $80
Power, light and water: $60
Marketing leaflets and order forms: $10

QUESTIONS

1 Leila is trying to decide how much money she needs to borrow for her business start-up. She would like to be able to pay her fixed costs for 3 months and her production costs for her first month. She is planning the following monthly production levels:

- celebration cakes: 37
- wrapped sweets: 70
- everyday cakes: 30

a) Work out Leila's total start-up requirement. [8]

b) Recommend how much Leila should ask the bank to lend her. Explain your answer. [12]

2 Leila is preparing to return to the bank with her business plan. In the meantime, her family and friends have said that they may be able to loan her some money.

a) Identify and explain TWO factors that Leila should consider before deciding whether to take a loan from the bank or borrow capital from friends and family. [8]

b) Leila knows that the bank manager will ask her for details of the location of her shop. Do you think this will be important in determining the success of the business? Justify your answer. [12]

3 Leila is analysing her market research and trying to decide on her product mix and marketing strategy.

a) Identify and explain TWO problems Leila would face in carrying out her market research by means of a questionnaire. [8]

b) Recommend a marketing strategy for the opening of Leila's new shop. [12]

4 Leila plans to carry out some break-even analysis, to try to predict how many cakes she will need to sell before she starts making a profit.

a) Identify and explain TWO aims that Leila might have when she sets up her business. [8]

b) Explain how useful break-even analysis might be to Leila in managing her business and making business decisions. [12]

5 Just as Leila is making a decision about her new business, she receives a call from the managing director of a large bake-shop company, offering her the chance to become a franchisee of his business.

a) Explain the main features of a franchise operation. [8]

b) Recommend whether Leila should accept this offer of a franchise operation. Explain your answer. [12]

CASE STUDY	ZooWorld Ltd

ZooWorld is a family-owned animal park, situated on a very large estate in the country near to a large African city. Day-to-day management is under the control of Edward Mavhinga, also one of the major family shareholders. During recent years, emphasis has been on environmental protection and education, targeting tourists and local people who want to see the country's indigenous creatures. Many of the animals and birds have been rescued from exploitation and cruel treatment. The park is well kept and the staff are a highly committed team of animal specialists, who work hard for very low wages. There is also a large number of volunteers who conduct tours for visitors, and staff the ticket kiosk and small café and souvenir shop. However, the park is struggling to cover its costs, despite charitable donations and grants from local government.

One resource ZooWorld is not short of is land, and the family is trying to decide on the best way to develop a large green area next to the current lion enclosure. There are eight family members who are equal shareholders. At present, four are in favour of a dedicated education and conference centre, and four would like to build an animal-themed amusement park, aimed at families with children up to the age of 12. Both of these options would also include a local market, with craft and textile stalls, open to all visitors.

The ZooWorld owners have carried out market research to try to find out which would be the most popular development. The amusement park will reinforce the business's current popularity with the family market, but the education and conference centre will be aimed at the business market. Edward is keen to break the deadlock and make a decision as soon as possible.

Appendix 1

Forecasted profit and loss accounts for the business after the two developments are as follows.

	Option A: conference and education centre	Option B: amusement park
	$	$
Ticket revenue	300,000	400,000
Other revenue	100,000	100,000
Total revenue	400,000	500,000
Cost of sales	50,000	100,000
Gross profit	350,000	400,000
Expenses	200,000	220,000
Net profit	150,000	180,000

Appendix 2

Memorandum

To: Fellow shareholders
From: E. Mavhinga, Managing Director
Date: 31 May 2010
Ref: ZooWorld Development Plan

We need to make a decision about the new development within the next month. Please find the forecasted profit and loss accounts for the business after each of the two development plans.

Other research has shown an upward trend in the use of business conference centres, but also an increase in the popularity of family amusement parks, and our guests may stay longer and visit more often with this facility. I have also had a very positive response from local craftsmen to the market stall opportunities.

We must also be aware of the current worldwide economic downturn, which is affecting families and businesses alike. Tourism to the country is stable at present, but is likely to be affected if the recession gets worse.

Appendix 3

Memorandum

To: E. Mavhinga
From: Jon Chilanga, Head Keeper
Date: 31 May 2010
Ref: ZooWorld Development Plan

I have been asked by the other members of the ZooWorld staff team, and also the volunteers, to communicate our views on the proposed development plans for the park. We love the park and the animals and feel very strongly that the character is worth preserving. We do not want to see an amusement area in the space next to the lion enclosure, which could frighten the animals and also attract people who are not interested in our environmental aims.

We think it is much better to consider the conference and education centre, which would attract a new market and also further the park's educational objectives. We do like the idea of the local market, and several of our volunteers would like the opportunity to sell textiles and other crafts.

We hope that you value us, as your loyal staff, and take our views into consideration.

QUESTIONS

1 a) The ZooWorld organisation has both business and social objectives. Identify and explain ONE business objective and ONE social objective of the park. *[8]*

  b) Consider the two development possibilities – Option A, the conference and education centre, and Option B, the amusement park. Analyse to what extent each of these options will help ZooWorld meet both business and social objectives. *[12]*

2 a) Employees at ZooWorld work hard for low wages and they are supported by a large team of unpaid volunteers. Identify and explain TWO factors that motivate these workers to remain loyal to the business. *[8]*

  b) To what extent do you think that ZooWorld management should take account of the views of their staff as outlined in Appendix 3? Explain your answer. *[12]*

3 a) Edward would like to carry out further market research in order to help make the choice between the two options. Explain TWO methods of primary market research that may help Edward. *[8]*

  b) If ZooWorld chooses Option A, the conference and education centre, then changes will need to be made to each element of the marketing mix. Identify the four elements and explain what will need to be changed. Justify your answer. *[12]*

4 a) Calculate and comment on the forecasted gross and net profit margins for each option, based on the figures in Appendix 1. *[8]*

  b) Based on the financial information and other case material, recommend whether the Mavhinga family should choose Option A or Option B. *[12]*

5 a) Explain the phrase 'economic downturn' from Appendix 2 and show the potential effects this could have on ZooWorld's local and overseas business. *[8]*

  b) Organisations such as ZooWorld need to ensure that they comply with government laws which protect consumers and employees. Identify and explain THREE relevant examples of legislation and how these will affect the ZooWorld organisation. *[12]*

Practice exam questions

LONGER CASE STUDIES

CASE STUDY	Playways Games

Playways is a manufacturer of toys and games located in rural China, close to the city of Shanghai. The company is a subsidiary of a large multinational corporation and is a major manufacturer of toys and electronic computer games for the European and US markets. The factory occupies a very large site, where products are assembled and packaged. Over recent years, the company's product mix has changed in response to consumers' increasing demand for electronics and decreasing, though still considerable, demand for traditional toys, such as dolls and board games. The company has invested large sums of money in new technology over the last few years and production equipment is highly automated.

Playways employs 4,000 production staff, spread among the 10 different production lines. Each employee is allocated to an area of work and remains in that job during their time with Playways. The method of pay is time rate, with occasional opportunities for overtime if a big order needs to be completed urgently. Michael Tang, the production manager, is strict with his staff and expects his orders to be carried out without question. Some of the more senior workers have asked about joining a trade union, but have been told that the company would not be happy and they may have to 'reconsider their employment'. Playways is also considering using ready-made electronic components bought in from other South East Asian countries, which will work out cheaper than making these on site.

One problem facing the company at present is the strengthening of the Chinese yuan against the US dollar and the euro. Angela Chung, the company's sales manager, is concerned that 'if this trend continues, we will be seriously affected'.

Appendix 1

Playways Games balance sheet for year ending December 2010

	$million	$million
Fixed assets:		
Buildings	200	
Equipment	450	
Total		650
Current assets:		
Stock	65	
Debtors	100	
Cash at bank	5	
Total	170	
Current liabilities	100	
Creditors	30	
Overdraft	10	
Total	140	
Working capital		30
Net assets employed		680
Financed by:		
Shareholders' capital		675
Retained profit		5
Capital at 31 December 2010		680

Appendix 2

Memorandum

To: All staff
From: Michael Tang, Production Manager
Date: 31 December 2010
Ref: Staff productivity

It has come to my notice that staff productivity has decreased by 2 per cent in 2010, as compared with 2009. This is not acceptable and I will be monitoring individual performance on a monthly basis this year. Any worker who does not reach given targets for 3 months in a row will lose his job.

You have been warned.

Appendix 3

Playways sales revenue

	2010 (%)	2009 (%)
Dolls	25	18
Board games	5	5
Toy cars	8	10
Construction toys	15	22
Electronic and computer games	47	45

1 a) Playways uses flow production. Identify and explain ONE advantage and ONE disadvantage of flow production to the Playways company. *[8]*

b) Consider the option for Playways of buying in ready-made components for their products from other South-East Asian countries. Do you think this will increase efficiency? Justify your answer. *[12]*

2 a) Employees at Playways are paid by time rate. Identify and explain ONE advantage and ONE disadvantage to employees of this method of payment. *[8]*

b) Consider the memo in Appendix 2 from Michael Tang to his production staff. Do you think this is the best way to increase productivity? Explain your answer. *[12]*

3 a) Angela Chung is carrying out a review of the product mix offered by Playways. Using Appendix 3, identify and explain FOUR trends in demand for toys and games. *[8]*

b) Using your knowledge of product life cycle theory and information from the case, recommend which product line, if any, should be discontinued. Explain your answer. *[12]*

4 a) Playways has made considerable investment in new technology in recent years. Explain why production companies such as Playways would choose capital-intensive methods. *[8]*

b) Based on the financial information in Appendix 1 and other case material, discuss whether Playways is in a strong financial position. *[12]*

5 a) Explain the phrase 'the strengthening of the Chinese yuan against the US dollar', and explain how this could affect sales of the Playways company. *[8]*

b) 'The future success of any business depends on its ability to bring out new products that meet customer needs.' Identify and explain THREE ways Playways could do this and indicate the ONE that you think would be the most successful. Justify your answer. *[12]*

Glossary

A

Acid test ratio sometimes referred to as the **Quick Ratio**. It is a ratio of the debtors and cash to current liabilities. It compares the size of the assets that can most quickly be turned to cash compared with debts the business may have to pay out in the very short period.

Adding value increasing the value of the product for the final consumer, through manufacturing processes, advertising, distribution, etc.

Annual General Meeting (AGM) yearly meeting of shareholders at which the Company Report is presented by Directors.

Appraisal formal evaluation of an employee's performance over a particular period.

Assets what a business owns, or is owed by others.

Automation operations controlled by machinery rather than people.

B

B2B business-to-business dealing through the internet.

B2C direct links between businesses and consumers through the internet.

Balance sheet account that shows a firm's assets, liabilities and sources of capital at a moment in time.

Batch production manufacturing items in sets for a particular length of time, before switching the manufacturing line to produce a different type of set.

Behavioural segmentation identifying segments of potential customers with similar behaviour patterns (e.g. those who like to be the first to try out new fashion clothes).

Benefits advantages, tangible or intangible, gained by customers from the product or service that they buy.

Board of Directors a body representing shareholders in a company, with the responsibility for looking after their interests.

Brand a product with a unique, consistent and well-recognised character. The uniqueness can come from a factual product detail or from its image.

Break-even analysis comparison of a firm's revenue with its fixed and variable costs to identify the minimum sales level needed to make a profit. The comparison can be shown on a graph known as a **break-even chart**.

Budget a plan, usually set out in table form, indicating how financial targets will be reached.

Business cycle up and down swings in the economy as indicated by movements in Gross Domestic Product.

C

CAD (computer-aided design) using a computer to design new products and processes.

CAM (computer-aided manufacturing) using computers in the control and management of machinery and processes.

Capital money or resources invested by the owner/s of an organisation; a source of finance used by the business to acquire assets.

Cash money in the tills and bank account of a business.

Cash flow forecast prediction of the flow of money into and out of a business.

Charity organisation whose purposes are to do good rather than to make a profit.

Closed question a question with a choice of prepared answers (e.g. in a market research questionnaire).

Communication the process by which information is exchanged between one group or individual and another.

Company a business that is registered as being owned by a group of shareholders and managed in their common interest.

Contract of employment legal document setting out terms and conditions of employment.

Corporate social responsibility (CSR) responsibility of a business to society.

Costs and benefits to determine the net benefit of an activity, all the benefits are added up and all the costs deducted.

Cost of goods sold the cost of making the products and services sold to customers.

Cost-plus pricing working out how much each unit of production costs to produce and then adding a fixed percentage for profit.

Costs the expenses incurred by a firm in producing and selling its products. They include expenditure on wages and raw materials.

Current assets shorter-term items such as stocks, debtors, money in the bank and cash in hand.

Current liabilities debts that a business needs to pay in the short term (usually less than 1 year).

D

Delegation passing power and authority down the hierarchy in an organisation so that decision making can take place at lower levels.

Demand consumers' wishes to purchase products, backed up by their willingness to spend money on them.

Direct competition the drive for market share between suppliers of products that are similar to each other.

Discrimination favouring or showing preferential treatment to one group or individual over others.

Diseconomies of scale the result of a firm becoming too large, when inefficiencies occur, leading to rising costs.

Glossary

Distribution channels the route through which a good or service is moved to the market.

Dividends the share of profits earned by an organisation that is paid to its shareholders.

E

Economies of scale the advantages of a larger firm over a smaller one, enabling it to produce larger outputs at lower costs per individual unit.

Economy the system in a particular country for creating goods and distributing incomes to those involved in production.

Entrepreneur risk taker in a business (e.g. the shareholders, a single owner or a partner).

Ethics sets of moral principles that guide behaviour.

Exchange rate the rate of exchange between one country's currency and that of another (e.g. the South African rand against the Ghanaian cedi).

Export sale of goods or service to another country.

Externality the spillover effect resulting from a particular activity, such as pollution caused by a production process. Externalities can be positive or negative.

F

Fair dismissal when a worker is sacked for reasons that are acceptable in law.

Fixed assets assets that stay within a business rather than being sold. Examples include building and machinery.

Fixed costs any costs that do not vary with the level of output (e.g. rent and rates).

Flow production continuous production of goods which 'flow' down a production line.

Forecast an estimate of what is likely to happen in the future.

Franchise permission to use a business's name and to sell using that name in a particular locality.

G

Gearing ratio ratio of capital used to finance a business that is raised from shareholders, compared with funds that are borrowed from outside the business.

Global warming rise in air and sea temperatures which may be caused by increasing industrial activity.

Gross profit the profit that a firm earns from trading or selling goods before the overheads and expenses have been deducted. It is calculated by: Sales – Costs of sales = Gross profit.

H

Hierarchy layers of decision making within an organisation. A hierarchical organisation has several layers and decision making is made in a downwards direction.

I

Import to bring in foreign goods to a country or use foreign services.

Income money received in return for providing a product or service, including labour time.

Incorporation establishing a business as a separate legal entity from its owners, and therefore allowing it to have limited liability.

Interest rate the price charged for borrowing money.

Internal communications communications that take place within an organisation.

International trade the process of buying and selling goods on international markets.

Intranet electronic communications system set up for and accessed by members of an organisation. The system is not accessible for those outside the organisation.

J

Job description a written document relating to a particular role, indicating, for example, job title, hours of work.

Job production a single piece of work produced for a particular customer.

Job specification the mental and physical requirements needed to carry out a role effectively.

Joint venture an organisation jointly set up by two organisations; frequently set up when one international company wants to enter a new market.

Just in time (JIT) production and distribution system which involves providing raw materials, components and supplies at the time when they are required by a customer rather than being produced earlier and stocked.

K

Kaizen system of making regular small-step improvements to production processes. *Kaizen* is Japanese for 'continuous improvement'.

L

Leadership the process of driving through change by persuading others to do what you want.

Lean production eliminating all forms of waste.

Liabilities what an organisation owes at a particular moment in time.

Lifestyle pattern of behaviour associated with particular groups of people.

Limited company one whose shareholders have a liability only to the extent of their investment.

Limited liability the greatest amount that a company's owners

Glossary

might have to pay out to meet debts, the top being the sum that they invested in the business.

Line production producing goods in a set of sequenced steps along a production line.

Liquidity the ease with which an asset can be converted into cash.

Location of business where a firm is set up, and exists.

Long-term liabilities debts that have to be paid, usually after 1 year.

Management style the predominant manner in which a manager acts. For example, a laissez-faire manager tends to stand back and let others make decisions themselves; an **autocratic** manager is much more controlling.

Manager someone with responsibility for resources and people within an organisation.

Market any situation where buyers and sellers come into contact.

Market economy economy in which decisions about what is produced and what is bought for consumption is strongly influenced by market prices rather than decided by the government.

Market research systematically gathering, recording and analysing data on the possibility of sales of a good or service.

Market segmentation grouping consumers into sections with similar characteristics, such as age, preferences, tastes, etc.

Marketing identifying and anticipating what the customer requires and then providing what they want.

Marketing mix a particular blend of price, product, promotion and place, designed to attract customers.

Maslow's hierarchy of needs a graded list of human needs. At the

bottom are **basic** needs such as food and shelter. At the top are **self-actualisation** needs of individuals to be totally fulfilled in their lives. Most jobs meet lower level needs; only a few jobs enable people to have their higher needs fulfilled.

Mass marketing activities designed to appeal to the whole of a particular market rather than a smaller segment.

Mass production producing a standard product in very large quantities.

Mixed economy economies in which decisions are made through a combination of buyers and sellers deciding what to buy, produce and sell, coupled with some government interference such as taxing or subsidising the production of some goods.

Monopoly a single seller in the market.

Mortgage a loan that is made and secured on property.

Motivation the desire to achieve a particular goal, backed up by the drive to perform.

Multinational a company with its head office in one country, but operating in at least two countries.

Nationalisation the taking over of a business by the government.

Negligence failing to carry out an expected duty or responsibility

Net profit the profit of a firm after trading costs and expenses have been deducted.

Newly industrialised country (NIC) countries such as Brazil, Russia, India and China that are currently experiencing rapid industrial progress.

Niche marketing activities designed to reach and appeal to a particular segment of a larger market.

Objectives clearly defined ends towards which an organisation works.

Off-the-job training training not specifically related to carrying out a work-based task.

On-the-job training instructing employees at their place of work while they carry out their normal work-based activities.

Open question in a market research questionnaire, a question that allows respondents to answer in their own words.

Operations the processes involved in producing goods and services.

Opportunity cost the next-best alternative that is given up when a decision is made.

Organisation chart a diagram setting out the relationships between people in an organisation.

Overheads costs incurred in the daily running of a business that do not vary with the quantity of production.

Owner's capital finance provided by the owner of a business.

Partnership a business owned by two or more people, often carrying out professional work or a business service on a local scale.

Penetration pricing charging a low initial price to win market share.

Piece rate payment according to the number of units or pieces produced.

Pressure group a group or association formed to promote a particular interest or cause by influencing businesses and public policy.

Price fixing groups of producers or sellers collaborating together to set prices rather than competing with each other.

Primary industry the first stage in a production process that uses natural resources (e.g. land for farming).

Glossary

Primary data use of first-hand sources (e.g. asking questions directly of respondents).

Private company a company whose shares are not up for sale on a stock exchange. Buying and selling shares may only be done with permission from the Board of Directors.

Private costs the costs to an individual of carrying out a particular activity.

Private sector the part of the economy that is owned by private individuals and organisations rather than the government.

Privatisation the switching of businesses from government ownership to private ownership.

Product life cycle the key stages in the life of a product, and how long the cycle lasts.

Productivity a measure of the output of a firm in relation to the inputs.

Profit the reward for risk taking; the sum which remains after all costs have been subtracted from revenues.

Profit and loss account (P&L) an accounting statement showing a firm's sales revenue over a trading period and all the relevant costs generated to earn that revenue.

Promotion money and effort dedicated to increasing the sales of a product.

Public limited company (plc) a company that is allowed to sell shares through the stock exchange.

Public sector part of the economy run and managed by a government.

Q

Quality fitness for purpose, when a good, service or process does exactly what the customer expects.

Quality assurance checking at the end of the line that the product meets a required standard.

Quality circle small groups of people who meet regularly to discuss work problems, usually with a leader.

Quota limitation on the numbers of items that can be exchanged between countries.

R

Ratio the relationship between one business variable and another (e.g. profit:sales).

Recession two or more consecutive quarters (three-month periods) in which GDP is falling.

Regulation supervision of the way in which a business or organisation can run; setting limits and rules relating to its activities.

Retail the final link in the chain of distribution from manufacturer to end-user. A retailer holds stocks at a location convenient to the customer and provides a choice of products. Retail outlets include supermarkets, small shops and street-corner sellers.

Revenue the value of total sales made by a business within a period, usually 1 year.

Risk the possibility of not reaching a desired outcome. For example, in setting up a business there is a risk that the expected profits do not result from business activity.

ROCE (Return On Capital Employed) Businesses invest capital in new projects. ROCE measures the return on these investments as a percentage on the capital invested.

S

Secondary industry the stage in the production of goods concerned with making or using raw materials from primary industries.

Secondary research using existing information sources to find out something for your own research.

Security Offered by borrowers when money is loaned, for example allowing the lender to take possession of some of their property if they fail to repay the loan.

Selling seeking to persuade potential customers that the business has the appropriate solutions to meet their needs.

Share a unit of ownership of a company, held by a **shareholder**, who can own one or many shares in a company. Shareholders receive a share certificate showing how many shares they own.

Shareholders part-owners of a company, with shares in the company.

Skimming creaming off successive layers of the market by charging an initial high price and then lowering it.

SMART the qualities of well written objectives: Specific, Measurable, Achievable, Realistic and Time-related.

Social benefit the advantages of a particular activity to members of a society.

Sole trader a business owned by one person.

Stakeholders people who have an interest in how an organisation or group is run.

Strategic decisions plans that have a major impact on the whole organisation.

Subsidy money granted by the state to keep down the price of goods.

Supply the quantities that producers and sellers are prepared to bring to the market at different prices.

Sustainable development growth of society in terms of what is produced and consumed. The nature of this growth is that it can be maintained over a period of time and that it does not take place at the expense of people and the environment.

T

Tariff a sum of money that an importer or exporter has to pay to trade goods across borders.

Glossary

Tariff barriers a tax on imports designed to protect producers in a particular country from foreign competitors.

Team people working together with a shared sense of purpose and commitment to achieve shared results.

Technology techniques involving the application of scientific principles to production processes.

Tertiary industry service industries concerned with providing value for people (e.g. postal services, insurance and banking services).

Total quality management (TQM) building quality into production at every stage in the production process, rather than checking for it only at the end of the line.

Trade union body recognised in law consisting of employees with common work interests who seek to further their collective interests through bargaining with employers.

Training enabling employees to develop the knowledge, skills and attitudes required to carry out the work needed to meet an organisation's objectives.

Uncompetitive practice carrying out activities designed to reduce the ability of competitors to compete, for example business agreeing with a buyer not to buy goods from a competitor.

Unfair dismissal loss of a job for reasons that are not acceptable in law.

Value added the increase in value of a product at each stage in production.

Variable costs costs which vary with the level of output (e.g. fuel costs, raw material costs).

Video conference a meeting that uses electronic connections so that participants in different locations can see each other and converse.

W

Website internet location providing information, advertising and details of an individual, organisation or topic, etc.

Key terms are in **bold** and also listed
in the glossary

Index

Index

The Musician's Guide to

Making & Selling
Your Own CDs & Cassettes

by Jana Stanfield

WRITER'S DIGEST BOOKS
CINCINNATI, OHIO

01 00 99 98 97   5 4 3 2 1

Library of Congress Cataloging-in-Publication Data

Stanfield, Jana.
    The musician's guide to making & selling your own cds & cassettes / by Jana Stanfield.
        p.   cm.
    Includes index.
    ISBN 0-89879-808-6 (pb : alk. paper)
    1. Sound recording industry—United States. 2. Music trade—United States—Marketing. 3. Popular music—Writing and publishing.
ML3790.S736   1997
780'.68'8—dc2   97-19883
                                                                                          CIP

Edited by Cindy Laufenberg
Production edited by Marilyn Daiker
Designed by Jannelle Schoonover
Cover designed by Design Mill (513) 651-3330

ABOUT THE AUTHOR

"I got tired of waiting for my big break in showbiz, so I went on without it."

She is no more famous than you, but with a little hard work and a knack for alternative marketing, Jana Stanfield sells over $40,000 in albums a year, performing paid concerts for appreciative pre-assembled audiences at non-traditional venues. Never one to be held back by obscurity, she supports a part-time staff and a full-time Jeep payment, travels "free" to great locations, and is frequently asked, "Are you working or on vacation?" Her answer is, "*Both!*"

After a long streak of losing at talent competitions (many of which were nationally televised), Jana Stanfield moved to Nashville and became a triple-platinum singer-songwriter with songs recorded by Reba McEntire, Andy Williams, Garry Morris, John Schneider, and Suzy Bogguss. Her music has been heard on "Entertainment Tonight," "The Oprah Winfrey Show," and "20/20." Her song "If I had Only Known" is the closing theme of the major motion picture *8 Seconds* starring Luke Perry of TV's "90210."

Even with tremendous songwriting success, Jana Stanfield knows the frustration of trying to get a record deal as an artist with a major label. "Finally," she says, "I stopped waiting for a record company to deem me worthy of living my dream, and I deemed myself worthy."

Once a signer-songwriter who talked a lot, she is now a professional speaker who sings a lot during her self-titled "Keynote Concerts." She has toured with best-selling authors including Wayne Dyer, Bernie Siegel and Deepak Chopra, and has written a story featured in *The 3rd Helping of Chicken Soup for the Soul*. She calls her unique brand of music "heavy *mental*" and says her goal is to give audiences a "*faith*-lift." In addition to television appearances on "The Nashville Network" and "TNN Country News," she is also reguarly featured on the Nashville's "Tennessee Crossroads." To help other artists who are tired of waiting for that big break in showbiz, Jana facilitates workshops for songwriters and performers called, "Start Small, Think Big, Live Large."

So most musicians were part-time entertainers and played for enjoyment. But some musicians are so fully committed that they are unable to become successful at any other work. *In the old days, these people might become itinerant musicians and make music wherever they could get a crowd together. Often they gravitated to the industrial centers like the mining camps and hoped that the collection they took after a performance might provide enough to sustain them.*

> —Edward A. Kahn II
> The Carter Family: A Reflection of Changes in Society

There's nothing base or ignoble about selling product, staying after shows to sign the product, and making a little extra money that goes a long way during the lean months we all know and dread.

> —Janis Ian
> Grammy Award-winning singer-songwriter

TABLE OF CONTENTS

INTRODUCTION

IS THIS BOOK FOR YOU?

This book could've been called, "I Couldn't Wait for My Big Break in Showbiz, So I Went on Without It—And You Can, Too."

Many of us started with the dream of having our music heard. (Okay, some of us also had our hearts set on sequined dresses, a private jet and a mantel loaded with Grammies, but that's something I'm better off discussing with my therapist.) It seemed that the only way to get our music heard by the people we wanted to hear it was to become a big star. The quest for *stardom* made some of us lose sight of our original, simple dream. We thought the only way to have what we wanted was to make music on a grand scale. It seemed too outrageous to think we could have success making music on a small scale, so we never truly considered it. The methods in this book will help you make music on a small scale and live your life on a grand scale.

- If you have ever dreamed of having a large following of people who like your music, this book is for you.
- If you have ever dreamed of pulling up at the concert hall and seeing a line of people waiting to get in to hear you, this book is for you.
- If you would enjoy spending an hour after your concerts signing copies of your new album, this book is for you.
- If you have dreamed of people telling you your music makes a difference in their lives, this book is for you.
- If you have ever dreamed of supporting yourself, your family and even an employee with your music, this book is for you.

• If you are a songwriter, musician or singer who has ever dreamed of having people enjoy and appreciate your music, this book is for you.

• If you already have your own albums and would like to sell twice as many as you're selling now, this book is for you.

All these dreams have come true in my life, because I was willing to open my mind to new ways of seeing my music, myself and my career.

There are lots of us out here making a great living with our own music. We started small by recording an album, and we are now living large . . . living our dreams. Our success on a personal and professional level is outrageously enjoyable. We're creating music we like; we're finding audiences who like our music; and we're having fun doing it.

You probably have never heard of most of us. We don't let that hold us back. You say most people have never heard of you? There's no reason to let that hold you back.

You'll see references in this book to folk music. Singer-songwriter-folk recording artist Christine Lavin lovingly and laughingly refers to it as the F-word of the music world. If you don't feel that you do anything like folk music, you may not understand the definition. *Contemporary folk* is the label for music that is impossible to label. *Folk music* can refer to blues, alternative, singer-songwriter, acoustic, bluegrass, zydeco, gospel or all of the above. In the past, this music was considered noncommercial. Few radio stations played it, and few record stores carried it, so these artists found their own way to bring their recordings to the people who appreciated their art form. Many of them are quoted in these pages.

When I read a quote from a working musician, it's easy to assume we have nothing in common, because they've probably been playing music all their lives. They probably don't know anything about working a day job in a demanding career while wrestling with the dream of playing music that gets heard and enjoyed by other people. The people in this book are people like you and me. Most of them have had other careers. Most of them have struggled to find a way to play the music they love. Now that they've found it, they are contributing their expertise. By sharing what we've learned, we hope it won't take you as long to get going as it took us.

Making your own album is like having the courage to toss a little pebble into the water. The first ring of supporters starts with friends and family. The rings grow from there to encompass thousands of people. Dozens of people can grow to hundreds, and hundreds can easily grow to thousands. You don't need millions. Thousands of people who like your music can abundantly support you in making a living doing what you love. The world is a great big pond with room for all of us to make our own brand of waves.

This book is written for anyone who wants to make a living making music. Some of you are professional songwriters who are just beginning to consider the possibility of putting ten of your songs together to make an album. Some of you are recording artists who are already selling albums and are looking for better ways to market them. If you'd like to sell at least $30,000 a year in albums, this book is for you.

For some, making an album of your own music is still just a dream. You're waiting for that perfect deal, the perfect time, the perfect songs, the perfect band, the perfect manager, the perfect situation.

Do you ever wonder if you've been waiting too long? Life is passing by so quickly that you're willing to change your strategy and try some new ideas. If you're ready to look at your career in a new way that can help you live your dreams faster than you ever imagined, read on.

CHAPTER ONE

DEFINE YOUR OWN OUTRAGEOUS SUCCESS

If someone told you that you could live in whatever town you choose, travel free or all-expenses-paid to the places you want to visit, bring in an unlimited amount of money and do it all by playing the music you love, you might call the idea outrageous. When I talk about *outrageous success*, I'm not just talking about money. The money is there in abundance for someone who is willing to step out on faith with their music and work hard for it, but there's more to outrageous success than that.

When I look at the musical freedom I have now, I think, *This is outrageous*. When I count out thousands of dollars for a bank deposit, I think, *This is outrageous*. When I consider that it's possible to do all this without being nationally known, I think, *This is outrageous*. If you're one of those who is determined to be the next big thing, maybe it would be hard for you to give up the idea of being big-time famous. It was hard for me at first, because that determination kept me going for a long time. It gave me the incentive to practice, to improve and to strive to be the best I could be.

I have a promise to make to you. When you sign dozens of albums after one of your concerts, and when many of those people want to have their photo taken with you, and when you later get letters from people asking how they can order more albums for their friends, it will feel so wonderful that you'll be saying to yourself, *This is outrageous*.

WHY ARE SO MANY PERFORMERS SUDDENLY MAKING THEIR OWN ALBUMS?

Only in the past several years has making albums become affordable to regular people like you and me. All this time, we thought it was too expensive. Making and marketing your own albums has never been so inexpensive. Now that the prices are low, people are waking up to the fact that a faraway dream is now clearly in sight. It may seem like a mirage, but it's not. You can make your own album. You can achieve it with less effort and less money than you ever imagined. You don't need anyone's permission or stamp of approval. You probably won't even need to take out a loan.

When you were growing up, did you know people who had albums out? Regular people who lived in your town and shopped at the local grocery store? Unless you grew up in Nashville or Los Angeles, you probably didn't know many people with albums out. When I was growing up, I only knew a few people who ever had an album, and that was quite a big deal. My dad had some singles out, but never an album. Back then albums were out of reach to regular people who didn't have big-time investors and recording contracts. All that has changed.

CAN I REALLY MAKE A LIVING MAKING AND SELLING MY OWN ALBUMS?

When I made my first album, I made only a hundred copies, thinking I'd have my whole lifetime to sell that many. Making my first album cost about $3,500. I had never saved $3,500 in my life, but I didn't have to, because I made the album as I had the money, $100 to $300 at a time. I was shocked at how easy it was to sell the first hundred within a few months.

Selling a hundred cassettes at $10 apiece, I made $1,000. As soon as I sold 350 cassettes, my investment was paid off. It took only five months to sell 350 cassettes. I have now sold a thousand copies of that album, for a total of $10,000, which amounts to $6,500 total profit. So far.

I was not famous, and I'm still not famous. I didn't have any *star-maker machinery* behind me, no manager, no booking agent, no public-relations director, no distributor and no computer (not to mention, no computer skills). I had no idea how I would sell my albums.

Four years later, my five albums are bringing in an average of $30,000 per year. I still don't have a distributor or most of the other stuff I just mentioned. I have sold each album myself, which gives me the opportunity to personally thank each person who buys one. I thank them because they are making it possible for me to make my living doing what I love.

Talented musicians, songwriters and singers come to me every week asking for advice about how to make their own albums. This book is filled with answers to questions they've asked about how I've done it and how they can do it. This is a book of ideas, insights and encouragement from me and many other artists who are making their living making music. If we can do it in our own way, you can do it in your own way. My goal with this book is not to be a technical adviser, but a friend who is sharing her wisdom, experience, strength and hope.

TIPS FROM THE PROS: LES SAMPOU

Les Sampou is a singer-songwriter who combines blues and folk into contemporary songs that are unique and on the edge. After years of working Monday through Thursday at the Secretary of State's office in Boston and playing music Friday, Saturday and Sunday, she got a loan from a relative to make her first album. When she was ready to release it, she sent out dozens of press releases and sample copies to the local media, which started a buzz in her town. This created so much interest that people who hadn't heard her before began coming to her shows and buying albums. As a result, she was able to begin playing music full-time and signed with a larger record company two years later.

When she's not doing concerts across the country, Les does private consulting and teaches workshops called "Ain't Nobody's Bizness But Yours." Here's Les's advice: "I'd recommend anyone interested in a career in music make their first CD if they haven't been able to secure a record deal right off. The immediate benefits are:

1. You have something to send to radio stations.
2. It becomes your calling card to whoever you want to introduce your music—record companies, agents, managers, other musicians, writers, etc.
3. A big benefit is *you can sell it off the stage* and make money to support you and your goldfish with."

DO YOU HAVE WHAT IT TAKES? YES!

"Listen for the whisper deep down inside
Listen for the whisper, a strong but gentle guide
With a thousand different voices ringing in my ear
I listen for the whisper that only the heart can hear."
—*from "Listen for the Whisper," Jana Stanfield and Tony Harrell*

It's hard to get a record deal. It's easy to start a record company. If you can get together enough money to buy a keyboard, a guitar or a saxophone, you can finance your own album.

In the days of vinyl, 8-track and cassettes, it took a record company-sized chunk-o-change to record, duplicate and release an album. Now, when your child says its first words, you can record it and send it to relatives on CD. Making your own albums has never been easier or more affordable.

If you are exploring the pages of this book, chances are you are exploring the idea of making and marketing your own music. Maybe you've been thinking this is a crazy idea. You're right. The good news is that it's a crazy idea that just might work.

I can promise the idea will pay off. It can pay off big in terms of money, and it can pay off in ways that may prove to be even more valuable. When you can honor the music inside you enough to record it and make it available, you will have a powerfully positive effect on your self-esteem. I can't guarantee that people will respect you more because you have an album out, but I will say it gives credibility to your music.

Jerry Penrod is a friend of mine who feels that the keyboard instrumentals he writes are ideal for someone like John Tesh. If Jerry sends John a cassette, or even a DAT (digital audio tape) demo of one of his songs, it would be fine, but if he sends a beautifully produced song on his own CD, that would probably carry more weight. It would be a pitch from artist to artist, instead of from songwriter to artist.

If you are hearing a call to record your music, I urge you to answer that call. It is my hope that this book will guide, support, enlighten and encourage you along your journey. You don't have to know your destination just yet; sometimes we don't know our destination until we get there. After making and marketing my own albums for years, I still don't know my destination. That doesn't keep me from enjoying the heck out of the adventure.

This adventure takes me to wonderful places along the way. As I seek out places to market my music, I always look for interesting towns I've been wanting to visit and faraway loved ones I've been longing to see. I have learned many things that can save you time, money and heartache along the way. This book will steer you around some of the pitfalls that can slow you down and help you avoid the detours that can pull you off course, so your journey can be easier and faster than mine.

Even though this journey hasn't always been easy, it has always been worth it. I encourage you to read further and, as you read, listen to the whisper of your heart to hear what action it is guiding you to take. I hope the first action it tells you to take is to turn the page.

START WHERE YOU ARE

The first step of any journey is always the hardest. You have taken the first step by turning the pages of this book to explore further the idea of making and marketing your own albums. The first thing you need to consider before you actually invest money in production is whether anyone out there will purchase your product. There is no way to know this for certain. The information in this section will help you make a pretty good guess. Even if, after digesting this section, you still don't think anyone would buy your albums, don't toss out the idea of making them. Loading a thousand CDs into your basement will give you all the incentive it takes to *find* people who will buy them.

You have a following (no matter how large or how small) of people who genuinely like either you or your music. I say "you or your music" because there's an important concept to understand here. Plenty of people are out there making a living with their music who have less-than-average musical talent and less-than-average vocal abilities. What these people often possess, though, is a charismatic personality or a way of delivering their material that makes you overlook their musical shortcomings. What matters is the overall effect. Often, the sum is greater than its parts.

Lyle Lovett has a limited vocal range. His songwriting is so unique that his songs are rarely the kind radio stations will play. On stage, he comes across as painfully shy and introspective. I personally find him very attractive, but some people find his looks unappealing. It is a good thing that Lyle Lovett doesn't let any of this hold him back. When you add his vocal style, his quirky songs, his looks and his shy, introspective persona together, you come up with a captivating performer who makes wonderful records that people buy in mass quantities whether radio stations play them or not.

If you could only hear Madonna's voice on tape, with no pictures or videos or choreography or special effects, it would not be something you would pay money to hear again. You might even pay money not to hear it again! This woman has made millions in music because what she lacks in vocal beauty, she more than makes up for in her skills as a dancer, a media manipulator and a marketing genius.

Neil Young. Bob Dylan. Am I the only one who thinks these guys are terrible singers? Fortunately, both have written songs that have endeared them to us, and that is the secret.

The secret is to appreciate and value those aspects of yourself that people find endearing. Maybe you're not the best singer in the world. Maybe you're not the best musician. I'm certainly not the best singer and, although I hack away at my poor guitar and continue to take lessons, I can't even call myself a musician. It's important to look deeper than your musical skills. You've got to assess more than just that about yourself, and when you do, you will be pleased with what you discover. Ask yourself these questions:

- Do I have something important to say with my music?
- Do people ask me if I have an album they can buy?
- Do people invite me to share my music at social gatherings?
- Do people stop and listen when I play my music?
- Does my music seem to touch people in a unique way?
- Is my music unique?
- Does my music promote important causes?
- Does my music make people think or help people relax?
- Is my music interesting?
- Is my music entertaining?
- Does my music appeal to the kind of person who buys music?

This test can be difficult, because it's hard to know what other people think of us. If you need help, find a few friends you trust who can help you with the answers to these questions. Be sure to tell them up front whether you want complete honesty. Maybe you don't. Maybe you want them to say yes to all these questions, because you really feel that making a record is what you need to do. If so, that's great. Go for it. If you can answer yes to even three of these ten questions, there probably is something that endears you to your listeners.

The most important element here is this: If you believe in your music enough to make records, you will find that there are people who will buy them. You have to believe before you start, because if you don't believe in your music, how can you expect anyone else to?

TIPS FROM THE PROS: DAR WILLIAMS

Dar Williams, who can now be found on tour with Joan Baez, in interviews on National Public Radio, and favorably reviewed in *People* magazine, started by making her own albums. For three years she played java joints, house concerts and pass-the-hat places before signing with Waterbug Records, then Razor & Tie. Somewhere along the way, she found time to write a book called *The Tofu Tollbooth* to help fellow travelers find wholesome meals in unknown towns.

"Know that there are two worlds out there: the audience-defined and the industry-defined careers," Dar says. "A person can have a full professional career in music that is defined by their live following and their self-released products. A person can submit demos to record labels and, if they get signed, let the label do a certain amount of the footwork. I do a mix of both now, but I'm very grateful for the years I did everything myself. It gave me more negotiating power when I signed with a label, and it gave me a sense of myself outside of how the industry defines *success*."

IF I WOULDN'T BUY THIS, WHY WOULD ANYONE ELSE?

If you weren't you, would you buy your album? The answer to this question just might be a big fat *no*. That's okay. At this point, maybe you wouldn't buy an album from anyone who created it themselves. But that doesn't mean a lot of other people won't buy it.

Take a field trip in your mind to your favorite record store. A large record store with good variety may carry a million different selections. You probably go to only one or two sections for your favorite music. If you look around, though, lots of people are in the other sections, too. There is something for nearly every taste. Maybe you wouldn't buy a jazz album. Maybe you wouldn't buy a hip-hop album or a gospel album. Fortunately, lots of people would, and there are enough people to keep the record stores and the recording artists in business. So what if you're going to make an album you wouldn't buy? There are lots of albums in the world that you not only wouldn't buy, but wouldn't listen to if someone gave them to you. This doesn't mean the music doesn't have value.

If I wasn't me, I probably wouldn't buy one of my albums. I always think so many people are more talented than I am, and I would rather listen to their music. When I listen to my albums, I can't help wishing I had sung that vocal one more time, put a little longer space between this verse and that chorus, or put a little shorter space between this song and that one. I have learned, though, that my albums do have value. If they didn't, my album sales wouldn't be paying my employee's salary, my salary and my Jeep payment. If they didn't have value, people wouldn't write me such nice letters and wouldn't ever buy a second, third, fourth and fifth one. I hope all those nice people understand when I say that, personally, I'd rather listen to David Wilcox, David Roth, Karen Taylor-Good, Greg Tamblyn, Susan Ashton and Shawn Colvin.

Value is in the eye of the beholder or, in this case, the cash-holder. If someone wants to buy your music, it has value. Many songwriters and performers are shy about what they do. Modesty, repeated rejection and/or fear have convinced them that their music isn't worthy of being in a record store.

Let's look at other kinds of artists. Few painters achieve exactly what they want with each painting. That doesn't mean the painting isn't beautiful and wonderful and valuable. Fortunately for art buyers, we have no idea what the artist was actually shooting for. We have no idea that the artist is disappointed because this painting is not what he or she had in mind.

Landscapers do their best to create something beautiful using plants. Unfortunately, plants are living things, and they cannot always be controlled. Sort of like an album. The landscape artist has an idea of what he or she wants to create and then works with the plants to help them reach their optimum potential for beauty. When the project is over, the landscape probably doesn't look just the way the landscaper planned it, due to a lack of cooperation by the plants. This doesn't mean it's not beautiful or that the person who owns the property won't be thrilled to see it.

There's a great saying about the way an artist feels about his or her creation when it is finished: "The disappointment that an artist feels at the completion of a creation is the seed of the artist's next creation."

We always want our creations to be better than they are, and we, as artists, have a tendency to judge our creations as worthless if they don't measure up to the high standards we hoped to reach. I know few artists who feel they absolutely reach their potential with every song. It's likely your album won't be as wonderful as you'd like it to be, but that doesn't mean it can't bring hours of pleasure to the people who buy it and listen to it. If people like your music enough to buy it, it has value you can measure.

A NOTE TO PROFESSIONAL SONGWRITERS

If "do what you love and the money will follow" was true for songwriters, we would all have bank accounts the size of songwriter Diane Warren's. We could all afford 24-track studios for our 22,000-square-foot homes,

Jaguars and guitar-shaped swimming pools. If wealth was measured by open hearts, hard-earned wisdom and pure talent, songwriters would be the richest people in the world.

While this book is written for everyone who has music they want to share, I hope my insights and experience will be especially helpful to you, my fellow professional songwriters. You are my brothers and sisters, my family and friends, my support, my inspiration, my peers and, at the same time, my teachers.

Each one of you has a spiral notebook or a computer filled with lessons of life in song form. Your heart is in each song. Your dreams are in each song. A picture from your soul that can never be re-created is captured in each song. For too many of us, those lovingly crafted lyrics go unheard while the demo tape of that song sprouts cobwebs on a publishing-company shelf. The publisher was really excited the week we wrote it, but now the song we were so proud of is a year old, or ten years old. It is quickly forgotten as new songs are turned in.

Remember the enthusiasm for your own music that started you on this journey into the music world? Remember what it was like to perform your songs for friends and family back when songwriting was nothing more than a beloved hobby? Your songs made the people around you laugh and cry and look at life differently than they did before.

Do people from your hometown still say that *you* ought to be singing your songs . . . that *you* ought to be an artist? You try to explain that you're too old, or that you don't have the right looks or that you just don't care to put your heart on the line for radio to accept or reject, but they don't want to believe that. People who love you and your music have probably told you that lots of people would buy your album. They are right.

When you make your own albums, you don't have to sell millions to make an unbelievable living from your songs. You don't need two hundred *Radio and Records* reporting stations to designate your song *hot* and *heavy* simultaneously to have a huge success with your own albums. If two hundred regular people buy your album, that's $2,000, and if those same people buy your CD instead, that's $3,000. Why invest so much energy jumping through hoops to impress radio and record company people when you can just be yourself and impress regular people?

Making your own albums from your demo tapes is easy, inexpensive and amazingly lucrative. The rewards are not only financial, but mental and spiritual. We all know the rejection we feel when someone listens through the verse and the chorus, then says, "I don't hear it." On the other hand, you won't believe the incredible rejuvenation you'll feel when someone says, "I love that song. Can I get your album?" Every time someone buys your album, they are saying, "I believe in you. I appreciate what you do. I want to support you in doing more of what you love."

Too often, when we think of success in the music business, we look right past all the non-music-business people who appreciate our gifts and talents. We can only see success in terms of a monumental hit song that will be adored by the masses. We ignore the trees in our quest to get to the forest.

You can still write the hits. You can still strive for that big-time record deal. At the same time, you can make your own albums and sell them whenever you perform. It's better than waiting tables, and I can say that from experience.

I'm not talking about becoming an independent artist competing with the majors to get on the radio. Forget radio. Forget charts. People out there in the real world couldn't care less about music charts, record label status or medium-rotation airplay. If they like your music, they'll buy your music, and they'll suggest their friends do the same.

Why put all your energy into the dream that one of your songs will make $30,000 someday, when your rejected, artsy-fartsy, these-just-ain't-commercial songs can help you make that much every year? You can still write to get cuts, but don't let those songs that haven't been cut (yet) go to waste. Put ten of them together, put your picture on the cover and let your songs put some beans on your table.

You can play concerts in all the places where you want to vacation. You can perform where you have family you've been wanting to visit, and you can write off every trip. You can enjoy the little luxuries of life, like insurance, regular dental visits and a car that starts every day. Soon, you can start shopping for that mutual fund you've been dreaming about. You can enjoy the rush of being a star and yet never suffer the inconvenience of getting accosted for autographs at Wal-Mart.

CHAPTER TWO

REASONS TO MAKE YOUR OWN ALBUM INSTEAD OF WAITING FOR A MAJOR LABEL DEAL

When I first arrived in Nashville to seek my fame and fortune as a recording artist, I was very lucky to get a good job in the music business. I worked for four years at Tandem Promotions, a company that promoted artists' records to country radio stations. We were hired by artists to call radio stations on their behalf. The job of a record promoter is to convince radio station music directors to play certain records and to play those records frequently. The more frequently a record is played, the higher it moves on the chart. We worked records for Garth Brooks, Vince Gill and just about every other country star you could name.

Working there provided me with a good education and a rude awakening. Lots of people find themselves asking, "How did *that* song become a hit?" but very few people understand how it really works. I thought if I really understood how it works, I could eventually make it work for me. I would know just what to do to make sure my own major label records would be huge successes. Unfortunately, no one in the record business has that power. Not me, not Garth Brooks, not Madonna, not the top music business attorney, not the top record company president, not the top manager, not anybody. The record-making machinery is too big and too unpredictable for any one person to have power over it.

WHAT THEY DON'T TELL YOU ABOUT A MAJOR LABEL DEAL

Honest Records recording artist Kate Wallace once said, "It's the music business. Not the music friends, not the music nice, but the music business."

"The word *art* is not in the title," says Michael Johnson, who has recorded for big and small record companies. "It's a business." After having huge success singing a song called "Bluer Than Blue," Michael's songs continued to make it to the upper reaches of the pop charts and the country charts through the '70s and '80s. As unpretentious as he is incredibly talented, Michael now laughingly says, "I've had more hits than anyone to be as obscure as I am."

TIPS FROM THE PROS: TOM KIMMEL

Tom Kimmel released two albums on PolyGram Records in 1987 and 1990 and has written songs for over thirty artists as diverse as Joe Cocker, Johnny Cash, the Stray Cats, the Spinners, Levon Helm and Linda Ronstadt. He explains that a major label release is a group process. Even though your name is on the record and your face is on the video, your final product will reflect the opinions of a large group of people. "Recording for a major label generally involves working with a team: a manager, a music-business attorney, an accountant or business manager who is involved from the first advance check you receive, and an A&R rep from the label. Later you'll work with others at the label—most likely a product manager, a video coordinator, promo (and perhaps even sales) staff, an agent and a publicist.

"In the recording stage, however, direction will be offered from your manager, your A&R person and your producer. As a general rule, these people expect to have a say—perhaps a large say—in what you record and how you record it for your project. And they deserve to have their opinions considered. If an artist is smart, he or she will let those team players know that their input is appreciated and important, and if it feels right, will utilize their best ideas. There are times when I have gone against my better judgment and agreed to what others wanted when it felt wrong to me, but I didn't feel like I could rock the boat too much by disagreeing, and now years later those mistakes still don't sound right, and they never will."

"In the end, you really don't have the authority to do your own art if you're signed to a big record company," says Michael Johnson. Now that he is producing his own albums on a smaller record label, Michael recalls the frustration of not being able to make his own artistic choices about what songs to record and release. "It's not like they say, 'shut up and sing and just do what we tell you.' They lobby. They're insidious, and they come at you more and more often about what they'd rather see you do. If the record company stylist gives you the choice between the skunk suit and this yellow jumpsuit, do you have artistic control?

"People expect major label execs to know how to sell you and to know what to do next. I was assuming it was going to be a very focused thing, and it's not. I thought they were going to have the answers, and they don't. As liberal as these record companies may seem, they're very conservative.

They're taking a gamble on you, and if it does work, they're proud. If it doesn't work, you blew it, and you're out."

Most of us dream of getting a deal with a major label. We think the major label will invest big bucks in a great producer, in recording our music and in promoting our music to the public. If our albums turn a profit, the major label gets paid back and we get all the rest (theoretically). If our albums don't turn a profit, we are under no obligation to reimburse the label for what was spent on our behalf.

What a deal. Nothing to lose and everything to gain. We have visions of television appearances, sequined jackets and never again having to draw pictures for our loved ones of what we would have given them for Christmas if only we had the money.

With all this positive visualization going on, it seems harsh to say that getting a record deal is no guarantee you'll ever have records out. I'll just mention some things that can keep your record from ever being released: The record company can change presidents; the person who signed you can leave the company; or the record company can keep you in the development stage with no record out for a few years and then lose interest. Every music town (Los Angeles, Nashville, Austin, Chicago, Boston, New York) is filled with wonderful artists who will tell you why their records never came out, why radio stations didn't play them or why they were eventually dropped from a company's artist roster.

Let's not be pessimistic, though. Let's move on and assume that you have landed the record deal and your singles are making it at least to the thirties on the charts. While most of us would be thrilled to be making such progress in our careers, the record company sees it differently.

AIRPLAY IS A TOUGH GAME, EVEN FOR THE MAJOR LABELS

In the world of commercial radio and big record companies, the life of a single song release is about three months. If the song hasn't made it to the top of the charts by then, it's not going to happen. "If a certain amount of time goes by after your single comes out, and only half the radio stations in the country are playing it, the label will stop working it," Michael Johnson explains. "They've got other artists waiting, other release schedules and quotas to meet. To them, there's no such thing as a regional success."

It's the reality of commercial music. "Trying to get your song up the charts on commercial radio is like trying to win *Star Search*," Michael says. "You're there singing some heartfelt ballad, or some great groove-oriented thing, and you're competing with somebody who sings, tap dances and twirls flaming batons with the lights out. That's your competition on *Star Search*, and that's your competition on commercial radio."

You might be shocked to know that in the commercial radio world, a record that doesn't make it to the top twenty is frequently referred to as a *stiff*. When describing those songs you were so thrilled to see listed in the thirties on the *Billboard* chart, radio station music directors would be likely to speak in deep tones of disillusionment about how they took a chance on playing you, and all your records have stiffed. At the record company, your future would be a large question mark.

You would logically think the next album will do even better after all the recognition you've gained. The accountants at the record company think a second album for you might be a case of throwing good money after bad, since they're still in debt from your last album. Your album would have to sell at least $150,000 to put them in the black, and chances are that your first album won't sell that amount in the first year. If you make it big, your first album will eventually sell that much, but that will be the result of people picking it up along with your second or third album, so it may take a while.

All this is leading up to the good news and the bad news. The bad news is that despite the fact that you would be overjoyed that people bought 100,000 units of your major label record, the label could consider you a failure, a disappointment and possibly even an embarrassment. You would be unlikely to see any of the money from the sale of those 100,000 units. The good news is that if you make your own albums and you sell 100,000 units, no one can call you a failure, a disappointment or an embarrassment. They will have to call you a millionaire.

To sell a thousand units on a major label is a joke (although, believe me, it has happened to some major label artists whose careers were subsequently short-lived). To sell a thousand units on your own label is to walk away with $10,000. In cash.

GOLDFISH BOWL

The traditional music business can be like a goldfish bowl under a spotlight. Everyone wants to get into that fishbowl. For those who are striving to get in, it's easy to overlook the fact that there's not enough water for everyone. It's easy to overlook the fact that a spotlight can fry the skin of a tender goldfish, especially if there's not enough water to get lost in, to explore in, to dive in, to thrive in.

Deciding to make your own albums is like heading into open water. You may not be as easily noticed as you would be in the fishbowl, but your swim will be more carefree, more fun and more rewarding. In the open water, you can go anywhere your fins will take you. There is plenty of water, more than enough for every fish who wants to swim there. The light that falls on the water is easy sunlight. You can swim close to the light or swim away at will. Yes, it's a little lonely. Yes, it takes more courage and confidence, but those are two things that build on each other. The more courage and confidence you can muster in the face of a challenge, the more you will have for the next challenge. Yes, it's a little scary sometimes. But it's worth it.

ROOM FULL OF SLOT MACHINES

While sitting in his therapist's waiting room, a record producer began thinking about how the music business can be like a room full of slot machines. The slot machines are all in a circle, so all the players are facing each other. One circle of slot machines is for producers, one is for songwriters and one is for people hoping to get signed to a major label artist deal. You have to have talent to get into the room, because talent is what you put into the slot machines. You put in a combination of talent, money, hard work, persistence, patience, love, energy and enthusiasm.

Everyone in the room full of slot machines is hoping for the jackpot, the big win that will change their lives. Most frequently, the machines make small payoffs. Sometimes the machines pay off in money, but most often, the payoffs are tokens, like "The record company really likes your stuff," or "Bonnie Raitt put your song on hold."

When someone who got into the business the same time you did hits the jackpot, you think, *Okay, I'm next. I'm good to people, I don't step on anyone, I was given this gift for a reason, and I'm sure I'll be next.* Then your best friend hits the jackpot, and you think, *Okay, I'm next.* Then someone who just walked into the room hits the jackpot, and you think, *Okay, I'm next.* Then someone you don't even respect hits the jackpot, and you think, *Okay, I'm next. I've worked hard, I'm connected to all the best people in the business, I have invested my heart and soul in this, and I'm just sure I'm next.*

Meanwhile, you continue to pump time, money, energy, enthusiasm and talent into the slot machine, and time quickly passes. Children grow up, understanding spouses continue to wonder how much longer it will take for the big break to come, opportunities for other career moves come and go, and the years go by.

The most important thing to understand is that the machines don't care. The person who gets the jackpot doesn't get it by being the most talented, the most brilliant or the most hardworking. The machines pay off when they're going to pay off, and if you're there, you win. The amount of time, energy and talent you put into the machine is not going to cause it to pay off. Yes, the longer you stand there, the more likely you are to be there when a machine pays off. On the other hand, your investment has no guarantees whatsoever. Many incredibly talented musicians, producers, songwriters and singers have played for years and years, with nothing but tokens to show for it.

This record producer noticed something that day. He noticed that when his therapist invested an hour's worth of time in a client, the therapist got paid. It was a new concept for a person in the music business. Invest, get returns. In the slot-machine business, it's invest, invest, invest, invest, and take a chance on getting a big return someday, maybe, if you know the right people, if you're there at the right time, wearing the right clothes and saying the right thing.

So how does this relate to outrageous success? When you invest in your own recordings, the returns are not left to chance. The reason I stopped playing the slot machines as a songwriter wanting a major label deal is because I didn't want my future to be determined by the odds of a slot machine. When I make my own records, I know that if I am willing to get out there and make them available, they will bring me huge returns. I no longer want to leave my career to chance, not any more than I have to.

You can make your own albums and still play the slot machines. There's time for both. It's like diversifying your investments. If you feel a strong desire to play the slot machines, honor that desire. You might just be a big winner. If the slot machine doesn't pay off in the time you hoped it would, listen for that whisper that only the heart can hear. It will tell you when it's time to diversify.

YOU CAN HAVE A SUCCESSFUL MUSIC CAREER WITHOUT A MAJOR LABEL

If you are a major label artist, you are the last person to see the money the public spent to buy your record. You are not only the last person to see it, but by the time it gets to you, the record company and everyone else involved will have taken their shares out first. Yes, you might have received an advance, but that is long gone, spent for rent, food and clothing suitable for a big-time recording artist to wear while waiting for that first album to come out. You may later wish you'd kept working until the record was released, but at the time it seemed tacky to be seen still waiting tables after everyone heard about you getting signed to a major label. The record company keeps every dollar that comes in from the sales of your album, subtracting it from the debt you owe them for the entire album production, the unbelievably expensive video, the lavish promotional tour and that advance you received. You see only the remains if there are any. Even if your records are successful, you'll be paying off what the label invested for a long, long time. If you have a five-album deal, record companies can use a *cross-collateralization* clause to hold the profits from your successful album just in case your other albums are less successful. If you choose, instead, to make your own albums, you reap the rewards of your efforts the moment you sell the first one.

You won't believe the incredible satisfaction you'll feel when someone hands you money for one of your albums. With each album a person buys, that person is enabling us to continue making music we care about. When we are at our sales tables signing albums after concerts, we have the opportunity to thank people for buying our cassettes and CDs, and that feels really good. As I hand them back each autographed CD, I say, "Thanks for your support. You're helping me to continue doing what I love for a living."

Karen Taylor-Good, a Grammy-nominated songwriter who has also been successful in making and selling her own albums, has a quote printed on all her checks that says, "Every dollar I spend enriches others." I'd like to have a quote on my checks that says, "Every dollar I spend supports what I support." It feels good to know that when we buy a book we like, we are supporting that author in doing more. By creating albums, we give people the opportunity to be part of our success. We all enjoy supporting causes we believe in. Our albums give people a chance to support us at the same time that they get some good music to listen to.

When we sell our own albums, we let people join in our success. It's sort of like when you have a waiter or waitress who admits it's their first day on the job. We are more forgiving in that situation, and often we are more generous. It feels good to be able to help somebody out. When people understand that it is through album sales that we are able to continue making music, they become very generous in buying gifts of our albums for their friends and relatives. They are also more likely to send in a mail order when they want more, instead of just running off a tape copy.

When a major label artist has a day in which $300 of her product was sold at Tower Records, the artist won't even know it happened, much less feel any positive reaction. On the other hand, if you sell $300 worth of albums off the stage after a concert, you will go away feeling rich, rewarded and fulfilled.

The Ongoing Saga of Sara Hickman
Sara Hickman is a wildly energetic Texas-based singer-songwriter who has had national radio exposure, national television exposure and even a slot as guest host on VH-1. Best known by the public for her songs "I Couldn't Help Myself" and "Simply," Sara is famous with those of us in the music community for her spirit, for her talent and for the legend of how people who believed in her helped buy her album back from a big record company.

Sara begins the story with her first homemade album project. "I made my first record, a 45 single, in 1986 with $400 my grandparents let me borrow. In 1988, I came out with *Equal Scary People* on Four Dots, the label run by [the band] Brave Combo, although they didn't really do any sort of label work. They just let me copy their logo off of one of their vinyl records and stick it on my album/jacket sleeve! Then Carl [lead singer in Brave Combo] let me come over to his house and rifle through his list of radio contacts. Ah, the good old days! Anyway, I kept it simple and didn't mail but maybe two records out. I just made this record for fans in Dallas who wanted a collection of some of my stuff. I wasn't thinking beyond the present. I had a record-release party and sold around seven hundred copies, and ended up selling about five thousand in the Dallas/Fort Worth area in a few months. I had borrowed money from five friends and subsequently was able to pay each of them back plus 5 percent interest."

In 1989, Sara's album *Equal Scary People*, which she had recorded for about $5,600, was picked up and licensed to Elektra. "This was cool because I got a huge chunk of change up front, but still owned the masters." What happened next gets talked about a lot among musicians but is told most concisely by Joe Mitchell in "Fertile Ground" published in the *Austin Chronicle* (5/13/96):

> *If you're unfamiliar with the story, it goes something like this: In 1991, a happy Sara Hickman signed with a really big major label known as Elektra. They put out her first two albums,* Equal Scary People *and* Shortstop. *Both sold respectably, moving about 50,000 units each, thus setting the stage for a third release, which Hickman handed over in 1993.*
>
> *But the folks at the label didn't like what they heard, and decided to shelve the LP and drop Hickman from their roster. They complained that the singer hadn't delivered a "radio hit," and said that none of the songs on her latest LP had such potential. Hickman asked for the masters back so she could release the album herself, but the label refused, claiming the masters were their property. It was then that Hickman's mother came up with the grand idea of buying the masters back from Elektra.*
>
> *When approached with this idea, Elektra's attorneys initially told Hickman that "this just wasn't done." But she persisted until the label finally gave in, putting a $100,000 price tag on the masters. Eventually the price dropped to $50,000 and finally landed at $25,000, but it wasn't like Hickman had this sort of scratch just lying around. So, it was at this point that Hickman cautiously asked her fans to help, and much to her satisfaction, money, and letters of encouragement, poured in.*
>
> *"It was a big bonding experience with my fans," says Hickman about the selfless generosity of her dedicated audience. She eventually sold her house and some guitars to raise the remainder of the $25K, and the masters were purchased. The result is* Necessary Angels, *the name Hickman bestowed upon all the fans who donated money to her cause. The album was released on Discovery Records in 1994.*

During the years of big-budget recording, promotional appearances and radio tours, Sara noticed that while she was selling more records than fellow artists like Ani DiFranco and Trout Fishing in America, they were doing much better financially on smaller labels.

"I now have my own label, Sleeveless, and my first album is a collection of songs previously unreleased. I licensed it to Shanachie Records, and it will be distributed through them to Koch International, so it will be available overseas." Sara's new album is called *Misfits*.

IF YOU STILL WANT A BIG-TIME RECORD DEAL

The great thing about making your own albums is that you can still pursue a record deal with a major or independent record label. Meanwhile, you can prove your selling power and increase your name recognition. Keep a mailing list of people who like what you do and build a following. That will be valuable to a record company and will help when a record company is interested in you.

After Dar Williams released *The Honesty Room* album successfully on her own, she was able to lease it for distribution to Waterbug Records, a tiny Chicago-area label that specializes in singer-songwriters. With success there, she was able to lease it to a bigger fish in the record pond, the Razor & Tie label. This paved the way for *The Honesty Room* to get national and international distribution. Two songs from *The Honesty Room*, "When I Was a Boy" and "The Babysitter's Here," became favorites in the Adult Album Alternative (Triple A) format. All this came from Dar's courage to record and release her own music.

If you're trying to get a record deal, your own albums will not conflict with that. A large record company is not threatened by the number of albums you sell. In fact, they will be impressed.

Let's say you get a record deal next week. It will take at least a year before your music hits the stores. If you have your own albums, consider this. You can spend the year selling all the albums you possibly can between being in the studio and doing publicity photo shoots and such. Let's say you work really hard and sell cassettes to four thousand people during the year.

First, this gives you $40,000 to spend on expenses the record company doesn't cover. Second, it shows the record company you have the hustle and savvy it takes to sell records. Even if you have the *exact same songs* on your major-label album next year, there are lots more than four thousand people in the world. There is room for you to sell your album to four thousand people and for the record company to sell it to all the rest.

HOW OLD DO YOU HAVE TO BE TO MAKE AN ALBUM?

You're never too old or too young to make an album, as long as you've got caring people to help you. I loved music as a kid and loved performing.

By the time I was in high school, singing in front of crowds got scarier and scarier as my self-esteem got shakier and shakier. Not that this was abnormal; after all, I was a teenager. Everyone's self-esteem gets shaky then.

Can you imagine the confidence boost for your musical dreams if you actually had an album out? As a child? As a teenager? Who cares if it's available only in town, because when you're a teenager, your town is the *only* town. Especially before you get your driver's license. Can you imagine all the skills you'd gain as you sang the vocals, worked with musicians, learned about microphones and began to understand a record company by starting one? It's okay if adults are helping and doing the more complicated stuff. You are watching, participating and getting an education.

I met Wilson Marks when I played a concert at his United Methodist church in Boerne, Texas. As I circulated after the concert, I noticed him, maybe fourteen or fifteen at the time, standing about a foot away from my guitar, just looking at it for a long time. When I encouraged him to pick it up, he acted shy for about a nanosecond, then strapped it on and quietly amazed me. His tasteful and intricate playing left my C, F and G chords in the dust.

Wilson is seventeen now and working on his second album. The first is with friends Chris Collie, seventeen; Dan Huff, seventeen; Aaron Huff, fifteen; and Kyle Nowakowski, seventeen, who formed a band called Circadian Rhythm. Their music could best be described as alternative/folk groove. They started with a $1,000 loan from some local patrons, which is nearly all paid back now. They play gigs in the area (when they're not quarterbacking football games or marching in the school band), and they use all the money from sales to pay off the loan.

Wilson remembers when he thought the idea of making an album was impossible. He doesn't want other young people to limit themselves with that belief. "It's not in the least bit impossible. You just have to have some self-motivation and a love for music. You don't need to be scooped up and paraded around by a record label to be able to hold a tape in your hands and know that your music and thoughts are on there. If nothing else, you can do a live recording with a small mixer and some mics. Churches usually have mixers and soundmen who would be happy to help if you explain your situation. Just don't dawdle and postpone. Go for it."

Wilson Marks lists these as being the most important benefits of making the Circadian Rhythm album:

- We can share our music with other people without them coming to a gig.
- When we play gigs, we can sell cassettes between sets.
- Older musicians actually take us seriously, knowing we've recorded.
- It feels good to release the expressive nature in us through our music.
- It's nice to be able to give tapes to people who book clubs.
- We've gotten many more gigs since we made the tape.

Although they're happy about having their loan paid off, financial success was not among the list of reasons for doing an album. "It wasn't done for monetary results. To us, music is much more than that, probably because we don't have to pay for rent or food yet."

If you are the parent of a young person with talent, my strongest piece of advice is to let the child or teenager be involved in the process of making the album as a learning experience. It's not a make-it-or-break-it activity. Make a good album for the sake of making a good album. It's a snapshot of your child's miraculous gift. Don't push the child to be perfect. My mom, an elementary music teacher, always says, "Music is not meant to be perfect. It's meant to be fun."

I got a letter today from an eleven-year-old who sent me a picture of herself playing guitar and singing in her school talent show. Her letter said, "My goal is to be famous by the end of the year." Ouch. Will she feel like a failure for every year this doesn't happen? My advice to her was, "A dream is a direction, not a destination. Be famous right now. Be famous right now for being a good entertainer and for being a good human being."

If you're convinced you've got the next LeAnn Rimes in your house, go ahead and try to get a bigger record deal with your child's album, but don't record it just for that. Record it because you want your child to experience the pleasure of creating an album and to have fun making music.

TIPS FROM THE PROS: SARA HICKMAN

Singer-songwriter Sara Hickman has this advice to share:

"First, a warning:

"Above and beyond anything anyone can tell you, believe in yourself. Have fun. Do this because you love it and stop when you get tired. Whether you are singing alone in your room or in front of thousands of people, you are unique and have every right to create in the way you want to create. Many people will give you 'free' advice, and you have the choice to believe, utilize, throw out or learn from that advice. You may grow from it, but don't let it hamper, strangle or destroy the gift that is yours. You don't need to make records to be 'good' at what you do. What you are doing is enough in itself; music is a gift you have received. What you believe of and do with that gift is up to you.

"OK. Now . . . advice time.

"1. *Think about what you want and how to get it.* What is your objective? Do you want to make an album to give to friends and family or make a record for posterity? You might want to consider this if your objective is just to collect your music together for a small audience. Be honest. Do you want fame and fortune?

"If you answered yes, don't worry, you're not the only one! Make cassettes, CDs or DATs to send to people in the industry you have met or can reach through a network. Make just as many as you need. Don't waste your time and money mailing out and making expensive product—no one is going to listen to unsolicited material. I promise you, it ends up in the trash, on a couch (seen it happen) or being taped over. You'll need to get your music into the hands of someone who can actually help you, so make a limited amount. This is the way to go if you want to have other people perform your songs, if you want to get a publishing deal, or if you want to skip the perform-ance world and maybe (*big* maybe here) go right to the top of some label, get signed off your homemade CD, and let the label make the kazillions of records you once only dreamed of.

"Want to create a buzz? Work hard, play lots live and become great in who you are. Get good press and play where you can get attention (the cooler the venue, the better the night; open for someone you admire with a big name; etc.). Create a demand for your music, then make CDs to sell at your shows and through local distribution. Make press or music-industry folks want to come see you. Let them see you live, let them see what kind of rapport you have with an audience, then slap a CD in their hand.

"Be sure to set goals. Don't be afraid to take risks, but make immediate and long-term goals so you won't frustrate yourself.

"2. *Expect to spend money.* If you are going to make a CD, there are a lot of costs involved. How will you pay for it? Save up from gigs, work, inheritance, rob banks, what? *Plan ahead.* Figure out a budget (engineer, studio, tape costs, musicians, DATs, food, etc.) and *stick to that budget.* You can make a great record with little money, but you need to be smart and find out ahead of time where that money is going to go and how you are going to get that money beforehand. Worst-case scenario: You are making a groovy record and right in the middle of production, run out of funds. No fun.

"3. *Network, network, network. Everyone* has the potential to be an ally in this business. Treat people with respect and you will see results. Send thank-you cards. Remember names. Ask questions. Get to know the club owners. Get to know people in touring bands. Open for touring bands. Smile. Listen to the conversations going on around you at festivals, between other songwrit-ers, etc. You can learn a lot when you shut up and listen.

"4. *Be persistent.* Don't give up. Persistence pays off when talent gets to the end of its rope.

"5. *Be prepared to give product away, but sell as much as you can (from the stage, online, mail, local book and music stores, through distribution, newslet-ters).* Help each other out; I list other musicians' stuff in my newsletters from time to time. You will end up with CDs in your garage if you make too many. Remember, you can always go back and make more.

"6. *Go back and read my warning.*"

CHAPTER THREE

FINDING THE MONEY TO MAKE YOUR ALBUM

The money to make your album can come in many ways. If you already have it, or if you can go down to the bank and get a loan easily, you can skip this section.

THE KARMA BANK

The rest of us will use other ways to bring in the money, including preorders, donations and loans. I call this the Karma Bank section, because most of the people who help us are doing it simply because they care about us. I believe that when we help someone we care about, it's like making an investment in the Karma Bank. If what goes around comes around, by helping a deserving person live a dream, we will also be helped in living our own dreams.

Before you begin collecting money, create a special account for it at your bank. Keep a list of the people who have contributed. Hang the list on your wall so you can constantly be reminded that those people believe in you enough to help you. This list will also be a constant reminder if you need to pay them back.

When dealing with funds from a Karma Bank, it's obviously important to be responsible with people's good faith. One option to help you maintain total integrity is to open an account that has to be signed by you *and* someone else in order to get the money out. If two signatures are required to write checks on the account, it will help you resist the temptation to use the money for that unexpected $1,000 new transmission your car required during the recording project. It is important to keep this the *Good* Karma Bank and not let it turn into a *Bad* Karma Bank.

Avoid spending this money for anything but the album. I don't have to tell you how rotten you'll feel if you use it for bills and then can't fill the orders. If you do this, you will wind up living in the same hell that my sister's been in for thirteen years. After her wedding, my sister never finished her thank-you notes. You do not want to live in that hell.

To really give yourself a confidence boost, keep your camera with you and get a smiling photo of everyone who donates, loans or preorders. Pin these on the wall wherever you hang out the most, so that when you're wondering if this whole album idea was a big mistake, you can look up and see the faces of all those people who have so much faith in you that they're willing to help you achieve your dream.

Karma Bank Donations

To simplify the process of gathering the money, look first for donations. You know who loves you, believes in you and wants to help you. Let those people know about your dream and give them the opportunity to be part of it. Start with those people who have told you time and time again that you ought to have a record out. If you had a niece who loved ballet and you'd been telling her for years that she should pursue it, when she came to ask you for help in getting professional training, wouldn't you help? If you had a nephew you'd been encouraging as a baseball player and he had a chance to join some big team if he could get the money together to get there, wouldn't you help? Of course you would, and you'd be happy to have the opportunity.

The reason it's good to go for out-and-out donations first is because when your album comes out, you'll be working to get sales. Times will be lean at first, and you may face that moment when you're doing half music/half day job. You have to make the choice to jump full time into music. If you have a lot of people you owe big sums of money to, you'll either be paying off lots of what you're making or feeling guilty every time you see those people until it's paid. For people who care enough about you to donate, seeing you work hard and thrive with your own albums will be the best way you can thank them for their kindness.

Karma Bank Preorders

Dig out your Christmas list. Start there. Write a letter to everyone you know, and maybe even some people you don't know, like friends of your parents, or friends of friends. Send it to everyone you can think of who might enjoy your music and/or like you as a person. Be creative. Be funny. Be humble. Tell them about your dream of making your own album. Tell them how much you expect it to cost. Let's say you expect it to cost $3,500. Tell them that even though it is impossible to store up treasures in heaven, it *is* possible to make a generous deposit in the Karma Bank, simply by supporting someone's dream. For a mere $10 now, they can get a copy of your cassette as soon as it is released. At that rate, you'll need 350 cassette preorders to pay off your album, plus a few extra to pay the postage for out-of-towners. If they're buying CDs, it will only take 250 preorders.

Christopher Williams made a smart move when he was in college. He wanted to be a professional musician, so he became the person in charge of booking the campus coffeehouse. He brought in all the people he admired, all the people who could teach him about making a living as a performing songwriter. To get the money to make his first album, Chris mailed out a card to family and friends who had encouraged him, saying that he'd made a decision to play music full time and was asking for preorders to help pay the recording costs. He got 150 orders, along with some loans, which he was able to pay back within a month of his album-release concert. He produced his first album for about $5,000, with help from friends on the instrumentation, graphics and photography.

Karma Bank Loans and Investments

I'm going to tell you the reason I have never solicited loans or investments before. I don't do it, because I'm afraid I wouldn't be regular enough with paying people back. I would wind up feeling bad every time I saw them, which would cause me to avoid them, which means, since they'd probably be my friends (or, now, former friends), I wouldn't be able to leave my house.

If you do feel you could be responsible enough to pay people on a regular basis, then consider asking for a grace period of a year after the album is released. You will be so swamped with the task of learning how to sell the albums that you'll need all the money from your album sales to keep going at times. It will be trial and error at first, as you see what works and what doesn't. You don't want to feel, whether it's true or imagined, that someone is looking over your shoulder or worrying that you're not bringing in enough money. You'll be worried enough about that, and you don't need any extra pressure. You'll be in a better spot financially in a year.

You can pay what you owe in one of two ways. One is to make regular payments in amounts that don't change from month to month. The other way is to take a certain percentage out of all your album-sale earnings and pay that portion of your earnings monthly or quarterly.

Chuck Pyle, a wonderful performer known as the Zen Cowboy, puts $2 from every album sale into a separate account. When that account has $500 in it, he sends that amount to one of his investors. Chuck says the best place to look for investors is in your audiences. "There are those people who always show up," he says. "A lot of times those people really want to support us and are willing to toss some money into the hat."

Chuck gives investors a demand note that says when he's going to pay them back and how much. The note says that if he doesn't pay back the entire amount in a year, he'll continue paying on the balance at 10 percent interest per year. He offers to pay back with 10 percent interest on the entire amount but says that offer is usually declined. He keeps a file with records about how much has been paid and how much is still owed.

Karma Bank Magic

There's one more thing about the Karma Bank. Once you begin this project of following your heart's desire, I predict that good things will happen to help you along the way. Watch for signs that your courage is being rewarded. Once you commit to the dream of making your own album, take any unexpected funds and put them in your new business account. You will be amazed at the number of helpful "coincidences" that will occur, logistically, musically or financially, which will help you along your way.

I believe our heart's desire will lead us to our individual purpose in the world—our unique mission. W.H. Murray said it best, with help from Goethe:

> "The moment one definitely commits oneself, then Providence moves too. All sorts of things occur to help one that would never otherwise have occurred. A whole stream of events issues from the decision, raising in one's favour all manner of unforeseen incidents and meetings and material assistance, which no man could have dreamt would've come his way. I have learned a deep respect for one of Goethe's couplets: 'Whatever you can do, or dream you can do, begin it. Boldness has genius, power, and magic in it.' "

Karma Bank magic is never static. Keep the flow going. As you make your album, the good karma is coming to you from others. Whenever you can, help someone else along the way. Pass it on.

HOW I WOUND UP MAKING MY FIRST ALBUM

In music towns there are *listening rooms* where songwriters are the stars. These are generally small clubs where people come to sip coffee, have a quiet meal and listen to song crafters share their latest works. After working on the business side of music all day, I'd spend evenings at these clubs, listening to other writers' creations and sharing my own.

Nearly every time I played in one of these places, people from the audience would ask if they could buy a copy of a song called "If I Had Only Known." I had written the song with Craig Morris, who is now lead singer of a group called Forerunner. This is the song that Reba McEntire later recorded and dedicated to her band members who were killed in a plane crash. The song is about coping with loss, especially the death of someone you love.

The people asking for copies were not music business people. They were regular people who had come out to listen to music. They would often tell me stories of a father or a brother or a sister they loved who had died. Many of them said they were unable to cry in a public place when they heard the song and wanted to take it home with them so they could be alone to cry the tears that needed to be shed. It broke my heart. Even though making tape copies was one of my least favorite things to do, I would make tapes of the song and send them out at my own expense to whoever asked.

My first idea was to make a small quantity of tapes of that one song. I had no plans to make an album. I just hated making tape copies and was trying to save myself some work and postage. I figured I could carry these with me when I played. If people wanted them, I could make them available for just a few dollars' reimbursement.

Here's my process from there. I started thinking about the other side of the tape. Instead of leaving it blank, why not put another song on there that people might also like? Instead of trying to type the cassette labels and card inserts myself, maybe I could make up something that looked nice and run it through a copier. I could put my picture on that card insert, too, and it would look cool and that would be worth the few dollars' reimbursement that I otherwise would feel kind of guilty asking for from people.

As I began to visualize this one- or two-song cassette, I started considering what it would be like to put ten songs on there. Before this positive visualization could even begin to take hold in my brain, it was blown to bits by all my negative thinking. See if any of this sounds familiar:

• You are going to look like a fool when people ask for a copy of that song and you whip out tapes with pictures of yourself on them.

• You will be an independent label artist, and people will assume you couldn't cut the mustard with the majors.

• You have got to be kidding. You must have a pretty inflated ego if you think people are going to buy albums from someone they never heard of.

• Your music business associates will laugh at you. People in the business of selling millions of albums will think you're a joke out there selling your albums one at a time.

• You barely have enough money to scrape by every month. You'll never be able to come up with the small fortune it would probably cost to make your own record.

While I could get past the other negative thoughts, the one about money kept coming back. I had no idea what it would cost and didn't even know how to find out, but I knew it had to be more than I could afford. I figured it would cost about a thousand dollars. That was more than a hurdle for me. It was a roadblock. Fortunately, a caring friend came through just when I needed her.

Her name is Rosemary Cathcart. One day Rosemary asked me why I wasn't making my own albums. Lots of people had asked me this before, but I always said, "No way, that would be like giving up hope that I'm going to get a major label deal and I know I'm going to get one and besides I don't want to be an independent label artist because I wouldn't have any distribution into the chain stores around the country and people in the music business would think I was a joke and besides I could never come up with that much money. . . ."

When I told Rosemary the same thing I had been saying for a long time, Rosemary did something I will always love her for. She completely ignored the rest of the list and said, "We could help you come up with the money."

"How?" I asked.

"We could get all your friends together to come to a concert to support your dream of making your own album. You could provide us with an afternoon or evening of music. Instead of charging admission, we would take a break during the concert to explain what you wanted to create and how much it would cost, and then we'd pass the hat to let people donate whatever they could to help you."

I was so touched by the idea of my friends being so kind to me that I developed a lump in my throat the size of a basketball. All choked up, I thanked Rosemary for the idea and told her I'd think about it. In light of Rosemary's generous and noble offer, my fears about what music-business people would think seemed silly. I ran through my list of reasons why I couldn't make my own album, and suddenly they all looked silly. If people cared enough about me or my music to do all that to help me make an album, maybe there would be people who would also buy the album. These warm thoughts about all my friends donating the money to make my album led me to this next thought, which is the reason we never held that concert.

If all my friends donated the money to make the album, *who would buy it?* I figured that on the outside, there were about a hundred people in Nashville who liked my music enough to maybe buy one of my albums. Chances are these would be the same people who would come to the fund-raising concert. I began to explore other options.

I thought about ways to make the album without outside donations. I considered going to a church with good acoustics and a good sound system on a weekday afternoon when no one was in the sanctuary and getting permission to play my songs live into the church's tape deck. I thought of finding the cheapest demo studio in Nashville and playing my songs live there. I was a worse guitar player then than I am now, so neither of these options was extremely appealing.

As I got out the demos of the songs I wanted to put on my album, it became clear that my best alternative was to put ten of those demos together to make my first album.

CHAPTER FOUR

CAPTURING YOUR UNIQUE SOUND WITH YOUR UNIQUE BUDGET

You could make a recording of yourself burping the words to "The Star Spangled Banner" and get ten thousand CDs made. Duplicating plants don't care what's on your album. Your money spends just the same as any other artist's. The quality of your original recording will be up to you. You get to choose.

Do you want it to be playable on the radio? If you do, go for as much quality in production as you can afford and definitely press CDs. Radio stations won't play anything else these days. Your cover artwork will need to be top-notch for radio, too. If you're not spending a lot of money on these things, your album will still need to look and sound like you did.

If you think only about what a radio station might play, you could be limiting yourself from creating a wonderful album you and many record buyers will love. If we think too much about what's on the radio, it's easy to get intimidated. It's easy to spend a lot of time second-guessing our own intuition and worrying about the opinions of radio people we don't even know. How can we know what they will think? Worrying about it can only hold us back. Don't let radio intimidation slow you down.

The marketing techniques in this book will give you the skills to market your music and make a living with it whether radio plays your music or not. When I made my first album, I didn't have any hope that radio would play it. This didn't keep me from believing my music had value. If this is your first album, consider the idea of making your album the best you can

TIPS FROM THE PROS: DAR WILLIAMS

Singer-songwriter Dar Williams offers some advice for recording:
"I try to persuade fellow artists to go low-tech at the start. I really like what Hewitt Huntwork did: He bought a 4-track and some mikes, recorded four songs at a time, put them on both sides of a cassette, and sold them for $4 or $5 each. Getting his own technology was a money saver in the long run, the simple voice-and-guitar [and a few extras] recordings made great demos as well as sale items, and the low price of the product really got his music out there."

afford. Don't worry about the radio right now. Use this as a learning experience. Once you get out there and gain a following, you will be able to create the kind of album radio is looking for.

A LIMITED BUDGET IS NOT A BAD THING

The style of your album and the budget will go hand in hand. Money will be the most powerful determining factor in your final product. This is not a bad thing. If you have unlimited funds, your options are unlimited. Your album could take forever and still not be good enough for you. Come to think of it, this is how you'll feel no matter how much money you have to spend. The difference is that when you're out of money, you have to stop and don't have the option of agonizing over whether to pump another few thousand dollars into the project to improve it.

With a limited budget, there are certain things you can and can't do. You will not have to decide whether this or that needs to be changed, whether to use this or that studio, or whether to get CDs or just cassettes. People with a lot of money will worry a lot about this stuff. With a smaller budget, these decisions will be obvious. Your challenge will be to make the money stretch so that your lower-budget project will look and sound like it cost more than it really did.

Your budget will include:

Recording costs
Recording facility
Engineer and Producer, or Engineer/Producer
Musicians

Cover costs
Photography and photo duplication
Graphic design and layout (color or black-and-white)

Duplication costs
Mastering
Cassettes, CDs or both

The style of your album will determine and be determined by your budget. Here are some tried-and-true ways to record an album, starting with the cheapest.

So Cheap It Might Be Free

Contact a church or synagogue with a good sound system, one that has the equipment set up to record the message every week. Ask the music director for permission to go into the sanctuary during off-hours to record your album live. This option might not work for a death-metal band or a group with a name like Armpit Aroma. If you have an affiliation with the facility, and if your music is basically wholesome, you'll have a better chance of making this option work for you.

Let's just assume you have found a church or synagogue that will allow you to come in during the day to record some songs. If you're using this option, it's best to keep your instrumentation simple, like guitar and vocals or piano and vocals. For every additional musician you add, you will multiply your recording challenges (and the number of things that can go wrong) by at least ten. In this setting, you probably won't have the option of recording the instrumental and vocal tracks separately. They will both need to be recorded together live. You can either hire an engineer by the hour to set the levels and run the recorder or you can have a friend do it.

Go ahead and laugh at this idea if you want. I did. After having a good laugh, I seriously considered this option for making my first album. A church I sang in frequently had a good sound system. Most churches are quiet, peaceful and have great acoustics, which are some of the same qualities you'd look for in a studio. Among the many differences between a church and a studio, you probably won't have to pay for the use of a church, and this little element alone can make the idea of recording in a house of worship incredibly attractive.

If you choose this option, please do all upcoming recording artists a favor and be respectful of the space and the equipment while you're there. If any of their equipment breaks or gets lost during your use of it, repair it or replace it so that it will be in working condition when they need it next. What you are saving on recording costs will more than pay for whatever that costs. You could buy the place a new sound system for what some studios charge per day. You'll probably be the first person who has ever asked to record an album in their facility. It is my hope that if you don't cause them any inconvenience or embarrassment during the time you're there, you won't be the last.

Pretty Cheap If You're a Songwriter

Some people reading this book are professional songwriters with stacks of demos. If you have sung some of your own demos, one option is to put ten of these songs together, add the cover artwork and make your album out of that.

My first album was done with this "pretty cheap" method. Over the years, I had recorded demos of all my songs. I chose ten songs that seemed to go together and made my album from these demos. Ideally, an album will have the same sound from song to song. This is usually achieved by recording the album all in one studio with most of the same musicians on each song. When you have ten demos, chances are they are all from different studios with different musicians. This was true in my case. Not only were all my songs from different studios, they were all on different qualities of tape. Some were on reel-to-reel, some were on cassettes. For some songs, the cassettes I had weren't even the original copy.

I had paid about $300 for each recording, which was an average cost for Nashville demos. That was $3,000 for the recording costs, which had been paid over the three or four years I had been making those demos.

After calling around about where to take the compilation tape, I wound up at National Tape and Disc (NTD) in Nashville. Friends had told me this was the cassette duplication facility they used. There, I learned that all the songs needed to be recorded onto a digital audio tape, or DAT. Many duplication facilities have sound engineers on staff who can be paid an hourly rate to put your separate song tapes onto a DAT with the proper spacing between songs. You can find out about tape duplication facilities in your town by checking the yellow pages or looking in local weekly newspapers that have coverage of the music scene in your area.

I paid $100 to an engineer to take all my tapes and put them together on a DAT. At NTD, I paid $130 for the cover artwork, a $50 mastering charge, and $101 for the duplication of a hundred tapes. My total cost so far was $3,381. By the time I sold 350 cassettes, my entire investment was paid off and all the rest was profit.

The duplication facility prints a thousand copies of your album artwork. They keep those on file. Every time you order a hundred more cassettes, all it costs is about $1 per cassette. Every time you order a CD, you pay less than $3. Is it becoming clear that making your own albums is a good investment in yourself and your career?

Affordable Recordings of Songs You Didn't Write

If you're a good singer but you don't play an instrument, write songs or know any musicians, you can still record your own albums. Karaoke catalogs like Sound Choice and Pocket Songs can send you the tracks and the necessary paperwork so you can record any popular song they offer. The tracks are sent to you on DAT so you can add your vocals. All you need is a microphone and a DAT machine. You can sing to the tracks in any place that has good acoustics, from a house of worship to a local studio. If you have a friend who works at a radio or television station, you could even do your album there after hours. To find information about local studios, check the yellow pages or ask at the nearest music store.

Reasonably Priced

One of the founding members of the Tuesday Night Music Club, which launched Sheryl Crow, was the late Kevin Gilbert. Gilbert was a singer-songwriter-instrumentalist who, by the age of twenty-nine, had worked in various musical capacities with Michael Jackson, Madonna and the Muppets. In the January/February issue of *Performing Songwriter* magazine Gilbert said, "The idea that you have to make a record in a big studio is gone. Get an 8-track, a couple microphones, a decent mic preamp. Start recording your stuff, then take it to a decent studio to mix it and it's going to sound every bit as good as a twenty, thirty thousand [dollar] demo."

If you don't have a Tuesday night music club and don't know where to get the musicians you need for your recording, ask at local music stores. They usually have bulletin boards full of players' cards. Before you call the players whose cards are displayed, ask the people behind the counter if they know the person you're considering. You'll be spending important time with these musicians, and it's important to learn about their character (reliability, flexibility, personality) as well as their musical skill.

TIPS FROM THE PROS: DAR WILLIAMS

More advice from Dar Williams:

"Take advantage of all the technology out there," she encourages. "When in doubt, you can do high-quality, low-tech recordings with simple arrangements. Sometimes you can find someone who has his or her own 4-track recorder. They'd probably be thrilled to let you come in at $5 to $10 an hour [or free donuts, or three pounds of onions from your garden . . .] when they're not home, throw down some tracks and have a solid demo or a beginning off-the-stage product."

If you keep your albums simple, you can record a quality album with a 4- or 8-track recorder. Eight-track studios and machines are easier to come by than 24-track facilities and cheaper to rent by the hour. You might even have a friend who owns a 4- or 8-track machine, and you can do your recording at home. You could buy one for what some people spend on their albums and still have enough money left over to buy a Mercedes.

Every album after my first one has been recorded at an 8-track studio. Recording an album with only eight tracks requires a lot more precision because you have only eight tracks to work with. If you've got guitar tracks and bass tracks and drum tracks, you can't record several tracks of vocals and pick the best one. You've only got two tracks left, one for vocals and one for background vocals. This means you can't put each background singer on a separate track. They have to be there all at once, singing into one microphone. It decreases your options to use only four or eight tracks, but it also decreases your recording costs. It will be important to keep your album uncomplicated if you choose this method. Focus on creating a good representation of your songs. You won't have all the bells and whistles of a 24-track studio, but do you really need them and can you afford them?

In many cases, the recording engineer at an 8-track studio is also willing to act as producer of the album. On my second and third albums (*Stop, Look & Listen* and *I'm Not Lost, I am Exploring*), Nashville studio guitar ace Jerry Kimbrough was the producer. Don Scott Hare, who co-owns the Country Club Studio 8, where we recorded, acted as engineer.

To save studio time and to make the best use of those eight available tracks, Jerry and I got together before the recording session to map out the arrangements of each song. We decided which songs would need additional musicians and which songs would be made of layered guitar tracks under the vocals. We chose to keep them all simple. *Stop, Look & Listen* is nothing but layered guitar tracks and vocals. *I'm Not Lost, I am Exploring* is made up of mostly layered guitar and vocals, with a few songs also featuring bass, keyboards and percussion.

As I began planning my fourth and fifth albums, *The Trick Is to Learn to Enjoy the Ride* and *Playing Favorites*, I saw how much it would cost to do two albums at one time and decided to cut my costs. Instead of paying one person to produce and another to engineer, I hired Don Scott to do both. Jerry would still be involved in creating the arrangements and playing all the guitar parts. Since Jerry is one of the top guitarists in town, he is also more expensive than other guitarists. To reduce the total bill, I had Jerry play on one of the albums, and I hired a new guitar player in town, Marco Rodriguez, to play on the other.

I have several reasons why I have continued to do my albums at an 8-track studio. It is affordable. I enjoy giving my business to people I want to support, and I am so comfortable working there I can't imagine being anywhere else. It's true that my albums don't have the thickness of twenty-four tracks, but people don't buy my albums for thickness. They buy my albums for the content of the songs.

More Expensive

Hire a 24-track studio, an engineer or engineer/producer, and a group of musicians. You can record locally, or you can travel to a music town to do your album. No matter where you record, do some price shopping before you start. Since the aim of this book is to help you make a good living making and marketing your CDs and cassettes, I'm going to suggest ways to get the job done at the lower end of the price scale. Unless you have an unlimited amount of money to spend, you should compare prices from studio to studio, and producer to producer.

Finding a Studio That's Right for You

Prices vary. The only way to know whether you're getting a good deal is to compare prices and compare what each studio has to offer for that price. In your research, you'll find that one studio charges ten times the rate per day that another studio charges. It's not that the studios are out to rob anybody. If the expensive studio has a great reputation and does a great job, its owners are justified in charging whatever they can get. The same goes for producers and musicians. It's up to you to find out what they charge and decide how much you can afford. From there, you can make the choice that best suits your budget. Before asking about prices, tell the person at the studio what your goals are with this album. If your goal is to make a good album at the lowest price, say so.

Most studios have a list of musicians they work with frequently, and if you aren't bringing in your own musicians, they can hire musicians for you. Studios often offer this, and it's a good deal if you don't know the musicians yourself. While some studios will include this as part of the overall cost of your album project, others may charge a fee for their services or ask for a percentage of what you're paying for the album. Don't be in the dark about the process. Learn all you can from whoever is doing the musician contracting, so next time you'll have the option of doing it yourself.

Get an education for your money. Before choosing a studio, go there in person if possible. You will want to see the facilities and make personal contact with the person who will be overseeing your project. Find out every cost that will go into the production, and make sure the person who is quoting prices is someone you respect. Ask what things this person can think of that might drive the price higher than you anticipate, so you won't be caught off guard by unexpected expenses. Ask what you can do to keep the price as low as possible. Before you open your checkbook, be sure the studio will have an open book about where your dollars are going.

The easiest place to record your album is in the nearest town with recording facilities. There are several good reasons for recording your album in your area. First, you're keeping the money in your local economy. Second, you can sleep in your own bed every night after the recording sessions. Third, you'll get to know the musicians in your town. Fourth, you'll have a better connection to the entire music scene in your area.

When you record locally, you'll come to mind when people at the studio hear of places you could share your music. Those who were involved with the album will probably talk it up to their friends and family, which will increase your name recognition. Word-of-mouth connections are less likely to occur if you're recording in a music town where you're there for a week, then gone like the wind. Recording locally makes you a more important part of the big music picture. If the newspaper does a story about you, the recording studio also gets publicity. If the story is about the studio, they're likely to mention the local artists who record there.

If you want to cut your album in Los Angeles, Nashville, New York, Chicago or any other towns known for their connection with the music industry, go where you know a local musician who can connect you with a good, reasonably priced studio. While you'll have to factor in your travel expenses, you can often cut an album much faster in music towns than anywhere else. Music towns are full of musicians who are used to working with material they've never heard and creating wonderful recordings in a matter of minutes or hours. In Nashville, studios can often cut four songs per day, and when you're paying per day to use the studio, that's a good way to save money.

How to Avoid Being Ripped Off on Recording

There are countless stories about aspiring artists who answered an ad placed in a newspaper by talent scouts in town for a limited time looking for talent for commercials, television shows and movies.

Keep this in mind: In every town where commercials, television shows and movies are shot, qualified singers, actors and models with incredible press kits wait in the lobby every day. Real producers don't waste time and money flying talent scouts to Port Arthur, Texas, to set up auditions in motels. No matter what credentials these "scouts" claim to have or how many famous names they drop, this is not the way it works in the real entertainment world.

What happens in these motel situations is that the "producer" or "agent" or "talent scout" says you look like the exact thing they're searching for. Pay a small fee (usually over $50) for them to videotape your audition, and you'll get a copy of the tape. They say they're taking the tapes back to Nashville or Hollywood and you'll be notified if yours is chosen. Guess what? If you seem to have the right amounts of enthusiasm, gullibility and access to money, you get chosen. All you have to do now is find the backers who'll put up the thousands of dollars for your big album. In return for this money, they say they'll produce the album, get you national airplay and make you the next big thing. These people sound very professional and convincing. They are professionals all right and may have actually had some success in the music business before they found they could make money much more quickly and easily in the "con" business.

Sometimes a "showcase" in front of the big record companies is included in your package price. One person I knew who fell prey to this ploy was even told he would be presented to the record labels in a show at a Nashville auditorium. He and the other victims (who didn't know yet that they would never get a piece of recorded music out of the money their backers paid) appeared in this concert, supposedly attended by record label executives. This acquaintance of mine had friends at a local radio station in Florida. The radio station chartered a bus and sold tickets to people who wanted to take a trip to Nashville to support the local boy in his big record company showcase. They thought they were going to be part of the next big thing. They were part of a big rip-off. There were people in the audience, thanks to all those victims who brought friends and family for a big concert, but no way to tell whether any of them really worked for a record company.

It's very confusing if you are one of the victims of these cons, because you actually did fly to Nashville (at your own expense), you actually did play a concert (supposedly for record-company executives and booking agents), and in some cases you actually did sing in the studio with musicians. The other common denominator of these situations is that at about the time your recording project is supposedly being shipped to radio for national airplay, you can't get the "scout" or the "producer" on the phone anymore. The phone has been disconnected. You call the Better Business Bureau (better late than never) but can't find anyone who's ever heard of any business by that name. The people you dealt with are probably still in Nashville (or Hollywood) going about their business with their real names, which you will never know.

I'm not saying that every talent search is a rip-off. If Disney does a nationwide search for the new Cinderella, it's probably a harmless publicity ploy so they can have huge crowds and get on the local news across the country. If you want to spend the time taking a shot at it, go right ahead. In any other situation, remember these guidelines:

1. Don't pay for the opportunity to audition. If they say the money is for a "professional videotape recording of your performance," make sure you see examples of their finished product, because that may be all you ever get for what you pay. Be aware that once these people leave town, you might never hear from them again.

2. These people stay in business by feeding off aspiring artists' egos, hopes and dreams. They tell you you're great, you deserve to have your dreams come true, they believe in you and that they can make it happen. You've been waiting so long to hear this from someone who can help you that it can impair your judgment and your business sense. Don't let it.

3. Check the Better Business Bureau before you start. If there's no record of this business, be concerned.

4. Check more references than those the person gives you. Call anyone who might know anyone who knows the person who is offering to make you the next big thing.

5. Call the person's former clients, especially those who have done the same kind of project you're planning. Make sure you're talking with a recent client. If there are no recent clients you can call, that should be a red flag.

6. Get a price breakdown of everything the person is promising, including the names of people who will be paid. It's your money, and you need to talk to each recipient before you pay it.

7. Pay as you go for services rendered. Don't make a big lump-sum payment before the project starts.

8. If someone really believes they can make you the next big thing and they want to share in the profits when that happens, they should also be investing time and money.

9. Don't sign away percentages of your future earnings. Pay as you go. Sign contracts for a year at a time, not a lifetime. A manager works for you. It's not the other way around.

If the individual or company loses interest in you as you check around, consider this a good thing. People who are on the level will think you're smart to do some checking and won't be threatened by this.

RECORDING THE ALBUM

This can be the most fun and the most trying experience of your life. You will simultaneously experience the rush of creativity flowing through your heart and money flowing through your wallet. It's quite a feeling.

After talking with everyone involved in the album, you'll get a good idea of how long the album will take to record. Block that time out and don't plan to do anything else during that time except record the album. When you get into the recording process, it will take every available cell of your right brain, your left brain and whatever parts are trying to remain neutral. Of course, life will present other things, like kids in need of emergency dental visits, a flat tire and unexpected houseguests, because that's how life is. So plan for it by clearing your schedule of all but life's necessities while you're recording.

No matter who the producer is, remember that you are the executive producer. The buck will stop with you, since all the bucks are coming from you. There will not be a single decision made that you will not be involved in, so plan to be there for all of it. You will be glad you did.

As you listen to each song on your finished album, you may like some parts, love some parts, or cringe at some parts, but after it's finished you'll be able to say with a feeling of accomplishment, "We did it my way."

One more thing. Ideally, this will not be your last album. Learn from it. Let it be your practice album. You can spend more and do more with the next one if you want to, or you can learn from this one how to save even more money next time. Keep a mental list of all the things you're going to do again and all the things you'll do differently next time. This one doesn't have to be perfect to be something you can be proud of for years to come. Pat yourself on the back for having the courage to affirm your talent.

What to Expect in the Studio

You've decided that you're as ready as you'll ever be to go to the studio and begin your project. Ideally, you have planned what you're going to do so you have some idea of how long it will take, how much it will cost and what your music will sound like when you complete it. After all this planning, it's time to let it be what it's going to be. Trying to make your music be a certain thing in the studio is like trying to guide a giraffe stampede.

In the studio, you can try to be in control of the sound, the budget and the time, but the project takes on a life of its own, and sometimes it's difficult to make it all come out just like you want it to. Even as you hold tightly to your plan, the whole thing can slip right through your fingers in the studio if you're not careful. For example:

• The guitar player comes up with a cool alternative way to play this one song. You love the groove, but it's going to take some extra time to rework it this way with the rest of the players.

• The day you have scheduled to do background vocals at the end of your project, dangerously close to your deadline, the background singer gets sent to the hospital with food poisoning, and puts you behind a day.

• When all the tracks are laid, someone comes up with the idea to put a zither on a few of the songs. You love the concept, but that takes more time and money.

• Once you've got the zither on two or three songs, it seems that the album lacks continuity. You've got to decide whether to take the zither off those songs (and lose the money you paid for the musician and the studio time) or shell out some more money to put zither on all the songs.

Given that unexpected challenges will cost unexpected dollars, the best thing to do is accept the fact that the project is going to become its own animal in the studio. If you can accept this and roll with it, you won't be devastated when the budget runs over and the deadline keeps being moved further out. Expect it. It's going to happen and you can save yourself a lot of grief if you're ready for it.

Cutting the Vocals

One of the most ironic things about recording an album is that the vocals usually go on last. By this time, you're usually over budget and out of time. The musicians had the luxury of time, but when it comes to the vocals (the part most vocalists think is a crucial element), time and money is running short, and you don't get to spend the time you'd like on your vocals.

This is a blessing in disguise. As vocalists, we tend to be perfectionists. We want everything that comes out of our mouths to be the absolute best it can be. If we didn't have a time and money limit, we could stay in the studio for a year doing vocals and still not be satisfied. If you're like most vocalists, you do most of your performing before a live audience, not a live studio microphone. When we're out in public, there's not so much pressure on us to reach perfection. We sing each note to the audience, and as each note is sung, it disappears into the air, leaving only a vague memory in the listener's mind. By the end of the song, live audiences judge your performance on whether they enjoyed the entire song. If they liked the overall performance, they don't think about whether this note could've been held out longer or that note went a little flat in the middle. They just know they liked what they heard.

Singing in the studio is a humbling experience. Unless you're a seasoned jingle or demo singer, you'll probably feel a little out of your element. You may have a lot of confidence in your live performances, which is like having beautiful hair. When you look at your hair, you admire the color, the style, the shine and the overall picture. Singing in the studio is like taking that beautiful hair and putting it under a microscope. Suddenly you are shocked to see eye-popping horror lurking in each hair follicle, along with things that look like mutant insects hiding underneath all that luster.

When you sing in the studio, it's like putting your voice under a microscope. What was once a beautiful sound in your head will now sound so flawed that you can't believe you ever thought you were a good vocalist. You will hear every morsel of phlegm on your vocal cords. You will come face to face with the disappointing reality that the human voice is an imperfect instrument. Still, the human voice is a beautiful instrument. Here are some ideas to keep you from making yourself miserable while you play this instrument in the studio.

Strengthen Your Voice Before, Not During

Cutting vocals can be strenuous for your voice. You're probably used to singing in short bursts, but during the cutting of an album you'll be singing for hours on end. First, you'll sing scratch vocals as a guide for the players to go with, and then you'll cut the lead vocals on each song.

As each line is repeated for perfection on the lead-vocal track, your voice can become tired and raspy. As you leave the studio, you think you should practice songs for the next day's sessions, but your voice is worn out. The next morning, your voice is still scratchy from overuse, and it's hard to sing vocal exercises before the session when you know you'll be using every ounce of energy singing lead vocals.

Marcia Jones, a former recording artist who is currently writing full-time, offers a great tip that she has used in recording her albums. In the weeks before recording, she vocalized, practiced and sang for long periods of time each day to prepare her voice for the studio process. She was getting those vocal muscles accustomed to singing in long stretches. After doing all this work in the weeks prior to the session, her voice was in better shape than usual and she felt more confidence in her abilities. When recording started, she stopped her long vocal workouts and threw that same amount of energy into singing that album.

Avoid Studio Self-Sabotage

I hope that this next part won't happen to you, but it happens to me a lot in the studio. Even though it's embarrassing to tell you about it, I feel a duty to share it so you won't be surprised if you experience it, too. What I'm talking about is that sick feeling you might get in the pit of your stomach when the producer or engineer says, "That was a little flat." Maybe they'll say, "That was a little pitchy." Sometimes they'll just say, "I think you've got a better one in you," and even though they didn't specifically say you were singing off pitch, you will know in your heart that's probably what they were thinking. You won't even believe what a few responses like that (or, in my case, a few dozen responses like that) can do to your confidence.

You can go into the studio feeling great about yourself, but when you find yourself singing the same line or lines over and over because you can't quite nail them, something takes control of you and you will begin to think that you must be the worst singer in the world. I pray it won't happen to you, but it happens to me in the worst way. I begin to lose confidence. Silently panicking, I start asking myself:

- What was I thinking?
- What in the world ever made me think I could do this?
- What about all those friends and family who told me I was talented?
- Were they all lying to me to make me feel good?
- Am I really as awful as I'm sounding on this line?
- Do I always sound this bad and just don't know it?
- Do people laugh at me behind my back?
- Is the engineer in there laughing right now?
- Will I ever be able to sing this line?
- Why did I choose this song?
- Why didn't I see that this was obviously out of my league in terms of range and ability?

With thoughts like these running through your head, it becomes harder and harder to sing that line or that song the way you'd like to. So how do we turn the tide and keep from drowning in all this self-defeating negativity?

Occasionally when I was so overcome by these negative thoughts and the subsequent loss of all confidence, I have said, "Let's take a break," and have gone outside to sit in the sunshine on the studio steps and cried. I remember one occasion in particular on which the producer and the engineer just sat in the studio (and on the clock, I might add) while I sat outside trying to get myself together so I could continue.

Take a break when you need it. When I get by myself with my tears and my thoughts, I finally realize that all I can do is my best. My desirable best and my achievable best are sometimes two different things. As I sit there, I come to accept that this album is only a snapshot of me on this day. I will be a better singer tomorrow and next year, but even then, I probably won't be satisfied with how I sound.

It's important to record as we are today and not wait until we're as good as we want to be. I don't know about you, but I don't think I'll ever be as good as I want to be. It's just not going to happen, so I might as well move forward and just do the best I can do with my imperfect instrument.

Remember that the producer's opinion that "you've got a better one in you" is merely an opinion. This person is not the expert on what's happening in your throat. This person cannot feel the strain as you sing the line over and over again. This person is not the one who is pacing tired vocal cords for the marathon of singing an entire album.

Your opinion about whether you can do better is what counts. On my earlier albums I wondered, "Gosh, what was wrong with that line? I thought it sounded pretty good, but obviously it wasn't." I'd keep pushing and pushing my vocal cords to try to make it better. Now that I have made five albums, I remind myself that I'm the one with the final say. If I think it's good enough, I say so, and if the producer still disagrees, I'll go into the control booth to see if I can hear anything wrong. If I'm not convinced that it needs to be resung or that I can do it better, we move on.

Ninety Percent or Better Is Good Enough

To boost your courage during recording of the vocals, or any other part of the album, remind yourself that this album can be excellent without being perfect.

Your vocals can be excellent without being perfect, and you could sing perfectly without being excellent. Sometimes I just have to use the 90 percent rule. The project (and especially my vocals) will never be 100 percent of what I want it to be. So I shoot as high as I can. I ask myself how close I got to what I was shooting for. Often, it's 97 percent. If I feel I've achieved 90 percent perfection or better, I call that good enough.

Others may disagree with my "90 percent or better" theory and believe that you should stay in that studio until every note of every instrument (including the vocals) is absolutely perfect, no matter how many weeks or months it takes to achieve this.

Each of us must decide how we're going to handle this situation. In singing, I feel better when I remind myself that the voice is just a section of muscles and there's no way I can make them constrict perfectly on every note. Maybe for you this is possible. For me it's not, but I don't let it hold me back.

I read a magazine article about k.d. lang, an incredible singer, who thought she was losing her ability to sing because she was trying to record her album and kept having problems with her pitch. She said it was terrifying to think the notes but not be able to make them come out that way into the microphone. This kind of experience wipes out our confidence if we let it, so it's important to try whatever method works for you to keep it from happening.

The "90 percent or better" formula will be important when it comes to finishing your album. Even after you have recorded the vocals, the

TIPS FROM THE PROS: JOYCE ROUSE

Joyce Rouse is a singer-songwriter who performs as "Earth Mama" at festivals, conferences and special events. She has three albums of environmentally sound music you can dance to. Her advice on recording:

"1. Make a budget, double it, then stick to it!

"2. Trust your gut. From tempos to tambourines, if you let yourself be talked into something on your tracks you instinctively feel is not right, you will not be happy with it, or you will have to pay to do it again. But, listen to the expertise of the people you are working with. They may have dynamite ideas you can use. And *you* are paying *them* for their best work.

"3. When your ears are tired, *go home* and rest them. I have paid dearly to learn this.

"4. Wear comfortable clothes. I can't believe I once wore pantyhose to the studio (along with other things, of course). Your physical comfort allows you to keep your mind on the music.

"5. Use the best musicians you can afford. Don't use players, however, who think your work is beneath them.

"6. Bonus tip: Enjoy each moment of the process of making your recording, even the uncomfortable ones. Being really present with the 'now' will make it a richer experience for you and a more focused work. It will all be over soon!"

percussion, the guitars, the background vocals and the tubas, you will still be wondering if you should have done it differently. Since we all set our goals so high, I believe that if you know with confidence that you achieved 90 percent or better, you can be proud of what you have accomplished. Your album could be perfect, without being excellent.

GETTING YOUR MUSIC READY FOR DUPLICATION

In the next chapter you'll find information about audio duplication facilities, also known as manufacturers. Before mastering your project, decide what format you want to use for delivering your project to the manufacturer. Guide sheets or booklets from the audio duplication facility you choose will tell you everything you need to know about what you'll need to turn in, from the music to the cover artwork. Most manufacturers can duplicate from anything, even a reel-to-reel or cassette tape. For better quality and easy handling, most artists turn in their music on DAT (digital audio tape).

Other artists turn their projects in on recordable CD (CD-R). Your album can also be duplicated from a "1630" (¾" U-matic), a ½" tape or a ¼" analog tape. Check with the studio where you're going to record to find out what formats they work with.

Mastering Your Project

Mastering means preparing the master tape for duplication. This involves laying down all the songs in order and going through the entire project with a fine-toothed comb to make sure it sounds as good as it possibly can. This can be done in the old-fashioned way by depending on the human ear, or it can be done by running the sound through a computer. When your tracks are examined as sound waves on a computer screen, flaws the naked ear could barely hear can be corrected. Sound levels can be balanced exactly, so you won't have to listen to your album after it's released and say, "Does it sound like this song is louder than the others?"

The studio where you record might offer this kind of high-tech mastering. Find out. Talk with the people at the studio you've been working in to see what they offer, and then call the professional mastering studios. See what they can do to improve your project and then ask these questions:

• What do you charge per hour for this kind of project? Be sure to tell them how many CDs and cassettes you plan to press and let them know you are a musician on a tight budget because you're funding this yourself.

• How long would you expect it to take for this kind of project?

• What condition do you need the project to be in before you start (what kind of tape, etc.)? Let them know you want to be fully prepared so you won't waste any time.

• Do you have a list of suggestions for me that can help the process move faster and save money?

• Do you have any openings in your schedule that will fit our timetable for completing the project? They often book way in advance.

• If they can't fit you into their schedule or the prices seem outrageous, ask if they can recommend a less expensive studio or any other options.

Duplication facilities often offer mastering services for an extra charge. When you inquire about this, make sure you are clear in describing what you want. The manufacturer has a process that's generally called "making the transfer master." This is the master copy they create from whatever you turn in to them (your "source"). They turn your source into a transfer master and that becomes the master from which they duplicate your cassettes and CDs. You're not ready for a transfer master yet. You are looking for information about creating your source at this point, not duplicating it.

Sequencing the Songs

The song sequence needs to be decided before you start mastering. When listening to someone's album, do you think about the song sequencing? I don't. It never even occurs to me. If it doesn't occur to you either, then just put your songs in what seems to you to be the most logical order. Don't stress out. There are plenty of other details to stress out on as you put this album together, so if the song sequence would not cause you to like or dislike someone's album, save your stress energy for something more important to you.

If song sequence on the albums you listen to is important to you, here's your chance to do it the way it should be done, whatever that is.

These are simple guidelines a lot of artists and producers use. Put your strongest song first, since this will be your first impression. If people don't like that first song, they might not listen further. Put a strong song as the first song of the second side, if you're planning to release a cassette. Put a great song at the end of the album, because that's the last impression you make, and ideally that last song will make people want to hear your album again. These are just basic guidelines; they are not rules, because there are no rules for song sequencing. Get together with the producer of the album and decide what order best represents your songs.

There is a high-tech and low-tech way to visually put the songs in order. Start by writing down the elements of each song. For example:

song title: "Butterfly"
tempo: ballad
key: A
lyric content: dealing with change

You can do this on a computer or on a piece of paper. For the low-tech version, cut the paper apart so each song has its own information on a little slip. This way, you can move them around in different orders. For the high-tech version, you can move these units around on the computer screen to see the desired order.

Try to avoid putting two songs in the same key side by side, but there are people like me in the world who would listen to your album and never even know if you violated that rule. On one of my albums, we had a song about a dog and a song about a butterfly, and while no rules say "two animal songs cannot live side by side," we separated the two. We also tried to avoid putting two sad songs together or two songs with the same message.

It's easy to start thinking that you have to get it just right and that people will judge your album based on how you put the songs in order. Don't let those thoughts get out of hand. One artist friend of mine says that there are two tried-and-true ways to get the perfect song order: Spend hours debating, deciding and rearranging the song order, or draw the names out of a hat.

WHEN IT'S COMPLETE, LET IT BE COMPLETED

After you've mastered your project and turned it in for duplication, the manufacturer will usually give you the first copy of your album to listen to one last time before they mass-produce it. This will either be a cassette or a CD. It is called a reference or a test copy. If a reference CD was not offered in your package deal, they might charge around $50 if you want it on CD. The cassette test copy is usually free.

This is your one last chance to proof the project. It is not the time to make changes. You are listening for any flaws in the production. What the manufacturers mean is that you're listening for any huge flaws on their part. If you hear flaws on your part, or things you wish you'd done differently, it is too late. The only way to fix them is to rerecord, remix and remaster, all of which will cost big bucks.

Try looking at it this way. Did you ever take a photograph of a magnificent sunset that filled the sky with blazing color? When you got your photos back, did you feel disappointed when all those colors were shrunk onto a piece of paper that barely filled your hand? That's what it's like when you hear your test copy.

The test copy is there to let you listen for any weird noises that may have wound up on the tape as it was being prepared at the duplication facility. Instead of listening for that stuff, we listen for all the things that it's too late to change.

When I turn my project in to be made into cassettes and CDs, I'm always thinking that some magic fairy dust will get sprinkled on my songs. With the help of this fairy dust, my whole album will sound even better than it did when I brought it in. I don't know if the magic stuff happens for anyone else, but it's never happened to me. In fact, I sometimes feel that the magic has been sucked out of the songs. I know many people who heard their test copies and had an overwhelming desire to start over.

Don't start over. Stop torturing yourself. Accept this as a learning experience. Don't go get out all your favorite albums and compare yours to theirs. Consider the idea that those same artists probably felt the same way when they got their test copies. No matter how bad you feel, I promise there will be people who will like your album. Just think, maybe some recording artist down the line will be comparing their test copy to yours.

After listening to the test copy, take note of how you'd like your next album to sound. Next time, you'll know even better what things you want to include and what things you want to avoid. The only way to learn is to do it. Give yourself credit for the courage it took to start this project, and the courage it takes to say, "This is it. This was our best. Imperfect as it is, I am proud of what we have created." I'm sure that the Beatles felt this same sinking feeling when they heard their test copies. When they considered the time and money it would take to start over, all they could do was break out in a new song—"Let It Be."

CHAPTER FIVE

DESIGNING THE ALBUM PACKAGE

J ust when you think you can't get any more decisions out of your studio-frazzled brain, you realize you'll have to be the executive producer of another project—your album cover. The credits. The graphics. The photos. If you hadn't already invested so much of yourself in figuring out the recording process, you might feel like quitting. Don't quit, just get a good night's sleep. You can do this, and you can do it in your own way.

SHOPPING FOR THE BEST DEALS ON GRAPHICS, PRINTING AND DUPLICATION

In nearly every music magazine, you can find ads for audio duplication services that manufacture cassettes and CDs. This is quite a change from a few years ago when no one knew where to go for this service. The question is, how much shopping do you want to do?

I will drive all over town to save a few dollars on shoes, but when it comes to comparing prices of audio duplication facilities, it's easy to get worn out fast. Each one offers a great deal that is broken down differently. One might give free jewel boxes (the clear plastic cases your CDs come in), and others offer free graphic design, while another one offers a compilation CD of their customers that they send to radio stations, and yet another gives you a free Web page on the Internet.

Since they all offer different package deals and bonuses, call around, get them to send you their information, and compare. If it all starts to sound the same to you, take into consideration the courtesy, helpfulness and accessibility of the sales reps at each company. You will be asking a lot of questions of your sales rep before, during and after your album is duplicated. As you're doing your research, pay attention to how you are treated and how quickly a company gets back to you. There is a learning curve here, and you may go off into the ditch a few times in figuring out how this process works. You will need someone who is helpful and won't make you feel like an idiot if you don't understand everything immediately.

For a comprehensive list of manufacturers who provide audio duplication services for cassettes, CDs and even vinyl records, look at yearly directories such as the *Recording Industry Sourcebook*, available from Mix Bookshelf at (800) 233-9604, or *International Buyer's Guide*, available from Billboard Directories at (800) 344-7119. For a less comprehensive list, pick up a musicians magazine and look through the ads for a few manufacturers that appeal to you. Whichever way you choose, call several manufacturers and ask them to send you their price lists and a guideline for submitting your material.

At this point, you have two choices. You can either contract all the artwork and the printing yourself, using the manufacturer only for the duplication of the music, or you can take advantage of a full-service duplication facility that will do everything as a package deal. The first thing to decide is how many units you want to produce. If you're making fifty cassettes, you can save money by designing the cover on a computer label program and copy it yourself using a laser printer or color copier. Copies of the tapes can be run individually on your home tape deck.

If you're making a hundred or more cassettes, they can be done at the larger duplication facilities, but check the prices before you decide. Some companies don't like the hassle of small orders, so their small orders are very expensive. Others cater to the small-order business, which for them is usually one hundred minimum, so they give price breaks for small orders and often provide graphic services.

The Benefits of Doing Graphics, Printing and Duplication in One Place

If you're not yet a pro at making CDs and cassettes, I recommend using one of the full-service audio duplication facilities for everything. They have great deals with graphics and printing included for five hundred cassettes or five hundred CDs. If you have a friend who's a graphic artist and will do it for you free, you can turn in the cover artwork with your music and still take advantage of the special deals. Making an album for the first time has many unexpected complications, and many details have to be just right, like the graphic design specifications for ensuring the J-card (for cassettes) and CD booklets fit perfectly inside the boxes. If they aren't right, you can lose a lot of time and money correcting the problem. If you're a computer-graphics whiz, you could do it yourself, or you could contract the work out to any graphic artist. But graphics are so inexpensive (often free) on a manufacturer's bargain package that it doesn't make sense to take on the extra challenges of having the graphics designed at an outside source.

If you have everything done at a full-service facility, you only need to call one number to check on the progress of everything at once, and your sales rep can guide you through every step of the process and advise you from every angle.

THE ALBUM COVER

Many people buy things because the item is visually appealing, so a good-looking album cover is essential. It needs to look professional so people will take your album seriously. No matter how you choose to accomplish this, it must be visually appealing.

People have bought my album based solely on the album cover and the appeal of the album title. It's hard for me to imagine that happening, because I don't think I would buy an album because of the cover and the title. But people come to my concerts and tell me that they originally chose my album simply because they saw it in a little bookstore somewhere and liked the cover.

Before you start planning your album cover, go to record stores and see what you like. Take these ideas with you to your photo shoot. If you want to save money, go for something that is simple and black and white. Album covers can range from a plain piece of white paper with your name on it to a slick multicolored design with expensive graphics and an even more expensive photo. You will have an album cover on your cassette (the J-card) and the same basic design in a different size configuration for your CD case (the jewel box). The album information on paper inside that jewel box is called the book or booklet.

I believe a great-looking album cover is important. Ideally, instead of costing a lot, it will look like it cost a lot. If you're going for low, low budget, these are the secrets of getting the lowest priced album covers:
- Go for black, white and gray.
- No extra pictures inside.
- No lyrics inside.
- Minimal liner notes.
- Keep your thank-yous short so you won't be charged for excessive typing.
- Do your covers on computer label software.

These tips will keep your costs down if that's important. On the other hand, consider this. Your album cover is going to sell the thing. Let's say you're going to get a thousand albums on your first run. Even if you pay $1,000 for the cover graphics, extra photos, lyrics inside, long thank-yous and a panel to advertise your other albums with a tear-off order form, you're paying only a dollar apiece for the artwork. Once the artwork is designed, you never have to pay for the design again, so you're paying only a small charge for additional copies of the cover. If you buy five thousand copies of that album over time, you pay $.20 for each cover. Since the artwork sells your albums, it's a good investment.

The price of your album cover will depend on the intricacy of your graphics, the number of colors you use, the cost of the photographer and the cost of the graphic artist. Let's start with graphics.

Graphics

Your least expensive option will be black and white with basic graphics. While the cost increases with the number of colors and the complexity of the graphics, those same elements will increase your album's visual appeal. Visual appeal is important, since this will be potential album buyers' introduction to your album.

With some ingenuity, you can make really great-looking covers that are also inexpensive. Ideally, your album cover will look like it cost more than it really did. One way to save money is to keep it simple and repeat the same design from album to album. Karen Taylor-Good (writer of Patty Loveless's "How Can I Help You Say Good-bye" and Collin Raye's "Really Not That Different") has made five of her own albums. On the first three, she chose a simple one-color background and used another color for cool-looking graphics that said "KTG I," "KTG II" and "KTG III." Using this method, she paid only for two-color printing instead of full-color, and paid once for the graphic design of "KTG." The design was not complicated. She paid $75 to a graphic artist for the original design, which she could also use as a logo, and with each successive album, she paid only a minimal fee to the artist to have the new number added in place of the old one.

Graphic artists usually charge by the hour. You can find graphic artists at most copy and printing businesses, and the duplication facility that handles your album will also have graphic design available as part of the package price. You can save money with graphic designers by following these simple rules:

• Type all the words that will go on the cover, from the title to your name to the credits. Ask if they would rather have this on a computer disk. Check and double-check the spelling of everything.

• Deliver your photos in the format they need. To do this, ask if they need the original photo, a slide or a negative, and find out what size they want it in. Take your photo to a photography shop to get these things done or to find out where it can be done.

My first album cover was as basic as it gets. I used a black-and-white head shot (*head shot*: a cozy, warm, friendly-looking close-up of the face, commonly used to get acting and modeling jobs). I cut a little zigzagging border off an ad in a New Mexico magazine, copied it a few times on a copy machine to get a longer piece, then pasted it around the photo. I typed my name, blew it up bigger on the copy machine, and spent nine hours with an X-Acto knife and a jar of rubber cement removing all the straight lines of my name and replacing them with this zigzag. I had no idea that when you take your music and your photo to the cassette production company, they will have a graphic artist do all of this for you, and the artist will even come up with original sketches of cover ideas for you to choose from. What a concept!

Before the album was completed at the duplication place, I needed about a hundred of them to take to New Mexico where I had some gigs. The cassettes were ready, but the J-cards weren't finished yet. I knew I could sell the tapes if I had them with me, but I didn't want to sell them without a cover. Michelle White, the graphic artist at National Tape and Disc, where I was doing my albums, came up with the idea of copying them on good copiers. She gave me a copy of my original X-Acto design in the size that would fit in the cassette cases. I took it to a copy place and got a hundred copies on card stock. Since I was able to fit two or more covers per page, I had to pay for only fifty copies at a few cents per page, plus pennies more to have them cut to size.

Since those first hundred J-cards didn't look as good as they could, I did something else to make them special to the first hundred people who were willing to buy them. I signed them inside and numbered each one like an artist would with a hundred prints of a painting. After signing them, I took the hundred signed J-cards back to NTD to have them packed into the cases with the cassettes, then had them shrink-wrapped so they looked a little more professional.

The reason for this whole story about doing album covers on a copier is to let you know that it is possible. You can create your own design by reducing a large photo, printing your name and the title of the album on your computer, and then making copies and having them cut at a copy center. With today's computers and software designed to make labels, you or a friend can do the entire job on a computer and print the labels yourselves.

Although it is possible to do your album covers on copy machines, computers and laser printers, use some caution. Print a few test runs and then compare your finished product with the J-cards in some of your favorite major-label releases. Ideally, your album cover will look and feel like it came from the same quality materials that the pros use. The pros use printed material on card stock with a little gloss to it. Their covers don't have little perforation marks where the cards were separated. If yours comes out looking homemade, consider whether that's the impression you want your album cover to make. Remember that for a potential buyer, the album cover will be a direct reflection of the music inside. If the outside looks amateurish, they might expect the music to be amateurish, too. As you compare yours with the majors, consider the weight and stiffness of the paper stock, the way the ink looks on the paper and the glossiness of the paper. Make sure yours looks professional.

Whether you have your graphics designed at the tape duplication facility or by a freelance graphic artist, it all starts with your general concept for the album. You take in a photo or other cover artwork, and describe the mood of the album and the audience you want to reach. The graphic artist will take it from there. Within a few days, the artist will present you with one or more mock-ups of what your album can look like. You will choose which you like the best. If you are working with the graphic artist at the duplication facility, you will see your design by fax or mail and approve it over the phone.

Another option is to have your J-cards and CD covers typeset and copied at a print shop. They will either have graphic artists on staff or they send the work out and then bring you in to approve the design. You can talk to your representative at the tape duplication facility to get the size and shape specifications along with anything else the printer will need to know.

Looks count. Potential buyers make assumptions about the quality of your album based on the quality of the cover. If a crummy, cheap-looking cover discourages anyone from buying your album, what's the point of investing all that money in recording it? Make sure your cover reflects all the quality you can afford.

Photography

You have several options if you want to use a photo on your album. The cheapest option is to use a photo you already have. Most people use a photo of themselves, but some use nature photos that they or their friends have shot. If you use a photo of yourself, make sure it is a sharp, clear image. The photo can be computer enhanced by whoever is designing your album cover, but it is best to start with a great photo. Even computer enhancing cannot make a cool photo out of a mediocre photo.

Photographers often have a sliding scale for their work, depending on what you're going to do with the photo and how many albums you intend to make. In other words, they will probably charge you a lot less for your photo than they would charge Madonna. I have friends who have paid thousands for their album photography, along with hundreds for the stylist and makeup artist on the shoot. I have paid from $50 to $300 for mine and have been very pleased with every cover.

Remember that this photo will be small on the cassette cover, so it's important that you not be a speck in the photo. Make sure you are prominently placed in the photo. You might have a great 8″ × 10″ of you on top of a mountain, or you on a boat in the middle of the lake, but by the time it's shrunk to the size of a cassette cover, we'll need a magnifying glass to recognize you. My suggestion is to put your face pretty big on the cover. If nothing else, it begins to plant the image of your face in people's minds and will increase your recognition, even with those who just look at and don't buy your albums.

Record producer Murray Krugman of Silverwolf Records suggests you avoid using two shots from the same photo shoot on the front and back covers of your album. If you have two different shots in the same clothes at the same location, it looks like this is the only photo session you've ever had. Artists on the big labels use two or more photos from the same shoot all the time (I'm looking at Enya's *Shepherd Moons* right now, which has all four CD photos from the same shoot and at the same angle), but his point makes sense, and I'll certainly be thinking of it for my own albums in the future.

You'll get more mileage out of your photography investment if you get a sharp simple photo of your face that copies well on a copy machine. You can use this photo for newsletters, press releases, brochures, posters and more. Every time you use the same photo that's on your album cover, you will be reinforcing that image in potential buyers' minds. You can even use the same image on stationery and envelopes, reinforcing your image to everyone who receives a written communication from you. If you get a really cool photo of yourself, you have a much better chance of having it printed in the newspaper when you send out a press release. Newspaper people like to have an eye-catching page, and if your photo is eye-catching, they'll be more likely to use your photo to make their page look good.

To get a good deal on your photo session, find a photographer who is just getting started or is in transition from amateur to professional. Photographers are always trying to build their portfolios with varied examples of what they can do. If you live in a place that's not known as a music town, a photographer might love to do an album cover to enhance his or her portfolio.

To find your up-and-coming photographer, ask friends if they know of friends who'd be interested in the job. If no one turns up in that search, ask at your nearest camera and photo store. Someone working there may be interested, or they can connect you with someone they'd recommend. Since they see everybody's photo-development projects, they'd know who is good and who isn't.

Here's a basic lesson of working with photographers that I learned the hard way. Make sure you write down all the prices you and the photographer agree on during your first meeting, especially if you are not used to working with photographers. After you have described what you want and what you'll be using it for, the photographer will quote you a price. The photographer may assume that you realize there will be additional charges for rolls of film, proof sheets and printing of the final photos you choose. These items are more costly than you'd expect and can quickly add up to a whole lot more money than you were planning to pay. Write it all down, along with your deadline, then have the photographer check it and approve it to make sure you've covered everything. This will help you compare prices between photographers and will also keep you from being unpleasantly surprised when you get the bill.

Cross-Promote Inside Your Albums

Once you have more than one album, be sure to advertise your first album in the cassette cover and CD booklet of every album after that. When you reorder covers of your original album, add a panel that advertises all your subsequent albums. The best way I've found to do this is to have the person doing your graphics do a small photo of your first album cover. Write a little blurb about the album, to be printed next to the photo of the cover. Include an address that tells people where they can order your other album (or albums) and be sure to tell them how much it will cost, including postage.

A panel of information inside your album costs around $40. If you're printing a thousand covers, that's only $.25 cents each. If you get mail orders for five cassettes, that will cover the $40 plus the postage to mail out the cassettes.

Some people include a panel in their cassettes and CDs that is a detachable order form. If you do this, don't ask for a perforation where people can tear out the order form, because making the perforation on each one will be very expensive. Just put a dotted line along the top with the image of scissors. People will get the idea that they're supposed to cut it there. With the order form, you can also do some market research. Obviously, you'll ask for the person's address. You can also find out where they heard of you, where they bought their album and whether they belong to a group that might be interested in sponsoring a concert. This information will be useful for your database and your mailing list.

Including instructions about how to get more albums is helpful even if you have only one album out. Make it easy for people to get more copies directly from you. Inside the album cover, just write, "To order additional copies or to schedule a concert, please write to: (Your mailing address)."

The Words Inside

Fewer words equals fewer dollars. On the other hand, extra panels inside your album covers are not expensive, and this album is a milestone in your career, so why not go all out?

These are some of the things that can go inside your album, listed in no particular order:

• List of songs, in order. As a writer, I ask you please to include the songwriters' names and the name of the publisher under each song title.

• The length in minutes and seconds of each song. Radio stations like this and need this.

- Thank-yous. The more you thank, the more you pay in terms of graphics, but the people who have helped you all these years probably deserve the space.

- Your other albums, if you have any. Advertise them with a photo of each album for visual appeal.

- Lyrics. As a songwriter, I believe the lyrics are essential. I didn't include them in my first album. I regretted it, so I've included them in all the rest.

- Copyright information. The duplication facility can tell you what you need here.

- The address for ordering more or for booking concerts. It can say, "For booking information or to order more albums, call or write this address," and then include your calling and mailing information.

- A request or threat (whichever is your personal style) regarding the copying of your material. You can be generic and use "Federal law prohibits . . . ," or you can be original and make up your own. I saw an album cover recently that said, in big letters, "WARNING: IT IS UNLAW-FUL, UNHOLY AND SINFUL TO COPY THIS TAPE." Mine say, "Please resist the urge to copy this creation." On some of my albums, I have gone on to say things like, "The proceeds from these songs go to pay for housing and pencils so I can write some more. For additional copies. . . ."

All this should be written neatly or typed and turned in to the graphic artist. The duplication facility will also need the song list so they can print it on your cassettes and CDs. With computers, you can now type out your song list, your inside lyrics, your thank-yous, your blurbs to advertise your other albums, and everything else that will go inside. You can do all the spell-checking on your computer, and then give your graphic artist a disk of every word, in order, that will go on the inside of the album. They can still move sections around, but they won't change spelling.

A lesson folk artist Crow Johnson learned the hard way is that all the proofreading of all the writing on your album is up to you, the artist. She also learned that proofreading is more than just checking for spelling errors. Crow's new album sounded great and looked great. The cover was beautiful. Anxious to get airplay on her new album, she did a mass mailing to all the radio stations that play her kind of music.

There was one problem. When a disc jockey introduced song number ten by announcing the title and pushing "play," a different song came on. The song order on the album jacket was not the same as the song order on the CDs.

The number of words to check when you do your album can be over-whelming, but it's our job to do the proofing. I have sat with a magnifying glass, going letter by letter over each word of the microscopic lyrics inside my cassette-jacket proofs. It's tedious and time-consuming, but it's up to you. Once you sign off on the job, meaning you've accepted it, that's how it will be.

Packaging

Shrink-wrap (the plastic around the outside of a new album) makes your cassettes and CDs look more professional, but the shrink-wrap is unnecessary and also clutters the environment with more trash. Although shrink-wrap is inexpensive, you can save a little money and reduce clutter in landfills by not having your albums shrink-wrapped.

I shrink-wrap mine because it follows my philosophy that our albums should look the same on the outside as everything else in a record store. Good news on the environmental front is that some new, cardboard CD cases are becoming available that will replace the hard plastic jewel boxes.

If you are not planning to have your cassettes and CDs shrink-wrapped, you can also save a very small amount of money by packing the music and covers into the cassette cases and CD jewel boxes yourself. This work is tedious, but if you order your cassettes or CDs in small quantities only, it might be worth the money you'll save.

Making Your Albums Radio-Friendly

If you want your album to be radio-ready, make sure you've covered these important things in your packaging. The easier you make it for radio stations to play your music, the better.

1. Include the length of each song in minutes and seconds.

2. Make sure lyrics are easy to read in your album so they can easily check out your lyric content if they're trying to decide which cuts to play.

Crow Johnson, entertainer, songwriter, recipient of the 1995 Kate Wolf Memorial Award and former publisher of *Zassafras Music News*, has found that airplay in the areas where she'll be playing concerts has greatly increased attendance. "Airplay is magic. In three and a half or four minutes, your little tune may reach more people than you will perform for 'live' in a whole year. You want to make it fun and easy for the radio world to support your work."

When Crow mailed her *Painting Stories 'Cross the Sky* album to radio stations that play independent releases, she included a postcard that asked for three responses from the disc jockeys:

1. Here are my thoughts on *Painting Stories 'Cross the Sky*:

2. Here is a printable quote:

3. Please refer to me as:

Crow says she got some excellent constructive comments, super quotes and a better understanding of what those radio stations look for.

FREEZE THE DESIGN

The hardest part about creating an album is knowing when to quit. Artists in other fields, like architects and engineers, face this same challenge. They solve the problem with a time limitation that will "freeze the design." At whatever stage the design is in when time is up, the design is frozen, meaning it has to stay in that form. Without a deadline for freezing the design, plans could be made and remade for weeks, months and years, holding back the completion of the project indefinitely. This is what can happen to your album if you don't plan a cutoff date and a budget limit.

Believe me, your album will *never never never* be as perfect as you want it to be. *Never.* No matter how much money or time you spend, you will always want to go back and change things. You might as well stay within your monetary and time limits, or at least try not to go *too* far over, considering that whether you spend $3,000 or $300,000 on the album, you'll wish you could do it better.

Advice is easy to give and often hard to take. As I write this, I am in the process of recording my latest album. We completed my album *Enjoy the Ride* and just got our test copy back today. The producer and I are checking the test for any flaws. As I have been listening to it, I hear some glaring flaws in one song. Unfortunately, these errors are no one's fault but mine. One song has some pitch problems. When we recorded it, it didn't seem so bad, but as I listen to it now, I am cringing.

To redo that song would run up $250 more in recording costs and would set my album back by at least a week. The CDs are ready to print any minute now, so we would have to notify the plant in another state to hold the presses while we take our master source (the digital audio tape of the album we originally turned in) back to the studio to resing and remix that one song. After that, we'd return the master source to the duplication facility to have it transferred to another test copy for us to approve. This will do more than delay the album. It will also delay everything else in my life that has been on hold for the weeks during recording.

If I resing and remix that one song, I might not have any new albums with me on my upcoming tour. I am playing in places where people have already bought my previous albums, and if I don't have new product, I won't do very well there in album sales. Even though it hurts me to tell you that I knew something was imperfect and chose not to correct it, that's what I'm going to do. I'm leaving the song as it is. I'm freezing the design, knowing there are things I could redo on *every* song on *every* album. You have to stop somewhere. I won't try to tell you it's easy to do.

CHAPTER SIX

MAINTAINING YOUR SANITY WHILE MAKING AND MARKETING YOUR ALBUMS

The biggest challenge in creating and marketing your first album won't be raising the money or finding a recording studio. As with most things in life, the biggest challenge is maintaining a positive attitude to keep you going when you want to give up. Creating albums can be overwhelming. You have hundreds of decisions to make, leads to follow up and information to chase down. If you set a deadline for making your album, such as a big show you're doing where you'll be able to sell a lot of them, that deadline creates other, earlier deadlines. You will need an unbelievable amount of personal motivation to get it all done.

The only thing that's as powerful as my drive to succeed is my fear of failure. Making and marketing an album, whether it's the first one or the fifth one, is still a challenge to my mental health. The album is a reflection of me, and when things about the album can't be the way I'd like them to be (due to limitations of time, finances, vocal abilities or other resources) it's hard to keep going. When the choices, decisions and unexpected setbacks get overwhelming, it would be easy to say, "This is too hard. What's the point? The world is not missing anything by not having an hour of my music on the market." In order to complete the project, sometimes having some good techniques for maintaining your mental health can be as valuable as having great songs to put on the album.

THREE STEPS, NO FAIL

Most people reading this book already have big commitments to think about and not much extra time to spend making and marketing an album. You may have a demanding career, a family to support or debts to pay. Lots of people have all three. You have invested a great deal of time, energy and love to get what you have, and you can't throw it all away. You have traveled a long way down your path. Giving up all you've got and starting over is not an option. Fortunately, there's a better way. Start where you are and begin building a bridge.

"Three Steps, No Fail" is the way to build a bridge from where you are to where you want to go. "Three Steps, No Fail" will show you the quickest way to keep from being overwhelmed by the ideas in this book so you can move forward and begin making speedy progress toward your dream. I learned "Three Steps, No Fail" when I was in Albuquerque, New Mexico, as a beginning television news reporter at an NBC affiliate. With a degree in broadcasting and the dream of being an entertainer, I intended to get one year of experience after college. That way, I could always fall back on broadcasting if music didn't work out.

As you might already be guessing, that one year of experience multiplied into four years quicker than you can say, "Jana Stanfield, Eyewitness News." The longer I stayed, the more demanding the job became. Along with the demands came the perks like awards, prestige and trips to cover interesting stories in interesting places. I was on the nightly news and was recognized at the mall. Some of my stories were sold to the network, and my parents got to see me on NBC News. I even got sent to Washington to cover the second inauguration of Ronald Reagan. The awful part was that young women all over the country were dreaming of having my job, and there I was living it but not wanting it.

With every passing day there were more perks and more demands. This career I had stepped into halfheartedly was now wrapping its tentacles around me so tightly I couldn't escape. I kept having this dream that I was hanging from a rope tied to a hot-air balloon that had lifted off and was heading skyward fast. With every foot the balloon rose, it increased the chances of my being killed or badly injured if I let go. Part of me wanted to jump and still have a chance of surviving. Caught between the fear of letting go and the fear of holding on, I felt immobilized as the balloon (my job) swept me away to a place I never intended to go. Every person caught in a career that keeps them from their art is familiar with this feeling.

Fortunately, I have a caring family. My father knew how much I wanted to pursue music, because that was always his dream too. He understood my feeling of being trapped in my job by my lack of knowledge about how to make my musical dreams come true. Dad called my uncle, Rev. Clyde Stanfield, who is a United Methodist minister and a professional counselor. Clyde, who was serving an Albuquerque church across town from the television station, called to see if I'd like to get together for lunch once a week. During these wonderful lunches, he taught me "Three Steps, No Fail."

During the first lunch, he listened patiently as I told him how I wanted to be an entertainer and how trapped I felt in my career.

He said, "What we need to do is build a bridge. You don't have to be able to see to the other side yet. You just need to be able to see the first three steps. Those first three steps will move you forward enough that you'll be able to see the next three steps." The great thing about "Three Steps, No Fail" is that you don't have to know exactly where you're going for its magic to work.

Clyde gave me an assignment for our next week's lunch: Make a list of three things you can do in a week that will take you closer to where you want to be. There's only one guideline for choosing the steps. Each one has to be something you couldn't possibly fail at in a week's time. Each step will begin building not only a bridge, but a feeling of confidence. Soon, you'll be able to believe you have the ability to make your dreams come true if you just take it one easy step at a time.

This was my first list:

1. Buy a book about making it in the music business.
2. Call a voice teacher to see how much lessons would cost.
3. Order cable television so I can watch The Nashville Network.

I had been thinking about doing all three of these things, plus many others, for a long time. The one thing holding me back was my feeling of hopelessness. Since I knew that none of them would make my dream come true, it felt like useless effort. Once I understood "Three Steps, No Fail" I began to understand that none of these things have to be the *perfect* thing that makes it all happen. Each one is building the bridge.

The Magic of the First Three Steps

When we can't see the road ahead, it can immobilize us. We can get caught between fear and faith. When we focus on doing the footwork, instead of worrying about the road ahead, amazing things can happen. The road unfolds little by little, a step at a time. Each small set of steps leads logically to the next small set of steps.

I didn't have to be a genius to know that when I came back with my list, my next week's assignment would be to do the things on the list. I was so excited about building this bridge that I arrived at our next lunch not only with the list, but with all three steps accomplished. I felt exhilarated at my accomplishments and anxious to take three more steps.

Each of the three steps will always lead to the next three. Here's what evolved from my first three steps:

1. Buy a book. After buying the book, my next step was to set a goal of the number of pages I was certain I could read in a week. I didn't put any pressure on myself to make it a large number. I was making progress and that felt wonderful. That feeling of progress was so new that it could be easily shattered by small failures, and it was not worth the risk to put anything on my list that I couldn't accomplish easily. Setting the number of pages I would read in a week as one of my three next steps taught me to break tasks down into small, accomplishable bits so that I could continue my pattern of success. This pattern of success is what builds a foundation of unshakable confidence.

2. Call a voice teacher. Calling a voice teacher was my second step, and it led me easily to the next step. For months I had been thinking of calling this wonderful singer in Albuquerque, Linda Cotton, who had her own jazz band and also taught voice lessons. In addition to the hopelessness that kept me from calling her, I also was intimidated by her enormous talent and scared of asking anyone for help in being a better singer. The whole thing made me feel so vulnerable. That's why I didn't set the goal of signing up for voice lessons. I just made it my goal to *inquire* about voice lessons. As I talked to her on the phone I found that her prices were affordable, that the place where she taught was not far from the station and that she was kind and caring and warm. Right then and there I took another step. I set up an appointment with her for a lesson.

I truly believe these steps are like magic if you choose to see it that way. Each step leads me to believe with all my heart that when we step out in faith, Providence moves too. The floodgates will open to bring us all the good that we have the courage to open our arms to receive. Goethe said, "Whatever you can do, or dream you can, begin it. Boldness has genius, power, and magic in it."

During the short time I spent with Linda that day, she encouraged me, told me a little about what her life was like as a full-time singer, and then there was one more thing. Here's where it became magic. She told me about a gifted piano player, Sid Fendley, who had left her band recently to play at a local country club. She suggested I call him, providing my next step. It turns out Sid was looking for someone to come out on weekends and sing with him in a beautiful country-club piano bar.

Meeting Sid turned everything around for me musically. For the first time in my life, I was making music as something more than just a beloved hobby. I was actually working in music and still doing the news. Sid was a wonderful mentor who taught me about living the life of a full-time musician, from practice and performance to professionalism and paychecks. With Sid playing piano and me doing most of the singing, we worked together for nearly a year, eventually moving from the country club to a job at a nice downtown hotel where all my friends and even my co-workers at the television station could come to hear us. I loved singing with Sid every weekend. I loved practicing every week. We made good money and it was a thrill for me to be learning the ropes of a career in music.

3. Order cable. After ordering cable, one of the steps that frequently showed up on my weekly list was to watch two programs on The Nashville

Network. One was *Nashville Now,* a nightly country-music talk show, and the other was *You Can Be a Star,* a daily talent contest that awarded a recording contract to the grand-prize winner. Each episode of *You Can Be a Star* was followed by an announcement that said, "If you'd like to appear on *You Can Be a Star,* simply call this number or write to this address for information." Of course, I put it on my list one week to call for information.

The producer of the show answered the phone. He was friendly and unpretentious, immediately putting me at ease. I'm sure he knew how nervous people are when they call. He told me everything I needed to know about how to send in a tape to be considered for the show, so I had plenty of little steps to take in the coming weeks. My tape was approved, and I was invited to appear. I used my two weeks of vacation time to be on the show, explore the Nashville music scene and look for a job. I didn't win the grand prize on the show, but I hit the jackpot with those job interviews. Soon after returning home, I got a job offer in the music business that paid as much as my job at the television station!

I won't say every single step brought a miracle. I won't mention the talent contests I entered and lost, the unsuccessful Opryland auditions that I flew to Memphis for that year or the horrible band I rehearsed with for months and performed with for two weeks. Most of it was mundane stuff, putting one foot in front of the other and making plodding progress. It was the progress that I loved, though, even when I was getting home at three in the morning from the band gig and getting up at dawn to be in full drag and make-up for my television job. Finally, I had learned how to give myself hope, by practicing three easy steps per week that I couldn't possibly fail at.

Within a year of practicing "Three Steps, No Fail," I was living in Nashville and working in the music business. I continued to take three steps a week to achieve my dream of becoming a recording artist. I had plenty of struggles ahead, but I was thrilled to be on my way.

ONE PROJECT AT A TIME

One way of organizing this journey in your mind is to take it one project at a time. Maybe all you know right now is that you're tired of waiting for a record company executive to wave a magic wand that will change your life. That's all you need to know to begin taking this journey one project at a time.

Your first project is to glean all the information you can from this book. Your next project might be to read other books that will tell you more of the specifics about making your own album. It's not necessary to make a decision yet about whether to make an album, because the decision itself can be a big project. One good way to make the decision is to break it down to just one segment at a time.

You might start by considering what songs you would do if you did decide to make an album. You might start by planning the cover. You could begin by thinking about who you would thank on your album.

Choose the project that seems the easiest. Starting with an easy project, like deciding what songs you'd put on the album, will give you two advantages. First, it will get you going and give you the confidence you need to take on a more complicated project. Second, it will help you visualize your project. This will make the project seem more real. With the real prospect of an album growing in your mind, other ideas about how to make it happen will sprout and spread like wildfire.

Too often we have been taught that we have to know the destination, that we have to have some ultimate goal. One option is to make it your ultimate goal to be exactly where you're meant to be right now, doing exactly what you're meant to be doing. When we set goals that are too far away, it's hard to take into account the everyday challenges and commitments of life. It makes it too easy to feel like we're not making any progress if we haven't achieved stardom yet. When we constantly judge ourselves by how far we are from the goal, we will always come up short.

With a goal of "one project at a time," you can go at your own pace. You don't have to know what the next project will be. If you decide to make an album, don't worry yet about how you will promote it. As you are in the process of each project, the next project will present itself to you. You will know what to do, and as you do it, the next project will begin to take shape.

FAME

A wise man named Larry Davidson once said, "It's just as fulfilling to be famous in your own community as it is being famous all over the world."

Larry Davidson was famous. Though he passed away a few years ago, he is still widely known. He was famous to all the people who knew him. He was famous in his own community. Larry had a contagious laugh and contagious enthusiasm. He was a tall man with gray hair, blue eyes and a striking appearance. He was once a luxury-car salesman. When I knew him, he was selling "modular homes." I was shocked to learn later that this meant "trailer houses." Not that anything is wrong with trailer houses, it's just so appropriate that Larry would wear his black pin-striped suit with the red or yellow pocket square and refer to them as modular homes.

I always felt like Larry was my greatest cheerleader. Back in the days when I was an unsuccessful songwriter struggling to get a record deal, he was constantly telling me I needed to make my own albums. He said more people needed to have the opportunity to hear my songs. He believed in me even when I didn't believe in myself.

Larry read *Think and Grow Rich* and was a big believer in the teachings of its author, Napoleon Hill. The book suggests getting a group together of like-minded individuals who can support each other's goals. A group like that is known as a Master Mind group. One day Larry said, "Jana, we need to put together a Master Mind group of people who believe that your song, 'If I Had Only Known,' ought to be on the radio." Larry held the meetings at his house. The group included me, my husband David, Larry and his wife Conneigh, and our friend Jennie. We met only about three times before we all had scheduling conflicts and the group disbanded. I don't know for sure that our prayers and faith had anything to do with it, but a year later Reba McEntire recorded "If I Had Only Known." If nothing else, I am grateful to Larry for being willing to do whatever small thing he could to support my dream.

At Larry's memorial service, people from all walks of life came down the aisle and stood at the pulpit of Nashville's First Church Unity to talk about how much Larry meant to them. People that Larry's wife and family had never seen before came forward to talk about the difference Larry made in their lives with his kindness and encouragement. Throughout the service, the same words were repeated: "I felt like Larry Davidson was my greatest cheerleader."

You probably never heard of him, and yet Larry knew a lot about being famous. He always told me the greatest success you can ever achieve is to be admired by the people you admire.

A NOTE OF ENCOURAGEMENT

If there is a longing somewhere deep inside you to let your music be heard . . . pay attention to that longing.

If there is a whisper somewhere deep inside you that is urging you to take the risk . . . listen to that whisper.

The longing and the whisper are there for a reason. If you pay attention to the longing and listen for the whisper, they will take you where you need to go and teach you what you need to know.

SELLING ALBUMS IS EASY

Once you've jumped through all the hoops on your album project, the real fun can begin. Selling albums is like receiving applause. Every person who wants to buy one is affirming that your music is important, has value and brings pleasure into someone's life. So why are we scared about making our albums available? I was pretty shy about my albums at first. Now, I'm proud, and I appreciate every purchase from every human being. These are the people who support me in doing what I love for a living.

My audience won't be the same as your audience. People will be drawn to the music of people like themselves. People who like your music might think mine is nothing but ear torture. That's okay. The great thing is that there are more than enough people out there to support us all in creating our music.

HOW I SOLD MY FIRST ALBUM, OR "YOU MEAN IT? YOU WANT TO BUY THIS?"

At first, I felt timid about making my album available. Heck, I had merely strung ten demos together. They were all from different studios, with different producers or no producers at all. There was little continuity, no identifiable theme, nothing that gave it cohesiveness except that I co-wrote and sang all the songs.

I knew it couldn't hold a candle to the major label products. I knew it was crummy in comparison. It was only a few steps up from making cassette copies of ten songs in my living room on that hand-me-down stereo one of my Music Row employers gave me that had a bumper sticker across the front that read "Disc Jockeys Do It on the Air."

I almost felt like I was stealing from people if I did anything to talk them into buying this album. If they wanted it, they would have to ask me for it to prove that it wasn't my idea; then, they could never come back and say I had tricked them into thinking this was going to be as good as the $50,000 albums they bought for the same $10 from "real" recording artists.

Then an amazing thing happened. People said they liked the album. They bought copies to give to their friends. They wanted me to autograph their copies and the copies for their friends. As shocking as it was then, it's even more shocking to me now. I'm making (in my opinion) much better albums, and people still come up to me almost apologetically like it's going to hurt my feelings, and say, "I still like your first album the best."

Gradually, I gained confidence enough to tell people about my album proudly. All it took was practice, along with a lot of people telling me they were glad they bought it.

HOW *NOT* TO SELL YOUR PRODUCT FROM THE STAGE

At first, you may find it challenging to make a good sales pitch for your albums from the stage. You may be more inclined to appear modest and say something like:

> *"Oh, by the way, if you really want one, I have some cassettes with me tonight. They're just some little things that I made up myself. No big deal. They're not on a major label or anything. I didn't really work with a producer or anything. It was just me and the band messing around in the studio. It's just done on a 4-track. I don't even really like them anymore, and they don't really represent what I'm doing now. We just made them real cheap so we'd have something available if someone really wanted to have some of our music. I can't blame you if you don't buy them. I know you'd have to feel about as foolish carrying one out of here tonight as I feel telling you about them. I know you probably don't want one anyway, but my husband/wife said he'd/she'd kill me if I didn't mention them this time. I don't know . . . I just forget about them."*

Don't get me wrong. This technique is effective. It is effective in *not selling your album.*

HOW TO *SUCCESSFULLY* SELL YOUR PRODUCT FROM THE STAGE

Every time we sing, we "sell" that song to an audience. We put in all the energy we can muster so that whoever is listening will "buy" the lyrics, meaning the audience will believe in the song. Folk performer Janet Feld, who has had her own CD out for a year, says that it is her goal during each performance to put that same vocal energy into selling her CDs. "I noticed that after all this vocal presence during the song, I would then back off the mic, duck my head and use this shy little voice to say, 'Oh, by the way, I have some cassettes and CDs in the back if you want any.' I'm trying to take that same voice the audience hears when I sing and use it when I'm telling them about these albums I'm so proud of."

Janet has found that mentioning a little bit about the making of her album is a good way to plant a seed in the audience's mind and make a smoother transition into the sales announcement. When we say, "Thank you very much. By the way, I have albums for sale," it can feel a little bit abrupt. The audience is thinking about how much they like your performance, and now here you are trying to sell them stuff. It takes the edge off if the albums have already been mentioned during the set. Janet talks about bringing all the recording equipment and musicians into her house to do the recording, and then finding that every time they wanted to record something, they had to turn off her noisy old refrigerator. Some artists might not want the audience to know the album was made in the living room, but for others, like Janet, that down-home quality makes audiences feel like they are part of her life when they hear this music made in her living room. It's like the difference between home cooking and gourmet food.

In the same way that a writer will often say, "I hate writing, but I love it when I have written," you may someday say, "I hate selling albums off the stage, but I love it when they sell." It's absolutely true that it's awkward to talk about your product onstage. I won't even say it's awkward at first, because I still find it awkward sometimes and I have been doing it for years. The great thing to remember is that many people will want to buy your album and they won't have the opportunity if you don't let them know they're available.

"But, Jana, What Do I Say?"

The most important tool in selling your albums off the stage is to help audience members feel that by buying your album, they are supporting someone in living a dream. Here are some ways to announce your album sales off the stage without sounding money hungry:

• "At the risk of jeopardizing my current level of obscurity, I will point out that all the songs you've heard tonight can be found on my albums at the back of the room. I've also got a mailing list you can sign if you'd like to know when I'll be back this way."

• "If you think these songs sound pretty good here tonight, you won't believe how great they'll sound coming out of your own stereo. All the songs you've heard tonight can be found on my albums, which are available at the back of the room and can be enjoyed in the privacy of your own home or car."

• "I'm having such a good time here tonight that I'd love it if we could all do this again sometime. If you'll come back to my table during the break, I've got a mailing list you can sign so I can let you know the next date I'll be playing here. I've also got all the songs you've heard tonight on cassette so the next time I come you can sing along."

• "If there are any songs you've heard tonight that you'd like to hear again or share with a friend, they are all available on my new album, which I'm really proud of. I'll be back there signing albums during the break, and if you've got time I'd love to have you sign my mailing list."

• "We've shared a special evening tonight, so even if you don't have a cassette player or a mailing address, at least come back so we can meet and I can personally thank you for making this a great evening for me."

• "Even if you don't want a cassette and don't particularly want me to know where you live, I hope you'll come back during the break to say hello."

Here's how some other people do it:

• "If you enjoyed the show tonight, please sign my mailing list at the back of the room. If you hated the show, you should also sign up. This way you'll know where I'm playing next, and you can avoid me with amazing accuracy."—Don White

• "These are soon to be collector's items, so you might want to buy several as a hedge against inflation."—Marita Brake

Nationally known recording stars use these techniques, too, because they know they can only keep their contracts if their albums sell well. In Nashville this fall, I saw a country artist perform an "unplugged" show at a local venue. In the introduction for several songs, she mentioned which albums they were on, and toward the end of her set, she said, "These albums are all out there in the stores, and a I just want to say one thing: It's never too early to shop for Christmas." Dolly Parton, who is recording for a smaller label these days, was on an awards show recently. In her brief moment on camera, she somehow managed to mention she had a new album out and encouraged people to get one.

Let the Introducer Do It

Your introduction will have a big effect on your album sales, whether the introducer mentions that your albums are available or not. The bigger the build-up before you perform, the stronger likelihood that the audience will think you're worth listening to before they even hear you. This also increases the chances that they'll buy an album after your performance.

Write a great introduction for yourself that highlights all your accolades.

This is very important. Carry copies of this introduction with you whenever you perform. I leave them in my gig bag with my cords, guitar strings and extra batteries. Often, the person who introduces you either won't need it or won't use it, but it is very helpful when they do. At the end of your intro, write something like, "Her latest album was released this fall. It's called, 'Whatever,' and it will be available near the door after her performance. And now, please help me welcome. . . ."

People in the audience need to know who you are and what you've done, because this determines their frame of mind for listening to your first notes. When the audience hears you have albums out before you even perform, they will consider the possibility of taking one home. If your performance is good, they'll be even more likely to buy than if they didn't know you had albums out until you mentioned it at the end of the set. By that time, they may be thinking about getting home, paying the babysitter, etc.

ADDITIONAL SALES TIPS

Notice that the words *for sale* were not included in any examples. People may want stuff, but they don't want you to *sell* them stuff. If you have to say something along those lines, say that your tapes are *available* at the back of the room instead of *for sale*.

If at all possible, have someone else take the money. That way you'll be free to shake hands, hug and sign albums. When you have to make change, you take time away from what people really want. They want to have some human contact with you. They want to talk to you for a minute. They come back to your table and often buy your albums just to be close to you, to feel that you're friends.

If you feel yourself balking at the idea that people would come to the back of the room and stand in line to have you sign their albums, just imagine your favorite artist for a moment. Pretend you were there when she was playing the kind of places you'll be playing. Pretend this artist was offering to sign her albums. You might be too shy to just go up and talk to the artist, but if you bought an album you wouldn't even have to ask. She's going to be there, and all you'll have to do is wait your turn and you can talk to her. Or him. Wouldn't that be worth a few dollars investment? Besides, if you don't buy one, you probably won't get to talk to her (or him) because she's going to be too busy talking to everyone who did. Wouldn't you buy one? Sure you would, and believe it or not, that's how a lot of people are going to feel about you and your albums. If you don't believe it, just try this at ten or fifteen shows and see.

WHEN YOU CAN'T MAKE A SALES ANNOUNCEMENT

If you feel too shy to say anything about your albums during your own show, use your albums onstage as a set list. In between songs, just hold one up as you look for what song to sing next. Obviously it is better to hold up CDs if you have them, because they're bigger and easier to see.

Sometimes you will be in performance situations where it is not appropriate for you to mention your albums. It might be on a variety show with other performers where each performer is doing only a few minutes of material. Though you can't promote your album on stage, there is an unobtrusive way after the show to let potential buyers know that you have albums available. As you mingle when the show is over, simply hold an album in your hand. If people come up to compliment you on your song, you can let them know the song is available on your album or you can say nothing about it at all. If they are curious about that shrink-wrapped thing with your picture on it that you're holding, they can take the initiative to ask.

It's possible to sell albums even if you're not performing. I have sold albums at places where I stopped to ask directions. In Wharton, Texas, where I'd played a couple months before, I stopped for directions and ran into someone who'd been at the concert. She said she'd tried to buy my albums at the local bookstore, but they were sold out. I had some in the car, even though I wasn't playing that weekend, and she bought several. Once when my car was towed (kidnapped by a ruthless tow-truck thug who saw me step away from it for three minutes), I sold an album to the guy at the car pound who collected my car's $140 ransom.

THE DUNKIN' DONUTS TECHNIQUE

You'll be amazed at the number of albums you'll sell simply by learning the Dunkin' Donuts technique. While I was working odd jobs (yes, some very odd jobs) during my "I'm Not Lost, I am Exploring" phase, I was hired as a Dunkin' Donuts secret shopper. I loved it, and I learned a lot about sales.

Dunkin' Donuts' research showed that the movement toward healthier eating was causing people to avoid purchasing big items like long johns, cinnamon rolls and filled donuts, especially after the morning rush was over. Dunkin' Donuts decided to test-market smaller versions, hoping that, like donut holes, people would buy multiple mini-long johns without feeling as guilty as they would feel buying one big long john.

My assignment every day was to go into a different Dunkin' Donuts and ask for coffee. While the coffee was being poured, my job was to see if the counter person said, "Would you like to try our new mini-donuts with that?" If the counter person asked me if I wanted to try the new mini-donuts, I got to give prize coupons to every employee on duty. This also made each employee eligible for the grand-prize drawing, which was an all-expenses-paid luxury vacation.

Obviously, anyone who comes into Dunkin' Donuts is a potential customer for their new product, just like anyone who listens to you play is a potential buyer of your albums.

Despite the posters on the door and the large cardboard stand-up of a goofy-looking Dunkin' Donuts man holding a tray of the stuff, most people had no idea that mini-donuts were available. Most people won't know you have albums available unless you tell them.

You wouldn't believe how many people I saw at Dunkin' Donuts who came in to get something else and left there enjoying mouthfuls of mini-donuts. I'm sure a lot of those people also came back to buy more and maybe even became regular mini-donut customers. I know I did. They weren't offended at being asked if they'd like to try the new minidonuts. Some of us like to try new donuts, and a lot of people like to try new albums.

Often people don't realize your albums aren't available at the record stores. In some cases they may not even realize you have records out. Wherever you go, let people know you have records out and where your records are available. If someone mentions enjoying your music, it's easy to say, "Well, I've always got them with me if you decide you want to take those songs home." That way, there's no pressure on the person to buy, but people often do buy because it's so easy, just like when it was suggested to them to try those mini-donuts.

A SECRET THAT WILL DOUBLE YOUR SALES

Do you have a song that has lyrics people would want to keep? Is there a line from one of your songs that could look good on someone's wall? Do you have a positive or thought-provoking message in one of your songs that people would want to have as a reminder of your concert? Print them on bright card stock, with all your booking information at the bottom. You can often get four per page and have them cut into 4¼″ × 5½″ cards. Offer this as a free gift at your concerts.

When you give out these cards in advance, you accomplish three important things:

• You give people something to remember you by, something they may even display for all the world to see.

• You give out your booking information, in case someone needs it in the future.

• You help people decide which albums they want before you even finish, so they won't feel so pressured by the crowd at the sales table that they go home empty-handed.

There are several ways to use these sheets. You can put them on people's chairs in a concert setting or their tables if it is a dinner show. If you use a bright color, this will look good on the table and lots of people will come by and pick one up. You don't have to give them out up front. You can use them to get people to your product table. From the stage, offer to make the card available as a gift to everyone who hands you their business card after the show or signs up on the mailing list.

Explorer's Creed
Jana Stanfield

I am exactly where I need to be today.
I have more than enough of everything I need
to meet the challenges of this day.
I am right on schedule, growing at my own pace.
As I come to appreciate the importance
of living at my own pace,
I am less likely to compare my pace, faster or slower,
with anyone else's pace.
I am learning exactly what I need to learn,
even though I may not have a clear understanding yet
of today's lesson.
What I'm learning today is preparing me for
all the good and all the challenge that lies ahead.
I am getting better every day
in every way that matters to me.
I can be excellent without being perfect.
I am letting go of the all-or-nothing perfectionism
which kept me coming up short,
finding joy instead of constant progress.
I'm making progress in my career today.
I'm making progress today in my personal life.
I'm making progress every day in my spiritual life.
I'm making progress in my health today.
It is important for me to invest my energy
in the things I care about
during the short time I have in this world.
I don't need to completely understand the big picture
to know that I play an important role.
Though I may not know where I'm going,
I'm not lost, I am exploring.

*For information about Jana Stanfield bringing her program
to your group, call 1-800-256-5458.*

This is what I print on bright card stock and give away at my performances.

TIPS FROM THE PROS: MICHAEL LILLE

Michael Lille is a singer-songwriter-guitarist who has been performing and touring throughout the world for twenty-three years. He is the *L* in the group SGGL, a foursome who've sold close to sixty thousand self-produced albums over the course of twelve years. He is a winner of the 1993 Kerrville New Folk Competition and 1996 Telluride Troubadour Songwriter Competition. Lille has opened shows for Alison Krauss, Bob Dylan, Little Feat, Leo Kottke, David Wilcox, Kathy Mattea, J.J. Cale, Warren Zevon and comedian Carrot Top. Here are his thoughts on selling product and performing:

"Making our albums available is the thing that gives a musician staying power, something for the audience to take home and, over time, make them want to come back and hear those songs live again. Recorded and live performances are two very different animals.

"Packaging is something that is often overlooked by the recording artist when in fact it's the first thing a consumer sees. I had a distributor in California who took my first record unheard because he said the packaging looked like a major label release.

"I always put a short personal note in the package when someone orders one of my records through the mail. People like to feel personally connected to an artist. Same goes with autographs after a show. Though many of us are not Sting, and signing feels silly, you have to remember they would not have asked if it didn't mean something to them.

"Don't overdo it from the stage, but be sure to tell the audience about the disc and where they will be after the show. I've had people come up after I've said something about my CDs twice and say, 'You should make a CD.' Make some sort of a reference joke from the stage, like, 'I happen to have three thousand copies with me,' or 'Only 150 shopping days 'til Christmas,' and of course when you play a song from the CD, you can easily introduce the song as being from your latest CD or whichever one it's on."

Make programs for your shows. Take a piece of 8½″ × 11″ paper and fold it in half. Put your photo on the front with your name at the top. If you're doing them show by show, leave a spot where you can drop in the date and the name of the place you're playing. For example, your program might say, "Mary Kerr Macey, Singer-Songwriter" at the top, and at the bottom it would say, "Presented by the Emmanuel Arts Center, May 9th, 19____." This will be a souvenir program.

Put the lyrics to one of your most popular songs inside the program. Another option is to put the lyrics to any sing-alongs you frequently perform. Make sure to include booking information, and maybe a paragraph or two about the kind of shows you do, to give people ideas about how easy it would be for you to do a concert for their group. On the back page, list your albums and the top songs from each one. This way, if you play some of those songs, they can be thinking about which album or albums they want to buy after the show.

THE SALES TABLE

At the same time that you make arrangements to perform somewhere, also make arrangements for a sales table (not a corner of the bar where you can put three cassettes). While we all know that in certain situations we have to take what we can get, do your best to arrange what you want.

Space and Browsing Room

Get the longest table you can find for your product table. I say "find" because in most places that you'll play, a table will be available. If you're playing at a hotel, you can arrange it in advance with the event planner. You'll need the biggest table you can find because if all goes well, your table will be swamped after your performance.

If the table is small, only five to ten people can gather around at a time. Anyone behind them will be prevented from getting a good view of what's on the table. After waiting a few seconds, people behind the first row might decide they're either in too big a hurry or that it's just too much trouble to wait to get to your table. Once you've stood behind a too-small table and watched people wait for a few minutes and then walk away, you'll understand why it's so important to have a long table that can accommodate more people wanting to look at the cassettes and CDs.

Round and square tables will work, but a long rectangular table is best. If you have a good idea that you'll have lots of sales, get two tables and set them up identically so that people at one table won't think they're missing anything at the other. You can also do this identical setup on either end of one long table so that you can have two buying areas. A solid color cloth will set off your tapes and CDs better than a plain wood or plastic table will. It's a good idea to carry one with you. You can buy really cheap tablecloths in plastic or paper at any discount store.

Face Forward, Not Up

Anything you can do to get your product up off the table will increase your sales. I used to lay my tapes flat. When I would go across the room after setting up, I'd notice that from a distance, it was hard to see that anything was on the table. Display companies (find them in the yellow pages) can supply you with several options for giving your product table that third dimension. If you don't have stands yet, place your product in neat stacks, then take one cassette or CD from each stack and put it face forward toward whoever might consider coming to the table to browse.

The manufacturers who do audio duplication are a great resource for display boxes. Call around to the same people you called when you were comparing prices and ask if they sell display boxes. The display boxes come as flat precut pieces of cardboard. Using their handy diagrams, you can fold this cardboard into a display box in a matter of minutes. As you get better at it, you'll be doing it in seconds. These boxes can hold two levels of product (twelve CDs, or six cassettes and six CDs), and they put your albums face forward. They even have a panel you can attach to the top where you can display information about the albums, like the prices or a song list. After the show, you take a few seconds to unfold the boxes and put them back in your luggage or product case.

Another good option for displays is to buy inexpensive photo frames. Take out the glass. (You don't want it to break as you haul it from show to show.) Inside one frame, put a colored sheet of paper with a list of what's available and your prices. Get another frame for each album. In these frames, list the songs you are most likely to sing from each album, and you can even color-copy your album cover in the size you want. Put the song list at the top and the picture of the album cover at the bottom, because the list of titles is what will sell the albums after your show. Make it easy for people to read by printing the letters as big as possible. To keep your sheets from getting dirty, laminate them.

You can get lots of options for displays by calling Paper Direct at (800) A-Papers. This company sells everything from decorative paper to press-kit folders to colored newsletter paper. They have a great cardboard frame with plastic instead of glass, so you don't have to laminate the sheets that go inside. Their frame has a foldout stand in back, so the whole thing folds flat. After six months of road wear and tear, my set of frames is still in great shape.

Displays can be made out of plastic or cardboard. Go for the ones that lie flat in your luggage, or you'll be replacing them after every plane ride.

Cards and Brochures

Some people like to put their cards and brochures on the table with their albums. It's a good idea to have something people can take from your show with your name and any other information they'd need to book you. Business cards are good for this purpose, and they're inexpensive.

There are good reasons for and against putting brochures out on your product table. Going for the positive first, you can put them there so that people will take them home, read all about you and remember who you are next time they want to book some music. When I got my first brochures, I was so proud that I wanted everyone to take one. It took a while for me to notice the two good reasons not to hand them out. First, they are expensive. My early brochures cost less than $1 apiece, but now that I'm running full color with intricate graphics, they cost me $3 each. (See page 80 for a look at my brochure.) Second, most people who take them are not in the business of booking entertainment.

Many artists choose to put a single brochure on display with their tapes. You can even laminate it to make sure no one thinks it's there to be given away. If someone wants the brochure, just take their card and mail it to them. As you're taking their card, ask if they have an idea for a place you can play. This way, you can decide whether you want to follow up with a phone call after mailing the brochure.

You can also put a spot for check marks on your mailing list that says "Please send me a brochure." That way, you can contact this person, and if they're interested in having you do a show for a group they're involved with, you can book it.

Mailing List

At the center of your table, place your mailing list. Some performers have two lists. One is for mailing addresses, and the other one says, "Call me about scheduling a concert." If you think people won't take time to sign your list, you can put out a basket or an empty goldfish bowl with a sign that says, "Mailing List . . . Drop Your Card In."

Instead of having people take the time to sign up at the sales table, hand out mailing-list cards that people can fill out during the show. Hand out the cards at the door or place them on the tables. This is better because the line at the table can get so backed up that only a few people have time to sign the list. While they wait in line to sign, they block others from getting close enough to choose the albums they want to buy.

With mailing-list cards that are handed out, you can also have fun with the space on the other side. I print them four to a page and cut them into 4½″ × 5″ rectangles. (See page 81 for my mailing list card.) On the other side, ask people to write their latest joke or favorite quote. Have them turn the cards in during the break to a basket, bowl or box top that does not block album sales. You can read some of them in the second set.

If you don't have access to a computer, you might wonder how to handle all those names from all those towns. Believe me, it will be worth the effort to collect them. If you don't have a computer, you can hire someone to type the names into a form a little easier to work with than a bunch of scribbles. With a computer list, the names can then be categorized by zip code. Mailing-list services (find them in the yellow pages) can handle your list and your mailings for just pennies per name. You can send them your scribbled lists, tattered business cards, names on napkins and scraps of paper, and they will turn it all into lists and labels.

Whether you do it yourself or use these services, the idea is to get as many names as possible on your mailing list. There are several reasons for collecting as many names as you can. The first reason is so that you can use the computed mailing list to mail *gig cards* or announcements of your performances in that area to everyone in the surrounding zip codes. The second reason is that if someone is thinking of booking you for an event,

Jana Stanfield RECORDINGS

5 tapes for $40 / 4 CDs for $50 (not available in stores)

Jana Stanfield. 1991. Cassette.
If I Had Only Known
Music On The Wind
Farther Down The Line
I'd Be Looking For You

Stop, Look & Listen. 1992. Cassette or CD.
Ready To Use The Gifts I've Been Given
Love Lines
We've Started A Conversation
If You'll Just Listen To Me
Wake Up & Dream
CD contains "If I Had Only Known"

I'm Not Lost, I Am Exploring. 1993. Cassette or CD.
I'm Not Lost, I Am Exploring
Waiting For My Happiness
Manuel Garcia
Listen For The Whisper
Little Red Book
Wings of Eagles

Enjoy The Ride. 1994. Cassette or CD.
Underachiever's Anonymous
U.B.U.I.M.E.
What Is Mine Will Find Me
The Trick Is To Learn To Enjoy The Ride
That Makes All The Difference To Me
Butterfly

Playing Favorites. 1995. Cassette or CD.
Turning My Stumbling Blocks To Stepping Stones
Secret O' Life
You've Got A Friend
Home On The Range
Lean On Me
Forever Young

Keynotes & Concerts
PO Box 60146. Nashville, TN. 37206.
615.226.4764

JANA STANFIELD
SPEAKER SONGWRITER STORYTELLER

Here's an inexpensive way to make handouts for people at gigs. This was printed on two sides of an 8½″ × 11″ piece of paper and folded.

Explorer's Creed
Jana Stanfield

I am exactly where I need to be today.
I have more than enough of everyting I need
to meet the challenges of this day.
I am right on schedule, growing at my own pace.
As I come to appreciate the importance
of living at my own pace,
I am less likely to compare my pace, faster or slower,
with anyone else's pace.
I am learning exactly what I need to learn, even
though I may not have a clear understanding yet of today's lesson.
What I'm learning today is preparing me for
all the good and all the challenge that lies ahead.
I am getting better every day
in every way that matters to me.
I can be excellent without being perfect.
I am letting go of the all-or-nothing perfectionism
which kept me coming up short,
finding joy instead in constant progress.
I'm making progress in my career today.
I'm making progress today in my personal life.
I'm making progress every day in my spiritual life.
I'm making progress in my health today.
It is important for me to invest my energy
in the things I care about during the short time
I have in this world.
I don't need to completely understand the big picture
to know that I play an important role.
Though I may not know where I'm going,
I'm not lost, I am exploring.

For information about scheduling a Jana Stanfield program, call
1-800-256-5458.

about Jana Stanfield

Jana Stanfield is a multi-million selling songwriter and an award-winning professional speaker.

Her songs of love and life have been recorded by Reba McEntire and many others. Her story is featured in the book *3rd Helping of Chicken Soup for the Soul.*

The songs she has written have been heard on Entertainment Tonight, 20/20, and Oprah Winfrey. As a performer, Jana has made numerous appearances on TNN and has shared stages with Louise Hay, Melody Beattie, Wayne Dyer, Dr. Bernie Siegel and Deepak Chopra.

Jana travels the country as a motivational performer, encouraging youth, educators, health care workers, businesses, & associations. "Difference-makers", she says, "can always use a faith-lift."

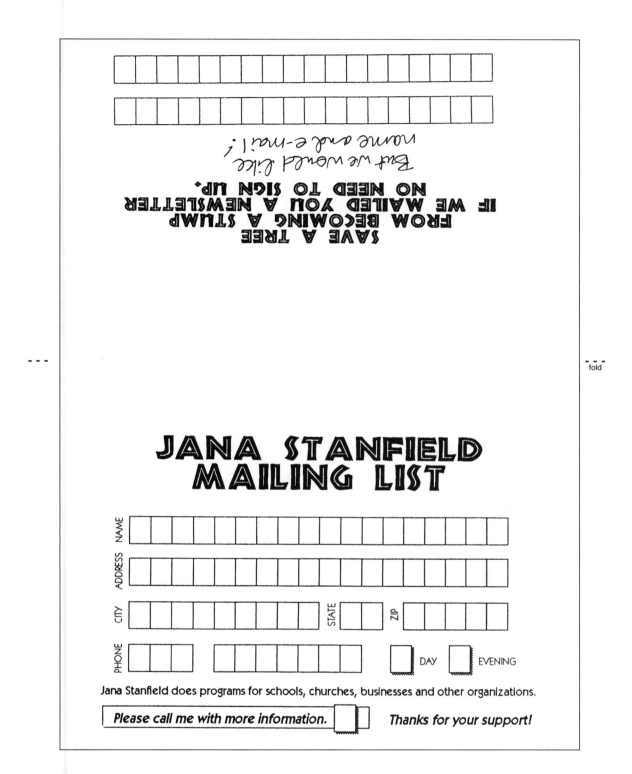

These mailing-list cards are folded in half and stood up like tents on tables at gigs.

it helps if you can say, "I have several hundred people on my mailing list in that area, and I'd be happy to send out a card asking them to come."

In your database, categorize people as *clients, potential clients, friends, family* or *bought product*. Be *sure* to put those who bought product in a special category, because they are the people most likely to buy again.

These categories will be important as your list grows, so name them carefully. I have been categorizing, but not enough. *Signed mailing list* doesn't mean as much now when I know that in the beginning I wanted *everyone* to sign the mailing list just for showing up. It could mean they just felt pressured to sign or they thought there might be a prize drawing. Many names from my first few years weren't categorized. With over six thousand names on my mailing list, a newsletter costs over $3,000 to mail to them all at once. Now I'd like to go back and delete names that would've been in categories like *Washington, DC, cabdriver who didn't overcharge* or *my sister's former dentist* or *met at baggage claim because we had identical black roll-alongs*.

Order Blanks

Some people put order blanks on their sales tables. I don't and here's why. Buying an album after a performance is an impulse purchase. Not that it's a bad purchase. At a large concert, you can buy T-shirts, tour jackets and color programs covered with the artist's name. I own some of these T-shirts. Now, I wouldn't go into a store and shop for an Elton John T-shirt. It was an impulse buy at the concert. It is not an impulse buy that I regret. Year after year, that shirt narrowly escapes donation to Goodwill because I have fond memories of sitting on a damp hillside in crummy lawn seating at an amphitheater, listening to Elton sing "Your Song."

If I can't decide which album to buy after someone's concert, and I pick up an order form instead, chances are I'll never send it in. If the impulse is not strong enough right after the concert to make me buy, it's only going to get weaker after I get home. There will always be somebody who wants an order form, and I keep a few with me for those who ask. On the other hand, I don't just put them out. It's better to have people deciding which album to buy than to have them deciding whether to buy now or decide later.

Once people have bought albums, they'll call to order more for friends and family, so put your phone number in your albums. They also write to the address in your album, inquiring about ordering more. If they call, we take the credit-card information over the phone and then ship the product right out. If they write to us, we send or fax an order form. We get several hundred dollars in orders every month from past customers.

Table Dressing

Table dressing is my term for anything that makes your album sale area more appealing, from free Cheez-Its (my favorite) to portable CD players with headphones so customers can sample your album.

Folk artist Susan Herrick carries a large laminated poster of herself that she places on an easel at her table. If you just need one poster to use in this way, it's easy and inexpensive. Take a good color picture of yourself to a copy center, have it enlarged to poster size, then laminate it. You should be able to do the whole thing at the copy center for less than $10 in less than ten minutes. If you'd like to put information on it, like your name and some credentials, this can also be done at a copy center, usually for a small per-hour layout charge.

When I was on tour with Deepak Chopra and Wayne Dyer, I learned some good table techniques from the other performers. The tour was sponsored by an organization called Future Visions. In each city, Future Visions would bring in four speakers, usually Deepak, Wayne, Dr. Bernie Siegel, Louise Hay or Melody Beattie, plus several performers to create a one-day educational and entertainment extravaganza. I was doing music on the show with some great talents. Randall Leonard is performer-composer of wonderful piano instrumental albums, and Debra Voltura is a fabulous vocalist and songwriter. Swami Beyondananda (alias Steve Bhaerman) is a humorist and author who parodies a hilarious Swami to lovingly poke fun at sacred cows like mental health, environmentalism and the New Age movement. Swami travels with (but would probably prefer I say "performs with") his wife, a dancer who calls herself Trudi Light.

Traveling performers like Swami, Trudi, Randall and Debra usually make much more from product sales than they make from their performances. This doesn't mean they don't make a lot for performances. It means they multiply their take-home pay with the huge amounts of product they sell. Here are some of their secrets of success.

While most of us have just tapes and CDs (or in my case now, tapes, CDs and books) available, Swami and Trudi have lots of other things, too. Trudi imports beautiful beaded scarves from Egypt and gives demonstrations of the dozens of ways the scarves can accent a wardrobe. She also sells a wide array of unique gifts, like long shiny ribbons on sticks, just like the ones you watch her use so beautifully in her dance routines. Swami sells his books, comedy tapes, a product called "Absolutely Nothing," which comes in a box that says, "Absolutely Nothing" on the cover. The idea is that if people are there to buy albums, they're often open to other purchases.

Randall and Debra don't have all the other products, but they have come up with good ways to sell their cassettes and CDs. Randall has several albums out. He combines packages of CDs by tying them together with bright ribbon. He sells these packages at a graduated discount. The more you buy, the cheaper it is per album.

Debra stacks her CDs in piles of fifteen or more, then when they are all straight, she twists the stack just a little to make this nice curve from the bottom to the top of each stack. When you look toward her table, you see

TIPS FROM THE PROS: ELLIS PAUL

Ellis Paul has three albums in distribution. He records for Rounder Records and has been doing between 150 and 200 shows a year for the last three years. His three recordings have sold over forty thousand units collectively in this period. He sells an average of four thousand units a year at performances.

"I used to put out my own recordings on a label shared with my manager," Ellis says. "My overhead was low because of this, and if I felt the crowd was young and might be light in the wallets, I would sell CDs for $10 apiece rather than $15; this way I would end up selling CDs in batches rather than individually. In one gig, opening for Patty Larkin with 250 in the audience, I sold 101 CDs! Everyone bought two because they were cheap, they knew I wouldn't be back for a while, and they wouldn't be easily found in stores.

"Keep promo stuff cheap for the consumer. T-shirts are billboards, like free advertising. They make money for you indirectly; every time someone sees the band name or your name it gets filed in the back of their brains until they happen to be in Tower Records, and lo and behold—there's that band Nirvana's CD who had the cool T-shirt. I give them away to other musicians who are recognizable and will wear them in public places. My friend Kristian Bush, from the duo Billy Pilgrim, wore his Ellis Paul shirt during a VH-1 interview! I wore Kristian's shirt on stage at the Kerrville Folk Festival. I'm less concerned about profit on promo stuff—you just want to get it out there. I sell T-shirts for $10 so more go out the door. Other promo stuff is only good if it gets attention, and buttons work well for that.

"When selling product, have volunteers help you and pay them with CDs. Your job should be to sign the CDs, not sell them directly. Don't sell and sign at the same time, because this clogs up the table. Have posters, reviews and bio info available to be seen. Elevate the product so people see that the table is for buying stuff, not for refreshments. Bring hangers to display the T-shirts. A little light on or candles near the product becomes a beacon for the audience, and a tablecloth from home dresses up a rickety card table nicely. Play songs from everything that is being sold. Every audience member has a different song that sticks in their head each night. Let them know what song is on what album, and make sure you print the song titles on the back of your CD so they can scan for their favorites."

this design she's made with her CD stacks that is visually interesting, and just might draw potential customers over to take a look. Debra used a cardboard backing to create a poster that also draws the eye (and therefore the customer) to her table. She covered the cardboard backing with brightly colored shiny paper, then decorated it with her CD covers and cassette J-cards photo to make a collage. She props this up on her table to provide visual appeal from across the room.

If your table is mobbed, the people in the crowd ten feet away won't even know a table is there unless you've got posters or a banner hung on the wall behind your table. Be sure that whatever you use is hung so the top of it is above the heads of the people who'll be shopping at your table.

Posters can be made for $.50 to $1.00 apiece. Use several of them to make a design. I've never bought a banner because I can't figure out what I'd hang it on in most of my performance situations. Posters are easier for me. They can be folded to fit in luggage and can be reused. I carry Handi-Tak (made by Super Glue, looks like Silly Putty and sticks your poster to the wall), which won't hurt walls and can be reused from town to town.

Site Selection

Janis Ian was nominated for a Grammy in 1993 for Contemporary Folk Record of the Year and is best known for her hits "At Seventeen," "Society's Child" and "Jesse." In the November/December issue of *Performing Songwriter* magazine, where Janis has a regular column, she describes her ideal site for a product table: "We choose a site as close to the stage as possible [though not so close as to interfere with load-out], or somewhere between the stage and the main entrance/exit. Ideally we have a six-foot, extremely stable table covered with a black drop cloth. Behind it are two chairs, one for me and one for the salesperson. The table must be somewhere convenient for gawkers, so people can see what you have for sale, but secure enough that theft isn't an overriding concern—we like to have a wall behind the chairs instead of an open space.

"In an ideal world there's enough room for people to exit the building and for us to form two lines with autograph-seekers: one for those who've already purchased or just want to say hi and one for those wanting to buy something. We hang our T-shirts on the wall behind, and either put up an easel with our display or hang that, too. We try to set it up so people exiting the show will first see the product display, then the salesperson, then me.

"The best place to put your product table is in an area where people can't miss it on the way in or on the way out. If they can see it on the way in, they know you have product available and they know where to get it. It plants the seed. If your table is on the way out anyway, it's easy to stop, browse and buy."

Checklist for Product Table
- Cassettes and CDs
- Tablecloth
- Photo, posters or backdrop sign
- Mailing list
- Goldfish bowl
- Your business cards
- Order blanks (not on display)

- Sharpie permanent markers or other pens that will write on CDs and cassettes
- Price list
- Display stands
- Change ($50)

PERSON-TO-PERSON SALES

So what is the difference between a musician and a savings bond? Eventually a savings bond will mature and make money.

At the risk of generalizing, I think it's safe to say that most professional musicians have a stronger interest in learning how to negotiate a key change than learning how to negotiate a business deal. At some point in our lives, there's this fork in the road where it seems we have to decide between the business world and the music world. When you make your own albums, you live in both worlds. This may sound like bad news to some. The good news is you'll probably benefit financially.

When music is something we love to do, it's very difficult to ask people to pay us to do it. While any working musician has already learned that it's vital to get paid to play, making your own album presents a new hurdle. Some big ethical questions are involved. These are just a few of them:

- Where do I draw the line in handing out free albums to my friends and family?
- What do I say when a friend asks for my album but doesn't offer to pay?
- Should my albums cost more than, less than or the same as major-label albums?

Let's take these questions one at a time.

Where Do I Draw the Line in Handing Out Albums?

Every person who has ever started a business that sells stuff has faced or is currently facing this challenge. It's a tough one, and everyone probably does it differently. The good news is that everyone who has ever started a business will understand.

If you had a restaurant, you'd have to decide which of your family members could eat free anytime they wanted and which ones would have to pay. If you didn't do this, all the people you care about or are related to could drop in for a free meal anytime they wanted and this eventually would "eat" your profits.

Some people give albums away to their immediate family members. It's up to you whether your immediate family includes aunts, uncles, cousins, etc. One hazard of this is the family member who says, "I want to get some more of those from you to give to my friends." They want to give your albums away because they are so proud of you. On the other hand, it not only costs you for every album you give to relatives and friends of relatives, but these are also albums you could have sold for full price.

We can't expect our family members to know in advance that the money we take in from the sale of each album is what keeps our lights on and a roof over our heads. A lot of people you know will see your cassettes as a $10 item and won't stop to consider that you paid thousands of dollars in recording costs to create each product.

Since cassettes and CDs are relatively inexpensive, most people have no idea that we could actually make a living from selling them ourselves. If they stopped to think about it, they'd know it takes quite a few ten-dollar bills to live on each month, and the only way to get enough of those ten-dollar bills is to have the courage to let people know that we can't give all our albums away to the people we care about.

Most people don't understand that the money we make from the sale of each album becomes our meat and potatoes, our bread and butter, etc., so it sometimes becomes necessary for us to explain it. It's always awkward at first, but I have found that once someone realizes I am attempting to make a living from my albums, they are very eager to pay for the album instead of asking me to give it to them.

My family and friends have been great about all this. I have immediate family members who buy my albums as gifts for their friends. I would gladly give my parents all the albums they want (and I usually do give them extra copies they can give away), but both my parents have bought copies from me when they want to give them as gifts to friends. I have family members (aunts, uncles, second cousins) who have generously bought my albums to give to their children as a way of offering their support.

Recording artist Bill Nash of Dallas spends his workdays as a Unix system administrator for Texas Instruments, Inc. Bill has no problem letting his friends and family help. His mom, who lives across the country, is his best sales rep. "When my mother goes out to visit her friends or attends functions, she carries several CDs and tapes with her, along with a tape player! When and if the conversation comes around to 'her son the musician who has a CD,' and people ask her how they can get one, she pulls out the CD and says, 'You can get them from me directly!' She has sold over $1,000 of my product for me in Illinois in the past eight months, without my even living there!"

In the past eight months, with his method and a once-a-month gig in the Dallas area, he has sold about $4,000 in product. He estimates that he could double that if he played out more often.

Bill Nash has found an innovative way to work his day job into his record business. "I think the most important way I've been able to sell albums lately has been through letting co-workers at my day job take a copy home with them to listen to. So far, everyone I've loaned a CD out to has come back in the next few days to put their money down. With the competition (like Blockbuster) allowing customers to listen to albums before purchase, I think it's become important to give them a listen to albums beforehand."

Here are Bill's best tips for person-to-person album sales:

"1. Don't forget to have product with you (at least in your vehicle) at all times. I've missed a few sales that I could have made if I had just kept a few in the car.

"2. Let people know you have a product to sell (without really saying it), even when you are just in casual (non-music-playing) situations. I think you will find they will be interested in purchasing a copy just because they've met you and find you to be an interesting person, and they want to take a piece of you home.

"3. Get on the Internet *now!* I am a continuous poster on several news groups, have gotten to know a lot of people personally through these, and when I announced I had an album for sale, many of them sent in orders. Through the newsgroups (and then regular mail), I have sold albums to people in other countries, so now I can say I'm 'internationally distributed!'

"4. Be willing to autograph everything. People want to own a copy of our CD with a signature on it, and besides, as Bill Ward from Houston always says, tongue in cheek, 'I can sign that for you and it might be worth fifty cents more at the garage sale next year.' People love to have personal interaction, and this is one of the best ways."

What Do I Say When a Friend Asks for My Album But Doesn't Offer to Pay?

It's very difficult when someone you love or even like a lot says, "I hear you have a cassette out. Hey, I need to get one from you." They probably don't have any idea how uncomfortable this is for you. They don't realize that they have just said the equivalent of, "Hey, I want to get $10 from you."

When someone says this, your natural reaction will be to pause as you search for something to say. You would gladly give them $10 if they needed it, but what we're talking about here is $10 that will help you make your living from your music. It's an important $10. Often during this pause, your friends or family members will realize that they've put you in an awkward spot and will ask you how much you charge for them as an indication that they are willing to support you by buying their copy. If they don't offer this, it's time to answer. Here are several options that people I know who make their own albums have used:

• Great. I'd love for you to get one of my albums. I've usually got them with me in the car so whenever you've got the money, I'm ready.

• Thanks. I'm so glad you want to get one. If you've got ten bucks we can do it today.

• That's sweet of you. I sell them for $10 . . . would you like a dozen?

TIPS FROM THE PROS: DAVID ROTH

Singer-songwriter David Roth's response to my questions asking for his input on the book is a lot more fun if you get to see the questions so here you have it:

1. What is your general philosophy of in-person album sales?

    "I have five albums at the moment, and a question I'm often asked at shows is, 'Which is your *best* album?' Resisting the temptation to answer back, 'Well, this one is really good and the other four suck,' I turn the question around. The dialogue might go something like this:

    'David, which is your *best* album?'

    'Ummmm . . . do you have any kids?'

    'Well, yes, we have three. . . .'

    'Which one do you love the most?'

    'That's silly—we love them all for different reasons.'

    'You've just answered your own question.'

    If they don't have kids, try pets, grandparents, etc. Be creative."

2. Please list five tips to help others have more success with product sales.

    "1. I give a free tape or CD to any volunteers who've helped me at that engagement: the product seller, sound person, etc. They are most appreciative, deserve the recognition, and it's a very small price for the amount of goodwill generated. You may even have a new fan for life because of it. Every supporter becomes a seed sprinkler, especially if they take a piece of you home with them.

    "2. I provide an inventory sheet with an accurate start count of each title. All I have to do at the end of the night (minus the ones I've given away) is count what's left, leaving an instant record of how many of each title sold at that engagement.

    "3. I offer a discount for multiple purchases—for example, I ask $15 for a CD but only $14 each for two or more. For anyone who buys five or more, I throw in a cotton tote bag. Tapes are $10 or three for $28. You'll be amazed at the increase in sales just for knocking off a buck or two.

    "4. I have an easy-to-read price list mounted in one of those clear plastic frames that stand up by themselves. They come in all sizes, and the one that measures 5"×7" will fit under the headstock in most guitar cases. Keep it covered with an old sock (washed) to prevent scratches. I also travel with a wrinkle-free table cover, and I have a bank—a wallet filled with anywhere from $25 to $50 in singles, fives and tens, to start the evening with. All the product money goes in there, so at the end of the night I subtract the starter amount and see what the sales total is.

    "5. I always ask the sponsor/emcee to announce that I have tapes and CDs available at intermission and after the show, and will stay around to sign 'em. This may seem obvious, again, you'll be amazed at the difference this will make, and the idea of an autograph may inspire another purchase."

Friends have been wonderful about understanding that I make my living by the sale of my albums. I'll admit, though, that when the first album came out it was difficult. They were looking to me to let them know whether I'd be giving albums away to all the people I hang out with, or whether I'd be offering them for sale. I was so thrilled to have albums out that I wanted to give them to everyone, but I knew my music could never support me if I didn't allow those who wanted my music to buy it.

SHOULD YOUR ALBUMS COST LESS THAN THE MAJOR LABELS?

Many artists who make their own albums believe in charging at least as much for their albums as the going rate for major label albums. When I first started, I was charging a little more than most albums cost. Prices of major label product have caught up now, and we charge about the same. Generally, $10 is a good price for cassettes and $15 is average for CDs.

Choose prices that are easy to work with, because that will be important when you're making change while answering people's questions. Think about the change you'll have to make if you charge $9.68 for a cassette and $14.32 for a CD. Work out the sales tax you expect to pay if you're selling in-state (you don't have to collect sales tax if you're selling out-of-state) and set your price so that with tax it comes out to an even number that is a multiple of five. If you have to count out dimes, nickels and quarters with every purchase, what will you do when you can't make change because you don't have the exact amount? It's easier to keep $50 in fives in your change bag.

It is not unreasonable to charge more for your albums than the majors charge for theirs. After all, your album is a homemade product. It is not mass-produced. It is unique and a thousand of a kind. You pay more for homegrown fruit, and you pay more for an artist's handmade coffee mug than you would pay for a stoneware mug at the grocery store.

Some artists feel better about charging less for the albums. What we charge for our albums is a reflection of what we believe to be their value. I think my albums have tremendous value for those who are interested in buying them, and I have no problem charging what the major labels charge. I have a friend, on the other hand, who is far more talented than I am who charges much less for his albums. Charge whatever price you feel good about.

If you make a cassette with only four or five songs, decide for yourself what you want to charge, maybe $5.

Price Breaks

It's good to give package deals once you get more than one product out, like an album and a T-shirt, two albums, etc. Some give a graduated discount that looks like this:

1 cassette. . . . $10	CD. . . . $15
2 cassettes . . . $18	CDs . . . $28
3 cassettes . . . $26	CDs . . . $42
4 cassettes . . . $34	CDs . . . $56

This works on paper but means heavy-duty brainwork when it's time to make change, and you will lose sales from those who can't get to the table because they're waiting behind those getting complicated change. It works only when you've got someone making change (assuming you've got enough dollar bills) who really knows your prices well. What happens when someone wants two CDs, three cassettes, and they have a cassette they bought at your last show which they found out they already had so can they exchange it, and will that count as one of the three cassettes?

As they say in Alcoholics Anonymous, "Keep It Simple, Silly." Okay, they don't say, "silly," but you get the point. Make it easy. Make it multiples of five. I make it even simpler than that. I only give price breaks for "the works" (all my albums) on cassette or "the works" on CD. Now that I'm promoting "the works" instead of this copy or that, it is making a big positive impact on my income. Many of those who can't decide which album to buy just get "the works."

CHAPTER EIGHT

MARKETING YOUR MUSIC AND YOURSELF

There's not much room at the top, but there's more than enough room for all of us at the bottom and in the middle. The music business is like a slippery pyramid with the smallest part at the top. You think you have to get to the top before you can put your music out, and then it trickles down to reach all those music buyers at the bottom. Yes, it does work that way for some, but fortunately, it's not the only way.

Why skip over all the record buyers at the bottom and the middle, just to get to the top? Why not go straight to the bottom and start there? That's where most of the music lovers and record buyers are.

During my first year in business with my new album, I rarely got paid for musical performances. That was okay with me back then. As a professional songwriter, I was used to working for free. I would play for any size audience, as long as I could make my albums available. At first, I was coming home from performances with anywhere from $10 to $100 in album sales. Now I charge a lot for my concerts, plus expenses, and sell anywhere from $10 to $2,500 per event.

All it takes to market yourself is to be likable, flexible, dependable, hardworking, willing to learn and hungry. Once you've made your own albums, you'll be very hungry. This hunger to support yourself with your music will help you develop all the other skills you'll need. If you're reading this book, you've already demonstrated that you're willing to learn.

As you turn the pages and learn these marketing methods, keep a pencil handy to jot down ideas. We all have to do it our own way, and your way will take shape as you read about how others have found success.

THE BEST SET IS YOUR MIND-SET

Why Musicians Need Revolutionary Marketing Methods

If you've invested money in your album, it is important to invest time and energy booking yourself in places where people will buy it. Lots of opportunities are out there that most musicians overlook. Either they ignore these opportunities or they don't know about them, because they can only see the *Big-Time Record Deal* method, the *Big-Time Songwriter Deal* method or the *Coffeehouse/Club Circuit* method of success.

The ideas in this book are revolutionary because they require a revolutionary shift in your thinking. We always thought we had to be big stars in order to have big-selling major label albums. With this shift in thinking, you'll begin to see ways that having a well-liked independent album can make you a star on a smaller, but maybe even more enjoyable, scale. With these methods, you can create your own stardom, right where you are, starting on a small scale and moving up steadily. Most of the ideas on the coming pages can be used successfully even if you are working a full-time day job outside the music business. You may be ready to move into this work full time when you begin to realize how much you can earn so easily.

Open Your Mind to New Ways of Thinking

Some musicians see poverty as a badge of honor. They fear they will get kicked out of the starving bohemian musician society if they provide themselves with a good living from their music. If this is you, don't read any further, because the rest of this book is filled with the latest ideas and information about performance opportunities and nonperformance opportunities that will help you earn a good living making and marketing your own music.

The information ahead will challenge your ideas about how you always thought your successful music career would look. The coming chapters may challenge your definition of success, especially if you have a limited picture of how people can be successful in the music business.

I used to think that the only way I could consider myself successful in the music business would be if I was a major label recording artist with a long string of number-one hits. I am so glad I finally got over that. My life has been better for it. Success is the ability to do what you love and love what you do.

You may read ideas in the coming chapters that cause you to say, "I could never do that." Don't let that hold you back. When I was shown how to play the guitar intro to James Taylor's "Secret O' Life," I said, "*No way! My hands will never be able to do that.*" Once I moved past my resistance, I tried it until my hands hurt, and then I'd try it again the next day. I'm proud to say I've nearly got it now, and I'm already working on the verses.

When we were kids, we didn't know how to drive a car, but that didn't stop us from dreaming of having one. Making your own albums and learning to market them is similar to buying a car and learning to drive it. For starters, your album is going to cost about as much as a car. Your album can cost the same as a 1973 lime-green Pacer, or it can be closer in cost to a brand new Silver Shadow Rolls Royce. As you learn to drive your "career," you may stall out at a few intersections. Once you get rolling, though, you'll be able to drive this "car" to many exciting destinations. You'll also be able to use the profits from your albums to buy a real car, truck or van to get you there, sooner than you could imagine.

Simple Music, Basic Math

Let's say that in order to start paying off your album and supporting yourself financially, you'd like to make $30,000 per year. That's $2,500 per month. For most musicians, this is an unimaginable amount of money to make in a year. Few musical performers make $2,500 per month. With your own albums, though, this dream can quickly come within your reach.

If you charge $10 for cassettes, you can make $30,000 in a year by selling 3,000 cassettes. If you charge $15 for CDs, it will take 2,000 CDs to make $30,000. If we break that down further, it's 167 CDs per month or 250 cassettes. That's without performance fees. All you need to do now is decide how much money you want to make each month. That will tell you how many units you'll need to sell. From there you can discover ways to make your music available to the people who might enjoy it.

When I made my first cassette, I never dreamed I could make $30,000 or more every year doing what I love. If you had asked me if I thought I could do it, I would've told you flat out that it was *not possible*. Obviously, I didn't set out with a goal of making a certain amount per year. I had no goal, no direction, and yet, it happened. I was out there on my journey, and I stumbled over most of the marketing ideas that will be described in the coming chapters.

When I started, I had no strategy. I had no techniques. I just had a hundred copies of my cassette that I hoped to sell in this lifetime. I was working a freelance television reporting job for $200 per week. The first time I sang two songs for a small gathering of people and sold $300 in tapes afterward, I was hooked on the idea of making my living with my albums. Finding places to play became my mission. My motto was, "Where two or more are gathered, I'll bring my guitar." Of course, this meant I'd be bringing my albums, too. Within six months, I no longer had time to work the television job, and I no longer needed the money.

It took a lot of energy and persistence to book myself into mainstream music venues. When I got there, I found that I didn't sell as many albums as when I played other kinds of gatherings. I started letting people know I was available to do concerts at barbecues, picnics, bonfires, twelve-step gatherings, church functions and service-club meetings. I was amazed at how much I enjoyed playing for small groups of people and selling my albums afterwards. It took only two years before I was making $30,000 per year from my albums.

This is not some do-it-yourself, get-rich-quick scheme. If you don't have the musical ability or the dedication to make and market your own albums, you're probably better off staying at your day job. However, if you have talent and dedication, there is no limit to how much you can make with your music every year. The only limitation is your imagination.

Find the Extraordinary in the Ordinary

The first revolutionary idea is to start small, start now and start where you are. Most musicians get their start playing their music for free at small social gatherings. Soon, we begin to get paid for it. By that time, we usually set our sights on gigs with higher status in the music world. We get in a band or we sing jingles or we compete to play Friday nights at the coolest local hangout. We go for gigs where we can be seen by more people and get more notoriety. Maybe we start thinking of moving to a major music center like Nashville, Los Angeles or Austin, where we can make it big. It doesn't take long before we don't want those jobs playing for small social gatherings anymore.

With your years of experience as an entertainer, songwriter, singer, guitarist or whatever, you can go back to those small social gatherings and blow people away with your talent. In music clubs, audiences come to expect a certain level of expertise, and they're harder to impress. At small social gatherings, the expectations are low. If you offer to come and do a small concert, people planning the event will be thrilled. It will be a big deal. Along with promoting their event, they'll be promoting the fact that you'll be performing. This will get more people there. Since no one is expecting much, they're going to think you are fabulous. They will want your album, and they will want you to sign it.

Let Your Friends and Family Help

You have people all around you who love your music. Give them the chance to support you by helping you find places to play where you can make your album available. Organize an album-release concert or a series of album-release concerts in different towns. Ask your family and friends to invite other family and friends who might like your music. These concerts can be held in someone's house or garage. Tell all the people there that your dream is to support yourself with your music. Tell them you're looking for people who might like this kind of music, and you're looking for places to play. Let them be the first to own your new album. Let them be part of creating your success.

Too often, artists take for granted the people who love their music the most.

- Oh, they don't count . . . we're related.
- We used to work together . . . they don't count.
- They don't count . . . they're my neighbors.

Chances are, you already have a strong base of fans among friends and family. If you will allow those people the opportunity to support you by buying your albums, they can help you live your dreams. Wouldn't you be willing to help make a dream come true for one of them? Especially if all it took was the purchase of a $10 cassette?

Every one of us is famous to somebody. In our quest to become a household name across the nation, remember that it all starts with being a household name across the street. It's not how many you know, but who you know. The best way to generate success with your albums is to focus first on the people you know. Believe me, the people who like your music will be proud to own your first album. They want to support you. By helping you become all you can be, they are affirming that their faith in you was well founded. They want to prove they have a good eye for talent, and they will go to amazing lengths to help you be successful in making your living performing and selling your albums. They'll even talk their friends into buying your albums.

Reclassify Performance Opportunities

When you make your own albums, you will see performance opportunities differently than you saw them before. While you will still play at many of the same venues you have always played, you will classify them by new criteria. You will look for more chances to perform in places where people are eager to buy music.

When you sell $100 in albums at an engagement, it will naturally take a step up on the list of places you enjoy playing. When you can sell $3,000 in albums somewhere, playing there again will become a major priority in your life.

If you're trying to get a big-time record deal, these are the criteria you use to classify a music venue:
- How likely is it that I will be discovered there?
- Is this a prestigious venue in the music world?
- Will a performance there make it likely that I can then be booked at other venues like it?

Many performers use these three things as their criteria for rating performance venues. They want to be seen by the right people for reasons of prestige and hipness. That's how I used to judge gigs, too, but priorities change. If your goal is to make a good living with your music, being discovered is no longer the object. Now, the most important questions are:

- Will people at this venue be likely to buy albums?
- Will the people there be the kind who would like my music?
- How much competition is there for the booking?
- Will I be well paid to play there?

High-visibility venues with prestige in the music world are certainly fun to play, and it feels good to see your name on the list of upcoming attractions. Many of them are also the hardest to book, the lowest paying and the greatest disappointments in terms of album sales. Every person who plays there is not only competing to get the job, but also competing to get the same audience. Those audience members can't go out every night of the week to hear all of us, no matter how good the music is. They also can't

TIPS FROM THE PROS: MICHAEL CAMP

Advice from singer-songwriter Michael Camp:

"There are only so many radio stations, with so many artists and so many songs, with commercials in between and so many minutes in a day. The mathematics alone rules out a lot of real fine, talented people, so if you want to make a living at it you've got to create how to do that for yourself. It can be house concerts or letting Mom and Pop get involved. When you pull the guitar out, people will gather."

afford to buy all the albums available from the traveling performers. Creating concerts outside the usual music venues is usually much easier because there is no competition. It's more rewarding both musically and financially. That makes playing concerts outside the boundaries of the known music world a high priority in my book.

WHY WE NEED AUDIENCES OUTSIDE THE MUSIC SCENE

When you are making a living with your albums, the bottom line for any engagement is, "Will my albums sell there?"

The easiest way to guarantee music sales is to do a concert in front of buyers who will enjoy your music. Groups like this are easy to find, easy to book, easy to please and a joy to perform for. Booking concerts outside the music-scene spotlights may seem less glamorous, but it depends on what you think is glamorous. I happen to think that doing a concert for an appreciative audience, then signing albums for an hour, is *extremely* glamorous.

House Concerts

All it takes to create a concert venue is a space and some listeners. If you are not yet familiar with the house-concert concept, get ready. This great idea is catching on quickly all over the country.

Have you ever noticed that lots of people in the world don't go out to hear music very often? Some people dislike the lines, the crowds, the smoke, the lack of parking and the cost of the door plus the cost of food and drinks, etc. It's just too much trouble for some people. Those same people *love* house concerts and will gladly give you the money they would've paid to waitresses and parking attendants, just to be able to hear you in a nice living room or backyard.

A house concert is as easy to put together as a neighborhood potluck, and twice as fun for the participants and the performer. House concerts are intimate musical performances for audiences of fifteen up to as many as you can fit into a given space. House concerts don't even have to be held in a house. They can take place in the great outdoors, libraries, church sanctuaries, twelve-step meeting rooms, bookstores, recording studios, community theaters, art galleries, VFW halls, corporate conference rooms and apartment-complex party rooms.

The most important thing about a house concert is that it be hosted by someone who likes your music. All this person needs to do is invite friends, and encourage friends to invite friends. The more crowded the room is, the better. House concerts are meant to be cozy.

After-Hours Business Concerts

An after-hours business concert is just a house concert at a business. If you have a friend with numerous employees, or if there is a company you frequently do business with, offer to do a concert right after work. People can bring snacks for the occasion, and maybe the business owner will pitch in to buy liquid refreshments. You can gather in the conference room, in the shop, in the auto-repair bay or any other room large enough to accommodate all the employees. They can even invite their families or friends. This works best if you have someone in the business who has heard you before and has wanted friends and co-workers to hear you. This person can set up the concert and talk it up so people will stay for an hour on Friday night to socialize and hear some music. Be sure to make it known in advance that you'll be bringing your albums, so people can be ready with enough money.

When you have your own albums, people don't think about whether you made them yourself or whether you're on a major label, especially if you put out a quality product and are a talented performer. If you're talented, they know you wouldn't put out a bad album. If they like your performance, they just want a representation of you, and they won't care what label it's on. The fact that you have albums will be a drawing card to get people to stay after work for the concert. You can even give the business an album in advance that some of the employees could pass around so they're familiar with your music before you get there.

Once, when I was on tour in Lubbock, Texas, the friend I was staying with asked me to play for a pizza party where she worked. They were having people come in from out of town for a training day. I had nothing to do at lunch, so I said, "Sure." We had a great time, and lots of people bought albums and asked to be on my mailing list.

Finding Sponsors for Your Concerts

Greg Tamblyn left his job at the newspaper circulation department in Kansas City about three years ago. He'd been doing music since his teen years. He is now playing music full time because he discovered ways to connect with groups of people who liked his music enough to help him put together concerts. He was able to do this on the side and keep his day job until his music could fully support him. It all evolved as Greg discovered his ideal audience, and his ideal audience discovered him.

Greg describes himself as a human being who sings and writes songs and tries to be funny. He says he strives to write songs that help people like who they are and live from their hearts. After a stint in his thirties as a Nashville songwriter and a stint after that as an entertainer in the Cayman Islands, Greg wound up back in his hometown of Kansas City, selling newspaper subscriptions while recovering from a medical operation. As he wrote songs about his humorous and heartwarming adventures in achieving better health, he found that others on this same path loved his music. He began playing music for self-help groups, medical conferences and churches. A local psychologist who did speeches about the healing power of humor asked Greg to add his music to the programs. In all these situations, the audience was already there, and they were going to gather anyway. Greg played, made their event better than they ever expected and made his albums available afterward. The groups were happy, and Greg was really happy. It took about two years of playing for these groups before he had the confidence to leave his job. He's been very successful and has a devoted following.

Do you belong to a group in your town that has branches in other towns? It might be a church group, a social group or a self-help group like Alcoholics Anonymous. I usually start with churches and ask if the choir or the singles group would like to sponsor my concert. In return for their willingness to publicize the show and do a little legwork, give them 10 percent of everything you make from the door and from tape sales. Offer to promote their group or any upcoming programs they're sponsoring during the show, if that would be helpful to them.

If you're a wholesome performer, many church groups will sponsor a concert as part of their outreach to the community. Churches know there are lots of former churchgoers who haven't darkened a church door for decades. Many of these "formers" got out of the habit or had a bad experience. Churches want to let people know that nobody is going to hassle them or pressure them if they want to test the waters again. Churches know that the reason many people get involved is because they like the other people in the congregation. The hope is that if "formers" or people searching for a place to worship can try out their church, these people will enjoy it enough to come back. Your concert doesn't have to be religious, just wholesome, good-natured and affirming.

Always ask a person who has worked hard to make the concert happen to be the master of ceremonies. During the concert, thank whoever sponsored you and let the audience know that the reason we're all able to get together and enjoy this evening is because of the hard work of the people who made it possible.

I find that people usually don't sponsor concerts for the money. They are glad to have it, but they usually do it just because they want to be involved. A lot of really good, kind people out there like music enough to do whatever it takes to share music they enjoy with their community.

Preassembled Audiences

Think of all the non-music-business kinds of gatherings where you could do a concert. I'll make my list and leave some room for you to add your ideas.

Family reunions	Singles groups
Picnics	School events
Barbecues	Church activities
Annual parties for clubs and service organizations	Banquets
	Business meetings
Conferences	

What we're looking for are preassembled audiences. In addition to your established music business performances, consider non-music-venue performances. The people at non-music-venues are usually really excited to have someone do a concert. They are great audiences and can become great supporters of your music. Since having music at their event is out of the ordinary, it's a big deal to them. They go away feeling fortunate that they ran into a recording artist they could enjoy up close, and you'll go away feeling fortunate that you found a group of people who like your music.

Ideally, they'll go away with lots of your albums to listen to and share with their friends. You'll go away with their financial support, which will help you continue to make your living doing what you love.

Great audiences are just waiting out there for you to ask if you can share your music with them. No matter what day it is or where you live, at least twenty such audiences are assembled in your state as you read this. At these gatherings, you may be the only person who has *ever* called with an offer to provide music. Often, the group has a budget for entertainment, but they don't know who to call.

Booking Basics for Preassembled Audiences

Preassembled audiences are usually gathered for one of three reasons:

1. They gather for business purposes, to network with like-minded individuals.

2. They gather to learn.

3. They gather to socialize.

Audiences gather every week for meetings, meals, workshops, conventions and athletic events. At each gathering, a coordinator is in charge of making sure everyone has a good time. This event planner wants the people at the gathering to remember it fondly. If you can present a short concert that will significantly improve the gathering, the coordinator will be thrilled. In many cases, the meeting coordinator will even pay you handsomely to do this.

It would be nice if booking agencies would call these groups and mail out our promotional materials, but on the lower end of the pay scale, 20 percent of your fee won't add up to enough to feed a booking agent, too.

Greg Tamblyn sees the value of learning to do your own bookings. "It hasn't been easy to find someone to book me, and that's probably a good thing because I've had to learn how to do it myself. I've learned marketing, business skills and public-relations skills that are invaluable, and it's just stuff you pick up by doing it. It's very important, critically important, to be totally professional, to do what you say you're going to do. It's also important to stay unemotional about booking, so you don't take it personally if someone cancels, and you don't get mad if someone is hard to deal with."

To sell a group on the idea of using you and your music, take these steps in this order:

1. Find out who is in charge of event planning. Let's assume the group has an upcoming event.

2. Call this person and introduce yourself as a performer who entertains at gatherings like this one. Say you want to explore the idea of whether music would be a possibility at this event. If it is, spend just a few minutes on the phone finding out the details of their upcoming event and ask if you can send your promo material. Ask about the best time to call back.

3. Call back on the day and time they specified. See if they've reviewed your materials and ask if this is a good time to take a moment to explore the idea of using music at the event.

The word *explore* is a good one, because you and the event planner can both throw ideas out without committing. Believe me, if this is not going to be a good situation for music and you commit to it, you will regret it.

The person who will book you for a show in front of a ready-made audience will usually be a professional worker. Sometimes it will be a member of the group who has volunteered to put together the group's annual gathering. In most cases, this person will be reasonably easy to get in touch with and will be friendly and courteous. The coordinator may not know much or anything at all about booking music, but they are usually interested in doing a good job at getting you whatever you need in terms of stage and sound.

The hardest part will be helping them understand your equipment needs, since most of them don't know a boom stand from a bandstand. Challenges like this are easy to overcome if you provide a detailed list of what you'll need to get the sound you want from your performance. If you have your own sound system and are willing to bring it, this will make everything run more smoothly. Your own sound system, or a system you take responsibility for renting, can be offered to the group for an added cost.

"There are an unlimited number of jobs out there," says Al McCree, a sought-after professional speaker who started out doing humorous after-dinner music programs at banquets. Al is a retired Air Force lieutenant colonel who always dreamed of a full-time career in music. During his Air Force years, Al was always the guy asked to play his guitar and sing at Air Force banquets. He began doing programs for community groups for a small fee. Starting at $50 to $100, and raising his fee as he gained a list of good references, it took Al only five years to begin making an annual salary of $80,000.

What does it take to book these groups? Booking a preassembled audience is easy to do, but there is one strong requirement: Be professional about everything you do, from returning phone calls promptly to being on time and ready to go on the day of the event. Club owners are used to dealing with musicians and their lovable eccentricities. Meeting planners are not. Professionalism is of extreme importance when dealing with people who don't normally work with musicians, especially if it was your suggestion to bring music to the event. You will need a good-looking brochure, business cards and a businesslike manner. You'll also need to collect letters of recommendation. If you do a good job with these groups, those letters won't be hard to come by. If you do a *really* good job, they'll advertise you to other groups.

Let the Group Handle the Publicity

If you do a concert for an organization's event, the organization will do the publicity. They do it for their organization, but the result is they advertise you. They will advertise the fact that you'll be performing in hopes that it will boost attendance.

There have been times when I have knocked myself out to get publicity when I was going to play at a music club, then received little or no mention in the media. It has been amazing how easy it is to get publicity when the

TIPS FROM THE PROS: GREG TAMBLYN

Some observances on performing live from singer-songwriter Greg Tamblyn:

"Small audiences can be the best audiences. I find that the smaller the audience, the greater the percentage of album sales. If I have an audience of twenty people, almost everybody will buy a tape, and some people will buy two things. If I have an audience of fifty people, I'll only sell to twenty-five or thirty. It's weird how the percentage of those who buy goes way up when the audience is small.

"While playing your bigger audiences on the weekends, don't overlook the opportunity to get a small group of people together for a show on a weeknight. Why not make a few hundred dollars on a Tuesday night instead of sitting in a hotel room or doing nothing? Doing a tour and working fourteen out of fifteen nights can be very productive.

"Rewards: It's great to be able to make a living. I take a lot of pride in saying I make a living as a concert performer. There's very little about it I don't enjoy. The monetary rewards are great, but the psychic rewards are great, too. Travel, meeting new people, making new friends, getting to write songs and sing them, not having to worry (like I did when I was a country writer) about whether it's okay to use the word 'dysfunctional' in a song. Being creative without restriction is wonderful. The challenge of taking it to new venues and new audiences is always fun."

organization I'm doing a show for just calls up the paper and tells them about the event.

It is important for you to provide good publicity materials. You will need to put together a good promotional package. This will include a bio, a press release (often just a reworking of the bio), articles that have been written about you, a good newspaper-friendly photo, posters and a brochure if you have one. Start with whatever you have. As you gain more exposure and more experience, you'll be able to make your package better and better.

Once you have secured an engagement with a group, they will direct your publicity material to the people who need to receive it. They have a better chance of getting something in their local paper than you will. Especially in small towns, people in the group will have friends at the paper and at the radio station. No one can guarantee that the media will cover or promote your event, but local news outlets often like to give publicity to events that will be of interest to the community.

Many groups have their own newsletters. When you provide good promotional materials, they can copy your press release inside it or create an ad for your concert that will go out to all the people on their mailing list.

Before you arrive, people in the group can hang posters around town or around the building where you'll be performing. They can also do a lot of word-of-mouth advertising to get people to your concert. Once you've played in town once, publicity will get easier and easier each time you return. If you're headed for a radio station when you get to town, tune your guitar before you go in and be ready to perform live. Be sure to mention the group that is sponsoring you or the people who have worked hard to get people to the concert.

NICHE MARKETING AND TURBO MARKETING

Why Niche Marketing Works So Well

Marketing to a specific group, or niche marketing, is the easiest way to get word-of-mouth referrals. You can quickly multiply your name recognition, your demand and your bookings. Niche marketing is a powerful tool. There are niche markets you'll choose, and maybe some that will choose you.

Here's an example of one that chooses you. Someone comes to a house concert where you're performing. This person is a school-bus driver. She recommends you as the entertainment at the inner-city school-bus drivers' annual awards banquet. You do a thirty-minute concert before they give out their safe-driving awards. They like you, so they tell the people who are organizing the county school-bus drivers' dinner. They like you and the word starts to spread to other counties. Next thing you know, you're doing an after-dinner concert for the state school-bus drivers' convention. The national school-bus drivers' convention chairwoman is in the audience. She wants you to come and do the national convention.

There are four tiers to any national organization—local, county, state and national—and there's a wealth of work for someone who is interested in doing these kinds of jobs. Marketing to these groups is a matter of letting them know you're interested and available, and that you'll do a good job.

You'll water down your marketing efforts if you sing at a self-help workshop one week, a Rotary Club picnic the next week and a church gathering the week after that. The people who enjoyed you might not think to mention it to a person in another kind of group. If you focus on one group, members will recommend you to more groups like theirs. They'll be doing the promotion for you.

Targeting Niche Markets

If you're trying to build name recognition in a certain niche market, consider advertising in the publications read by the members of that group. The group might have a newsletter you can advertise in inexpensively. Advertising in private-interest publications is often much more affordable than advertising in nationally known magazines. Once you know where your music has the largest appeal, you can focus your advertising dollars there.

Tiffany Snow is a composer and visual artist who has found a way to combine her talents and interests into a career. Tiffany creates music popular with nature lovers. Along with the twenty-four instruments she plays, she records live nature sounds to enhance her instrumentals. She is also a painter, using oil and an airbrush to create beautiful artworks with aquatic and nature themes. The paintings are featured on her album covers. She sells her music in dive shops, metaphysical shops and seaside tourist gift shops. She also has a strong following of health-care professionals who buy her music for its stress-reduction qualities.

Tiffany rarely performs her music. She has found other ways to introduce it to potential buyers. She advertises in magazines, newspapers and newsletters belonging to organizations of people in her target markets. She finds out about these newsletters at the library and says there is often little or no charge for an ad. She says that she does a good mail-order business this way. To keep track of which ads are selling the most product, Tiffany gives each one a code she can recognize. Let's say her box number is 411. She gives each state she advertises in a number from one to fifty. If she advertises in a newspaper in California, she lists her box number as 411-1NP. That means the mail order came from California (#1) and that the person saw the ad in a newspaper. If she advertises in *Scuba Diver* magazine, she lists the box number as 411-MGSD for "magazine" and *Scuba Diver*.

Turbo Marketing

The best kind of fame is to be admired by the people you admire. Think of the kind of people you like to hang out with. Chances are, you have similar interests, similar values and similar personalities. You probably feel very comfortable with certain groups.

Turbo marketing is marketing your music to preassembled audiences who are interested in things you have a passion for. It might be psychology, hunting, golfing, biking, motorcycles, tennis, running, the environment, children's issues, education, spirituality, sales or sailing.

As an example, maybe you are like performing songwriter Jeff Pearson and you love bass fishing. I'll use Jeff in this invented example, just to spark some thoughts about how you can combine your music with the other things you enjoy doing. There are bass-fishing tournaments all over the place every summer. At each bass-fishing event, lots of bass-fishing enthusiasts are in one place. There are also boat dealers trying to sell boats to all those people. The boat dealer wants people to come look at all those shiny boats. If you were Jeff, you could get the boat dealer to sponsor you (*sponsor* here means *pay*) to do a concert. The boats could be parked in prime viewing area all around.

During Jeff's concert, the bass-fishing enthusiasts learn from Jeff that he is a bass-fishing guy, too. They are happy to have their own entertainer who is also "one of the guys." They buy Jeff's albums afterward, which makes Jeff happy, and they hang around looking at boats, which makes the boat dealer happy. Jeff doesn't have to sing fishing songs. The fact that he is an entertainer will be enough to draw interest, and when they find out that he's also a bass fisherman, he will be even cooler in their eyes.

The people who bought Jeff's albums take them home and enjoy them. They begin talking to their buddies who weren't at the tournament. "Hey, there was this guy there who did a concert. He was real good, and he's a bass fisherman like us. You need to hear him." When Jeff plays at the next tournament, the people who heard him before will come to enjoy his music again, and they'll bring their friends. Jeff's name recognition spreads like wildfire.

Soon, Jeff is the official troubadour of the bass-fishing world. He does a little advertising in *Bass Master* and has a steady mail-order business going. Whenever people are planning national bass-fishing events, they want to be able to advertise that Jeff will be there, because they know Jeff will draw his bass-fishing audience. Event organizers will pay Jeff to do shows for them. He'll be a big hit at the trade shows, sponsored by a pontoon dealer who provides the most high-tech pontoon boat as Jeff's stage. Dealers give him free bass-fishing equipment and ask him to endorse their products. Jeff becomes a celebrity in the bass-fishing world. All his bass-fishing trips are tax deductible. He becomes a big star among people he likes, makes his living hanging out with bass fisherpeople and has a blast doing it.

The scenario about songwriter Jeff Pearson illustrates the concept of turbo marketing. When you begin doing concerts for groups of people with a common interest, you are niche marketing. When you choose a niche in which you have an interest that connects you with the group, you have turned niche marketing into turbo marketing.

How to Turn Niche Marketing into Turbo Marketing

Joseph Campbell said, "Follow your bliss." He explained that the way to do this is to do what you care about. Niche marketing becomes turbo marketing when you have a passion in common with the group you're performing for. When you care about the same things the group cares about, all your marketing to that group will be turbo marketing. It will be turbocharged.

Shriners, for example, contribute enormous amounts of time, energy and money to help children. If this is important to you, too, then you and the Shriners are working side by side for a common goal, and you're entertaining them along the way. If you were a Shriner, or even if someone in your family had been a Shriner, they would do everything they could to feature you at other Shriner events. They would go out of their way to call other Shriners in other towns to help you get jobs.

You can double your progress in half the time when niche marketing turns into turbo marketing. The way to do this is to find groups of people who believe in what you believe. Focus your marketing efforts toward this group. You will enjoy them, they will enjoy you, and you'll have a win-win situation.

Turbo-Marketing Power

You can't buy word-of-mouth advertising. The only way to get it is to earn it. You can earn it faster if you focus your efforts on one kind of group or one type of event. In its simplest form, this is niche marketing. You can turbocharge it if you have an affinity for the group's goals and ideals.

One easy way to begin focusing on one area is to start with your strongest interests. You might have an interest in psychology and self-help. Maybe you even worked in that field before you started wanting to play music full time. Psychologists have an annual dinner for their state association. You could do a show there. If they like you, they will tell the psychologists in the next state who are planning their annual dinner.

When you market to groups of people who are interested in things you have a passion for, you multiply the power of everything you do. Your shared interest with the group puts you on the inside instead of the outside. There are also many other benefits:

- You're performing for people with whom you share a common bond.
- Bookings are easier to get, because you're the only musician with any knowledge of things they're interested in.
- It's easy to become a celebrity among these groups.
- The audiences are appreciative, and in many cases they're very large.
- These audiences buy more albums. They want to support you, because your music relates to them.
- The pay can be five to ten times higher, because you are seen as a unique commodity in their field.
- The groups will often pay your travel expenses in addition to your performance fees.
- You can easily start playing for a certain kind of group at a local level, then move up to the state level and national level.
- You can travel around the country to play for these great audiences at the same time as you pursue personal interests like vacationing, visiting friends, skiing or beach bumming.

Turbo Marketing in Your Own Town

So many meetings, events and gatherings go on every week that you can afford to be selective. You can choose to be involved with groups that focus on topics that interest you.

For example, if you enjoy riding motorcycles, find out from your local cycle dealerships about events they are planning. In Albuquerque, New Mexico, for example, a popular dealership, M&M Honda, sponsors a motorcycle ride at least once a month. The group gathers for breakfast on Saturday morning, takes a scenic ride to a designated outdoor spot and has lunch. It's a time for the riders to socialize and a good time for you to offer a concert, with your albums for sale afterward. After you've done concerts for the riders, they'll tell other motorcycle groups about your music, and you can do more concerts for motorcycle groups. Every time you do a concert for motorcycle riders, include any humor you've picked up about motorcycle riding. Share funny stories of things that happened in other groups of motorcycle riders you've performed for. Pretty soon, you can play the national Gold Wing convention, then the national Honda convention. After that, you can go anywhere in the country and play at Honda events. You'll be a big star to them.

Many businesses have an annual dinner to thank their employees. Do you have an interest in computers? Your favorite computer store probably has an annual picnic or banquet for its employees. You could be the entertainment. After seeing you in the store all those times, the employees will love hearing your music and will probably want to take home a few of your albums. Soon, they'll be referring you to other computer operations who have annual get-togethers. When a computer-equipment expo comes to town, you'll know all the people to talk to and can book a concert there. They will love you, and you can do shows for computer events for the rest of your natural life.

You don't have to stick with just one. If you are a computer enthusiast who likes to ride motorcycles, do both. At the same time, market to any other groups you have a passion for. It's your shared interest with members of the groups that turns niche marketing into turbo marketing. Wherever you have a passion, go for it.

Targeting Your Turbo Markets
Here are some ideas to help you identify groups you'd have a common interest with. Jot down notes as they jog your memory about other groups.
  • What church, synagogue or other spiritual group do you belong to?
  • What clubs or social groups do you belong to? Are you a twelve-stepper, do you go to a singles group or are you into contra dancing?
  • Is there any kind of equipment, service or product you buy frequently? For example, if you are a skier and you buy a lot of gear from one sporting-goods store, what about doing a show in connection with the store's annual ski sale?
  • What organizations do you or your family members belong to? Start with groups like Rotary, Kiwanis, Lions Club, etc.
  • What would you like to promote in the world? You might be interested in protecting the environment, improving our schools or joining forces with a political candidate.
  • What activities do you enjoy? Are you an in-line skater, cyclist, runner or bowler?
  • In what kind of places do you enjoy socializing? Do you park your boat at a certain dock every summer? What about a sunset concert on the dock?

- What organizations provide a service you support? (Mothers Against Drunk Driving, battered women's shelters, rape crisis centers, hospice programs)

You don't have to choose just one. Choose several groups to target. As you go along, you'll discover which ones are the most suitable for the kind of music you do.

Turbo Name Recognition

You know the old sayings, "There's no such thing as bad publicity" and "I don't care what they say about me, as long as they spell my name right." You'll be amazed at the power of name recognition. Obviously, it's more helpful if you have positive name recognition.

Name recognition is easiest to get if you turbo-market, or at least niche-market. When you shot-gun, which means you send out promo materials to all kinds of groups, becoming known will be a slow process. When you target your efforts to groups of people who have common interests, they will talk to each other about you. Your name recognition will multiply.

The power of name recognition works even if people can't remember where they heard of you. This concept is called *perceived importance*. It works like this. If you tell the person in charge of hiring entertainment that you are an incredible entertainer, it won't have much impact. On the other hand, if someone they know says you're an incredible entertainer, it's going to be taken seriously. You will now have perceived importance. The next time you call, even if they can't remember who told them good things about you, you'll probably be hired. If they have heard of you, that gives you a certain credibility in their eyes.

When a potential client books an event, your name recognition will help you in several ways. First, it helps you get the booking. It will also help you get a better fee. Another way it will help is that the person who books you wants you to have a certain celebrity status or perceived importance so that people will want to come to the place where you're playing. If they know that a lot of potential attendees have heard of you, they know they'll have a good crowd.

ONE TOWN AT A TIME

Being famous in Muleshoe, Texas, can be just as rewarding as being famous in Minneapolis, Memphis or Miami. You can still strive for worldwide fame. At the same time, allow yourself to consider the benefits of being a celebrity in one town at a time.

When you play in a town once or twice a year, your popularity grows with every concert. As your popularity grows, your audiences grow in size. This increases your sales. Every time you come back to town, people who have heard you before will bring friends. Your old customers will buy new albums, and their friends will buy your old albums. Every time you return to this group will be a homecoming. You will become part of the culture of that town. In more than one town I go to twice a year, in my introduction, the master of ceremonies will describe me as "one of our own," or "like one of our family." That feels so good. It is a huge compliment. You will develop friendships in each town that you'll want to continue for a lifetime. Twice a year you'll get to go back to see these friends and swap stories. Being thought of as an important part of a community you don't live in is an honor. This is one of the greatest "living large" parts of this business.

As a ten-year veteran of the singer-songwriter highways, recording artist Jimmy Landry knows you have to start somewhere. He was living in Washington, DC, playing music around town whenever he could. Another recording artist, Jonathan Edwards, had advised him to "play anywhere you can, for anybody, anytime for any amount of money." When Jimmy complained to Jonathan that he'd probably never get out of Washington, Jonathan said, "You'll never get out of Washington until you leave." For some reason, this had a life-changing effect on Jimmy, who immediately began booking himself in Charlottesville and Richmond, Virginia. He said he was additionally inspired by a band called Eddie From Ohio. Eddie developed a following in Washington, then branched out 100 miles until they built another following, and then branched out 200 miles. Jimmy has now toured Germany, played for two weeks in Paris, and went on to log 328,000 American-highway miles on his most recent vehicle.

Start in Your Hometown
Michael Camp is a 1994 New Folk winner at the Kerrville Folk Festival but doesn't consider himself *new*. As a performing songwriter with several albums out, he plays 50 to 150 dates a year at house concerts, coffeehouses and music festivals. At forty-three, he says, "My teeth aren't perfect, and I don't wear a cowboy hat, and my hair's falling out. I don't play music for the glory or glamour. I do it because I love it." Michael grew up in Michigan, started as a cabinetmaker and built his vocation into a company and then a factory. On the side, he played his music. He had his first solo gig at nineteen. "Wherever there's a crowd, there's an audience," he says. "When I was getting started, I'd walk into a bar or restaurant that didn't have music and say, 'Would you mind if I play a song for your audience, and if you don't like it, I'll quit right in the middle and leave?' I'd just pull the guitar out and start singing, with joy in my heart, because I love to sing. And I was making a living singing table to table and singing for tips. The old-fashioned troubadours went farm to farm and sang for their dinner because people loved music," Michael says. "My mother taught me a long time ago, 'Make it your life's work to get the guitar out of the case as many times as you can, and play it. Forget about who you're impressing or who you want to impress and just play from the heart.' "

Most people think they have to be famous all over the world in order to be famous in their hometown. Deep down, it's possible that all most of us really, really want is to be famous in our hometown. You don't have to sell your soul for major label success just to be famous in your hometown. Being famous in your hometown is easy. If you're already living in your hometown, finish this book and get started. If you're living somewhere else, start making plans for a trip down memory lane.

Take some inspiration from the story of Nashville songwriter-singer-producer-publisher Wood Newton. Wood grew up in Hampton, Arkansas. He arrived in Nashville with plans to follow in the footsteps of other troubadours like Kris Kristofferson, Johnny Cash and Willie Nelson. After a stint as a recording artist on Elektra/Asylum, Wood settled into the songwriting life and has had a great deal of success.

A few years ago, Wood decided to go back to his home state to play a few concert dates for friends and family. He put twelve songs together and made an album. His hometown hosted him for a big homecoming concert held at the local softball field. Six hundred of the town's sixteen hundred people showed up. With that concert, a New Year's Eve party engagement, and a few other concerts here and there in the area, Wood sold twelve hundred albums. If all those were cassettes that he was selling for $10 each, he made $12,000. If those twelve hundred albums were CDs at $15 each, he'd make $18,000. Chances are, he sold a mixture of both, so the total fell somewhere in the middle.

One town at a time, starting with your hometown, is a great method for artists who are struggling to make it in the larger music centers. They often left behind a base of fans when they decided to try to make it in the big time. Most of these struggling songwriters and singers have lots of demo tapes around. They ignore these because they are waiting for that magical mystical music deal that's going to turn their lives around. Meanwhile, they hardly ever get to play more than one or two songs at a writer's night, and the rest of the time their music is trapped inside their hearts.

Start with the town you live in or start with the town you grew up in. You might choose a town where you have friends or relatives you would like to see, or you may prefer a town you'd like to vacation in. The idea is to do some shows, collect a mailing list and make your albums available. Don't worry about getting a perfect start, just start.

Don't forget that you can write off your travel expenses. As long as you are doing work in that town, you can write off the expense of getting there and eating food on the day of your show. Of course, you can't write off hotel bills and rental cars for two months if you did only one show, but writing off the cost of getting there is certainly a wonderful thing. Along with your receipts, be sure to save any proof you can find (programs, check stubs, recommendation letters) to prove to your friendly IRS person that you did do a show in Cancun, Mexico.

Small-Town Fame

The smaller the town, the easier it is to draw a crowd. This may take one of those revolutionary shifts in thinking, but it's true. In a large city, people have endless options of things to do. Metropolitan newspapers have pages of listings of artists you can go hear any day of the week. In small towns, live music is unique. A recording artist in town to do a concert is an event. In a city, it's nearly impossible to get an article written about your show in the local paper. In a smaller town, the paper may come out only once a week, and they're glad to have something new to write about. In many small towns, they'll take the press release you send them and print it word for word, along with a big picture. You can put your posters up right there on the door of the 7-Eleven. If they have a radio station, you can do an interview to promote the show, and chances are, most people in town will hear it since it's the only station. That kind of stuff doesn't happen in large cities. Most radio interviews are pretty short, but I went to a small town recently where they kept me on the air for forty-five minutes and played four or five of my songs while I was there. We also had a contest where people could call in to guess my age and get a free CD.

Start your fan base one small town at a time. Choose towns that are close together so the publicity for your show in one town will be talked about in the next town. Play each town at least twice a year. This will increase your name recognition, your audience size and your album sales. Every time you play a concert in that area, ask people to bring friends next time. Sell albums at all your concerts. Even when you're not there, your albums will be reminding people of you and your music. When people see that you're coming to town to play again, they'll be there.

Create Your Own Circuit

One of the most popular myths in the performing world is the belief that there is "a circuit." Maybe a long time ago there was a Holiday Inn circuit where a band could play Holiday Inns from town to town for weeks or months in each place. In our minds, the Holiday Inn probably did all the work of setting up the tour. We'd like to think a folk-festival circuit, a coffeehouse circuit or a dance-hall circuit exists out there just waiting for us. We think that maybe if we do well at one of these places, they will tell their fellow venue owners and we will be fully booked for the next five decades without lifting a finger. I wish! The myth is popular because we want to believe it's true.

The bad news is that a circuit that you can step into does not exist. The good news is that you can create one. You can stay on it for years. It can grow and grow. It can take you back to the same performance venues twice a year, giving you the opportunity to make friends in those areas and really enjoy their towns.

Maybe you have commitments to family or a job. Maybe you are pursuing

TIPS FROM THE PROS: MEGON MCDONOUGH

By age nineteen, singer-songwriter Megon McDonough had an album on RCA, was on tour opening for John Denver and played Carnegie Hall. Unfortunately fame, according to Megon, can be as fleeting as a pair of bell-bottom hip huggers with a peace patch on the butt.

By her early thirties, Megon was living in Chicago, performing in musicals, doing stand-up comedy and learning to appreciate what life had to offer. She longed to release albums again but wasn't willing to do it the way she did before, with agents and lawyers and managers and stylists and stress.

"I thought, *I'm not signed to a label, and I don't have the time or money to make great demo tapes and then find an attorney and/or manager to shop it around for a record deal.* I'm married to a roofing contractor, and I like living in the Midwest, and I thought, *What can I do with what I have right where I am?* Before we married, my husband said, 'I really like your music, and so do a lot of other people. What would it take to get your music out there on tape?' And I said, 'Well, money.' He said okay, and gave me the money to do *Day By Day*, a tape where I played everything; it's a very simple bare-bones production. It's a favorite among people who have my records. It will never be a CD, and it was not intended for that. It was always meant to be a simple cassette."

Later Megon began touring with three other well-known singer-songwriters, Christine Lavin, Sally Fingerett and Julie Gold, who call themselves the Four Bitchin' Babes. "When I started traveling with the Babes, we were selling our product, and I recorded *American Girl*, which is a full-blown production and an album I really like." Megon has now recorded a jazz album for Shanachie Records, the label that also releases the Babes' compilation albums.

After experiencing "stardom" at an early age, Megon tries to keep life in perspective. "I don't think it's ever going to be different if and when I get the major record deal, major distribution and major gigs. I'm still going to have to pick up my dry cleaning, take my son to Montessori school, make dinner, do my laundry, write a song, bake a cake, go to a wake. Life goes on, and everything is really the same."

She says fame doesn't make you a different person than you were before. "Everyone has the same stuff going on and I think it's a mistake to think it's going to be different if only *this* happens. I don't think that's the case anymore. I think you have to live life. In the process of that, things come to us. My philosophy is, 'Pray to catch the bus, but run like hell.' "

a music deal and don't want to leave town for very long. Here's a way you can use this method to travel only once a month. If you can do this well, you can quit your day job and make your entire living on these once-a-month trips. This will give you more time for your family or more time for pursuing other interests, like a large-scale record deal.

Let's say you are a performer from Jackson, Mississippi, and you have made your own album. You don't like to travel much, so you want to be gone only once a month. You can play a Friday night in Grenada, Mississippi, and a Saturday night in Greenwood, Mississippi, twice a year. In each town, you can either get a cheap hotel room or stay with the friends you'll be making at your show. Each time you play, remind people when you'll return and ask them to come back and bring friends. Since you don't want to drive back to Jackson after your show on Saturday, you can get an inexpensive place to stay. Why not sing in a church the next morning? You can sing in church, collect a soloist fee, possibly make your albums available (depending on the church) and be home Sunday afternoon.

All you need to find are five more Friday/Saturday/Sunday situations in small towns close together like that. If you have six one-weekend-a-month areas and you perform in each set of towns twice a year, you'll be booked twelve months of the year. After that, all you need to do is maintain your relationships with the people who book you in each of the six areas. Every time you play, you'll have more and more people at your shows, and you'll sell more and more albums. Those who already have your albums will be back for anything new you've produced, and they'll bring friends to buy your original album.

If you don't want to spend the night away from home, find small towns within driving distance. Your circuit can be as big or as small as you want it to be. The less you spend on travel expenses, the more you'll keep in take-home pay.

In small towns, if people like your music, they like you. They are flattered you would come out there and play. You are an honored guest. I get nervous sometimes when I'm playing a big city, but I get nothing but excited about playing a small town.

Create Your Own Audience

Here is an example of how you can create your own audience in a new town. A few years ago, I sang at a wedding in Steamboat Springs, Colorado. Steamboat is a beautiful little ski town full of great people. I liked it so much I wanted to go back. My friends, whose wedding I sang for, helped me organize a concert on my next trip. We held the concert at the local arts center, an old train depot. It cost $25 for me to join the arts council, which gave me access to the building for an art project (my concert). My friends put signs up all over town, told the radio station about it and took my publicity material to the local paper. The paper did a nice front-page blurb. A blurb is smaller than a story, but, what the heck, it was on the front page. As I recall, we had about thirty people at the concert at $5 per person and had a great time.

By calling ahead to Denver to let them know I'd be in the area, I found a church there where I could play. In Denver and Steamboat, I told the audience that I was hoping to make this a regular stop when I was out on the road. I asked them to come back next time and asked them to bring friends.

I go back to Steamboat Springs and Denver an average of twice a year now, and each time I play, the concerts are bigger and bigger. The trip is so enjoyable that I usually stay as long as I can. I have good friends there. In the winter, there are mountains to ski, and in the summer there are horses to ride up those mountains.

When you perform in any town you want to return to, be sure to ask people to come back next time and bring friends. They won't know you want that unless you ask them. When they bring a friend next time, they will know that they helped you and that you appreciate it. In Steamboat, my first audience consisted of friends of my two dear friends, the couple who invited me to sing at their wedding. The audiences have grown so much in Steamboat that my last concert nearly filled the hall.

Michael Camp built a following in his home state of Michigan; Colorado, where he lived for thirteen years; and Texas. It all started the same way he got his first job at nineteen. "I'd look at places and think, *This is a nice place. I wonder if they'd like to have music in here?* I'd ask, and they'd ask, 'What would it cost?' and I'd say, 'Would you feed me, or give me $50,' or whatever I needed. What I did was I went places and made friends and played music. I've got venues that I've played for twenty years. And all I have to do is call up and tell them when I'd like to come out, and they'll close down the back room, put up the folding chairs and set up a little spot for me to play."

Create Your Own Concert Venues

This may be a mind stretch, but stay with me. You're probably wondering by now where you are going to perform in all the places I've suggested. It's great to say, "Yes, I'll do a show in this town on Friday and the next town over on Saturday, but how do I do that? Where will I play? How do I do a concert in a town if they have never heard of me?"

We've got to open our minds to alternative performance venues. It doesn't have to be a place where they've ever had music before. A lot of ideas for performance spaces were covered in the section about house concerts. All you have to do is find a place in each town where people can gather. Part of the location's appeal will be in its uniqueness. While people might not be the type to go out to a bar or listening room on a Friday or Saturday night, the idea of going to a concert at the town library will be a novelty.

It's all going to start with the people who like your music. I'm not suggesting that you call the local library and ask them if you can do a concert. It starts by having someone in town who likes your music enough to help you find a place and get some people together. Since people know their community much better than you do, let them use their contacts to find a place.

Create Your Own Stardom

You don't have to be nationally known to be a star. In fact, you can be a star and still not be nationally known. When I do concerts in other cities,

I often ask the audience what kind of music they like and what artists they like. I also ask if they know who Suzy Bogguss is, since she recorded one of my songs. I am shocked that even though Suzy is very popular in country music and was awarded the 1992 Country Music Association Horizon Award, most people I ask have never heard of her.

When Garth Brooks performed at the Super Bowl along with Travis Tritt, Wynonna Judd, Tanya Tucker and others, I was watching with a group of doctors and lawyers from the Northeast. The only person they knew was Tanya Tucker. They didn't know who Wynonna was, but when I described the mother/daughter duo she had been part of, they thought maybe they had heard of the Judds.

When I went to London in 1993, I quizzed every cabdriver in an informal survey to find out how much they knew about country music. They knew about as much about country performers as I know about thrash metal artists. They had heard of Garth Brooks and Reba McEntire but didn't really know any of their music.

I'm telling you this because even big-time artists aren't known everywhere and you don't have to be either. You can start marketing your music one town at a time.

I always wanted stardom on a large scale. I thought the only way to be a star was to be nationally known. I didn't realize how great it can be when someone calls and says, "Jana, your name came up in my therapy group today. We were talking about listening to music that makes us feel better and someone said, 'Get some of Jana Stanfield's albums. Her music helps me a lot.' " It felt great to hear that. So what if I'm a star only in small towns and therapy groups? I love it.

Before reading this book, had you ever heard the name Jana Stanfield? Most people haven't. So, you probably never heard of me, and yet you now have my book. This proves we don't have to be famous in order for people to buy (and even enjoy!) our creations. I have a successful music career performing and selling my albums (and now books). If I am doing that and most people have never heard of me, then we have something in common, because they've probably never heard of you either.

Let the Audience Come to You

In Clark, Colorado, there is a great entertainer named Ken Jones. Ken played in bands since he was a teenager, while pursuing a career in ranching. At some point, he realized the ranch was his true calling. Still, he couldn't turn loose of the music, and I'm glad he didn't.

This man has created the most unique and wonderful performance situation I have ever seen. He has found a way to let audiences come to him. Ken is the owner of a Colorado guest ranch called the Home Ranch. Guests stay for a week at a time, and during that time they get their own horse, their own saddle, their own brushes and bridles, with plenty of wranglers available to lead rides up into those gorgeous mountains. If they'd rather fish or hike, there are fishing and hiking guides. All the kids get to have their own rodeo at the end of the week, with numbers on their backs, a rodeo announcer calling out their scores and cheering fans (their families). On one night of each week, dinner is served in the top of the huge barn. After dessert, the guests are treated to genuine live cowboy music.

Ken built a stage in the second story of that barn. When he hires ranch hands, he looks for people who play instruments and sing. He has a great band called Cowboy Ken and the Ranch Hand Band. Ken has two albums out of his own music and popular cowboy tunes. He even did comedy between songs on his first album, making it sound like an old-time radio show at KATL Radio.

Ken gets a new audience every week, summer and winter. Every week, guests leave the Home Ranch with copies of Ken's albums for themselves and for their friends. Another member of the Ranch Hand Band, Michael Moon, has also created his own albums now. The weekly hootenannies allow Mike to showcase his music, too, and Mike's albums are sold alongside Ken's at the Home Ranch Store.

The thing I admire most about Ken is that he has created a situation in which he combines his love of ranching with his need to make music. His music doesn't support him financially, but he doesn't need it for that. It supports his need for a creative musical outlet. He didn't give up his day job; he just incorporated his skills as an entertainer into his job description. His albums give him the opportunity to share his unique blend of humor and cowboy songs.

Ken doesn't tour the band. He gets to sleep in his own bunk every night. This is not to say that the band doesn't travel. Cowboy Ken and the Ranch Hand band are so popular with the guests that one of them saw to it that the band got to play on Farm Aid, right up there with Willie Nelson and The Spin Doctors.

Of course, creating a Colorado guest ranch is an expensive way to draw a crowd, but maybe someone in your area is already drawing the crowd for you. Is there a bed-and-breakfast, a guest ranch or a retreat facility in your area? Consider doing a weekly show there. Do you have a friend who has a business that caters to tourists? You could put up a sign that says, "*Your Name*, Local Musician, Next Show One Hour," and do fifteen-minute miniconcerts throughout the weekend. This would draw traffic into the store, and your friend could sell your albums.

The Power of Selling at Local Record Stores

Let's say you live in Clovis, New Mexico, a town of about thirty thousand people with several record stores. Most local record stores carry records by local artists. They often take the records on consignment, meaning that when the records sell, they will keep a sizable percentage (usually 60 percent or less) and give you the rest. The majority of the record buyers in your town shop at these local record stores. If your albums are there, the people of your town will see you on the shelves just an aisle away from Garth Brooks, Babyface and Alanis Morissette. This will increase your name recognition in town whether people buy your albums or not.

Many artists make good money from the sales of their albums at their local record stores, but the money is not the only good reason for placing your product in local stores. Your name recognition will jump significantly when your records are in the local record stores. This will help you with your bookings and will also increase sales at your concerts.

Getting Small-Label Releases on the Radio

Bill Wence works for artists who are trying to get their music heard and played by Americana stations. He says, "If you create a good album, you've got a real good chance of getting airplay in this format, because they will play you and give your new music a chance. The disc jockeys really care about the music, that's why they're there. They want to share it with listeners. They get excited about a good record or a good artist. They're not going by a computer printout from a consultant. These stations also have more freedom to support a local act if the act puts out a good record. They don't care so much about the size of the record company that put out the record. They care about the quality of the music."

As a promoter to Americana stations, Bill is first contacted by an artist who wants to go for national airplay. Radio stations often refer local acts to him so he can get their music played in other parts of the country as well. The first step is to mail albums to all the stations simultaneously to create a buzz. Bill handles the mailing, then begins calling the stations to get them interested in the record. These are the objectives of record promoters in this format:

1. Get the music director who chooses albums to listen to the record.

2. Get the album moved into the control room where the disc jockeys can play cuts off of it.

3. Get the album added to the station's official playlist, which will then be submitted to a national trade magazine like the *Gavin Report*, which tracks how much each album is being played across the country.

4. Get the album moved from light rotation (a few plays a week) to medium and then heavy rotation (many plays per week).

If enough airplay can be received from the stations that report to the trade magazines, the artist will also be able to add a line to his or her biography that says, "This artist has had a nationally charted record in the *Gavin Report*."

For Americana and other alternative formats, Bill Wence says it doesn't matter whether you're on a small label, a large label or your own label.

"They couldn't care less about what you spent on your album, because they're listening to what you have to say with your music and how well you say it. Be honest with your music. They look for music that is from the heart."

Finding Information About Radio Stations, Venues and Publications That Feature Small-Label Artists

For many years, albums didn't get made if a record company didn't think it would get radio airplay. Record companies, record stores and radio stations were like a dog chasing its own tail. Radio airplay advertised the records and then, ideally, those records sold at record stores. If radio wouldn't play a certain artist on the record company's roster, that artist's music wouldn't sell, and that artist was subsequently dropped from the label. Radio tastes had tremendous power over record company output. When radio consultants entered the picture, consultants claimed to have the best expertise to pick and choose which artists and songs radio stations would play. The consulting firm dictated airplay for many stations simultaneously. Now the consultants had the power. Do you see any place here where the artist has the power? No. Do you see any place where the public has the power? No.

The bottom line with commercial radio stations is the word *commercial*. Commercial radio stations sell commercials. With every station competing to get advertising dollars from local businesses, they all want to have the guaranteed hottest music. They don't want to take chances on good songs. They want megahits and only megahits. Consultants claimed they could predict and guarantee which songs would become megahits. In the end, they were right, because when a consulting firm told all its stations to play a certain song instead of other songs, the songs selected by the consultants had a good chance of becoming megahits.

Fortunately, the public finally became disenchanted with stations that play the same songs over and over. People began asking their friends for recommendations of what albums to buy instead of letting radio tell them what records were hot. The public enjoyed a variety of music of their own choosing because they listened to cassettes and CDs.

Alternative radio formats emerged in the '90s. These formats were often adopted by college and public radio stations which didn't depend heavily on advertising dollars. Two of the formats feature singer-songwriters: Americana and Adult Album Alternative (Triple A). Both are artist driven, meaning they choose entire albums for airplay instead of single songs. Air personalities are given the freedom to play whatever cuts they like off these albums. The public is encouraged to call in and request favorites.

These radio stations are going back to what radio was like long ago. The air personalities usually work there because they love the music. They are there to be like that friend you have who checks out all the latest music and advises everybody about what's good.

The Kerrville Folk Festival, named for the town of Kerrville, Texas, where it takes place each summer, is one of the oldest and strongest U.S. folk festivals, featuring music that doesn't easily fit into a common category. There are many references to this festival in this book, because it is well known as an event where acoustic musicians and acoustic-music fans converge for weeks of camping out, playing music and networking.

The Kerrville Music Foundation, Inc., has compiled a comprehensive guidebook called *The Kerrville Directory.* Inside you'll find over twenty-five hundred listings of music venues, media contacts, publications and organizations useful to singer-songwriters or anyone involved in acoustic, folk or self-produced music. The listings include agents, record producers and manufacturers as well as performers. It doesn't cost anything to list yourself in the directory. I've never had anyone call me as a result of being listed as a performer here but it is a great reference book. Many sections are broken down into individual zip codes so you can find all the media contacts in Albuquerque or all the suitable music venues in Dayton. For more information, contact the Kerrville Music Foundation at P.O. Box 1466, Kerrville, Texas 78029, (210) 257-3600.

ADVERTISING

Is advertising in magazines or on the radio worth the cost? There are several ways to evaluate that. The easiest way to measure an ad's effectiveness is to divide the cost of the advertisement by the number of albums you think it will sell. If the ad costs $300, for example, you'll have to ask yourself whether the ad would sell thirty cassettes or twenty CDs. If you're advertising a concert, divide the cost of the ad by the ticket price to see if you think it will bring in more ticket sales and CD sales than it cost.

Even if it won't sell enough product to pay for itself, that doesn't mean an ad isn't worth the price. Remember that some people have to hear your name three times before they are inspired to buy. That doesn't mean you have to buy three ads. Maybe the people who read the magazine or listen to the station have heard of you twice already, and this will push them over the edge.

There's a value to advertising that reaches beyond recouping your investment right away. You might advertise on the radio for a community concert and find that half the town doesn't come to the concert. That's okay. Maybe some people will feel like they missed something (especially if friends tell them they did), and they'll come next time. Maybe you will be sending one of those no-shows a promotional package about something they are in charge of booking in the future. If they have heard your name on the radio, or if they've seen it in a magazine, they won't necessarily remember they heard of you in an ad. They'll just know they've heard of you, and this will make it more likely you'll get the booking.

For performing songwriter Nancy Moran, advertising first paid off in name recognition, then in bookings, which led to album sales. After placing her ad in *Performing Songwriter* magazine, she found club owners saying, "Yes, I've heard of you." They didn't treat her like a nobody trying to get a booking at their clubs. She knew, since she had never been to the areas she was calling, that they must have seen her ad. She felt she was being shown a little more respect, simply because they had heard of her. It's hard to measure the specific effectiveness of an ad, but Nancy believes advertising made people more aware of her and made it easier to get bookings.

CONFERENCES, SEMINARS AND CONVENTIONS

A great deal of information is taught at conferences, seminars and conventions. The main reason people attend them is to schmooze, also known as networking. If you're interested in getting your name out there, it's smart to attend any gathering of people who can book you, buy your albums or advance your career in any way. It can also be expensive.

Consider whether you can afford to make this investment, knowing it might not pay off immediately and might not pay off at all. With so many people crammed into one hotel, you won't get much time to spend with anyone you'll want to talk to. Making lasting connections at these events sometimes requires repeated attendance over a period of years.

Every conference has its own culture, complete with its own customs, taboos and character. Find out about these before you go. An example of a taboo is that if you are an aspiring country singer attending the Country Radio Seminar, it would be completely uncouth for you to play guitar and sing in the hotel hallways, trying to give radio DJs a sample of your music. It can only take a moment to create a bad impression that will take years to live down.

When attending an event for the first time, consider it an experiment. You're going there to find out if this organization is a good one to join. You're going there to find out if this is a gathering that could be beneficial to you. Learn all you can and put that knowledge to use if you decide to continue attending.

Booths at Conventions

In addition to attending conventions of people in the music profession, I have also tried attending conventions of people who might like my music. In exchange for my participation in a presentation called "Music and Humor: Just for the Health of It," I was given a free booth at the conference of the Tennessee Alcohol and Drug Association for two days. Or was it three? It seemed like five. Those were some boring hours, because everyone was either in training workshops or networking, and neither activity brought them near my booth. To make my booth more appealing, I played my CDs, played my guitar and had people put their business cards in a fishbowl for a drawing for a free house concert. The house concert turned out to be a really good thing in the long run, but as far as CD sales went, let's just say I spent more on junk food to get me through those days than I made.

When the book you're reading first came out in its self-published version, I paid for a booth at Folk Alliance, which has a lively booth situation. Here are some tips:

• When the booth area is packed with exhibitors like you, passersby will have little time to spend at your booth, so plan in advance what you'll do to make your booth appealing.

• Give away food, and not just the red-and-white hard-candy peppermints like everybody else. People get picky as they see the same food at every booth. Fork out the money for chocolate or good cookies or packs of Pez. At one conference, I passed a booth (repeatedly) that had really exotic, expensive cookies. My friend and I felt so guilty about accepting the cookies that we stayed and heard the sales pitch for their catering service.

• The best booth artist I've ever seen was Ratsy at Folk Alliance. She gave out Cheez-Its from a huge box. Of course, to get the Cheez-Its, you couldn't be grabbing without stopping. After all the sugar you snagged at other booths, it was great to stop and reach for some carbohydrates. Ratsy's booth had four to six portable CD players with her CDs cued to certain songs in each one. While you munched, you could put the headphones on and listen to her music. She had all kinds of stuff to give away, including pins and buttons. On a related note, there is a rumor that she has been known to hand out homemade brownies at her concerts. It must work, because it started a rumor and now she's in a book.

• If your food is good, it gets people to stop and consider what you're promoting at your booth. Once you've got them, have some sort of giveaway they can put their card in for, and make sure they know they'll have to stop back on the last day to see if they won.

• Booths are not for introverts.

GIG CARDS

Gig cards are inexpensive postcards that can let the people on your mailing list know:

• that you're coming to town
• that you have a new album available
• that you're going to be featured in the national media

If your mailing list is on a computer database, you can send gig cards to people in the area of the country you're going to be playing in. You can let them know when and where you'll be playing so they can come and bring friends. (See facing page for my gig cad.)

Chuck Pyle sends cards to the people on his mailing list about three times a year. For three thousand cards, he spends about $1,000 for copying

Print upcoming gig information on two sides of brightly colored card stock to use as postcards to mail to people on your mailing list.

JANA STANFIELD

FRIENDS...I'm headed your way, playing some of these places for the first time. With your support, they could be regular events! Hope to see you there... Continued blessings,

Jana

The new album is ready: **ENJOY THE RIDE**

To order, send $15/CD's or $10/tapes to us at:
Music With Meaning. P.O. Box 60146. Nashville, TN 37206.
Or E-mail your order to jana@songs.com

Tuesday, July 18
Steamboat Springs, CO
Strings in the Mountains, 7:00 pm
(303)879-5056

Sharing the stage with Riders in the Sky, my favorite cowperson band...it'll be a great night.

Saturday, July 29
Lubbock, TX
Songwriting and Music Business Workshop. 2:00-5:00 pm
(806)762-3233

Expanded from the Kerrville Folk Festival workshop, based on my new book, "Start Small, Dream Big, Live Large: A Guide to Making and Marketing Your Music." Invest in the possiblities. Cactus Theater. $20.

Saturday, July 29
Lubbock, TX
Cactus Theater Concert.
 8:00 PM
(806)762-3233

You won't believe the beauty of this gorgeous, renovated old theater. I can't wait to do a concert there.
1812 Ave.H.

Friday, August 4
Dallas, TX
Uncle Calvin's Coffeehouse
8:00 PM
(214)214-363-0044

Uncle Calvin's is one of the finest listening rooms in the country. Susan Lindfors is opening and Richard Berman will be my special guest. Richard is the winner of songwriting contests at South Florida and Napa Valley Folk Festivals. He captivates audiences at Kerrville campfires. When you hear him, you'll understand.

Please send your E-mail address to me at: jana@songs.com
My WWW address is: http://songs.com/noma/janahome.htm

and stamps. The information is printed from a computer, then pasted onto an original so both sides of an 8½″ × 11″ sheet of card stock can be run through a copier and cut into four cards. He says there are three benefits to the cards:

1. The same people start showing up to see you, so it makes you get better every time. It makes you responsible.

2. He usually gets $600 to $800 in sales from a mailing, plus lots of people coming to the shows and buying product there.

3. The cards develop a life of their own. "People put them away and order sometimes a year later," he says. "The jury's still out on whether I get back the exact amount I spent, but I think it's a good investment in the long run."

NEWSLETTERS

A newsletter is the best way to keep in touch with people who support your music. It lets them know what's going on with you and when you'll be back to see them. If you don't have much to say, just go with one page. Make it like a letter. If people have enjoyed you as a performer, they will enjoy hearing from you, even if it is a newsletter that goes to thousands of other people.

A newsletter serves several purposes. It keeps you in people's thoughts if they have an event they could use some music for. It's also a good way to advertise your cassettes and CDs. Be sure to put an order blank with each newsletter and a description of the product that is available.

Newsletters get categorized as advertising instead of money-making projects, because I don't know anyone who has received enough product orders from their newsletters to pay for itself. However, you can do some things to make it more likely that people will order product.

First, *do not discount your albums in your newsletter*. If you normally sell albums for $10 and in your newsletter you offer them for $7, people will never want to pay $10 for them at shows again. Even if they didn't buy from the newsletter, they'll remember they can get it cheaper that way, so why buy at full price when you play live? It may seem like a subtle difference, but instead of discounting your albums, offer a bonus. You can say, "With three items (at full price) you get something (maybe your original four-song demo tape) free," or "Buy two (at full price) and get one free." Of course, leave off the part that says "at full price," because that is implied.

Second, put in a time limit, so your "special" is like a coupon that expires. If you have a coupon that never expires, you'll forget to use it. If you have only three more days to get that discount, chances are you'll use it. Give it a deadline.

Third, be sure to suggest ordering "For yourself or for your friends." If you have three albums out and the people who get your newsletter already have one or more, it may seem to them that they can't take advantage of the special. If they have friends they want to share your albums with, this is a good time to complete their own collection and also get a couple of copies of the albums they like for friends.

Other things to put in your newsletter:
- All the latest news about what you've been doing
- Photos of people you've met along the road
- Your upcoming schedule
- How to get in touch with you for bookings
- Ideas about how to use your music
- Funny letters you've received, especially if they are from kids

BUTTONS, BUMPER STICKERS AND OTHER PROMO ITEMS

Buttons, bumper stickers, pens, fans and coffee cups with your name on them are inexpensive, especially if you buy them in large quantities. Every city has showrooms full of these items. Find them by looking in the yellow pages under "Advertising Specialties." You can have your name and number printed on anything that will stand still. Even with the printing charge, the items usually cost less than a dollar apiece.

For my money, they are best used as promotional items, not as moneymakers. While each item costs less than a dollar, I find that as income generators, they are more trouble to haul around than they're worth. Maybe you make a dollar every time you sell one. If you sell ten of them at each performance, you walk away with the same money you'd make from selling one album. I'd rather use the promotional items to increase the chances of selling ten albums.

A good way to measure the effectiveness of promotional items is to calculate how many albums you'd have to sell to pay for them. Let's say your promo buttons cost $500. If you think they will help you sell more than $500 in albums, then you'll at least break even. As an added benefit, lots of people will remember your name. Even if they don't buy an album now, they may buy one in the future.

Garth Brooks had his first single, "Much Too Young (To Feel This Damn Old)," out just as the annual Country Radio Seminar rolled around. Country Radio Seminar used to be known as the Disc Jockey Convention. It is now attended by people who work in every area of the country music field. It draws hundreds of music industry leaders from the U.S., Canada, England and even Australia. They are the country music decision makers, and their decisions determine the fate of each record and each artist.

Even though people were just becoming familiar with Garth's first record, which was faltering at the bottom of the charts, Garth walked every inch of the convention, day after day, wearing that broad hat and a broad smile. He had pins made that read, "Much Too Young to Feel This Damn Old . . . Garth Brooks." Garth personally pinned one on nearly every person at that seminar, and as he did, he spoke to them, shared eye contact and made a strong connection with them. Before his record was even halfway up the chart to number one, it lost its "bullet," meaning that it no longer had the momentum to move upward. I was working in record promotions then, and we were working his record, trying to get it to the top of the chart. Because of the strong connections he made with those radio programmers, those of us who worked the record were able to do what has rarely been accomplished. We were able to get the bullet back. The record went on to the top and got Garth's career off to a great start. In that case, the buttons were worth whatever small price he paid for them.

Buttons and bumper stickers aren't going to turn the rest of us into Garth Brooks, but they can be helpful. Here's an example of how they helped on a much smaller scale.

When I was in the New Folk contest at the Kerrville Folk Festival in 1992, I had a new album coming out. I had it announced in my introduction that I was having an album-release party in the hospitality tent (the place where they sell the performers' albums) immediately after the contest. I sold a lot of albums that way.

In 1993, with another new album ready, I wanted to sell even more, and I made it happen with buttons. In the announcement during my introduction at the 1993 contest, I offered a free gift as part of the album-release party that would follow in the hospitality tent immediately after the contest. The free gift was a cool-looking bright green button with my name on it that read, "I'm Not Lost, I Am Exploring." That was the name of the album I was releasing and the name of a song I had just performed in the contest. Many people came to get the free gift and wound up walking away with the album as well. I gave those buttons out during the week that I was at the festival. The majority of the Kerrville audience hadn't heard me at the contest, but they knew my name. When I gave out buttons, people would say, "Oh, that's you? I've been wanting one of these." The button advertised my name and my product. I sold a lot of albums that week, lots more than I sold the year before.

Posters

Posters are good promotional tools. They look good to the person who'll book you when you send out your promotional package. The posters show your level of professionalism. They show that you have invested money in increasing the number of people who will come to each concert. They show that you take your performances seriously. When people are considering the idea of booking you, they'll be able to see instantly that it will be easy to advertise your concert with the posters. They won't have to think of their own ideas for letting people know about your show.

Good-looking posters not only get people to your shows but increase your name recognition wherever they are placed. Even if someone can't possibly come to the concert because of schedule conflicts, they will remember your name (and possibly your face) from the poster and will be more likely to come to your next event.

If you get posters, make them artsy, bold and easy to read. Most copy centers can color-copy the poster you create for less than $2 each. Posters can be professionally printed for even less if you make them in black and white. Making them white plus a color other than black will increase the cost one step, and making them full color will make them much more expensive. If you have them printed, you can get your posters on regular paper, card stock or glossy paper. Glossy will look most expensive, probably because it *is* most expensive.

Make sure your poster is eye-catching, without too much stuff written on it. While it's important not to write too much, do put something on the poster that gives people a clue about what kind of music you do. This way, people who like your kind of music will show up, and people who hate your kind of music won't.

Be sure to leave a large space where the date, time and location of the concert will be written, since that is the reason for putting up the poster.

Here are two money-saving tips:

1. Print your posters in black and white. Make them color by using highlight markers, which come in everything from pastels to neons. Highlight markers will work better than the darker markers, because you can see the lines where you've colored something in with a dark marker. The lighter highlight markers blend better without showing lines. You don't have to color them all at once. Color a few at a time as you send them out, or color a dozen at a time while you're on hold. When my stepdaughter Crystal brought a friend to visit for the week, they colored about a hundred of them one night while watching overnight trash-talk reruns.

2. Print lots of them. The most expensive part is the graphic design and the setup of the printer. After that, copies are cheap. Check prices for a thousand and two thousand. The cost per poster will drop drastically in larger quantities, and you can use these posters freely to advertise all over the place. If the posters are cheap and plentiful, you can also use four or five of them in a design on the wall behind your product table to attract attention. If you use the posters on the wall behind your table, you can use the open space on the posters to write your album prices, so people can see them if they can't get to the table.

Double Your Graphic Mileage for Half the Cost

Color graphics on slick paper are expensive. Your CD booklets will be in color on this kind of paper, so look for opportunities to use them in more than one way. You're going to pay for five hundred or a thousand CD booklets anyway. Since printing costs go down quickly when you buy in large quantities, you can order extras inexpensively when you order your CD and use them for more than just CD booklets.

If you plan it right when you're doing the photography and graphics, your CD booklet can fold out into a small poster. To do this, use a full-body photograph for the poster and use just your head for the CD cover. When it folds out, it is a small poster. If you leave plenty of open space on the bottom or bottom right, the time and location of your concert can be written in there. On the back of the poster, you'll have all the lyrics to your songs.

You might not be ready to turn your CD booklets into brochures and posters, but you can still get double use out of the booklets. Ask the album production facility to give you any extras that are printed. These are called overruns. You can glue a CD booklet or even a cassette cover to your promotional pieces to make them full-color. I glued my CD covers to the front of my promotional-packet folders. Greg Tamblyn glued his cassette cover to his one-page marketing piece.

Buddy Mondlock has a great way to get more than one use out of his posters. He has his booking and brochure information printed on the back. That way, he can use nice glossy paper if he wants and can get two uses out of each sheet for less than he'd pay for a poster on plain paper and a brochure on plain paper.

TIPS FROM THE PROS: CHRISTINE LAVIN

Christine Lavin has released nine solo albums, three albums with a group called the Four Bitchin' Babes and five compilation albums. Her earlier albums are on Rounder Records, and the latest are on Shanachie Records. Always on the cutting edge of musical humor, Christine was the first to write a song (along with John Gorka) popularizing the term *Sensitive New Age Guys*, also known as SNAGs.

Christine is known as the queen of product sales and promotional giveaways. She believes that anything you can inspire people to take home with your name, your address, your album titles, your face and your phone number is a good investment.

After eight years of doing temp work as a New York secretary and music on the side, Christine knows how hard it is to create a full-time career doing what you love. "I'm in this for life," she says. "Anything that helps people know who you are will come back to you down the line. People who remember you with a smile will come to your concerts and buy your next album."

Christine's business cards are baseball cards. She puts them on every seat when she's doing a show and finds that people keep them because they think the card is funny. Although they're saving it as a souvenir, the card has her picture, address, phone number, record company logo and a bio.

To promote her funny-song compilations, Christine found a dental-floss dispenser that is the size and shape of a credit card and holds 12 feet of floss. On the outside she had printed, "Compliments of Christine Lavin and Laugh Tracks. Now you can laugh with confidence because your dental floss is always near." The listing for Christine's website was also included. She's given away over twenty-five hundred so far.

Christine says it's important to know your audience. Hers is made up of grown-ups, she says, so maintaining health and good looks is important to them. She's considering a line of jar openers next. Christine learned the hard way that neon-colored bicycle caps are not high on their list of priority accessories when she had five hundred made to promote a new album that included the song, "What Was I Thinking?" She asked herself that when it turned out her audience enjoyed the hats as giveaways but wouldn't buy one.

While she says it's difficult to tell whether the promotional items pay for themselves in concert tickets, word-of-mouth advertising and album sales, Christine believes the most important reason for doing it is to create goodwill. She gives promotional items away free with albums, gives them out as prizes during a show, gives them out to occupy the attention of noisy children in the audience, and authorizes the person doing sales to give them away to any kids who seem to want one. She sees the goodwill created as an investment in her long-term career.

CHAPTER NINE

MARKETING YOUR MUSIC ON THE INTERNET

Computers are revolutionizing the marketing of albums. Here's a simple example: You hear a song by an artist you've never heard before. You get the artist's name, and you make a mental note to look for that artist's music next time you go to a record store. You don't get to the record store for a few months, and by that time, you can't remember the artist's name or even the title of the song. You don't get the album, and the recording artist fades into obscurity as the result of dismal album sales.

With a computer, you can hook up to the Internet the same day you hear the song. There you can seek out an online record store where you can listen to clips of other songs by the artist, order the CD and have it mailed to you. You can visit the artist's home page to find out about television appearances, upcoming local performances and additional albums by the artist. You can even send an e-mail to get yourself on the artist's mailing list so you'll be the first to know about new releases.

Here's another great thing about the Internet. We know the best kind of advertising is word of mouth. The Internet is like a big foghorn. If you find an artist you like, that artist's home page can connect you to other artists who play that kind of music. If you visit my home page (http://songs.com/jana), there's a line that says, "If you like Jana Stanfield's music, we recommend you also try the music of Karen Taylor-Good, Greg Tamblyn and David Roth." If you click on one of those names, it opens up their home pages so you can find out more about them.

The future is wide open for independent recording artists on the Internet. To get a sense of what is on the horizon, here's an interview with Paul

Schatzkin of the National Online Music Alliance, a service that promotes the music of many fine artists through the Internet.

Q. Paul, computer marketing is changing everything. How did this kind of music marketing get started?

A. What we're talking about is more than just "computer marketing." It's a whole new science of "digital commerce." Regardless of what you call it, the landscape is definitely changing and will continue to change in the foreseeable future, in ways we can hardly imagine from our current vantage point. As with any frontier, you never know what lies over the next horizon.

However, I think it is safe to say that we will see two important trends emerging as these new technologies penetrate farther into the marketplace. First, we will see an almost infinite number of "channels" emerge, which will eventually bring to the music business the sort of diversification that cable brought to the TV business. Remember, twenty years ago, if you wanted to produce a television program, you had only three places to go: ABC, NBC and CBS. Now there is a cable channel for every imaginable taste and special interest.

Likewise, with radio, there are only a dozen or so formats, as defined by the various charts in *Billboard*. That's it—either your music conforms to one of those charts, or it doesn't get played. The multiplicity of channels made possible by the Internet can circumvent those constraints.

More importantly, the Net not only increases the number of channels to infinity, it also shortens the distance between the artists and their audience. For example, there are already a couple of sites on the Web that act as huge jukeboxes, with direct connections to the artists' home pages. Tune in, listen, and when you hear something you like, you click an icon that is linked to the artist's home page and order the CD online.

You can do the math on that yourself and see that what I'm talking about has implications at every level of the music business: artists, labels, distributors, retailers. Right now, the music business is controlled not by the artists or their audience, but by those intermediaries. As the new technologies command more attention, the control is going to shift back to the artists and the audience.

Q. What new technologies are we talking about here?

A. There are two systems that have converged in the past two years to create something entirely new. The first is the home-based, high-speed, multimedia-capable desktop computer. Sales of these computers, complete with CD-ROM drives, sound cards, speakers and enhanced video capabilities, have dwarfed every other segment of the computer industry.

The second piece of this puzzle is a vast, global data-transmission network called the Internet. Add to the system I just described a device called a modem, and you have the ability to retrieve virtually any kind of information with your computer, including sound and pictures. Together, these two systems have begun to merge into a new medium, the true nature of which we are only beginning to grasp. It's like an egg has been laid here, and we're all waiting to see just what manner of beast will emerge when it hatches.

Q. The Internet is certainly a buzz word these days. It seems we can't pick up a magazine or newspaper without reading about it. Just what is the Internet, anyway?

A. Strictly speaking, the Internet is a "network of networks." Its origins stretch back to a Defense Department project in the '60s that was intended to decentralize military command and control operations. In the '70s and '80s, this network was reconfigured and expanded to connect hundreds of university, national laboratory and government mainframe computers to a huge data internetwork. That network has evolved into what we now know as the Internet. But in the past few years, with the emergence of the World Wide Web, the Net has evolved from mere data transmission into a communications and entertainment system the likes of which the world has never seen before.

Q. But how did that network become a way to market music?

A. For the first twenty years of its existence, the Net was pretty much the exclusive domain of pocket-protector types who exchanged information about quantum physics and exotic computer languages. But its presence on university campuses gave rise to a wide range of bulletin-board-like discussion groups that deal with everything from art to zoology. These discussion groups eventually became a major subsection of the Net called UseNet and were the first step in the popularization of the Internet.

Q. And this is where music marketing on the Net started?

A. Where it started, yes, because with the UseNet *newsgroups*, as they're called, people started to create discussion groups about their favorite bands and recording artists. There are discussion groups for everybody from the Beatles and Beethoven to Springsteen and Metallica. But in this context, *marketing* is really a misnomer. Nobody was really promoting their music through these channels; interested fans were just using this means to discuss artists they were already familiar with.

Actual, promotional marketing became possible with the emergence of another subdomain of the Net, the World Wide Web. The Web is this marvelous new technology that comes darn close to making "all information, all the time" a reality. And much of that information takes the form of sound and pictures, which presents a whole new world of opportunities for independent musicians.

Q. How has the World Wide Web changed things?

A. The Web makes the Internet a consumer medium, with its own graphical user interface. But that's just the beginning. In just the past year, the previously silent network has been given sound.

When we started the National Online Music Alliance (NOMA) in 1995, there was no real-time sound on the Net. If you wanted to hear a sound file, you had to wait in silence for the entire file to download before you could listen to it. That could take five, ten, maybe fifteen minutes to retrieve just a couple minutes of sound.

But now we have what is called *streaming* audio, which in effect begins playing a file as it is still being received. The result is real-time audio, or *audio on demand*, and it changes everything, because it makes it possible to provide real audio-based entertainment on the Net. We have now entered the era of "desktop broadcasting" where everybody can have their own "radio station" sending programming around the world.

When the technology first surfaced, the quality was pretty poor, about as good as the sound you get stretching string between two tin cans. But the quality has improved steadily and dramatically—and quickly. As this is written, the newest technologies can deliver near FM radio quality over a 28.8KB modem connection. But that information will probably be obsolete by the time your readers read this. I'm sure something new will surface next week.

Q. What about CompuServe and America Online? Are they part of the Internet?

A. In a sense, yes. You might consider America Online and CompuServe, as well as Prodigy and a few other services, "neighborhoods" within a larger, global community. Those services can provide the neophyte with an excellent introduction into this strange new world. Their services are more organized and more structured than the Net itself and make it easier for a newcomer to find his or her way around.

The actual Internet is considerably less structured, to the point that it borders on global "info-anarchy." The structure is much harder to discern, and there is *so* much information out there—with more becoming available every day—that there is a learning curve involved in finding the information you want.

In an effort to maintain their subscriber base, all three of the major services have added access to the World Wide Web for their subscribers. So the Web audience is still growing exponentially. And now Microsoft, the Goliath of the personal-computer industry, has launched its own online network with Internet access. Some industry watchers have suggested that as many as a hundred million more people could be cruising down the information highway by the end of this decade.

Q. What can we expect from our computers in connection with album and artist marketing in the next five years?

A. You want to know about five *years* from now in a business where it's impossible to predict what might evolve in five *months*! About twenty years ago, Alvin Toffler first described the condition he called *Future Shock*, where the rate of change in our society becomes so rapid that no one can keep up. That has never been truer than it is today, especially in the area we're talking about. Not only is the rate of change accelerating, but it seems at times that the rate of acceleration is accelerating!

The World Wide Web is a perfect case in point. Three years ago it didn't exist. Today, virtually every corporation and business interest in the world is trying to define and create their presence on the Web. You don't see a TV commercial nowadays that doesn't display a Web site address before the final fade-out. We're witnessing the electronic equivalent of the Oklahoma land rush, or, if you will, the second Big Bang.

But for the music industry, high-fidelity real-time audio could well be the asteroid that destroys the dinosaurs.

Q. What difference will real-time audio make?

A. It really is a whole new ball game. Because you'll be able to use your computer like a radio, only you'll have hundreds, thousands, maybe *millions* of stations to choose from! You won't be limited to what the taste makers at big radio stations dictate in their endless effort to assemble the largest possible audience.

Remember your lessons from Big Media 101: The purpose of big media is not to deliver programming to its audience. Radio is in business not to deliver music to its listeners but to deliver the audience to its advertisers. How else can you explain the push for the highest ratings, the largest audience?

But all that changes when each member of the audience has the ability to seek out the music he or she wants to listen to and have it delivered into their receiver right *now*. The market is no longer supply driven, it's demand driven. That's a major paradigm shift.

Q. OK, so you've painted the big picture. Can you narrow it down to what it means for an artist or band trying to make a living from their music?

A. Well, Jana, I honestly believe you are the right person to be asking that question because you are a prime example of how an artist—a musician, a speaker, a performance artist—has to consider new possibilities in order to find an audience and earn their living. When you gave up your big-media-induced hallucination about becoming a "star," you liberated yourself to become an artist. And I think that's the example that artists in the future are going to have to live by.

So the first change is a metaphysical one that performers are going to have to find within themselves—to cast off the delusion of stardom and proceed as a professional performer. Then they can begin to use computer-mediated marketing as one component of an overall marketing program.

Q. And how would they use the computer for that?

A. There are basically two ways to use a computer in your marketing. You can use it to promote yourself, i.e., make your music accessible to a wider audience, or to gather information about your audience and your markets. Let's take the second example first.

Let's suppose you want to plan a tour in, say, New England. Where can you play? What sort of venues can you find that offer the kind of music you play?

Just recently, a man named Scott Russell finished compiling the Folk Venue Database Version 1.0. This is a listing of over forty-two hundred venues in North America that offer acoustic music in all its broadly defined forms, including contemporary folk, traditional folk, blues, bluegrass, Cajun, Celtic, African, etc.

Right now, this database exists in the form of a huge file that can be downloaded from America Online and CompuServe, or off the Web (http://www.hidwater.com), and sorted, using commercially available software, by region, type of music, room size—whatever criteria you select. So you could, in effect, query the database for the names, addresses, phone numbers and contact names of all the venues within 250 miles of Boston. And the program will give you a list of those venues.

Armed with such a list, you can very easily focus your marketing by geographic area. So, let's say you succeed in setting up a dozen dates in the area. Assuming you are adequately equipped, the next thing to do is get on the World Wide Web and find a site called Musi-Cal (http://www.calendar.com), which is a calendar and database of music events around the country. It's sort of the flip side of the Folk Venue database, in that it's designed for audience queries.

As an artist with an itinerary, you go into Musi-Cal and enter the dates and locations where you will be performing. Using the example I used before, you might go in and ask, "Who's playing this weekend within 250 miles of Boston?" Or you could ask, "Where is Jana Stanfield playing in the next thirty days?" And the program will print out a listing. It's really a very elegant program and could become the focus of the live-performance business in months if not years to come.

Q. Beyond simply listing my performance dates in a database, can I actually promote myself with a computer?

A. Yes, you can, but first a word of caution is in order. Marketing on the Internet is still controversial; it is an art and science still very much in its infancy. The rules are still being defined. But there is one rule that has clearly emerged: Hype—as we have all come to know and love it— just does *not* work in these circles. This is not a broadcasting medium where a mass audience is constantly being exhorted to buy-buy-buy. The Internet is, first and foremost, a communications medium. The traffic goes two ways. It's hard for hype to survive in that kind of environment.

Q. So, if hype doesn't work, what does?

A. The answer, in a word, is buzz. When a new artist begins to find an audience, you'll hear about it on the Net. There are mailing lists and discussion groups where people discuss their common interests. The discussion groups are like giant, global electronic bulletin boards; the mailing lists are participatory, electronic newsletters.

When a new artist begins to reach an audience, you'll hear about it in discussion groups and mailing lists. Perhaps the best example is Dar Williams, who some have called "The Darling of the Internet." Dar has an enormous following on the Net, and I bought her CD without having heard any of it because I had been reading so much about her in the newsgroups and mailing lists.

Q. Can you be more specific about these mailing lists and newsgroups?

A. In the acoustic/folk music arena, the nuclear center of it all is a mailing list called the F_M Digest which is moderated by Alan Rowoth from some mysterious place in upstate New York. Alan publishes an electronic newsletter which is distributed by e-mail daily. If you have any kind of Internet access at all, either a direct Net connection or through a service like CompuServe, you can subscribe to the F_M Digest by sending a message to: listserv@nysernet.org, with the message "SUBSCRIBE FOLK_MUSIC *Your Full Name*." The next day, you'll start getting a daily digest of messages from all over the world, with reviews, performances, albums and discussions of emerging artists, as well as familiar ones. That's a good place to begin your education. A couple months of the F_M Digest and you'll begin to understand the full scope of what's going on around the country.

On the newsgroup side of the equation, the parallel to the F_M Digest is called rec.music.folk. But whatever your specific area of interest, you'll find a newsgroup somewhere devoted to it.

Q. Are mailing lists and news-groups a good way to promote myself?

A. They can be an effective way of simply letting people know you exist, but like I said before, you want to avoid a lot of hyperbole.

Probably the most effective way to promote yourself, to give a curious audience a more thorough idea of what you are really about, is through a site on the World Wide Web. Already, hundreds of artists are creating home pages that include everything from press clippings and biographical sketches to photos and actual sound clips from their recordings.

But it's not enough to simply create a home page for yourself and put it out on the Net; you have to do something to draw people into your site. And with the vast and rapidly increasing number of sites out there, that's no easy trick.

The service I operate, the National Online Music Alliance, was created to draw together a pool of musicians to create a unified site that could promote them, and support the effort through direct sales of CDs and tapes. We are also developing our own Internet radio station that not only plays a continuous program of music by NOMA artists but provides direct links to the artists' home pages and our virtual record store, where CDs and tapes can be purchased online with credit cards.

You need two things to get attention, which I call *mass* and *focus*. By mass I mean you need to be part of a larger presence, to be affiliated with other similar artists within a single site. In a sense, it's like Newtonian physics: The more mass your site has—the "gravitational pull" it generates—the more people get pulled in to see what you have to offer.

By focus I mean that your site, in addition to having a fair number of participants, should have a clearly defined focus. With NOMA, our focus is clearly the independent singer-songwriter. It started as a Nashville-based operation, but the scope of the operation expanded quickly to include artists from all over the country, so we changed the name from "Nashville" to "National." But the focus remains on the singer-songwriter, as exemplified by the vast pool of relatively unrecognized talent that simmers just beneath the surface of Nashville's more familiar country-music industry.

Finally, there is no substitute for active promotion, through whatever means and channels are appropriate without pegging the hype meter. Unlike some services that just put up home pages, we are actively engaged in the promotion of our site and our artists. We're doing benefits, promotions, giveaways, and we've created an interesting, interactive site that provides some entertainment in its own right.

Q. Some of us (or maybe I was the only one) didn't pay attention when this whole computer thing started. What basic equipment will we need in order to catch up?

A. Basically all you need is a computer and modem, which is a device that attaches to or is built into the computer and enables it to send and receive data over normal telephone lines.

For a traveling musician, I highly recommend a laptop or notebook-type computer. The power in these little things is just amazing, and the prices are pretty reasonable. I realize that $1,500 may sound a bit rich for your average itinerant troubadour. But for maintaining and promoting your career, the computer is every bit as essential a piece of gear as your guitar, and these days a good wood guitar costs at least that much. But when you consider all that today's computers can do, it's almost indispensable.

Take booking for example. A lot of venues now have e-mail accounts as well as Internet sites, so a lot of booking correspondence can be handled through those channels. And a home page can in many cases substitute for mailing out expensive press kits and CDs. If the venue you're soliciting has Web access, just invite them to visit your home page, read your bio and press clips, and listen to the music. Do that a couple dozen times and you've more than paid for the cost of your home page.

Using contact-management software like Act! or Microsoft Schedule +, an artist can easily maintain their database of venues and keep track of which ones they've contacted, which have been sent tapes and press kits, which have booked them and which shows have been well received. You can easily maintain a mailing list, manage your itinerary, juggle your books. There are even electronic rhyming dictionaries that could expedite your songwriting.

I'll rattle off some technical specifications here, which may be foreign to some, but it'll provide a benchmark of what to look for when you start shopping. These specs apply to the Intel/Windows platform. I strongly discourage people from buying a Macintosh-based computer these days. Especially since Windows 95 was released, I don't see that the Mac offers any advantages over the Intel/Windows platform; the Mac's share of the market has shrunk to the point that new programs for the Mac are very slow to come to market. I'm sure some people will take exception with these sentiments, but I firmly believe the Macintosh is the Betamax of the '90s. What's a Betamax, you say? My point precisely.

1. CPU (that's central processing unit—the brains in the computer) should be no less than an Intel Pentium processor running at at least 90MHz.

2. RAM (random-access memory—the working memory) should be at least 8MB and preferably 16MB if you're running Windows 95.

3. At least 800MB of hard-disk storage (the permanent memory, where all the programs and files you create are stored).

4. An internal modem running at a minimum of 28.8KB/sec.

5. Some kind of SoundBlaster-compatible audio card (preferably the SoundBlaster itself, since it's a de facto standard).

6. CD-ROM drives are nice, especially since they double as an audio CD player.

7. Look through your local press and find a *local* Internet service provider (ISP) for your primary Internet connection. Nowadays, you can

subscribe to a local service for less than \$20 per month, which in many cases provides unlimited access, along with an e-mail address and all the software you'll need to log on, send and receive e-mail, and surf the Web.

8. Assuming you're running Windows 95 (or its latest descendant), I also suggest you sign up for the Microsoft Network (MSN), which comes built into the operating system. It may seem redundant to have both a local ISP and MSN, but you'll discover the advantage if you ever take your computer traveling with you. MSN has hundreds of phone numbers that provide access for the cost of a local call all over the country. MSN is actually a large, nationwide ISP; once you've logged on to MSN, you can use your regular e-mail software to retrieve e-mail from your local ISP server. You can't do that with America Online, CompuServe or any other online service. Of course, you could choose to use MSN as your ISP, but I generally recommend going with a local service for the majority of your online services and using the big networks like MSN only when you're traveling.

Q. What advice would you give to an artist who is working to find an audience for his or her music?

A. The short version? Sign on with NOMA, then get yourself a laptop and a modem . . . and hit the road.

Q. How can people reach you with questions? Of course, they'll understand when you charge them a fee for your excellent advice.

Paul Schatzkin, President
National Online Music Alliance
848 Mountain Valley Dr.
Nashville, TN 37209
(615)256-7121
e-mail: perfessr@songs.com
Web address: http://songs.com

CHAPTER TEN

TAKING CARE OF BUSINESS

SCHEDULING ALL THOSE UPCOMING GIGS

Even if you have no gigs yet, start visualizing them and planning for them. To do this, you need to buy a few things. All of them are cheap and easy to find at an office-supply store. Here's what you'll need:

- A Plan-A-Month calendar. It's a big wall calendar that's about 3' × 2', and it's best to buy the laminated one so you can mark on it with a dry-erase marker.
- Three dry-erase markers, one in red, one in blue and one in black.
- Colored dots. I use Avery ¾" Round Color-Coding Labels. Buy at least 250 of each dot color and get them in black, green, yellow, red, dark blue and pink. If you can't find all these colors, just make sure you get green ones, and then get five other colors of your choice.

With this wall calendar, you can see the whole year at a glance. (When I first started, all I needed was a "decade at a glance.") Don't worry, you will start filling it. Here's how we distribute the dots:

- Green dots are for income-producing dates.
- Black dots are for travel. Whether you're traveling for family events or gigs, these dots cannot be booked.
- Yellow dots are dates that are on hold but not fully booked yet.
- Red dots are for free gigs.
- Blue dots are for education days, like seminars and conferences.
- Pink dots are for personal days.

Let's fill in the dates you know first, so it starts to look full. Start with the personal days like family holidays, your daughter's homecoming pageant and the play-off game your husband hopes his team gets to go to. Now fill in all the other dates you know, with the necessary travel dates blocked out around them.

The markers are the fun part. First, estimate the amount of money you need to live on each month. Write it in blue on an open space for each month of the calendar. Think about how many tapes or CDs you need to sell each week or each month to make that amount. How many gigs would it take to sell that many units? If your ratio of gigs to album sales is like mine, it will be one-third fees and two-thirds album sales. How much do you need to make in performance fees to make it one-third of your monthly income and be able to sell two-thirds of your income in albums afterward?

It may feel overwhelming to think about how much you need to sell and/or get paid to make your money through your music every month, and it may seem impossible. Don't be discouraged. In working out how much you want and need, then figuring out what it will take to earn that amount, you are visualizing it. Visualization is powerful. We've all heard the phrase, "I'll believe it when I see it." Author Wayne Dyer has a book called *You'll See It When You Believe It*. I have visualized things I couldn't even get the courage to believe in, and they came true. It will happen to you if you can just be open to it.

The black marker is for money you make. On each green dot, use a pen or pencil to estimate the amount of money you think you'll make from that engagement. When you get back from the gig, use the black marker to write in the exact amount, and revise the month's total to reflect the current amount. Your goal will be to meet and then exceed the amount you need per month. Keep a running total; this will be encouraging.

The red marker is for business-related expenses. Keep a running total of that, too. This will give you a visual image each month of how much you are spending, how much you are making and how much you need to make to break even or get ahead. If this number is larger than what you're making, you can set a goal of bringing it down and you can see your results.

Hang the calendar where you can see it while you make booking calls. If you don't have enough action in a certain month, you can see that from three months out, and it will give you the incentive to make those calls and get some dots up.

In the beginning, I told myself I would do whatever it took to make the necessary dollar amount every month, even if I had to go work some hours at Taco Bell. The thought of me in a Taco Bell outfit gives me the push I need to start creating some gigs when I see there's going to be too much month at the end of the money.

This calendar method will accomplish many things:

• It will give you a visual goal to shoot for every day, every week and every month.

- It will give you a sense of whether you're spending more or making more.
- It will spur you to action when you need to get the courage to make some booking calls.
- Once you start seeing that dollar amount climb for the amount you've made every month, it will no longer be a matter of "How much do I need?" It will become a competition with yourself to see just how much you can make. It starts to be fun.
- It will give you a feeling of progress and pride in what you're accomplishing.

KEEPING TRACK OF DETAILS

You'll need at least three books to keep track of your bookings. These books will be three-ring binders to hold your presentation sheets and all the other information about each gig.

Presentation Sheets

Make up a form that has a lot of fill-in-the-blanks to keep track of your clients and potential clients. I call these *Presentation Sheets*, and I have included a sample. Every time you perform, keep a record of the details. This will help you remember pertinent information about the group for future reference and will help a lot if you want to play there again.

Starting with the name of the person to contact about the booking, fill in all the information you'll need to put them on your mailing list. If the person is a potential client, get all the information you can about the event. Get the date and find out whether they have a sound system. Find out what kind of people will be there, what the age range is and whether or not it will be predominantly men, women or an evenly mixed group. Find out how dressy the event will be.

Learn everything you can about what they want before you talk about money. Let them visualize how the event will look before you hit them with your fee. Most important: Write down the fee you quote them. Sometimes people call back months or years after you first spoke with them, and it will be important to remember all the details.

Once you get the job, fill in the directions to the location, the amount of time they want you to play, and whether there is a certain time they absolutely want you to stop or whether your quitting time is open ended.

Use these sheets to keep track of promotional materials you mailed. If you mailed them a promotional copy of your cassette or CD, write it down so that you don't accidentally duplicate your efforts. Press kits and albums are too expensive to mail out twice to the same person.

If you are mailing albums to the engagement, make sure to note how many boxes you mailed, so you can call ahead to make sure they all got *a nicer word for "gig"* ———→ PRESENTATION INFORMATION

Today's Date _____ Presentation Date _____

Organization/Company _*Who is sponsoring or hiring you?*_____

all this will go in your data-base {

Phone # _____ Fax # _____

Address _____

Contact Name _____ in Audience _*Expected #*_____

Referred By _____ Audience Age _____ M/F Ratio_____/_____

Location of Presentation/Directions _____

(Start time)↓   *(How long do I play)*
Presentation Time _____ Length _____ Title *(or theme)*_____

↱ *I send out a list of my equipment needs but bring my own for an added fee*
→ P.A. System Required? Y   N   Boom Stand? Y   N   Regular Stand? Y   N

Fee Quoted _____ Deposit _*usually 1/3*_ Received ____*Balance paid at performance.*____

Expenses Paid? Y   N   Tape/CD Sales Permitted? Y   N   Mailed Contract _____

Promotional Materials: _____
                        Press Release *Poster* *Did we send them a promo copy of one of these?*↰
Broch   Fact   P Rel   Photo   Post   JS (T)   SLL (T) (CD)   Exp (T) (CD)↰

Ride (T) (CD)   Faves (T) (CD)   Product (Shipped) or Carried ← *Circle one*

This helps in tracking late boxes↱
Shipping Agent _*UPS or USP?*_ #of Boxes _____, Cost _____, Date _____

Return Agent _____ #of Boxes _____, Cost _____, Date _____

How many shipped vs. How many sold

Available		Sold	Available		Sold
_____	Exp (T)	_____	_____	Ride (T)	_____
_____	Exp (CD)	_____	_____	Ride (CD)	_____
_____	SLL (T)	_____	_____	Faves (T)	_____
_____	SLL (CD)	_____	_____	Faves (CD)	_____
_____	JS (T)	_____			

Product Sales _____ Tithe _____ Tithe Mailed _____ Total Earned _____

ACT _____

Attire _*People will notice if you wear the same outfit next year. I've done it, so I know.*_

there. I used to make a big mistake. Sometimes I used United Parcel Service (UPS), and sometimes I used the U.S. Postal Service. I often forgot which one I used and couldn't track my boxes if they weren't there. That was embarrassing as well as inconvenient. I now write down the shipping agent on the sheet. I write down what day they were mailed, too, so I can track them down if they don't arrive on time.

In addition to all the other mailing information, write down what it cost you to mail them out. This will help you measure your expenses against profits. If you don't sell out and you need to mail product back, add that price to the sheet. Again, make note of what mailing service was used.

After the job, write down what you wore. Those people stared at your clothing for an hour or so, and they will notice if you happen to wear the same thing next time.

Booking repeat business takes only a fraction of the effort required to book something for the first time. With everything you need to know about an engagement all in one place, you can easily rebook the same gig at the same time of year, year after year. Keeping your presentation sheets and everything that goes with them will make this easy to do.

Place each presentation sheet in a transparent plastic sheath. The official name for these is top-loading sheet protectors, and you can get them at any office-supply store. Anything that has to do with this gig can be slipped into the plastic sheath, along with your presentation sheet. Any receipts you collect for gas or food on your way to and from the event can be stored in here. After the gig, you can put your song list in with the presentation sheet. Maybe you'll want to sing the same songs again next time, or maybe you won't. Either way, you'll know what you sang before.

For each gig, write down anything unusual or unexpected that you experienced. If there were any unexpected things, like an awful sound system, a woman who went into labor during your performance, or a thunderstorm that turned off the electricity, take note so you can refer to it next time. In my notes, I usually jot down information about what the venue looked like and what the sound system was like so I can be prepared for it next time.

When you're first making your living from your albums, you may not think you'll ever forget each gig. I hope your career will move so fast that you can't keep up.

Book One: Potential Clients

The first book will be for potential bookings. When you have made a contact that might develop into a gig, make a presentation sheet with the basic information like their phone number, address, who to contact and when the gig might take place.

Keep your sheets in order according to the probability that you'll get the gig, or you can organize them by the dates you're negotiating for. Obviously, the closest dates will be at the front of the book with dates that are further out at the back. Every Monday morning, or whatever day you choose, go through the book and call anyone who needs to be called.

Book Two: The Bookings Book

When a potential booking turns into an actual engagement, move the presentation sheet to the second book, which is the bookings book. Organize the book with your next gig at the very front, and the other gigs in order by date. In the sheath now you'll also put your letter of agreement. If you mail product to the gig, you'll put that information in the sheath, too.

Go through the bookings book once a week, too, leaving self-stick notes to yourself about things like the date you need to book airline tickets for the gig and the date you need to mail your albums out in order to take advantage of cheaper rates.

Take notes on the presentation sheet if anything changes before the event happens. They may change the time at the last minute or even the location. There may be a special birthday they want you to acknowledge during the concert. Keep track of all this by keeping it in one place: on that presentation sheet.

If people mail you material about the town you're going to or about the place where you'll be playing, keep that in the sheath. Some might even mail you a map. Keep everything there that you'll need when it's time for the show. When it's time to leave the office, you can lift that sheet out and carry it with you. I usually put a printed introduction in, just in case the person introducing has lost the one I mailed to them.

Letter of Agreement

People are sometimes a little nervous about contracts. Their fear of signing something that could cause them problems later often causes them not to sign at all. There's a better way to show the terms of your agreement with the person who has hired you. This method works well because it doesn't scare either party.

Before you finish the phone call in which you book the engagement, tell the person you're talking to that you're going to jot down all this information in a letter. This will not be a contract but a letter of intent or letter of agreement. Tell the person who has booked you that if he agrees that you have accurately reflected what you talked about for the job, he can sign it and send it back. If there's anything left out, he can add it to the letter before signing it.

If the person you're talking to is apprehensive about the letter, you can assure him that this will not be a binding contract but will serve as a reminder to both parties of what is expected from your performance. Be sure to ask in your letter of agreement that the person booking you will write you a recommendation telling what they liked best about your performance.

As soon as you get off the phone after booking the engagement, write the letter detailing what you talked about. Include fee, date, time, place and any other pertinent information. Send two copies. Sign and date both, leaving a blank for the person to sign it and send it back. Mention in the letter that the person can add his own notes if any of the information needs to be changed. At the end of the letter, write, "Please keep one copy for your files, and return the signed copy to me by _____ in order to hold the date on my calendar. The date will not be considered 'held' until this letter is signed and returned."

Some artists ask for a one-third deposit to hold the date on their calendar. Although there's not much chance you will double-book that day without the deposit, there's a good chance they'll cancel the event at the last minute. This happens sometimes when the organizers fear there won't be enough people for the event or when they think they haven't done enough to promote it. If you haven't received a deposit, they have nothing to lose if they cancel at the last minute. On the other hand, if they have already sent you a deposit, they will have the incentive to do the promotion needed to get people there.

Book Three: Completed Bookings

When each gig is completed, file the entire sheath, filled with the presentation sheet, the product sales sheet and any other information you acquired, in the third book, which is the completed-bookings book. This will be a handy reference for rebooking the same groups and will also provide valuable information. You may find, after it's all said and done, that it cost you more to get to a presentation (product shipping, airline tickets, rental car, meals and time away from home) than you made. In that case, it will be important to raise your fee for next year.

If people from that group write to you or mail you a gift, keep their letters in the plastic sheath with the rest of the information. Also make a note about what that person looked like, if you can put a face to the name. When you're traveling to so many new places, it's easy for the faces and names to get separated from one another.

I really felt bad when I arrived in Atlanta to play at a place I had played before and found myself in an awkward spot. In my rush at the sales table, I saw a woman I recognized and asked if she could help me. She was a great help, and I remembered that she had helped me before and that I really liked her. What I *didn't* remember is that she was the person who, after that previous Atlanta appearance, sent me a beautiful beaded scarf. I not only forgot to bring and wear the scarf when I returned to Atlanta, but I couldn't remember which person there had given it to me. I had sent her a note when I received it but was embarrassed that hours went by before I thanked her in person because I couldn't connect the gift and the name.

When you're heading back to play the same venue for a second or third time, look at your notes from your previous concerts there. In many places where I play, there will be a young teenage girl who hangs on every word and wants to be a singer someday. My heart goes out to them, because each one reminds me of me when I was their age. If I have time to make a connection with the girl, I'll often offer to let her sing a song with me next time I come to town. I *do not* want to forget this, because it would be so disappointing for her after she has practiced with my albums and told her friends that she's going to sing with me when I come back. You can remember things like this a lot easier if everything from each gig is kept together in your plastic sheath and you can review it before you go back.

At the end of every year you'll need a new book. After you've done this for a year, you will have your potential-client book, your bookings book and your completed-bookings book. In January of each year, start a new book to keep track of completed bookings so that each year's presentation sheets have their own books. Keep the sheets in order by date and the three-ring binders in order by year, so you can locate a sheet quickly just by remembering the year. If you'd like to keep all this in files instead of books, that will certainly work, but I hope you'll have so many presentation sheets that you can't hold them all in a file.

Reconciliation Sheets

After each trip, fill out a reconciliation sheet. These can either be kept in the completed-bookings book or you can keep them in a file so you can see all of them together. Since I usually do my sheets by trip, I keep them in a file.

Let's all be honest here and admit that when we are first making music, we don't care if it costs more than we make. We do it because we love it. In the second stage of a music career, we are striving to get ahead and are completely thrilled if we break even. In the third stage of our careers, we want to get ahead because we know there are lean months, and we don't want to have to spend those lean months flipping burgers to pay the bills. In the fourth stage, getting ahead means putting money away for the future, for a new house, for the kids' college education.

No matter which stage you're in, it's important to know whether you're falling short, breaking even or getting ahead. Filling out reconciliation sheets for your gigs can help you do that.

You can fill out the sheets either by job or by trip. For example, if you go to Seattle for a week, you can add all the fees together and subtract all the expenses to get your Seattle total. Some cities are expensive to fly to, so you may find out when you get back that a week in those cities is not cost effective. Airfare to Denver can cost $500 to $650, so you'll need some high-paying gigs if you want to play there.

To fill out the sheet by gig, divide the airfare by the number of gigs you

JOB RECONCILIATION

Client   _____

Location   _____

Gig Date   _____

INCOME   (total = $ _____)

fee	$ _____	cash	$ _____
album sales	$ _____	checks	$ _____
t-shirt sales	$ _____	credit card	$ _____
book sales	$ _____		
misc	$ _____ (bumper stickers, etc)		

EXPENSES   (total = $ _____)

airfare	$ _____
gas	$ _____
car rental	$ _____
shuttles/taxis	$ _____
lodging	$ _____
food	$ _____
tips	$ _____
commission (agent)	$ _____
preshow mailer	$ _____
product shipping	$ _____
incidental cash items	$ _____
other	$ _____

ADDITIONAL BENEFITS (other than financial)

TOTAL PROFIT $ _____

(income minus expenses)

played. That number goes in the airfare slot for each gig. Do the same with lodging, car rental, gas and product shipping.

Tracking Album Sales

There are several reasons for keeping track of how many albums you sell at each performance. It will help a lot at tax time, and it will also help in other ways. By looking at which albums sold the most, you will begin to get a sense of what your audiences like the most from your shows. You'll get a sense of where you sell more CDs and where you sell more cassettes. I find I sell more CDs in large cities, more cassettes in smaller towns. This is helpful when I'm planning how much product to haul or mail to a performance.

When you mail your product out in advance for performances out of town, you'll want to know how many to send. If you are playing for the second time at the same location, you can look back and see how many albums you sold last time. This will give you a good indication of how many to send this time. If the audience bought a large quantity of one album, they'll probably want you to play songs from that album so they can sing along.

One way to keep track of how many of each album you sold at a show is to buy several colors of stick-on dots. Put red dots on all of one kind of album and blue dots on another kind. Some people write the album prices on each dot. As each album is sold, take the dot off and stick it on a sheet of paper. At the end, you will have a record of how many you sold.

The drawback to this method is that people may pull the plastic off the album (with the dot still attached) and throw it away so you can sign the album. If you have someone helping you sell, they might forget to take dots off, and if you're anything like me, you'll be talking and hugging people and you'll forget to take dots off, too.

A system that has worked better for me is to let my cassette and CD cases do the counting. I buy the largest canvas cases I can find at local discount stores. I fill the cassette and CD cases to capacity, noting by rows how many I'm carrying of each album. After the gig, I put all the remaining product back in the row it came from. I measure how many I've sold of each one by counting the empty spaces.

Now that I have so many albums out, I can't carry enough of each one in my cases. This limitation pushed me to create a bookkeeping sheet that can be used by me or anyone who helps me sell.

Product-Sales Sheets

When you are ready for a system more advanced than colored sticky dots, create your own product-sales sheet. Make up a simple sheet (use the one on page 152 as an example) that will help you keep track of how much product you sold at each gig.

Put instructions on your sheet that will help your sales volunteers know what to do. Ideally, you arranged all your cassettes and CDs before the gig. Put out the same number of each one, just because it's easier to keep track that way. Count how many you put out and write it on the sheet. Let your volunteers know why you are doing this. If they need more, have them put out more in quantities of ten, putting " + 10" on the sheet next to the "10." When you are ready to leave, all you need to do is count how many are left, then subtract that number from the number you put out. This will tell you how many of each kind you sold.

The only challenge with this system is that it is important to make anyone who's helping you sell be aware that they don't pack everything away before you get a final count. Let your volunteer know how this works so they can handle it if you can't be right there. Ask one person to be in charge.

Often, people start buying while you're still onstage, and you can't be there to supervise. After the sales have been completed, you may notice that someone is "helping" you back at the stage area by putting away your guitar, cords and tuner. Since you'd rather do this yourself, so that nothing is misplaced or overlooked, you run to the stage to take care of that, and meanwhile, the sales volunteers are packing away your albums before doing inventory. Everyone is just trying to be helpful. This sheet will let sales volunteers know that they can be most helpful by counting how many cassettes and CDs are left in each stack so you can see how many sold.

CREDIT CARDS

Consider taking credit cards. People are much more likely to carry a credit card these days than they are to carry cash. If you take credit cards, you'll increase your sales, especially if people want to buy in large amounts.

After years of reluctance about taking credit cards, I am now a believer. At first I didn't apply because I thought I couldn't get approved to take them. It took numerous credit applications, a couple of weeks and a couple of different vendors before getting the OK. My bank, where I have a long history of good records, turned me down cold because I don't have a storefront. They couldn't approve me because I don't have a place where people can walk in and purchase cassettes and CDs. They referred me to another vendor with lower standards and higher rates.

The credit-card companies charge a fee to get you set up, and they charge a rental or purchase fee for the knuckle-busters, which are the metal plates with your company name, and electronic terminals that check credit-card numbers to give you instant approval. After that, they take a small percentage of the dollar amount you've sold.

I thought this would be so expensive that it wouldn't be worth it. I went ahead and bit the bullet, and we've been doing hundreds of dollars in monthly credit-card revenue ever since.

Here are some credit-card tips:

*********Jana Stanfield*********

Product List

Album title	Cassette or CD	# On table to start	# Remaining after event	# Sold
Jana Stanfield (black & white)	Cassette only	10 + 10	12	8
Stop, Look & Listen	Cassette	10 + 10	13	7
Stop, Look & Listen	CD	+10 10 + 10	4	26
I'm Not Lost, I'm Exploring	Cassette	10 + 10	6	14
I'm Not Lost, I'm Exploring	CD	+10 10 + 10	5	25
Enjoy The Ride	Cassette	10 + 10	2	18
Enjoy The Ride	CD	+10 10 +10	3	27
Playing Favorites	Cassette	10	5	5
Playing Favorites	CD	10	6	4
Cassette 5-Packs		5	1	4
CD 4-Packs		5	2	3
T-shirts		10	5	5
Books		5	1	4

Volunteers: Thank you for your help with sales. Inventory is easy with this system. This is all there is to it:

1. **Count # of each item out for sale. Enter in left column.**
2. **If we run out of one kind, put out ten more of the item we're out of and make note on chart.**
3. **At the end, count what's left. <u>PLEASE DO NOT PUT ALBUMS AWAY BEFORE COUNTING WHAT'S LEFT.</u>**
4. **Subtract the # of each item remaining from the # we started with for the total sold** of each kind.

Starting cash: ___$50___
Total at end: _____

• Shop for the best rates. Don't just compare the percentage they take from your sales dollars. Check their equipment rates and the rate they charge for charge-backs.

• Find out about their charge-back policy. Charge-back is what it's called when a customer says, "I never bought this." The money you got from that customer's credit card is charged back (deducted) from your account, along with a $10 to $25 handling fee. If you challenge it and produce the person's signed sales slip, you may get the money back for the product but could still be charged the handling fee.

• To avoid having customers say they never bought anything from you, make sure that the metal plate the company issues you has your name on the first line. If your record company is called Big Black Dog Productions, then "Big Black Dog" is what will show up on someone's credit-card bill. They call the credit-card company and say they never bought a big black dog. The company researches it, thus the handling fee. If the company who approves you insists on putting your company name on the first line of your metal plate, then take each credit-card slip and write your name on it, so they've got their receipt and you've got your copy in case of a challenge.

• Get people's phone numbers on the credit-card slips. This way, you can call them to say that "Big Black Dog" was really the albums they bought, and you can ask them to drop the credit-card challenge.

• Some artists charge a credit-card surcharge. If people want to buy by credit card, they have to pay a little extra to cover the percentage the artist pays.

• Think about the character of your customers. If you are getting a few hot checks already, you do not want to take on the expense of getting set up for credit cards without fully researching the idea. One artist I know has great customers and never got bad checks, but he's had three charge-backs in the past few months and he's wondering whether taking credit cards is worth the expense.

When considering which equipment to rent or buy, these are the options:

• Imprinter (nonelectronic): This is the swiping gizmo that imprints the credit-card number onto the slip. They usually cost less than $50 to purchase. You've probably seen the model that's commonly known as a knuckle-buster. These come in several sizes and shapes. One is about the size of a checkbook and comes with what looks like a Baskin-Robbins sample spoon to press onto the credit-card numbers.

• Electronic terminal: These need batteries or electricity and are much more expensive than the nonelectronic imprinters. They require a phone line because they approve or deny credit cards on the spot. As soon as you call the purchase in and it flashes "approved," the money is frozen in the customer's account. While the electronic option is costly, it can be paid per month (rental or purchase) and does have an important advantage. With the nonelectronic devices, you have to wait until you get home to submit the numbers, and by that time, the customer could've overspent the credit limit, leaving you with a worthless receipt.

• Phone setup: I tried to explain to the credit-card vendor that it would be hard enough to get an electrical outlet at my sales table and next to impossible to get a phone jack to go with it. "No problem," he says, "we'll rent you a cellular phone." As you can see, the electronic option can add up. I did not choose this option.

• Computer verification: The method I chose was a knuckle-buster and a computer program. With computer verification, they sell you a computer program that secures the amounts when you program them in from your home computer. We swipe the cards at the table, give customers a receipt, then program the numbers as soon as I get back. The computer program was $1,200, but in the long run (and I'm in this for the long run) it seemed less expensive than the rental or purchase of the other machines being offered. With phone orders, we can get approval before shipping product.

HOW TO GO FROM SEMI-EMPLOYED TO PRESIDENT OF A BUSINESS IN ONE DAY

More than anything else, these next two steps will empower you and help you see your music as a valid business endeavor:

1. Get business cards with your name and the name you will call your business. Under your name, put "President." There is a big difference between being an occasionally employed freelance musician and being the president of your own business.

2. Go to the bank and set up a separate account for your business. I ran the business out of my personal account for about two years, and everything began running better when I stopped doing that. The best thing about having separate personal and business accounts is you can see whether you're making a profit and you can make corrections as needed by spending less on the business and making more from it. Get separate checks, separate savings accounts and a separate credit card for the business. If you don't have a federal tax identification number, you can use your Social Security number. Tell your banker what you're doing and why. They can answer questions and advise you.

As you set this up, your banker can tell you about the tax forms you'll need to fill out to run the business. If they don't have the forms, they can tell you where to get them. The banker will tell you that you are going to pay more per month to have so many accounts and will try to get you to consolidate your money. It is true that you're paying a small fee to keep your money in separate piles, but to me it's worth it so I can also keep the money separate in my brain. Don't worry. No one at the printshop or the bank will check to see if your business is actually a pile of papers on your dining-room table.

ACCOUNTING FOR YOUR ART

There are great computer programs you can use to do your bookkeeping, your inventory, your billing and your taxes. These programs can do amazing things. If you enter the information into Quick Books Pro that you bought a thousand albums, it will subtract albums from the master inventory every time you bill someone and will alert you when it's time to reorder albums.

If you plan to take your music career seriously and you want it to grow into a business that supports you, I'd recommend going straight to Quick Books Pro or some other high-level bookkeeping software. I started out using Quicken, then Quick Books and now Quick Books Pro. If you begin with an inexpensive starter program like I did, you'll just have to spend time learning the better program later. Unless you enjoy reading manuals for new accounting software every year, spend more for a good program that your business can grow into.

If you'd rather do your bookkeeping on paper, there are some great books to help you with accounting for your art. To find one in a bookstore, don't go to the accounting section first. Go to the music business section. This way you can get a book written in your language instead of accountant-speak. These books answer all your questions about what tax forms you'll need and where to get them. Several even come in a workbook style with big envelopes to hold all your receipts. These are helpful and effective if you will use them.

If you think you can't do any of the bookkeeping yourself, look around for a freelance worker who can do that for you. This could be a bookkeeping service, an hourly worker who comes over twice a month to enter figures into your accounting program on computer, or just someone who organizes your receipts for you so you can do the rest. When I first moved to Nashville and was looking for additional hourly work, a woman hired me to put hundreds of receipts in order. She gave me a big bag of receipts, and I categorized them, first by years, then by other categories like advertising, office supplies and entertainment. Once I had the totals, she could take those totals to her accountant. When I started running my operation as a business, I paid someone per hour to do that same kind of organization for me. If you have a fifteen-year-old nephew who is trying to raise money for a car, get him to come over and organize piles of receipts on your floor.

"Should I Get an Accountant?"

Whether you do your bookkeeping on paper or computer, you still need to decide whether you want the help of an accountant when it comes to your taxes. To find a good one, ask musician friends who they use. You need someone who is familiar with your business. If you can't find an accountant who works with musicians, get one who works a lot with small businesses or freelance workers. The amount it costs to go to an accountant for financial advice will be only a fraction of all the money this person can save you in taxes. Some people say they can't afford an accountant. I don't know how anyone can afford *not* to have an accountant.

Accountants work on an hourly rate. Many offer free consultations for first-time customers. Let's say it costs $70 per hour after that. In your first visit, you can ask everything you ever wanted to know, plus the accountant can tell you what you need to bring and what you don't need to bring (like a trash bag full of receipts) to get your taxes done by him or her. Many accountants have handouts with blanks to fill in that give them the information they need for your taxes.

The first time I went to an accountant was the first time I had my taxes done when I was no longer employed full time on Music Row. At the same time I met with him about my taxes, I asked every question I could think of about running my own business. The accountant was very helpful. While they only officially charge for the hours you're in their office or they're doing your taxes, an accountant is also available for a quick question here and there over the phone.

An accountant can help you estimate how much you'll need to pay each quarter in self-employment tax. Most accountants will even give you little slips with the amount filled in for each quarter and envelopes to put your payment in.

Without an accountant to answer to in terms of keeping track of how much I spend and how much I earn, I probably wouldn't have any idea of those amounts. I probably wouldn't keep track of my receipts, wouldn't keep track of my income, and it would be difficult to estimate my taxes. For that reason, having an accountant is a good thing. An accountant makes one accountable.

If you can't think of any other reason to get an accountant, consider the time it will take you to do all the financial figuring yourself. Add that to the time you will spend procrastinating and feeling like garbage before you get it done. Wouldn't you rather pay someone to do it? This frees you up to do things that will bring in more income.

Taxes

At first, you may have another job while you get your music business going. Running a small business on the side just means that you fill out some extra tax forms along with your regular forms. You can ask your banker or an accountant, or you can get a book that will tell you which deductions you can take and which forms you'll need.

When you are self-employed, you'll need to estimate what you're going to make from the business and pay taxes quarterly. If you don't make as much as you thought, you get some of your money back. If you make more than you estimated, the IRS expects you to pay a penalty for the money you hand over. The hardest part about being self-employed is that the taxes are really steep. Still, it's worth it. When my taxes are high, I just look at it as a measure of a great quarter.

My records may not be perfect, but I do my best and get better every year. I find that keeping good records for my business is helpful. I like knowing how I'm doing and figuring out where I can improve. I report everything.

The reasons I choose to report everything are varied. First, obviously, I don't want to get audited. Second, I want to have a strong business. I have bills to pay. I want to have an accurate representation at all times of what is coming in and what is going out. I am proud of what I do, and I want everything to be on the up-and-up. I consider myself a small-business owner, and I want to be good at that, just like I want to be good at making music.

Royalties

Keeping track of how many albums you sell will help you pay your co-writers accurately. It is important for you to get permission from your co-writers on anything you record. Once a quarter, once every six months or once a year, figure your royalties and send them a check. The royalty rate often changes, so I won't list it here, but you can easily find the current rate by calling the BMI, ASCAP or SESAC office in any major music town.

I recommend paying your royalties as often as possible, so the checks seem small to you. I do a lot of co-writing. When I have twenty co-writers to pay from my five albums, those small checks can add up to a large amount if you don't pay regularly.

One easy way to keep track of how many albums you have sold is to ask the tape duplication facility to give you an annual printout of how many you have ordered. From these totals, you can estimate how many were promotional copies and how many were actually sold. Pay your royalties on the amount sold.

Using Credit Cards in Your Business

We all know that credit cards can be dangerous if they are used to buy what is beyond our means. If we can't pay it off every month, we end up paying huge percentage rates on the money we owe.

The only way to use credit cards safely in your business is to pay the entire bill each month. You can get an American Express card which requires this, or you can use a regular card and just do it.

Many of us believe it would be better if we never used credit cards, but unfortunately, it's pretty hard to rent a car without one. The credit card is needed because it gives the rental company some security that you'll bring the car back in one piece. If you're going to try to rent a car without a card, you'll need to call the rental company in advance to find out how much they need as a security deposit so you can take that amount with you in traveler's checks.

There is one big benefit to using credit cards, now that they have cards that award you frequent-flier miles for every purchase. If you know you have the money and will pay the bill off every month, you can use this card and get the miles. Just make sure you use the card only when you have the money to pay it off on time when the bill comes. When you reorder CDs, pay your accountant, buy a new printer or even pay the phone bill, you can use the card and get airline miles. Remember that the only way these miles will be free is if you pay that bill off on time every month. If you think you might let that bill slide for a month or two, by all means don't use the card. It's not worth the anxiety. Just pay full price for your airline tickets, and you'll come out ahead.

SETTING UP YOUR MAIL-ORDER OPERATION

A mail-order operation is easy to run. It starts with having order blanks made for your first album. When you're in situations where you can't sell albums, hand out order blanks. Be sure to note that discounts are available for large quantities. This way, if someone wants to buy ten copies and sell them to friends, you can provide them at a lower cost.

Many of your orders will come from people who bought an album and noticed inside how you promoted your other albums. At first, you can fill the orders yourself. Later, you might be willing to pay someone to take care of it for you. When people order by mail, put their addresses on your mailing list so you can let them know about future releases. Put an order form in with their order, in case they want to order more. I also include a bumper sticker and a little note thanking them for their support. I paste up these notes four or six to a page and copy them on a copier.

Be sure to charge a shipping-and-handling fee per item. I was so happy to get orders for the first few years that I paid the postage. With shipping product to gigs and mail order, my postage bill was outrageous. Now I charge $2 shipping and handling per item. Even though the postage may be less than that, the rest of the money goes for the bubble mailers and the time it takes to put packages together.

The only time I pay postage is when I have run out of product at a concert. In that situation, I take prepaid orders. People pay there, and I mail them the albums as soon as I get home. I used to keep up with this by using the mail-order cards. A person would write their name on the cards, and I marked what they wanted and that I had received the money, and then I put the cards in with the cash. Recently, I was very short on product at a concert, so I made up prepaid forms that were similar to order forms except they didn't have my address where they could be mailed in.

CHAPTER 11

STAYING ORGANIZED ON THE ROAD

HOW TO GET YOU, YOUR ALBUMS AND YOUR GEAR TO PERFORMANCES

At most discount stores, they sell cassette cases and CD cases covered with brightly colored, lightweight canvas. The CD cases generally hold thirty CDs and the cassette cases hold sixty. I like to keep my cassettes and CDs loaded into these. They are easier to carry into a gig than several cardboard boxes because they have shoulder straps. They also look less obtrusive than several cardboard boxes. You can carry them into places even where you're not going to have a sales table, just in case you have people who want to buy something. I carry a small case of my CDs and cassettes in my car, even when I'm not headed for a gig. I frequently run into people who say they want another album, so I've always got some available. My husband gives me a hard time about always having cassettes and CDs with me wherever I go. He says, "Honey, if you ever get asked to sing at a funeral, don't you think maybe instead of carrying tapes you could hand out order blanks?"

The important thing to remember is you never know when you'll run into someone who wants your album. Whether you have cassettes in your purse or order blanks in your pocket, be ready.

Mailing Product in Advance

When you first start out, you can carry your product in a suitcase if you're flying to a gig. Get suitcases that roll, because cassettes and CDs are heavy, especially if you're also going to be hauling your guitar and clothes. After a while, you'll either get tired of lugging all that luggage or you'll have so many albums to sell that they won't fit in the bags. That's when you'll need to start shipping.

Always ship at least a week in advance. This will save a whole lot of money. Make sure your product will arrive at the venue at least three days before you do. This way, you can call ahead and make sure it arrived. If it isn't there, you can track it down with the delivery service and make sure it is delivered on time.

If you are sending by UPS, pay a little bit extra to get a tracking number. I lost out on about a thousand dollars in product sales once in California because:

- I didn't realize you have to put in a special request for Saturday delivery.
- Even if your brother is a UPS guy like mine is, he can't help your CDs get there faster if you didn't get a tracking number so he can find your boxes in transit.

My boxes of CDs got there on the Monday after my big Saturday gig. I was headed for the airport when they arrived. I couldn't even ask the UPS person to send them back to me; they can't do that. I had to take possession of the boxes, drive to a San Francisco UPS location and pay to have them shipped back to me. In the end, I spent a fortune on shipping and had no sales.

If you're mailing three boxes, write "1 of 3" on the first box, "2 of 3" on the second box and "3 of 3" on the third box. Even though you will write down on your presentation sheet the number of boxes you'll be mailing, this will make it easy for whoever receives the boxes to make sure they're all there.

Always mail directly to the venue, not to the home or office of the person who booked you. If you mail to the person, there are two problems. First, you are requiring that person to load heavy boxes and bring them to the venue. Second, they might forget the boxes and arrive at your gig with nothing but apologies. Even though they can go back and get the boxes, this may put you behind in setting out your product table, and that always needs to be set out in advance.

Mail your boxes to yourself, in care of whoever is going to be responsible for them. If you mail them to another person, they might be forwarded on to that person's home address. You want them to stay at the venue where your show will be so they'll be waiting for you when you arrive. The best person to be responsible is someone who receives mail at the venue. This doesn't have to be anyone connected with the show. It could be the custodian of the building, as long as this person knows in advance what your boxes will look like, how many there will be and where to put them so they can be easily accessible when you get there.

Leave home with room in your suitcase, so you can carry unsold product home with you. After I mail the product out, I pack my empty canvas-covered tape and CD cases into my luggage. Use the cases to carry your product while on your trip so you don't have to haul it in cardboard boxes. When it's time to go home, you can load the remaining product into the cases, which already have a place in your luggage.

If you have waited too late to mail your boxes, and you are not sure they will arrive in plenty of time before the gig, take backup albums in your luggage. Load them into your cassette and CD cases. You don't need to carry enough for the entire trip, just enough for the first day or two until you think your boxes will arrive. If you fly with backup albums in your bags, check your baggage with the skycaps outside the airport. They don't use scales like they have at the ticket counter, and they are often less strict about bag weight. If they say your bag is too heavy and there is a $40 charge you have to pay at the counter, you can usually offer a $5 tip, and they'll go ahead and check it there.

Tips for Schlepping Guitars, Clothes and Product on a Long Tour
In the beginning, you'll have one album out, and you'll probably drive to most shows. Driving is usually the cheapest route, even if you're going several states away. Lots of performers choose to drive everywhere so they can haul their preferred sound gear with them. I don't like to be gone that long or drive that far, so I fly and rent cars for a week at a time. If you choose the flying/renting method, here are some ideas for making life easier on the road.

If you play guitar, invest $50 to $100 in a gig bag, which is a padded guitar case you can carry like a backpack. Make sure you get one that can hang like a hanging bag. On larger airplanes, you can carry it on and stow it overhead. Just make sure you sit under it so you can watch and make sure no one puts a metal briefcase on top of it and tries to use the door of the compartment as leverage for forcing the briefcase through the top of your guitar.

Here are some tips for flying with an instrument in a gig bag:
• Get to your gate as soon as possible, at least an hour before your flight leaves. This will be especially important on airlines like Southwest that board by numbers they hand out in order as you get to the gate. If the bins are full before you get on, it's hard to find space for a larger item.
• If your flight is going to be crowded, do your best to get on when they call for passengers who need assistance. Let the strollers and wheelchairs go first, and if anyone stops you, explain that it will be a lot easier to get everyone's bags in if you can put your guitar in first. If they won't let you board early, ask if they would at least take the guitar on now and put it in an overhead bin or closet. Remind them that it can hang like a hanging bag.

• Sympathy is your only hope, so be as cooperative as possible. Avoid getting in an argument because:

    a. The airline people will win.

    b. If you make them mad, they can put your bag down below and have gorillas stomp on it all the way to your destination.

    c. Your choices will be to either sign a release that says the airline doesn't have to pay you if they smash your guitar in the cargo area; buy a seat for your guitar; or get off the plane.

• Always check with your travel agent to see what size plane you're flying on. Anything smaller than a fifty-seater probably won't have an overhead bin large enough to accommodate a guitar. Some small planes have a cargo net where they can put fragile things in the cargo area, but don't count on it. For a smaller plane, carry your guitar in a hard-shell case.

For the rest of your gear, invest in the biggest, hard-shell rolling suitcase you can find and a roll-along (like the flight attendants use) that fits in the overheard compartments or under the seat.

Always take a larger suitcase than you need. On the way back home, you can fill it with unsold albums. This will save you the hassle of getting to a post office on your way out of town to ship your albums back home and will save you a lot of money on return shipping.

As you map out each trip to decide what gear to take, remember that there will be times at an airport when there will be no one available to help and no available carts. If you cannot single-handedly haul all your bags at once, part of your gear will remain unattended while you carry things out in shifts. If you have a gig bag on your back, you can carry two rolling bags. If you have your guitar in a hard-shell case, it's going to take up half your available hands. In the other hand, you can have a big hard-shell rolling suitcase.

If you leave room inside your big bag for product on the way home, put a hanging bag or small canvas bag inside the big suitcase on the outbound trip. This serves two purposes. First, with it inside the big bag, there's one less bag to keep up with at the airport. Second, if you're staying with friends, you can put your overnight gear in the small bag and leave the big bag in the trunk. If you have product to take home, you can check the small bag.

It may seem extreme to carry so much. Some of it will be sound gear, like wireless mics, pedals and effects boxes. Some of it will be your display gear, like cardboard stands, posters, signs for your table. Some of it will be empty space that you can fill with unsold product on the way home. The rest will be stuff that makes your trip more enjoyable, because you get to set up your tours to include places and friends you've been wanting to visit. You might have a pair of ski boots in your bags for Colorado, shorts and a swimsuit for southern New Mexico and a sleeping bag for a camping trip in south Texas. If you ski in Colorado at the beginning of a trip, you can mail your ski gear home so you don't have to lug it the rest of the trip.

Many artists have one bag loaded all the time with the things they'll need at each gig. For me, this is the black roll-along like the flight attendants use. It has pockets for all the things I need. In the front lower pocket, I keep my cardboard signs, posters and other things that need to stay flat. In the upper pocket, I keep the credit-card machine and mail-order sign-up cards. Inside, I keep my wireless gear, extra batteries, extra strings, cords and every cord adapter I own, so my gear can work with any sound system. I used to have a lock with a key on it, but I kept losing the key so now I use a combination lock.

One of the hardest things to fly with is a guitar stand. They are either too big and heavy for a suitcase or they don't lie flat or you have to take them apart and put them back together for every gig. The best flying stand I've found is made by Gruvin. It is sturdy, light, folds flat and fits easily inside a small bag.

IT'S NOT HOW MUCH YOU MAKE, IT'S HOW MUCH YOU KEEP

One of the guys in the folk duo The Billy's was dating an accountant, and she was helping them with their finances. When they came to Nashville and we met for dinner before their show, there was a good-natured ruckus between them over a missing receipt. They were given only a certain amount of cash for food on their tour, and they had to come back with a receipt to account for every penny that was missing. While we all laughed about this, I also thought it was great. I was wishing I had someone watching out for my funds like that.

When you're on the road, it's too easy to grab $20 out of the album-sales money to buy a burger. You plan to put the change back, but it somehow winds up in your pocket. Pretty soon you're grabbing another $20 to replace the mascara you lost and the shampoo you left in the last shower, a few bucks for wool socks since it got colder than you thought, a few bucks for skycaps, a *People* magazine, *USA Today*. The next thing you know, you get home and you know you sold thirty CDs over the course of the week, but where's the cash? It disappeared. So what happens to the $3 from every album sale you promised to pay Aunt Emma since she loaned you the money to make your CDs? That's $90 out of your pocket.

One good way to keep the money together from each gig is to take envelopes with you for each one. When the job is finished, put the cash in the envelope, write the amount on the outside and seal it. It's not that this will stop you from breaking into the money, but it will slow you down.

I usually take a small amount of cash on the road and a credit card. I put all the travel expenses on the credit card because:

a. It keeps me from breaking into the profit from albums sales.

b. The bill and receipts provide a written record of what I spent.

c. Since I have the kind that gives me frequent-flier miles, it provides free future airline tickets.

A PLACE FOR EVERYTHING AND EVERYTHING IN ITS PLACE

With every stop on a tour, it becomes harder to keep up with important pieces of paper. Lost receipts, phone messages and tickets can turn precious sleeping time into agonized searching time.

Here's a tip for keeping up with these things. Put them all in the same place, every time. They don't have to go in the same place together. They can all go in their own separate pockets of your bags; just make sure each item is always in the same place from day to day, trip to trip. It's better to put them in pockets of your bags than pockets of your clothes, because you will probably change clothes on a trip more often than you will change bags.

I know that any organized person is laughing like a hyena that I think this idea is worth putting in a book. I'm laughing myself that putting receipts in one place is really a stretch for me. I'm a dozen-little-balled-up-pieces-of-paper-that-look-like-trash-falling-out-of-my-pockets kind of gal. Empty your pockets every night (jacket, pants, shirt) and put the receipts in one spot so you can find them when you get home and you won't have to spend time wondering what you were wearing the day you rented that car in Columbus, Ohio.

The same goes for airline tickets. Keep your ticket in the same pocket of the same bag all the time. The few minutes it takes to put it there every time you get it out to look at it or use it will save many hours of searching for it. Not that anything like that ever happens to anyone but me.

Phone messages can be really difficult to keep track of, because you're checking your messages from pay phones. Don't be like me and write your messages on the back of magazines you will accidentally leave on the plane. When you go to the phone, take something to write on and with, and put that piece of paper, along with the complimentary Holiday Inn and Motel 6 message pads, in the same pocket of your bag every time. This is brilliant, I know, and I wish I could take credit for this amazing technique, but it was taught to me by my husband, who has a real job.

C H A P T E R   1 2

LIVE LARGE

''Words like these set me free: What I seek is
seeking me. Life's a journey, not a race. What
is mine will know my face. I can live each day,
and let it be. What is mine will find me. Live
each day, let it be. What is mine will find me.''

—from ''What Is Mine Will Find Me,'' by Jana Stanfield

The benefits of making and marketing your own albums are powerful and many.

Not so many years ago, I was a frustrated recording-artist wannabe who had been turned down by every major label. Some had passed on me more than once. A publisher I wanted to be signed by to write songs for a living had told me to keep writing and come back in another year.

Within weeks of that meeting, I lost my job on Music Row. I began supporting myself as a freelance television reporter while I sorted out my life. For the next year, I reexamined everything that was important to me.

I considered giving up trying to make it in the commercial music business. Getting back to the basics of my dream, I found that, at the core, what I wanted was not just the opportunity to share my music but the opportunity for self-expression. I considered writing short stories, like Robert Fulghum does in *All I Really Need to Know, I Learned in Kindergarten*. After I wrote a few of those stories, it became clear to me that I hated being alone for long hours with nothing but a typewriter to talk to. Self-expression alone was not enough.

I asked myself if singing would be enough. If someone gave me a job making great money singing at weddings three times a week, would it quench my need to share my musical gift? I would have audiences who would enjoy listening and would appreciate my talents. Would that be enough? Never. It wasn't just singing, and it wasn't just self-expression I wanted. I could not settle for one or the other. I needed both, and more.

For a while that year, I considered getting a real job, going back into television full time. That would fill my need for fame. I could really work hard at it, maybe get a regular slot at The Nashville Network. I would be well known, and that would feel good. I could do my music just for fun, like a lot of people do, having friends over on weekends for informal jam sessions. It broke my heart to think of that kind of life. I didn't want to let music be put aside again in my life. I had spent too many years as the interviewer, but always wanting to be the interviewee. I didn't want to ask other people about their fulfilling lives. I wanted my life to be fulfilling.

Nothing I considered felt right during that year. I went to a lot of self-help group meetings, prayed a lot and did a lot of soul-searching. Through clenched teeth and frequently through tears, I kept saying to myself, "I'm not lost, I am exploring."

Someone asked me what I was going to do with myself. I made a joke, saying, "It would be great if I could find a job where I could get paid to be myself." We laughed.

A few months later, I decided to complete a chapter of my life by putting my songs together on an album for friends and family. In making that album, my dream job found me.

When I am onstage, I look around at the faces of people who have come to hear my music. In that moment, I know my music has found its audience and we are having a wonderful time together. I am so happy in those slices of time that sometimes I become overwhelmed, thinking, *I am at my job.* When I go to play at a college and find myself sitting outside on the lawn afterward, having a '70s-song jam session with a group of students, I am overcome with gratefulness, remembering, *I am at my job.* When I am signing albums for an hour after a concert, and having people ask to get a photo with me, my smile is always genuine because I'm reminding myself, *I'm at my job.*

The first benefit is self-affirmation. You show that you care enough about the songs you created to let them have a life. It is not necessary for songs to appeal to billions of people in order for them to be worthy of being heard. Once I affirmed the value of my songs, people affirmed their value by buying them. In addition to the mail orders I receive, I get kind letters every week that remind me I did the right thing in making my own albums.

Through this process, you will learn that the best kind of fame is to be famous to the people you admire. My music did not appeal to a major-record label, because it did not appeal to the masses. That's fine with me. I have found something better than appealing to the masses. I have discovered that the people who are drawn to my concerts and my albums are really fine people, people I am proud to count as friends. I am honored that these people like my creations enough to support what I do. Your music doesn't have to draw millions. It will draw people to you who are like you, people you will like being friends with.

When you make your own albums, you have absolute, total creative freedom to write and sing whatever you want, in your own way. That freedom is intoxicating. It nourishes the soul and nurtures the creative spirit.

After being a professional songwriter trying to get cuts by other artists, I find it wonderful to know that you don't have to get approval of your songs from anyone before you record them. If you say they're worthy of recording, they are. It's empowering.

When I began my first album, I had no idea how it would all work (sort of like this book). I just knew it was important for me to do it (sort of like this book). All I knew about making my own albums was what I'd heard from two friends who were local songwriters at the time and now are people you've probably heard on the radio. Both these friends were living in Nashville but making their living going back to their home cities once a month or more to perform. Both people told me the same thing. They said, "Compared to how much it costs to make my records, I make an obscene amount of money selling them." Their words are absolutely true. Your albums can provide a life that is rich beyond your wildest dreams, in more ways than money.

I love my life. I love doing concerts in places I have always wanted to visit. I love not having to leave that place immediately to get on a bus in the middle of the night that will take me to the next town. I love being able to stay a few days and enjoy all that each place has to offer. The great thing about the methods outlined in this book is that if you don't like to travel, you don't have to. My perfect life might not be your perfect life. You can create your life in whatever way is best for you. There are hundreds of ways to do this, and all of them will work.

Be true to who you are. If it doesn't feel right to you to make and market your own albums, I am not offended. I had to learn what wasn't right for me before I could learn what was right. Each step we take brings us one step closer to where we need to be.

If what you've read feels right, go for it. Have faith that the path is already there, just waiting for you to take a step down the road. The hardest part is doing what it takes (booking the dates, staying organized, keeping records) to make it all work. I didn't know how to do any of this when I started. You can learn as you go and grow as you go. You'll get better and better at it every day, every month, every year.

My hope for you is that you will be able to experience the joy I feel in making my living by making my music. Listen to your heart and learn to trust the process. Your road will take you exactly where you need to go.

> "I'm not lost, I am exploring,
> Life is an adventure worth enjoying.
> Though I may not know where I'm going
> I am not lost, I am exploring
> I am not lost, I am exploring."
> —from "I'm Not Lost, I Am Exploring," by Jana Stanfield

INDEX